Greek Beyond G<

SHREWSBURY SCHOOL
CLASSICS FACULTY

Name....~~Mark Oswald~~ Theo Price....

House......~~G~~ G...... Set.........................

GREEK

Beyond GCSE

John Taylor

Bristol Classical Press

This impression 2011
First published in 2008 by
Bristol Classical Press
an imprint of
Bloomsbury Academic
Bloomsbury Publishing plc
50 Bedford Square, London WC1B 3DP, UK
and
175 Fifth Avenue, New York, NY 10010, USA

A catalogue record for this book is available
from the British Library

ISBN 978 1 85399 704 4

Typeset by John Taylor
Printed and bound in Great Britain by the
MPG Books Group

www.bloomsburyacademic.com

Contents

Chapter 3

Chapter 4

Chapter 5: Readings

Chapter 6: Summaries of syntax

Reference Grammar

Appendices

Vocabulary

Index

Preface

This book is a sequel to *Greek to GCSE* (two volumes), but can be used independently. It appears simultaneously with a revised second edition of *Greek to GCSE: Part 2*, geared to the current OCR specification for GCSE Greek (*Part 1* remains unchanged). *Greek Beyond GCSE* covers all the language requirements for AS-level, and the grammar needed for A2.

When *Greek to GCSE* was first planned (in response to a JACT survey of over a hundred schools), both OCR and AQA offered GCSE Greek, with combined coverage significantly in excess of present needs. Some of the displaced material appears in Chapters 1 and 2 of *Greek Beyond GCSE*, which continue in the same style, with grammar explanations and exercises interspersed with reading passages of lightly adapted Herodotus (words beyond the GCSE requirements continue to be glossed, to ease the transition to sixth-form work). From Chapter 3 onwards everything is new: more advanced language features are introduced, and glossing now assumes knowledge of the vocabulary prescribed for unseen translation at AS-level. Chapter 4 completes the coverage of grammar, and passages of unadapted Greek begin to be introduced. Chapter 5 consists of extended and unadapted extracts from a range of Greek prose authors. Chapter 6 provides a brief summary of syntax, including revision of constructions covered in *Greek to GCSE*, and some practice sentences. This is followed by a comprehensive Reference Grammar, Appendices and Vocabulary (English-Greek and Greek-English). I happily acknowledge debts to James Morwood's *Oxford Grammar of Classical Greek* (OUP), to the JACT *Reading Greek* course (CUP), and to H.W. Smyth's monumental *Greek Grammar* (Harvard University Press). My aim throughout has been to make the study of Greek accessible and enjoyable, in the belief that this is best achieved by tackling its grammar head-on, uncluttered as far as possible by minutiae but without compromise in the understanding of principles.

I have received welcome feedback on *Greek to GCSE* from a wide range of schools and from a heartening number of individual learners; I have tried to act on their advice, both in the revision of that book and in *Greek Beyond GCSE*. As before, I am grateful to Deborah Blake and Ray Davies at Duckworth for their help and advice.

John Taylor
Tonbridge School

Abbreviations

1, 2, 3	first, second, third person
acc	accusative
adj	adjective
adv	adverb
aor	aorist
comp	comparative
dat	dative
f	feminine
foll	follows, following
fut	future
gen	genitive
impf	imperfect
impsnl	impersonal
impv	imperative
ind	indirect
indecl	indeclinable
indef	indefinite
indic	indicative
inf	infinitive
intrans	intransitive
irreg	irregular
lit	literally
m	masculine
mid	middle
n	neuter
nom	nominative
opt	optative
pass	passive
pf	perfect
pl	plural
plpf	pluperfect
pple	participle
prep	preposition
pres	present
qu	question
refl	reflexive
rel	relative
sg	singular
subj	subjunctive
sup	superlative
usu	usually
voc	vocative

Greece and the Aegean

Glossary of grammar terms

absolute   grammatically unconnected with the rest of the sentence (literally *separated off*), as in *genitive absolute* and *accusative absolute*.

accidence   the part of grammar that deals with word endings (as distinct from *syntax*).

accusative   case of direct object; used with some prepositions, usually expressing *motion towards*; used to express *time how long*; used for subject of infinitive or participle in indirect statement and other constructions, if different from subject of main verb; the (neuter) participle of an impersonal verb unconnected with the rest of its sentence is an *accusative absolute*.

active   form of verb where the grammatical subject is the doer of the action (one of three *voices,* as distinct from *middle* or *passive*).

adjective   word describing a noun (with which it *agrees* in number, gender and case).

adverb   word describing a verb (or an adjective, or another adverb).

agent   person by whom an action is done, usually expressed by ὑπό + *gen* after a passive verb (but dative alone always after verbal adjective/gerundive, and optionally after perfect/pluperfect passive).

agree   have the same number (agreement of subject and verb); have the same number, gender and case (agreement of noun and adjective).

ambiguous   can mean more than one thing.

antecedent   person or thing in main clause to which relative pronoun (or adverb) refers back.

aorist   tense of a verb referring to a single action in the past (as distinct from *imperfect, perfect* and *pluperfect*); in all uses of the aorist imperative and subjunctive, most uses of the aorist infinitive and optative, and some uses of the aorist participle, the aorist is used by *aspect* (rather than tense) to express simply a single action, not necessarily in the past.

apodosis   the main clause of a conditional sentence, expressing the consequence (i.e. not the *if* half, which is the *protasis*).

apposition   use of a word or phrase parallel in grammar to another, to give more information (e.g. *Sophocles, the poet,* ... : two nouns *in apposition*).

article   (see *definite article*).

aspect   the expression of *type of time* (single or repeated/extended action), as distinct from actual time (past, present, future) which is *tense*.

attraction   in a relative clause, the process by which a genitive or dative antecedent makes the relative pronoun agree with it (overriding the normal rule that its case is determined by its job within the relative clause).

augment   epsilon put on the front of a verb to denote a past tense.

auxiliary   a verb (usually part of *to be*) used with a participle to form a tense of another verb.

breathing   symbol above a vowel or diphthong (or rho) beginning a word, indicating presence (*rough* breathing: ἁ = *ha*) or absence (*smooth* breathing: ἀ = *a*) of *h* sound or *aspiration*. Either breathing comes on the *second* vowel of a diphthong (αὑ, αὐ).

cardinal   ordinary numeral (1, 2, 3), as distinct from *ordinal* (first, second, third).

case	form of a noun, pronoun or adjective that shows the job it does in the sentence (e.g. accusative for direct object); cases are arranged in the order nominative, (vocative), accusative, genitive, dative.
clause	part of a sentence with its own subject and verb.
common	(referring to gender): can be either masculine or feminine according to context (e.g. ὁ/ἡ παῖς boy/girl).
comparative	form of an adjective or adverb meaning more, -er.
complement	another nominative word or phrase describing the subject.
compound	verb with prefix (e.g. ἀποβάλλω I throw away); adjective or negative made up of more than one element.
concessive	expressing the idea although or despite (expressed by καίπερ + pple).
conditional	expressing if or unless (the clause beginning if or unless is the protasis, the other half - expressing the result - is the apodosis).
conjugate	go through in order the different parts of a verb: first, second, third person singular, then plural (as distinct from decline, used for a noun, pronoun, adjective or participle).
conjunction	word joining clauses, phrases or words together (e.g. and, but, therefore).
consonant	letter representing a sound that can only be used together with a vowel.
construction	pattern according to which a particular type of sentence or clause (e.g. indirect statement) is formed.
correlatives	set of linked interrogative/indefinite/relative/demonstrative adverbs or pronouns (e.g. where?/somewhere/[the place]where/there).
contraction	process by which two adjacent vowels (or vowel plus diphthong) coalesce into a single vowel or diphthong.
crasis	process by which a vowel or diphthong at the end of a word coalesces with another at the start of the next word, the result written as a single word instead of two separate ones (e.g. ὤνδρες for ὦ ἄνδρες).
dative	case of indirect object, often translated to or for; used with prepositions, often to express position or rest (as distinct from motion); used to express time when.
declension	one of the patterns (three main ones, also used for pronouns, adjectives and participles) by which nouns change their endings.
decline	go through a noun, pronoun, adjective or participle in case order, singular then plural (as distinct from conjugate, used of tenses of a verb).
definite article	ὁ ἡ τό (equivalent to English the, but used more widely).
deliberative	use of the subjunctive to express a thought process (e.g. should I do X?)
demonstrative	pronoun, adjective or adverb pointing out some feature of a situation (e.g. this, that, there, then).
deponent	verb which has only middle (or sometimes passive) forms, but is active in meaning.
diphthong	two consecutive vowels pronounced as one syllable (e.g. αυ, ει, ου).
direct object	noun or pronoun on receiving end of the action of verb.
direct speech	actual words of a speaker, usually enclosed by inverted commas.
dual	special set of endings expressing two items, or two subjects of a verb (relic of an earlier stage of the language when plural implied three or more).
elision	dropping of a (usually short) vowel at the end of a word before another

	beginning with a vowel, indicated by an apostrophe (e.g. τ′ for τε).
enclitic	literally *leaning on*: a (usually short and unaccented) word which cannot stand alone but must follow another word (e.g. the indefinite τις).
ending	last bit of a word, added to the stem to give more detail and show its job.
feminine	one of the three genders, for females or things imagined as female.
finite	form of a verb with tense and person ending (as distinct from infinitive or participle).
future	tense of verb referring to something that will happen in the future.
gender	one of three categories (masculine, feminine, neuter) into which nouns and pronouns are put according to their actual or imagined sex or lack of it.
genitive	case expressing possession or definition, often translated *of*; used in expressions indicating e.g. *part of*, *some of*; used with some prepositions, usually expressing *motion away from*; used after a comparative to mean *than*; used to express *time within which*; noun and participle phrase grammatically unconnected with the rest of its sentence is a *genitive absolute*; follows some verbs expressing ideas such as *take hold of*.
gerund	a verb made into a noun (*the act of doing X*), expressed by τό + *inf*.
gerundive	adjective formed from verb, expressing the idea *needing to be done*.
historic	set of tenses (imperfect, aorist, pluperfect) referring to the past (as distinct from *primary* ones referring to the present or future), and determining the *sequence* according to which subordinate clauses are constructed (e.g. use of optative rather than subjunctive); *historic present* is the use of the present tense for a story set in the past (to achieve vividness), usually better translated as past in English.
homonym	word coincidentally spelled in the same way as another unconnected word.
idiom	distinctive form of expression within a language, established by common use but going beyond what can be worked out from the individual words.
imperative	form of verb used for direct command.
imperfect	tense of verb referring to incomplete, extended or repeated action in the past.
impersonal	third person singular verb whose subject is *it*.
indeclinable	does not change its endings.
indefinite	(1) *indefinite article*: the English *a(n)*, which has no direct equivalent in Greek, though the indefinite τις (*someone/a certain*) can be used. (2) *indefinite adverb* or *pronoun* (in the table of correlatives): usually the same in form as the equivalent indirect interrogative word, but with no accent or different accent; the indefinite relative is ὅστις (*anyone who*). (3) *indefinite construction*: clause expressing an unspecific *whoever*, *whenever* etc, expressed in Greek by ἄν + subjunctive in primary sequence, and by optative alone in historic sequence.
indicative	form of verb expressing a fact (as distinct from other *moods* expressing e.g. possibilities).
indirect	indirect statement, command or question is the reported form of it (as distinct from quotation of the speaker's actual words); indirect object is person or thing in the dative indirectly affected by object of verb, e.g. *I gave the money* (direct object) *to the old man* (indirect object).

xiii

infinitive	form of verb introduced by *to*, expressing the basic meaning (e.g. παύειν *to stop*). Greek verbs have several infinitives to express differences of tense and voice (e.g. future passive infinitive παυσθήσεσθαι *to be going to be stopped*).
inflection	technical term for *ending*: as an inflected language, Greek depends heavily on word endings to express meaning.
intransitive	verb that does not have a direct object (e.g. βαίνω *I go*).
irregular	word that does not follow one of the standard patterns of declension or conjugation.
main clause	clause which makes sense on its own, and expresses the main point of a sentence (as distinct from *subordinate* clause).
masculine	one of the three genders, for males or things imagined as male.
middle	form of a verb expressing a relation of subject to action which is thought of as midway between active and passive, but is often actually both (e.g. reflexive *I wash myself* or causative *I get something washed*); *deponent* verbs have only middle forms, but often with simply active meaning.
mood	set of forms of a verb showing whether it is indicative, imperative, subjunctive or optative.
negative	expressing that something is not the case or should not happen.
neuter	one of the three genders, for things imagined as neither male nor female.
nominative	case used for subject of sentence, or of any finite verb, or of infinitive or participle (in indirect statement and other constructions) if the same as the subject of the main verb.
noun	word naming a person or thing (e.g. πόλις *city*); a *proper* noun with a capital letter gives its actual name e.g. 'Αθήναι *Athens*).
number	being either singular or plural (or sometimes dual).
numerals	numbers, either *cardinal* (one, two, three) or *ordinal* (first, second, third).
object	noun or pronoun acted upon by a verb.
optative	form of verb (often expressed in English by *might*) expressing a wish or a not very likely possibility (as distinct from the indicative for a fact, and the subjunctive for a more likely possibility); in many constructions the subjunctive is used in *primary sequence*, the optative in *historic sequence*.
ordinal	type of numeral expressing order (*first*, *second*, *third*), as an adjective.
part of speech	category of word (noun, adjective, pronoun, verb, adverb, preposition, conjunction).
particle	short indeclinable word (often conjunction or adverb) connecting things together, or giving emphasis or colour (e.g. οὖν *therefore*; δή *indeed*)
participle	adjective formed from a verb (e.g. παύων *stopping*).
partitive	of the genitive to express *part of*, *some of* etc.
passive	form of verb where the subject does not do the action but is on the receiving end of it (e.g. παύομαι *I am stopped*).
perfect	tense of verb referring to a completed action in the past, whose effects still continue (e.g. *our friends have arrived*); in Greek a *primary* tense, often virtually equivalent to present. (A single action in the past is expressed by the much more common *aorist*.)
person	term for the subject of verb: first person *I*, *we*; second person *you* (singular

	or plural); third person *he, she, it, they* (or a noun replacing one of these).
phrase	group of words not containing a finite verb (as distinct from *clause*).
pluperfect	tense of verb referring to something that had already happened by a particular point in the past, and whose effects were continuing when something else happened.
plural	more than one (as distinct from singular, or sometimes from dual).
positive	not negative; (of adjectives) the ordinary form, indicating simply that the person or thing has the quality described (as distinct from *comparative* and *superlative*, expressing the degree to which they have it).
possessive	adjective or pronoun expressing who or what something belongs to; *possessive dative* is the idiom e.g. *there is to me a dog* for *I have a dog*.
potential	something that *might* happen (often expressed by ἄν and the optative).
prefix	word or syllable added to the beginning of another word.
preposition	word used with a noun or pronoun in the accusative, genitive or dative to focus more closely the meaning of the case (e.g. *into, away from, on*).
present	tense of a verb referring to something that is happening now, or of a participle referring to something happening at the same time as the main verb.
primary	set of tenses (present, future, perfect) referring to the present or future (as distinct from *historic* ones referring to the past), and determining the *sequence* according to which subordinate clauses are constructed (e.g. use of subjunctive rather than optative).
principal parts	first person singulars of important tenses of a verb, from which other forms and necessary information about it can be worked out.
prohibition	negative command (*don't do X!*), expressed by μή + *present imperative* for a general prohibition, or μή + *aorist subjunctive* for one occasion).
pronoun	word that stands instead of a noun, avoiding the need to repeat it.
protasis	the *if…* half of a conditional sentence (in negative form *if… not* or *unless …*).
reduplication	process by which the initial consonant of a verb is added again on the front followed by epsilon, to make the perfect tense (e.g. παύω, *pf* πέπαυκα).
reflexive	word referring back to the subject of the verb.
regular	a word which forms its endings according to a standard pattern.
relative	subordinate clause (or pronoun/adverb introducing it) relating to person or thing just mentioned in the main clause (who or which is the *antecedent*).
root	basic stem of verb, or element from which a group of related words are derived.
sentence	group of words with subject and verb (and often other elements), which can stand on its own (as distinct from *phrase* or *subordinate clause*).
sequence	process by which the tense of the main clause determines the construction of a subordinate clause (e.g. whether its verb is subjunctive or optative).
singular	just one (as distinct from dual or plural).
stem	the part of a word which stays the same: different endings are added to show the job it does in the sentence.
subject	noun or pronoun in the nominative case, expressing who or what does the action (with active verb) or is on the receiving end of it (with passive verb).

subjunctive	form of verb (often expressed in English by *may*) referring to an idea or possibility (as distinct from *indicative* for a fact, or *optative* for a more remote possibility); in some constructions the subjunctive is used in *primary sequence*, the optative in *historic sequence*.
subordinate	of secondary importance to something else; a subordinate clause cannot stand alone but only makes sense in relation to the main clause.
suffix	word or syllable added to the end of another word.
superlative	form of adjective or adverb meaning *very, (the) most, -est*.
syllable	part of a word forming a spoken unit, usually consisting of vowel with consonants before or after or both.
syntax	the part of grammar that deals with sentences and constructions (as distinct from *accidence*).
tense	form of a verb showing when the action takes place (in the past, present or future).
transitive	verb that has a direct object.
understand	provide in translation a word which is not separately represented in Greek but must be worked out from the grammar and context (e.g. *men* or *things* from the gender of an adjective or part of the article).
verb	word expressing an action.
vividness	principle by which past events, words or thoughts are envisaged as present (to give a sense of immediacy), so that a primary construction is used rather than the historic one strictly required (e.g. indicative in indirect statement/question, or subjunctive purpose clause, rather than optative).
vocative	case used for addressing someone or something.
voice	one of three sets of verb forms (active, middle, passive) showing how the subject relates to the action.
vowel	letter representing a sound that can be spoken by itself: α, ε, η, ι, ο, υ, ω.

Chapter 1

Direct and indirect questions

We saw in *Greek to GCSE (1)* that any sentence can be made into a question simply by adding a question mark (;), but that *open* questions (asking whether a statement is true, so that the answer will be *yes* or *no*) are commonly signalled by ἆρα at the beginning:

> ἆρα ὁ παῖς μῶρός ἐστιν;
> Is the boy stupid?

The word ἆρα cannot be translated in isolation (think of it as, but do not write, *Is it the case that ...?* - like French *Est-ce que ...?*): you need to look first at the tense and person of the verb.

• By adding οὐ after ἆρα (elided to ἆρ' οὐ, and with οὐ changing to οὐκ or οὐχ according to the usual rule if a vowel follows) the question is *loaded* to expect or invite the answer *yes*:

> ἆρ' οὐχ ὁ παῖς μῶρός ἐστιν;
> Isn't the boy stupid?
> *or*   Surely the boy is stupid?

• With the alternative negative μή, the question is loaded in the other direction, to expect or invite *no*:

> ἆρα μὴ ὁ παῖς μῶρός ἐστιν;
> The boy isn't stupid, is he?
> *or*   Surely the boy isn't stupid?

The easiest way to remember these is to think of ἆρ' οὐ as *surely* and of ἆρα μή as *surely not*. They correspond respectively to Latin *nonne* (expecting *yes*) and *num* (expecting *no*).

We also met direct questions asking for specific information, introduced by one of a number of *interrogative* or question words (mostly beginning with π-, where the equivalent Latin words often have *qu-* and the English ones *wh-*, all of which are historically related):

πότε;	when?
ποῦ;	where (at)?
ποῖ;	where to?
πόθεν;	where from?
πῶς;	how?

These are all interrogative adverbs; we also met two interrogative adjectives:

ποῖος -α -ον;	what sort of?
πόσος -η -ον;	how big? *pl* how many?

And the interrogative pronoun/adjective:

τίς; τί;	who? which? what?

Any of these automatically begins the question (regardless of case, with those that decline).

1

We also saw that *indirect* (or *reported*) questions operate in a similar way to indirect statements using a ὅτι (*that*) clause: the tense of the original direct speech is retained (with adjustment of the English if the introductory verb is past tense). They are most commonly introduced by the verb ἐρωτάω *I ask*, with its alternative aorists ἠρώτησα (first aorist active) and the more common ἠρόμην (second aorist middle).

Note the distinction between ἐρωτάω *I ask (a question)* and αἰτέω *I ask (for something), I beg*.

Open indirect questions (asking whether a statement is true) are normally introduced by εἰ:

> ἠρωτήσω τὸν γέροντα εἰ ὁ παῖς μῶρός ἐστιν.
> I shall ask the old man if (*or* whether) the boy is stupid.

(εἰ is the normal Greek word for *if*, used in other contexts too; *if* is perfectly possible in English to represent an indirect question, but *whether* often sounds better).

Note that the loading of the direct question to expect *yes* or *no* cannot be reproduced in the indirect form: ἆρα, ἆρ᾽ οὐ, and ἆρα μή all have to be represented by εἰ.

• *Whether* implies *or not*. If an alternative is actually expressed, Greek uses paired introductory words:

| | εἴτε ... εἴτε | whether ... or |
| or | πότερον ... ἤ | whether ... or (rather) |

(πότερον ... ἤ implies the second alternative is more important or likely, and is also used if the second half is simply the expressed negative ἤ οὐ *or not*)

> ἡ παῖς ἠρώτησεν εἴτε ὁ ἀδελφὸς εἴτε ὁ δοῦλος ἔλυσε τὸν ἵππον.
> The girl asked whether her brother or the slave had released the horse.

> ὁ κριτὴς ἐπύθετο πότερον ὁ ἄγγελος αἴτιός ἐστιν ἢ οἱ πέμψαντες.
> The judge enquired whether the messenger was guilty or (rather) those who had sent him.

πότερον ... ἤ can be used in a direct question too, but this cannot be represented in English, so πότερον here just signals that an alternative question is coming:

> πότερον οἱ σύμμαχοι πρῶτον ἀφίκοντο ἢ οἱ πολέμιοι;
> Did the allies or the enemy arrive first?

• The interrogative words asking for specific information are used in indirect questions too. At GCSE we saw these words used without change; this reflects the practice of Greek authors, particularly when they want to give a vivid idea of the direct question lying behind the reported one. But in more formal grammar the interrogative words add ὁ- onto the beginning in an indirect question. Hence:

| *direct question* | ποῦ ἐστιν ὁ ἵππος;
Where is the horse? |
| *indirect question* | ὁ ξένος ἤρετο ὅπου ὁ ἵππος εἴη (*or* ἐστίν).*
The stranger asked where the horse was (*literally* is). |

* We saw in *Greek to GCSE (2)* that if the introductory verb is in a past tense, the verb in the indirect question is in strict grammar put into the optative. But the indicative is often kept, to give a vivid sense of the original words, similar to that also achieved by using the normal π- form of the interrogative word rather than the ὁπ- form. Whether the indicative or optative is used, the verb in the indirect question has the tense of the original direct one, which needs to move back a tense in English if the introductory verb is past.

Although verbs such as ἐρωτάω and πυνθάνομαι commonly introduce indirect questions, many other verbs can do so. The question need not have actually been spoken, but may be only implied:

> βούλομαι γνῶναι ὅπως ἡ τριήρης ποιηθείη.
> I want to know how the trireme was made.

> οὔποτε ἠγγέλθη πότερον ὁ αἰχμάλωτος ἔφυγεν ἢ ἀπέθανεν.
> It was never reported whether the prisoner ran away or died.

This can mean that indirect questions are less easy to spot than some constructions, but the presence of an interrogative word usually gives a clue, even if there is no verb of asking. *I will ask who the stranger is* is obviously an indirect question; but so too is *I know who the stranger is* (because it means *I know* [the answer to the implied question in my own or someone else's mind] *who the stranger is*).

Exercise 1.1

Translate into English:
1 ἆρα μὴ πάντα τὸν σῖτον ἐφάγετε, ὦ παῖδες;
2 οὗτος ὁ ἄγγελος ἐρωτᾷ εἰ ἴσμεν περὶ τῶν ἐκεῖ γενομένων.
3 πότερον τόδε τὸ πλοῖον ἀμείνων ἐστὶν ἢ ἐκεῖνο, ὦ ναυτά;
4 ἀρ’ ἐπύθου ὁπότε οἱ νέοι στρατιῶται ἀφίξονται;
5 χαλεπόν ἐστι γνῶναι εἰ χειμῶνός ἐστιν ἀσφαλὴς ἡ ὁδός.
6 αἱ ἐν τῇ πόλει ἤροντο ὁπόθεν οἱ σύμμαχοι πέμποιντο.
7 βούλομαι μαθεῖν πότερον ἱκανά ἐστι τὰ χρήματα ἢ οὔκ, ὦ δοῦλε.
8 ἀρ’ οὐ φιλεῖς τὴν λόγοις οὕτω χρωμένην, ὦ νεανία;
9 αἰτήσω τὸν ῥήτορα εἰπεῖν ὅπως τὴν ἐκκλησίαν ἔπεισεν.
10 βουλόμεθα γνῶναι εἴτε νομίζεις τὸν δοῦλον αὐτὸν εἴτε τὸν δεσπότην
     αἴτιον εἶναι.

Exercise 1.2

Translate into Greek:
1 This woman asked whether I had seen the slave running away.
2 Surely the citizens do not trust that politician?
3 Do you know who wrote the best letter, teacher?
4 The stranger is asking where it is possible for him to find food.
5 I want to find out whether the enemy damaged the fields or the houses.

Correlatives

• We saw in *Greek to GCSE (1)* with the use of τίς and τις that the interrogative form (*who? which? what?*) has an equivalent *indefinite* form (*someone, a certain*), and that these are distinguished by accent. The interrogative adverbs similarly have indefinite forms:

interrogative		*indefinite*	
πότε;	when?	ποτε	sometime, once, ever
ποῦ;	where?	που	somewhere
πῶς;	how?	πως	somehow, in some way

On the same principle it is possible to build up whole sets of words.

Hence with a pronoun:

direct interrogative	*Who* escaped?
indirect interrogative	He asked *who* had escaped.
indefinite	*Someone* escaped.
relative	The man *who* escaped is my brother.
demonstrative	*This* man escaped.

And similarly with an adverb:

direct interrogative	*When* did the ship arrive?
indirect interrogative	He asked *when* the ship had arrived.
indefinite	The ship arrived *at some time.*
relative	I was away *when* the ship arrived.
demonstrative	The ship arrived *then.*

These sets of words are called *correlatives*. They are formed (apart from a few irregular exceptions) according to a distinct pattern. The words in each set typically begin:

direct interrogative	π-
indirect interrogative	ὁπ-
indefinite	π- , but with no or different accent
relative	drops the π-
demonstrative	τ-

The table on the facing page shows the correlatives in common use.

The most complete and regular set is provided by πότε; (*when?*) with its entirely predictable derived forms ὁπότε (indirect), ποτε (indefinite), ὅτε (relative) and τότε (demonstrative).

We have met some of the demonstratives already:

τότε	then, at that time
τοιοῦτος	of such a sort
τοσοῦτος	so big, *pl* so many
and οὗτος	this (where the expected τ- is seen after the nominative).

Again there is a parallel with Latin (*tam, tum, talis, tantus* etc).

4

Table of correlatives:

(note how accents affect the meaning)

direct	indirect	indefinite	relative	demonstrative

pronouns/adjectives:

direct	indirect	indefinite	relative	demonstrative
τίς; who?	ὅστις	τις a certain	ὅς (the one) who	οὗτος (*or* ὅδε), ἐκεῖνος this (this here), that
πότερος; which (of two)?	ὁπότερος			ἕτερος one /the other (of two)
πόσος; how big? *plural* how many?	ὁπόσος		ὅσος the size which as many as, all those who	τοσοῦτος* so big so many
ποῖος; what sort of?	ὁποῖος		οἷος the sort which	τοιοῦτος* this sort of

adverbs:

direct	indirect	indefinite	relative	demonstrative
ποῦ; where?	ὅπου	που somewhere, anywhere	οὗ (the place) where	ἐνθάδε, ἐκεῖ here, there
ποῖ; where to?	ὅποι	ποι to somewhere	οἷ to (the place) where	δεῦρο, ἐκεῖσε to here, to there
πόθεν; where from?	ὁπόθεν	ποθεν from somewhere	ὅθεν from (the place) where	ἐνθένδε, ἐκεῖθεν from here, from there
πότε; when?	ὁπότε	ποτε sometime, ever, once	ὅτε (at the time) when	τότε then, at that time
πῶς; how?	ὅπως	πως somehow	ὡς how, as, in the way in which	οὕτω(ς) *or* ὧδε so, in this way

* the more predictable forms τόσος and τοῖος also exist, and are common in early Greek, which also has a word τοῦ for *there* (making the ποῦ set completely regular).

5

• Indirect questions and relative clauses can seem similar, but they are distinct. Consider the following colloquial saying (mocking a stick-in-the-mud attitude):

> We know what we like, and we like what we know.

The two halves seem parallel, but one is an indirect question (*we know [the answer to the implied question] what it is that we like*), the other a relative clause (*we like those things which we do in fact know*).

• The use of a relative adverb (e.g. οὗ *where*) is equivalent to that of the pronoun in an ordinary relative clause (e.g. ἐν ᾧ *in which*). The use of a more specialised relative pronoun (e.g. οἷος *the sort which*) is exactly the same as that of the normal relative pronoun ὅς (*who*), i.e. it agrees with the antecedent (the word in the main clause it refers back to) in number and gender, but takes its case from the job it is doing in its own clause. For example:

> ἔχω βίβλον οἷα οὐ πολλάκις εὑρεται.
> I have a book of a sort which is not often found.

• Note the use of ὅσοι (lit *as many as*) for *all those who* (equivalent to πάντες οἵ).

• The phrase οἷός τ᾿ εἰμί + inf (*I am able to*) literally means *I am of the sort to*.

• Exclamations introduced by ὡς *how ... !* are common; οἷος and ὅσος can also be used in exclamations: *what a ... ! what a great ... !*

• Note the use of co-ordinated relative and demonstrative neuter datives (used like adverbs) in the idiom:
> ὅσῳ ... τοσούτῳ   *lit* by as much ... by so much, *i.e.* the more X ... the more Y

These are used with two comparatives for things that increase in proportion:
> ὅσῳ πλουσιώτερος τοσούτῳ μωρότερος γίγνεται.
> *lit*   By as much as he becomes more wealthy, by so much he becomes more foolish.
> *i.e.*   The more wealthy he becomes, the more foolish he becomes.

• Distinguish τότε *then, at that time* from ἔπειτα *then, next*.
They correspond respectively to Latin *tum* and *deinde*.

• ὅστις (the indirect question form of τίς) at first sight resembles the indirect version of other interrogative words by beginning with omicron. But in fact it is the relative pronoun ὅς stuck onto the front of τις, and although it is normally written as one word, both bits of it decline separately. Hence:

		masculine	feminine	neuter
sg	nom	ὅστις	ἥτις	ὅ τι
	acc	ὅντινα	ἥντινα	ὅ τι
	gen	οὗτινος	ἧστινος	οὗτινος
	dat	ᾧτινι	ᾗτινι	ᾧτινι
pl	nom	οἵτινες	αἵτινες	ἅτινα
	acc	οὕστινας	ἅστινας	ἅτινα
	gen	ὧντινων	ὧντινων	ὧντινων
	dat	οἷστισι(ν)	αἷστισι(ν)	οἷστισι(ν)

The neuter nom/acc sg is written as two words to avoid confusion with ὅτι *that/because*.

Because some of the resulting forms are rather cumbersome, alternative versions of the masculine and neuter genitive and dative singular and plural (ὅτου, ὅτῳ, ὅτων, ὅτοις) are formed as if from a second declension nominative singular ὅτος (the ὁτ- bit staying the same).

6

• The sentence *I know who the stranger is* could be translated into Greek literally as:

οἶδα ὅστις ὁ ξένος ἐστίν.

But note the common idiom whereby the subject of the indirect question is extracted and put before the question in the accusative, as direct object of the introductory verb:

οἶδα τὸν ξένον ὅστις ἐστίν.

Literally *I know the stranger* (as to the question) *who he is*: the sentence was grammatically complete and could have stopped after *the stranger*, but then an indirect question is tagged on specifying in what regard he is known. This cannot be reproduced in modern English, but Shakespeare (in an identical idiom) often writes *I know you who you are*.

• ὅστις has another important job, as an *indefinite relative*. Compare the difference between:

ὁ ῥήτωρ ὃς νῦν λέγει μωρός ἐστιν.
The politician who is now speaking is foolish.   (*definite individual*)

πᾶς ὅστις ταῦτα λέγει μωρός ἐστιν.
Everyone who says these things is foolish.   (*indefinite*)

The other indirect interrogatives (both pronouns and adverbs) can also be used as indefinite relatives, often with ἄν (which itself gives an indefinite flavour: see further pages 83-4 on indefinite clauses).

Exercise 1.3

Translate into English:
1   οὐκ οἶδα ὅστις τὴν ἐπιστολὴν ἔπεμψεν.
2   ὁ διδάσκαλος ἐβούλετο γνῶναι ὁπόσοι τῶν παίδων παρεῖεν.
3   ἆρ᾽ οὐχ οἱ νεανίαι τοσαῦτα ἆθλα ἐκτήσαντο ὥστε ὑπὸ πάντων θαυμάζεσθαι;
4   χαλεπόν ἐστι πυθέσθαι ὁπόθεν ἡ νόσος ἤρξατο καὶ ὅπως.
5   ποῖ φεύγεις, ὦ δοῦλε, καὶ διὰ τί;
6   ἆρα μὴ ἡ παῖς τοιαύτη ἐστὶν ὥστε ταῦτα πράσσειν;
7   τοσοῦτοι τότε ἀφίκοντο ὥστ᾽ οὐχ οἷοι τ᾽ ἦμεν μαθεῖν ὁπόθεν ἦλθον.
8   ἆρ᾽ ὅδε ἐστὶν ὁ τόπος οὗ ἡ συμφορὰ ἐγένετο;
9   ὁ στρατιώτης ξίφος ἔχει οἷον οὔποτε πρότερον εἶδον.
10   καίπερ εἰδὼς οὔτε ὅπως οὔτε ὁπότε ταῦτα τὰ τείχη ἐποιήθη, νομίζω αὐτὰ ὑπ᾽ ἀνθρώπων πως ποιηθῆναι.

Exercise 1.4

Translate into Greek:
1   What sort of food do you like, children?
2   The old man asked the stranger where the temple was.
3   Who are those slaves, and where are they running to?
4   Does the judge know how many of the women helped the man guarding the gate?
5   From where did these slaves whom I saw in the marketplace come?

Exercise 1.5

Libyans and Pygmies

In the course of his description of Egypt and North Africa, the historian Herodotus tells a story he has heard about some young Libyans who crossed the Sahara and discovered the pygmies who lived around a river which he and his informants presume to be part of the Nile but was probably in fact the Niger.

ὁ δ' Ἐτέαρχος, ὁ τῶν <u>Νασαμώνων</u> βασιλεύς, ἄνδρας <u>Λιβυκούς</u> ποτε
ἠρώτησε περὶ τῶν τῆς <u>Λιβύης ἐρήμων</u>. ἤθελε γὰρ γνῶναι πότερον
ἄνθρωποι ἐκεῖ <u>οἰκοῦσιν</u> ἢ οὔ. ἐκεῖνοι οὕτως ἀπεκρίναντο· "νεανίαι τινὲς
τῶν <u>Λιβύων</u>, πολίτων πλουσίων υἱοὶ ὄντες, <u>ὑβριστικῶς</u> ἔπρασσον. διὰ δὲ
5 τοῦτο οἱ πατέρες <u>ἐβούλευσαν</u> ἀποπέμψαι αὐτοὺς ἵνα οἱ μὲν ἄλλοι
πολῖται <u>ἡσυχάζωσιν</u>, οἱ δὲ νεανίαι αὐτοὶ ἔχωσι χρήσιμόν τι ποιεῖν.
πρῶτον μὲν οὖν διὰ τῆς <u>οἰκουμένης</u> χώρας ἐπορεύοντο. ταύτην δὲ
<u>διεξελθόντες</u>, ἀφίκοντο εἰς <u>χωρίον</u> οὗ ἄνθρωποι <u>οὐκέτι</u> ἦσαν, <u>θῆρες</u> δὲ
πολλοί. ἀσφαλῶς <u>ὅμως</u> διαβάντες, πέντε ἡμέρας τὴν ὁδὸν ἐποιοῦντο διὰ
10 τῶν ἐρήμων· τέλος δὲ δένδρα εἶδον. πρὸς δὲ ταῦτα ὡς τάχιστα
προσελθόντες, ἐλήφθησαν ὑπ' ἀνδρῶν μικρῶν. οὗτοι δὲ πολλῷ μικρότεροι
ἦσαν ἢ πάντα ἄλλα <u>ἔθνη</u>. καὶ δὴ <u>μέλανες</u> ἦσαν. καὶ οὔθ' οἱ Λίβυες οἷοί
τ' ἦσαν μαθεῖν ὅ τι λέγοιειν ἐκεῖνοι, οὔτ' ἐκεῖνοι τοὺς τῶν Λιβύων λόγους.
ἀγαγόντες δὲ τοὺς νεανίας πρὸς τὴν ἑαυτῶν πόλιν, οἱ μικροὶ αὐτοῖς
15 <u>ἔφηναν</u> τὸν ποταμὸν διὰ τῆς πόλεως <u>διαρρέοντα</u>. καὶ οἱ νεανίαι ᾔσθοντο
οὐ μόνον τοῦτον τὸν ποταμὸν μέγιστον ὄντα, ἀλλὰ καὶ ἐν αὐτῷ <u>νέοντας</u>
<u>κροκοδείλους</u>."

	Ἐτέαρχος -ου ὁ	Etearchus
	Νασαμῶνες -ων οἱ	Nasamonians (*a North African tribe*)
	Λιβυκός -ή -όν	Libyan (*adj*)
	Λιβύη -ης ἡ	Libya
2	ἔρημα -ων τά	desert
	οἰκέω	I live (in)
	Λίβυς -υος ὁ	Libyan, Libyan man
	ὑβριστικῶς	arrogantly
	βουλεύω ἐβούλευσα	I plan, I decide
6	ἡσυχάζω	I am quiet, I live in peace
	οἰκέω	I inhabit
	διεξέρχομαι διεξῆλθον	I go right through
	χωρίον -ου τό	place
	οὐκέτι	no longer
8	θήρ θηρός ὁ	wild beast
	ὅμως	nonetheless
	ἔθνος -ους τό	tribe
	μέλας -αινα -αν (μελαν-)	black
	φαίνω ἔφηνα	I show
15	διαρρέω	I flow through
	νέω	I swim
	κροκόδειλος -ου ὁ	crocodile

Exercise 1.6
Crocodiles

The confusion between the Niger and the Nile in the story about the Pygmies may have arisen because the Nile was famous for its crocodiles. Herodotus describes the crocodile for Greek readers who had never seen one. He also shows his usual interest in the cultural and religious significance of what he describes, and the different customs in different places.

ἡ τῶν <u>κροκοδείλων</u> <u>φύσις</u> τοιαύτη ἐστίν· τοὺς τοῦ χειμῶνος <u>μῆνας</u>
τέσσαρας ὁ κροκόδειλος ἐσθίει οὐδέν. τέσσαρας δὲ πόδας ἔχων, καὶ ἐν
τῷ ποταμῷ καὶ ἐν τῇ γῇ <u>οἰκεῖ</u>. ἡ δὲ <u>θήλεια</u> <u>τίκτει</u> μὲν <u>ᾠὰ</u> καὶ <u>ἐκλέπει</u> ἐν
τῇ γῇ καὶ ἐκεῖ <u>διατρίβει</u> τὴν ἡμέραν, τὴν δὲ νύκτα πᾶσαν ἐν τῷ ποταμῷ·
5 <u>θερμότερον</u> γάρ ἐστι τὸ ὕδωρ τῆς <u>δρόσου</u>. πάντων δὲ ζῴων περὶ ὧν ἡμεῖς
ἴσμεν ὁ κροκόδειλος ἐξ ἐλαχίστου μέγιστον γίγνεται· τὰ μὲν γὰρ ᾠὰ οὐ
πολλῷ μείζονα τίκτει τῶν τοῦ <u>χηνός</u>· <u>αὐξανόμενος</u> δὲ ὁ κροκόδειλος
γίγνεται καὶ εἰς <u>ἑπτακαίδεκα</u> <u>πήχεις</u> καὶ μείζων ἔτι. καὶ ἔχει ὀφθαλμοὺς
μὲν <u>ὑός</u>, <u>ὀδόντας</u> δὲ μεγάλους· γλῶσσαν δὲ μόνον <u>θηρίων</u> οὐκ ἔχει, οὐδὲ
10 τὴν <u>κάτω</u> <u>γνάθον</u> <u>κινεῖ</u>, ἀλλὰ τὴν <u>ἄνω</u> γνάθον προσάγει τῇ κάτω.

τοῖς μὲν δὴ τῶν <u>Αἰγυπτίων</u> ἱεροί εἰσιν οἱ κροκόδειλοι, τοῖς δὲ οὔχ· οὗτοι
γὰρ ὡς πολεμίοις <u>χρῶνται</u>. οἱ δὲ περὶ τὰς <u>Θήβας</u> οἰκοῦντες τοὺς
κροκοδείλους μάλιστα τιμῶσιν. ἐν γὰρ ἑκάστῃ κώμῃ ἕνα κροκόδειλον

	κροκόδειλος -ου ὁ	crocodile
	φύσις -εως ἡ	nature
	μήν μηνός ὁ	month
	οἰκέω	I live
3	θῆλυς -εια -υ	female
	τίκτω	(*here*) I lay
	ᾠόν -οῦ τό	egg
	ἐκλέπω	I hatch (something)
	διατρίβω	I spend (time)
5	θερμός -ή -όν	warm
	δρόσος -ου ἡ	dew
	χήν χηνός ὁ	goose
	αὐξάνομαι	I grow bigger
	ἑπτακαίδεκα	seventeen
8	πῆχυς -εως ὁ	cubit (*lit* forearm: *as unit of measurement, about* 45 cm)
	ὕς ὑός ὁ	pig
	ὀδούς -όντος ὁ	tooth
	θηρίον -ου τό	wild animal, beast
10	κάτω	(*here*) lower
	γνάθος -ου ἡ	jaw
	κινέω	I move (something)
	ἄνω	(*here*) upper
	Αἰγύπτιοι -ων οἱ	Egyptians
12	χράομαι	(*here*) I treat
	Θῆβαι -ων αἱ	Thebes (*i.e. Egyptian Thebes, not the Thebes in central Greece; = modern Luxor*)

τρέφουσι σίτῳ καὶ τά τ' ὦτα καὶ τοὺς πόδας κοσμοῦσι χρυσῷ. οἱ μέντοι
15 περὶ τὴν Ἐλεφαντίνην οἰκοῦντες καὶ ἐσθίουσι τοὺς κροκοδείλους,
οὐδαμῶς νομίζοντες αὐτοὺς ἱεροὺς εἶναι. ὁ δὲ βουλόμενος κροκόδειλον
αἱρεῖν δελεάζει νῶτον ὑὸς περὶ ἄγκιστρον καὶ εἰσβάλλει εἰς μέσον τὸν
ποταμόν· αὐτὸς δ' ἐπὶ τῆς τοῦ ποταμοῦ ὄχθης ἔχων ὗν ζῷόν, τύπτει
τοῦτον. ἀκούσας δὲ τὴν φωνὴν ὁ κροκόδειλος σπεύδει πρὸς τὴν φωνὴν
20 καὶ τὸ νῶτον καταπίνει· οἱ δ' ἐν τῇ ὄχθῃ ἕλκουσιν. πρῶτον δὲ πάντων ὁ
θηρευτὴς πηλῷ καλύπτει τοὺς ὀφθαλμοὺς αὐτοῦ· τοῦτο δὲ ποιήσας ῥᾷστα
ἀποκτείνει τὸν κροκόδειλον.

	τρέφω	I nourish, I support
	ὦτα -ων τά	ears
	κοσμέω	I decorate, I adorn
	Ἐλεφαντίνη -ης ἡ	Elephantine (city about 200 km further up the Nile
15		than Thebes)
	δελεάζω	I put (something) as bait
	νῶτον -ου τό	back
	ὗς ὑός ὁ	pig
	ἄγκιστρον -ου τό	hook
17	μέσος -η -ον	middle, middle (part) of
	ὄχθη -ης ἡ	bank
	ζῷός -ή -όν	living
	σπεύδω	I rush
	καταπίνω	I swallow down
20	ἕλκω	I pull, I drag
	θηρευτής -οῦ ὁ	hunter
	πηλός -οῦ ὁ	mud, clay
	καλύπτω	I cover

Use of the subjunctive

We saw in *Greek to GCSE (2)* that the subjunctive form or *mood* of the verb usually
expresses a *possibility* (often represented by a translation such as *may*), in contrast to the
ordinary indicative form which states a *fact*. We saw that it is simple in formation and easy
to recognise: subjunctive endings always have a *long vowel*, and are lengthened versions of
the normal primary active and middle/passive endings (see page 177).

We also saw that the distinction between present and aorist subjunctive is entirely by *aspect*
(present for something that may happen often or generally, aorist for something that may
happen on one specific occasion). At GCSE the subjunctive was met with μή as a
prohibition (*don't do X!*), with ἵνα in a purpose clause (*in order to do X*), and with ἐάν in a
future open condition (*if you do X*). The subjunctive also however has a number of other
jobs, which further illustrate its character. Because they deal with possibilities, the negative
used is μή (rather than οὐ, which applies to facts).

Jussive subjunctive and prohibition

• When the subjunctive is the main verb in a sentence, it is often some kind of command: a *jussive* subjunctive, named from the Latin *iubeo* (supine *iussum*) *I order*. It is typically seen in the first person plural (an *exhortation*: the speaker invites others to join him or her in doing something):

> φύγωμεν
> Let's run away! *(aorist, hence implying* now, on this occasion*)*
>
> μὴ τοῦτο ποιῶμεν.
> Let us not do this! *(present, hence implying* generally, ever*)*

Note that *let* in English here means *come on, let's ...* (addressed to others who are going to do it with you) rather than *do please allow us to ...* (addressed to someone else).

In second person, *imperatives* are normally used for commands. But for *negative* second person commands (prohibitions) we saw in *Greek to GCSE (2)* that, although μή is used with the *present* imperative for a *general* prohibition (*don't ever do X*), if the reference is to one occasion μή is used not (as might be expected) with the aorist imperative, but with the second person of the aorist subjunctive. Hence:

> μὴ διώκετε τοὺς δούλους, ὦ στρατιῶται.
> Don't (ever) chase slaves, soldiers! *(μή + present imperative)*
>
> μὴ διώξητε τοῦτον τὸν δοῦλον, ὦ στρατιῶται.
> Don't chase this slave, soldiers! *(μή + aorist subjunctive)*

Deliberative question

Another important use of the subjunctive is for a *deliberative* question, where the speaker is debating with himself or herself what to do (often conveyed in English by *what should I do?* or *what am I to do?*):

> τί ἀποκρίνωμαι;
> What am I to reply?
>
> ποῖ φύγωμεν;
> To where should we flee?

Note two possible ambiguities with the -ω ending: in the present active first person singular, the subjunctive is the same as the indicative (e.g. παύω); and the first aorist active subjunctive first person singular is often the same as the future indicative (e.g. παύσω). In such cases a deliberative question can only be inferred from the context (though if it is negative, it is identified by the use of μή rather than οὐ).

For a summary of the various uses of the subjunctive see page 149.

11

Exercise 1.7

Translate into English:
1   τὴν δικαιοσύνην ἀεὶ ζητῶμεν, ὦ πολῖται.
2   ποῖ φύγω, ὑπὸ τούτων διωκόμενος;
3   μὴ λάβητε τὰ τοῦ γέροντος χρήματα, ὦ παῖδες.
4   ἐν δεινῷ κινδύνῳ ὄντες, τοῖς θεοῖς νῦν θύσωμεν.
5   ἀεὶ τῷ στρατηγῷ πιστεύετε, ὦ στρατιῶται, καίπερ οὐκ ἀεὶ εἰδότες
       ὅ τι μέλλει πράξειν.
6   παρὰ τῷ ποταμῷ καθίσωμεν ὡς ἐδόμενοι.
7   ἀποβάλετε πάσας τάσδε τὰς βίβλους, ὦ δοῦλοι.
8   μὴ λίπῃς τὰ ὅπλα ἐγγὺς τῆς θύρας, ὦ φύλαξ.
9   ὁμολογοῦμεν περὶ τῆσδε τῆς βουλῆς, ἀλλὰ τί εἴπωμεν περὶ ἐκείνης;
10   μὴ ἀκούσητε τοὺς τοῦ ἀγγέλου λόγους, ὦ πολῖται.

Exercise 1.8

Translate into Greek:
1   What am I to reply to the teacher?
2   Do not steal this book, boy!
3   Let us always drive the enemy out of our city!
4   Always bury the dead, citizens!
5   Let us lead these allies up the mountain.

Exercise 1.9 (Revision)

Translate into English:
1   τούτῳ τῷ ῥήτορι μηδαμῶς πιστεύσητε, ὦ πολῖται.
2   πόσας ναῦς ἔπεμψαν οἱ Ἀθηναῖοι;
3   φάγωμεν ὡς τάχιστα πάντα τόνδε τὸν σῖτον, ὦ φίλοι.
4   οἶδά σε ὅπως ἀνδρεῖος εἶ.
5   μὴ κρύψῃς τὸν χρυσόν, ὦ δοῦλε.
6   σοφός ἐστι πᾶς ὅστις τοῖς νόμοις πείθεται.
7   ἆρ' οἶσθα ἐκεῖνον τὸν ξένον ὅστις ἐστίν;
8   λυσώμεθα τοὺς ὑπὸ τῶν πολεμίων ληφθέντας.
9   ἆρα μὴ ἀληθῆ ἐστι τὰ ὑπὸ τοῦ ἀγγέλου λεχθέντα;
10   ἠρώτησα τὸν στρατηγὸν ὁπόσους στρατιώτας ἄγει καὶ ὁποῖα ἔπαθον.

Use of the optative

We saw in *Greek to GCSE (2)* that, in addition to the subjunctive, Greek verbs have a mood called the *optative*. It is *like the subjunctive but more so*: more remote in likelihood or time. Where the indicative states a fact (*we are doing X*), the subjunctive indicates an immediate possibility (*we may do X*) and the optative indicates a more remote possibility (*we might do X*). As this last example shows, it is often represented by a translation such as *might*. We saw that the subjunctive always has a long vowel in its ending. The optative is even more easily recognisable by a *diphthong* (οι, αι or less commonly ει) in its ending.

At GCSE the optative was met with ἵνα in a purpose clause set in the past, and also in an indirect statement or question set in the past (*she asked what had happened*), in the latter case with no difference of meaning from the indicative but illustrating the *historic* character seen also in some of the optative endings (e.g. -μην). But as with the subjunctive, the optative shows its nature more clearly when it stands alone.

Wishes

When the optative is the only or main verb of a sentence, it usually expresses a *wish* for the future, often introduced by εἴθε, literally *if only* ... ! (or, in more formal and old-fashioned English, *would that* ... ! - compare εἰ, the normal word for *if*). The optative here operates (like the subjunctive constructions we have looked at) by *aspect* (i.e. present for a generalised wish, optative for a wish for one specific occasion). The negative in a wish is μή.

> εἴθε οἱ βάρβαροι ἀπέλθοιεν.
> If only the barbarians would go away!

It would also be justifiable to translate e.g. *I wish* ... (even though there is no first person verb), or *may* ... :

> μηδέποτε τοιαῦτα γένοιτο.
> May such things never happen!

• The optative operates by aspect except in indirect statements and questions (where it keeps the tense of the original direct speech, explaining why there is a future optative).

For a summary of the various ways in which the optative is used see page 150.

Exercise 1.10

Translate into English:
1   εἴθε αἱ τῶν συμμάχων νῆες ἀφίκοιντο.
2   εἴθε οἱ ῥήτορες ἀεὶ δικαίως λέγοιεν.
3   ὑπὸ τῶν πολιτῶν ἀεὶ τιμῷο, ὦ γύναι.
4   εἴθε μὴ νικήσαιεν οἱ πολέμιοι.
5   μηδέποτε τοιαῦτα αὖθις ἴδοιμι.

Exercise 1.11

Translate into Greek:
1   If only those women would send us money!
2   If only the allies would always fight bravely!
3   May wars of this sort never happen!
4   If only you would learn these words, boys!
5   Would that the king might always honour the citizens!

Exercise 1.12

Peisistratus (1)

We saw in Greek to GCSE (2) *that Herodotus gives much attention to the 'tyrants' who ruled many Greek city-states in the seventh and sixth centuries BC. They were not necessarily (as the word now implies) cruel despots: many enjoyed strong popular support. The old hereditary monarchies had long since given way to the rule of aristocrats. A tyrant typically came from the fringes of this privileged group: he seized power for himself, promising benefits to the ordinary people. In Chapter 5 we shall read of the unsuccessful attempt by Cylon to establish a tyranny in Athens in 632 BC. It was to stave off further attempts that Solon was invited to reform the constitution and economy. But despite his efforts Athens did eventually get a tyrant, for in 560 BC (when tyranny was already going out of fashion elsewhere) Peisistratus made his first and temporarily successful bid for power (we read subsequently of his second). This passage is a digression within Herodotus' account of the Lydian king Croesus, seeking allies in Greece against the rising power of Persia. 'Tyrant' was a loan-word from Lydian, attesting perception of a similar style of rule: we saw that Croesus' ancestor Gyges had seized power in a dramatic way, as Peisistratus does here.*

τὸ δὴ οὖν τῶν Ἀθηναίων ἔθνος κατείχετο ὑπὸ Πεισιστράτου τοῦ
Ἱπποκράτους τότε τυραννεύοντος. Ἱπποκράτει γὰρ ὄντι ἰδιώτῃ καὶ
θεωροῦντι τὰ Ὀλύμπια τέρας ἐγένετο μέγα· θύσαντος γὰρ αὐτοῦ τὰ ἱερὰ
οἱ λέβητες κρεῶν τε ὄντες ἔμπλεοι καὶ ὕδατος ἄνευ πυρὸς ἔζεσαν καὶ
5 ὑπερέβαλον. Χίλων δὲ ὁ Λακεδαιμόνιος τύχῃ παρὼν καὶ τὸ τέρας ἰδὼν
εἶπε τῷ Ἱπποκράτει· "πρῶτον μὲν γυναῖκα μὴ ἀγάγῃς τεκνοποιὸν εἰς τὴν
οἰκίαν· εἰ δὲ ἤδη ἔχεις, ἀποπέμψον αὐτήν. καὶ εἰ ἔστι σοι παῖς τις,
δεῖ ἀπειπεῖν τοῦτον."

ὁ μέντοι Ἱπποκράτης οὐδαμῶς ἤθελε πίθεσθαι τῷ Χίλωνι ταῦτα
10 παραινέσαντι. ἐγεννήθη οὖν μετὰ ταῦτα Πεισίστρατος οὗτος, ὃς ἀνὴρ
γενόμενος ἐβουλεύσατο ἵνα τυραννίδα λάβοι. στασιαζόντων γὰρ τότε τῶν

	ἔθνος -ους τό	people
	κατέχω	I control
	Πεισίστρατος -ου ὁ	Peisistratus
	Ἱπποκράτης -ους ὁ	Hippocrates (*gen indicates* son of)
2	τυραννεύω	I am tyrant
	ἰδιώτης -ου ὁ	private citizen
	θεωρέω	I watch
	Ὀλύμπια -ων τά	Olympic games
	τέρας -ατος τό	portent, miraculous event
3	ἱερά -ῶν τά	victims, sacrificial offerings
	λέβης -ητος ὁ	cauldron
	κρέας -ως τό	meat, piece of meat
	ἔμπλεος -ον	full
	ζέω ἔζεσα	I boil
5	ὑπερβάλλω ὑπερέβαλον	(*here*) I overflow
	Χίλων -ωνος ὁ	Chilon (*Spartan politician famous for his wisdom*)
	τεκνοποιός -όν	to bear children
	ἀπεῖπον	(*aor with no pres*) I disown
	οὐδαμῶς	in no way
10	παραινέω παρήνεσα	I encourage
	γεννάω *aor pass* ἐγεννήθην	I give birth to, *pass* I am born
	βουλεύομαι ἐβουλευσάμην	I plot
	τυραννίς -ίδος ἡ	tyranny, tyrannical power
	στασιάζω	I am in a faction, I quarrel

14

παράλων καὶ τῶν ἐκ τοῦ πεδίου, ὁ Πεισίστρατος ἤγειρε τρίτην στάσιν. συλλέξας οὖν στασιώτας καὶ προστάτης τῶν ὑπερακρίων λόγῳ ὤν, ἐμηχανήσατο τάδε. τραυματίσας ἑαυτόν τε καὶ τοὺς ἡμιόνους ἤλασεν τὸ
15 ζεῦγος ἐς τὴν ἀγορὰν ὥσπερ φεύγων ἀπὸ τῶν ἐχθρῶν· καὶ εἶπεν ὅτι οὗτοι βούλοιντο ἀποκτεῖναι αὐτόν. ἐδεῖτο οὖν τοῦ δήμου φυλακὴν πορίζειν. καὶ διότι δόξαν πρότερον ἐδέξατο ἐν μάχῃ ἐπὶ τοὺς Μεγαρέας γενομένη, ὁ δῆμος ὁ τῶν Ἀθηναίων ἐξαπατηθεὶς ἔδωκεν αὐτῷ ἄνδρας ἐξαιρέτους τῶν πολιτῶν οἱ δορυφόροι μὲν οὐκ ἐγένοντο τοῦ Πεισιστράτου,
20 κορυνηφόροι δέ· ξύλων γὰρ κορύνας ἔχοντες εἵποντο αὐτῷ. οὗτοι τε καὶ ὁ Πεισίστρατος ἔσχον τὴν ἀκρόπολιν. ἔνθα δὴ ὁ Πεισίστρατος ἦρχε τῶν Ἀθηναίων, οὔτε τιμὰς τὰς οὔσας ταράξας οὔτε τοὺς νόμους μεταλλάξας, καὶ ἔνεμε τὴν πόλιν κοσμῶν κάλως τε καὶ εὖ.

	πάραλοι -ων οἱ	men of the coast (*getting moderate living from fishing*)
	πεδίον -ου τό	plain (*rich agricultural land*)
	ἀγείρω ἤγειρα	I gather together
	στάσις -εως ἡ	faction
13	στασιώτης -ου ὁ	member of a faction
	προστάτης -ου ὁ	leader
	ὑπεράκριοι -ων οἱ	men from beyond the hills (*poor backwoodsmen*)
	λόγῳ	nominally, in theory
	μηχανάομαι ἐμηχανησάμην	I contrive
14	τραυματίζω ἐτραυμάτισα	I wound
	ἡμίονος -ου ὁ	mule
	ἐλαύνω ἤλασα	I drive
	ζεῦγος -ους τό	carriage
	δέομαι	I ask for (*+ gen*)
16	φυλακή -ῆς ἡ	bodyguard, group of guards
	πορίζω	I provide
	δόξα -ης ἡ	glory
	Μεγαρεῖς -έων οἱ	Megarians, people of Megara (*neighbouring state and enemy of Athens*)
18	ἐξαπατάω aor pass ἐξηπατήθην	I deceive
	ἐξαίρετος -ον	chosen, selected
	δορυφόροι -ων οἱ	spear-bearers (*normal word for bodyguards*)
	κορυνηφόροι -ων οἱ	club-bearers (*implied to be rougher and more formidable*)
20	ξύλον -ου τό	wood, piece of wood
	κορύνη -ης ἡ	club
	ἀκρόπολις -εως ἡ	the Acropolis (*citadel of Athens*)
	τιμή -ῆς ἡ	(*here*) office, magistracy
	ταράσσω ἐτάραξα	I disturb
23	μεταλλάσσω μετήλλαξα	I change
	νέμω	I manage
	κοσμέω	I arrange

Peisistratus (2)

μετὰ δὲ οὐ πολὺν χρόνον οἱ ἄλλοι στασιῶται τὸ αὐτὸ φρονοῦντες
ἐξήλασαν τὸν Πεισίστρατον. οὕτως ὁ Πεισίστρατος τὴν τυραννίδα πρῶτον
κτησάμενος ἀπέβαλεν. ἔπειτα δὲ οἱ ἐξαλάσαντες αὖθις ἐπ᾽ ἀλλήλους
ἐστασίαζον. καὶ ἐν τῇ στάσει κακῶς πράσσων Μεγακλῆς ὁ τῶν παράλων
5   ἡγεμὼν ἠρώτησε τὸν Πεισίστρατον εἰ βούλοιτο τὴν θυγατέρα ἔχειν
γυναῖκα καὶ τὴν τυραννίδα. καὶ ὁ Πεισίστρατος ἐδέξατο τὸν λόγον.

μηχανῶνται οὖν ἐπὶ τῇ καθόδῳ πρᾶγμα εὐηθέστατον (ὡς ἐγὼ εὑρίσκω)
μακρῷ, ἐπεὶ ἀπεκρίθη πάλαι τὸ Ἑλληνικὸν ἔθνος τοῦ βαρβάρου,
δεξιώτερον ὂν καὶ ἄνευ εὐηθείας ἠλιθίου. ἀλλ᾽ ἐν τοῖς Ἀθηναίοις τοῖς
10   πρώτοις λεγομένοις εἶναι τῶν Ἑλλήνων τὴν σοφίαν* ὅμως μηχανῶνται
τάδε. ἐν τῷ δήμῳ τῷ Παιανιεῖ ἦν γυνή τις ᾗ τὸ ὄνομα ἦν Φύη, μέγεθος*
ἀπὸ τεσσάρων πηχέων ἀπολείπουσα τρεῖς δακτύλους καὶ ἄλλως εὐειδής.

	στασιώτης -ου ὁ	member of a faction, faction-fighter
	φρονέω	I think, I hold an opinion
	ἐξελαύνω ἐξήλασα	I drive out
	Πεισίστρατος -ου ὁ	Peisistratus
2	τυραννίς -ίδος ἡ	tyranny, tyrannical power
	ἀποβάλλω ἀπέβαλον	(here) I lose
	ἀλλήλους -ων	each other
	στασιάζω	I quarrel
	στάσις -εως ἡ	faction
4	Μεγακλῆς -έους ὁ	Megacles
	πάραλοι -ων οἱ	men of the coast
	μηχανάομαι	I contrive
	ἐπί	(+ dat) (here) to achieve
	κάθοδος -ου ἡ	return
7	πρᾶγμα -ατος τό	thing, business
	εὐήθης -ες	foolish
	μακρῷ	by far
	ἀποκρίνω aor pass ἀπεκρίθην	I distinguish
	Ἑλληνικός -ή -όν	Greek
8	ἔθνος -ους τό	people, nation
	δεξιός -ά -όν	clever
	εὐήθεια -ας ἡ	foolishness
	ἠλίθιος -ον	silly
	ὅμως	nonetheless
11	δῆμος -ου ὁ	(here) deme (district of Athens)
	Παιανιεύς -έως	of Paeania (a deme)
	Φύη -ης ἡ	Phye
	μέγεθος -ους τό	size, stature
	πῆχυς -εως ἡ	cubit (lit forearm, as measure - about 45 cm)
12	ἀπολείπω	(here) I fall short by
	δάκτυλος -ου ὁ	(here) finger's width (about 2 cm)
	ἄλλως	otherwise, generally
	εὐειδής -ες	well-shaped, beautiful

* Examples of the 'accusative of respect' - lit with respect to, i.e. in wisdom, size, etc.

ταύτην γυναῖκα παρασκευάσαντες <u>πανοπλίᾳ</u> <u>ἐς</u> <u>ἅρμα</u> <u>εἰσβιβάσαντες</u> καὶ
πάντα πράξαντες ἵνα <u>εὐπρεπέστατη</u> φαίνοιτο, <u>ἤλαυνον</u> εἰς τὴν πόλιν,
15 <u>προδρόμους</u> <u>κήρυκας</u> <u>προπέμψαντες</u>. καὶ οὗτοι ἀφικόμενοι <u>ἐκήρυξαν</u> τάδε·
"ὦ Ἀθηναῖοι, <u>εὐμενῶς</u> δέχεσθε τὸν Πεισίστρατον, ὃν ἡ <u>Ἀθήνη</u> αὐτὴ
τιμήσασα ἀνθρώπων μάλιστα <u>κατάγει</u> εἰς τὴν ἑαυτῆς <u>ἀκρόπολιν</u>." οἱ μὲν
δὴ κήρυκες ταῦτα περιβαίνοντες ἔλεγον. <u>αὐτίκα</u> <u>φάτις</u> <u>πανταχόσε</u> ἀφίκετο
ὅτι ἡ Ἀθήνη τὸν Πεισίστρατον κατάγοι, καὶ οἱ ἐν τῇ πόλει νομίζοντες
20 τὴν γυναῖκα εἶναι τὴν θεὰν αὐτὴν <u>προσηύχοντο</u> τὴν ἄνθρωπον καὶ
ἐδέχοντο τὸν Πεισίστρατον.

	πανοπλία -ας ἡ	full set of armour
	ἐς	(= εἰς)
	ἅρμα -ατος τό	chariot
	εἰσβιβάζω εἰσεβίβασα	I put (someone) into
14	εὐπρεπής -ές	impressive
	ἐλαύνω	I drive
	πρόδρομος -ον	running ahead
	κῆρυξ -υκος ὁ	herald
	προπέμπω προὔπεμψα	I send in advance
15	κηρύσσω ἐκήρυξα	I proclaim
	εὐμενῶς	favourably
	Ἀθήνη -ης ἡ	Athene
	κατάγω	I bring back
	ἀκρόπολις -εως ἡ	the Acropolis
18	αὐτίκα	immediately
	φάτις -εως ἡ	rumour, report
	πανταχόσε	(to) everywhere
	προσεύχομαι	I pray to

*Peisistratus' second tenure of tyranny was also short-lived: he was unwilling to have children by the
daughter of Megacles because of a family curse resulting from events surrounding the earlier attempted
coup by Cylon (as we shall see in Chapter 5). Megacles was offended, the alliance collapsed, and
Peisistratus again went into exile. But a third attempt was more lastingly successful, and Peisistratus was a
generally popular ruler for about twenty years. He passed on power to his son Hippias, but the position of
second-generation tyrants was insecure: after a botched rebellion in which his brother was assassinated,
Hippias became a cruel despot (a tyrant in the modern sense). The ending of his regime (by Athenian
aristocrats with Spartan help) led in due course to the establishment of democracy.*

Conditional sentences (1)

In *Greek to GCSE (2)* we saw that a conditional sentence is made up of two elements, a protasis (*if X*) and an apodosis (*then Y*), and we met two particular types:

future open	If X happens, Y will happen.
	ἐάν + subjunctive, future indicative
past closed	If X had happened, Y would have happened.
	εἰ + aorist indicative, aorist indicative + ἄν

In the nature of things, these are the most common forms of conditional expression. In all however there are six different types, which divide into two categories.

Open/unknown conditions

Open conditions carry no implication about whether the condition is fulfilled or not. They can be any tense, and are normally indicative and straightforward to translate:

present	εἰ ταῦτα λέγεις, σοφῶς λέγεις.
	If you say these things, you speak wisely.
past	εἰ ταῦτα εἶπες, σοφῶς εἶπες.
	If you said these things, you spoke wisely.

Similarly it is possible to find:

future	εἰ ταῦτα λέξεις, σοφῶς λέξεις.
	If you say these things (*i.e.* in the future), you will speak wisely.

Note however that in this example, English has a *hidden* future in the first half. In a similar way (as we saw in the examples met at GCSE), Greek commonly expresses the first half of a future condition with a distinctive idiom, using (instead of the future indicative) a subjunctive (determined as usual by aspect, not tense), and a special word for *if* - ἐάν:

> ἐάν ταῦτα λέξῃς, σοφῶς λέξεις.
> If you say these things (*i.e.* in the future), you will speak wisely.

This use of the subjunctive is in line with other uses where it expresses a *possibility*, and is an example of the *indefinite construction* (see page 83), emphasising a necessary characteristic of future time.

• The ἐάν + subjunctive construction can also be used for an indefinite present condition (*if ever you do X*).

In contrast, the type of open future condition using εἰ and the future indicative stresses the unavoidable nature of the consequence, so it tends to be found in threats and warnings:

> εἰ ταῦτα λέξεις, κολασθήσῃ.
> If you say these things (*i.e.* in the future), you will be punished.

All these conditions are *open* (as distinct from the type where fulfilment is unlikely, or already ruled out, as in the past closed *If you had done X, Y would have happened*). But the sense in which they are open varies according to tense. A *future* open condition is genuinely open: *You may or may not do X, but if you do, Y will follow.* Clearly a *past* condition cannot be open in this sense. We cannot go back and change the events; what is *open* or unresolved is simply the speaker's knowledge: *I don't know whether you did X or not, but if you did (it follows that) you did something stupid.* This type of condition can therefore be thought of as past *unknown.* A *present* open condition can also be unknown in this way (*If you are working for five hours every evening, you are doing too much*); or it can simply state an axiom (*If a number is divisible only by itself or one, it is a prime number*).

• The word *protasis* (the actual *if* clause) literally means *put forward* (as a premise), and *apodosis* (the main or *then*) clause literally means *giving back,* i.e. providing an answer.

• In any conditional sentence, the negative in the protasis is μή and in the apodosis is οὐ.

• The protasis usually comes before the apodosis, but can come after:

σοφώτατός ἐστιν ὁ γέρων εἰ τοιαῦτα λέγει.
The old man is very wise if he says such things.

• It is also possible to mix tenses:

εἰ ἐκείνην τὴν βίβλον διέφθειρας, μῶρος εἶ.
If you destroyed that book, you are stupid.

• The apodosis can be replaced by e.g. an imperative:

εἰ τοιαύτας ἐπιστολὰς πέμπεις, παῦσαι.
If you are sending such letters, stop (doing so)!

Exercise 1.14

Translate into English:
1   εἰ ὁ ῥήτωρ ταῦτα λέγει, καλῶς λέγει.
2   εἰ πάντες οἱ αἰχμάλωτοι ἐκ τοῦ τειχίσματος ἔφυγον, εὐτυχεῖς ἦσαν.
3   εἰ τὸν ἵππον ἔτι ἔχετε, λύσατε αὐτόν.
4   ἐὰν τὴν παῖδα ἐπαινέσῃς, ἑκοῦσα βοηθήσει σοι.
5   εἰ ὁ στρατηγὸς μὴ σοφός ἐστιν, οὐχ οἷός τ' ἐστὶν σοφῶς βουλεύεσθαι.
6   εἰ πᾶν τὸ ἔργον τῇ πρώτῃ ἡμέρᾳ ἔπραξας, εὐτυχὴς εἶ.
7   μῶροί ἐστε εἰ ταύτην τὴν βουλὴν φιλεῖτε, ὦ πολῖται.
8   εἰ τιμᾷς ἐκείνην τὴν γυναῖκα, τί λέξεις περὶ ταύτης;
9   ἐὰν τὰ αὐτὰ αὖθις ὑπίσχηται, μὴ πιστεύσῃς τῷ ῥήτορι.
10   εἰ ἡ πόλις τοιαῦτα τείχη ἔχει, οὐδαμῶς φοβοῦμαι.

Exercise 1.15

Translate into Greek:
1   If the old man says this, he is foolish.
2   If the citizens waited all night, they were very brave.
3   If that slave is in the house, send him to the marketplace, mother!
4   If you stop the battle, general, we shall never conquer the enemy.
5   If you learned all the words, you are very wise.

Exercise 1.16

The Infancy of Cyrus (1)

Cyrus the Great (who conquered Croesus' kingdom of Lydia) was the founder of the Persian empire, and king of Persia 559-529 BC. This story takes us back to the beginning of his life. His father was a Persian noble, but his mother was daughter of Astyages king of the Medes. The Medes were for a century or so the leading power in the Middle East (after their rebellion from the previously dominant empire of the Assyrians, and before the rise of Persia). Cyrus was to shift power decisively from the Medes to the Persians. As often in ancient literature, stories akin to myth are told about the childhood of an historical figure in order to demonstrate his significance. The prophecy given at the beginning to his grandfather Astyages is strikingly similar to the one Acrisius receives in the Perseus story in Greek to GCSE (2). The 'exposure' of unwanted babies (leaving them in a lonely place to die, rather than incurring religious pollution by actually killing them) was undoubtedly practised in the ancient world, though it is unclear on what scale; in stories, it is often the context for an unexpected rescue or miraculous deliverance.

οἱ δὲ τῶν <u>Μάγων</u> <u>ὀνειροπόλοι</u> εἶπον τῷ <u>Ἀστυάγει</u> τῷ τῶν <u>Μήδων</u> βασιλεῖ
ἐξ <u>ὄψεώς</u> τινος ὅτι ὁ τῆς θυγατρὸς υἱὸς <u>βασιλεύσει</u> <u>ἀντὶ</u> ἐκείνου. ταῦτα
οὖν μαθὼν ὁ Ἀστυάγης, ἐπεὶ ἡ θυγάτηρ <u>Μανδάνη</u> ὀνόματι παῖδα <u>ἔτεκεν</u>,
ἐκάλεσε τὸν <u>Ἄρπαγον</u> ἄνδρα <u>συγγενῆ</u> τε καὶ <u>πιστὸν</u> ᾧ πάντα τὰ ἑαυτοῦ
5   <u>ἐπέτρεπεν</u>. τῷ δὲ Ἁρπάγῳ παρόντι ὁ Ἀστυάγης εἶπε τάδε· "ὦ Ἄρπαγε,
<u>πρᾶγμα</u> μέγιστον βούλομαί σε πρᾶξαι, ὃ μὴ <u>ἀποκνήσῃς·</u> λαβὲ τὸν τῆς
Μανδάνης παῖδα, καὶ εἰς τὴν σὴν οἰκίαν ἐνεγκὼν ἀπόκτεινον. μετὰ δὲ
ταῦτα θάψον αὐτὸν <u>ὥσπερ</u> βούλῃ." ὁ δὲ ἀπεκρίνατο· "ὦ βασιλεῦ, εἰ
φίλον ἐστί σοι τοῦτο οὕτως γίγνεσθαι, χρὴ τὸ ἐμὸν <u>ἐπιτηδείως</u> ποιῆσαι".

10 ταῦτα δ' ἀποκρινάμενος ὁ Ἄρπαγος, ἐπεὶ τὸ <u>παιδίον</u> ἐδέξατο, ἀπῆλθε
δακρύων πρὸς τὴν οἰκίαν. καὶ ἀφικόμενος εἶπε τῇ γυναικὶ πάντα τὸν
λόγον τὸν ὑπ' Ἀστυάγους λεχθέντα. ἡ δὲ εἶπε, "τί οὖν μέλλεις νῦν
ποιήσειν;" ὁ δὲ ἀπεκρίνατο, "οὐχ ὡς ὁ Ἀστυάγης ἐκέλευσεν. οὐδὲ γὰρ
ἐὰν <u>μαίνηται</u> κάκιον ἢ νῦν μαίνεται τοῦτο ποιήσω. διὰ δὲ πολλὰ οὐκ
15 ἀποκτενῶ τὸ παιδίον. πρῶτον μὲν συγγενές ἐστί μοι, ὁ δὲ Ἀστυάγης

	Μάγοι -ων οἱ	Magi (*caste of wise/holy men*)
	ὀνειροπόλος -ου ὁ	dream-interpreter
	Ἀστυάγης -ους ὁ	Astyages
	Μῆδοι -ων οἱ	Medes
2	ὄψις -εως ἡ	vision
	βασιλεύω	I am king
	ἀντί	instead of (+ *gen*)
	Μανδάνη -ης ἡ	Mandane
	τίκτω ἔτεκον	I give birth to
4	Ἄρπαγος -ου ὁ	Harpagus
	συγγενής -ές	related
	πιστός -ή -όν	loyal, reliable
	ἐπιτρέπω	I entrust (X *acc* to Y *dat*)
	πρᾶγμα -ατος τό	matter, business
6	ἀποκνέω ἀπέκνησα	I shrink from
	ὥσπερ	just as
	ἐπιτηδείως	suitably, properly
	παιδίον -ου τό	baby
	μαίνομαι	I am mad

20

γέρων ἐστὶ καὶ ἄπαις ἄρσενος τέκνου. ἐὰν δὲ τὴν ἀρχήν, ἐκείνου
ἀποθανόντος, κτήσηται ἡ παῖς, ἧς τὸν υἱὸν ὁ Ἀστυάγης νῦν βούλεται
ἀποκτεῖναι δι' ἐμοῦ, λειφθήσεταί μοι μετὰ ταῦτα κινδύνων ὁ μέγιστος.
ἀλλὰ δεῖ φυλάσσειν τὴν ἐμὴν σωτηρίαν· δεῖ οὖν τὸν παῖδα ἀποθανεῖν.
20 ἄμεινον μέντοι ἐστὶν εἰ ἀποθανεῖται πρός τινος τῶν τοῦ Ἀστυάγους, καὶ
μὴ πρὸς ἐμοῦ."

ταῦτα εἶπε καὶ εὐθὺς μετεπέμψατο βουκόλον τινὰ τῶν τοῦ Ἀστυάγους,
ὃν ᾔδει ὄρη ἔρημα νέμοντα. καὶ τὸ ὄνομα τούτῳ ἦν Μιτραδάτης. ἐπεὶ
οὖν ὁ βουκόλος τάχιστα ἀφίκετο κληθείς, εἶπεν ὁ Ἅρπαγος τάδε· "κελεύει
25 σε ὁ Ἀστυάγης τοῦτο τὸ παιδίον πρὸς τὸ ἐρημότατον τῶν ὀρῶν φέρειν,
ἵνα ἐκεῖ ταχέως ἀποθάνῃ. λέγει δὲ καὶ τόδε ὁ βασιλεύς, ὅτι ἐὰν ὀκνήσῃς
καὶ μὴ ποιήσῃς τὸ κελευσθέν, ἔσται σοι θάνατος κάκιστος."

ὁ οὖν βουκόλος ταῦτα ἀκούσας καὶ τὸ παιδίον ἀναλαβὼν ἐπανῆλθε τὴν
αὐτὴν ὁδόν. καὶ ἐκείνῃ τῇ ἡμέρᾳ ἡ τοῦ βουκόλου γυνὴ παιδίον ἔτεκεν.
30 τὸν δ' ἄνδρα ἀφικόμενον ἡ γυνὴ εὐθὺς ἤρετο διὰ τί οὕτω προθύμως
μετεπέμψατο αὐτὸν ὁ Ἅρπαγος. ὁ δὲ εἶπεν, "ὦ γύναι, εἶδόν τε εἰς τὴν
πόλιν ἐλθὼν καὶ ἤκουσα ὃ ἤλπιζον μηδέποτε ὄψεσθαι. πᾶσα γὰρ ἡ τοῦ
Ἁρπάγου οἰκία κλαυθμῷ κατείχετο. ἐγὼ εἰσῆλθον φοβούμενος, καὶ εἶδον
παιδίον χρυσῷ τε καὶ ἐσθῆτι καλλίστῃ κεκοσμημένον. καὶ ἐδάκρυε τὸ
35 παιδίον."

	ἄπαις -αιδος	childless, without offspring
	ἄρσην -ενος	male
	τέκνον -ου τό	child
	σωτηρία -ας ἡ	safety
20	πρός	(+ gen) at the hands of
	μεταπέμπομαι μετεπεμψάμην	I send for
	βουκόλος -ου ὁ	herdsman
	ἔρημος -η -ον	lonely, deserted
	νέμω	pasture (animals in)
23	Μιτραδάτης -ου ὁ	Mitradates
	ὀκνέω ὤκνησα	I hesitate
	ἀναλαμβάνω ἀνέλαβον	I pick up
	ἐπανέρχομαι ἐπανῆλθον	I return, I go back
	τίκτω ἔτεκον	I give birth to
30	προθύμως	eagerly
	κλαυθμός -οῦ ὁ	weeping, mourning
	κατέχω	I occupy
	παιδίον -ου τό	baby
	ἐσθής -ῆτος ἡ	clothing
34	κεκοσμημένος -η -ον	adorned, dressed elaborately

Conditional sentences (2)

The second category of conditional sentences (including the *past closed* ones met at GCSE) consists of *unfulfilled* conditions, and those which the speaker implies are unlikely to be fulfilled, often marked in English by the use of *would*. For the past and present we can call these *closed* (the possibility of fulfilment is already closed off). But just as the past cannot be truly *open* (so we say *unknown*), the future cannot ever be *closed*: possible future events can only be described as unlikely or *remote*.

Future remote conditions

A *remote future condition* expresses something which might possibly happen, but which the speaker implies is unlikely (the nearest the future can get to being *closed*). It uses the optative (present or aorist by aspect) in both protasis and apodosis, εἰ for *if* in the protasis, and the indefinite particle ἄν in the apodosis (ἄν generally gives a flavour of *would* or *might*: here it reinforces a sense which the optative already has).

> *future remote condition*
> εἰ ταῦτα λέγοις, σοφῶς ἂν λέγοις.
> If you were to say these things, you would speak wisely.

Present and past closed conditions

Closed or unfulfilled conditions in the present and past envisage situations which are already known not to be true. They do not involve any subjunctive or optative (this may seem surprising, especially given the use of the subjunctive for the equivalent construction in Latin), but rely instead on the indefinite particle ἄν with tenses of the indicative to give the flavour of *would*. A *present closed* condition uses the imperfect indicative in both protasis and apodosis, εἰ for *if* in the protasis, and the indefinite particle ἄν in the apodosis.

> *present closed condition*
> εἰ ταῦτα ἔλεγες, σοφῶς ἂν ἔλεγες.
> If you were saying these things, you would be speaking wisely.

• The use of *were* here is a good mnemonic for the imperfect, though it is actually an English subjunctive.

A *past closed* condition (as we saw at GCSE) normally uses the aorist indicative in both protasis and apodosis, εἰ for *if* in the protasis, and the indefinite particle ἄν in the apodosis.

> *past closed condition*
> εἰ ταῦτα εἶπες, σοφῶς ἂν εἶπες.
> If you had said these things, you would have spoken wisely.

Notice in both these examples that the indefinite particle ἄν does not just put a *would* into the apodosis but affects how you translate the whole sentence. The protasis εἰ ταῦτα εἶπες could (if there were no ἄν in the apodosis) be the first part of a past open/unknown condition (*If you said this, you spoke wisely*). You cannot translate the protasis until you

22

have looked carefully at the whole sentence and decided (from whether ἄν is present or not) what kind of condition is involved.

• As with open conditions, it is possible to have mixed tenses (protasis and apodosis different), but it is not normally possible to mix types of condition (closed/remote with open/ unknown).

εἰ ταῦτα ἔμαθον, εὐτυχὴς ἂν ἦν.
If I had learned these things, I would be happy.

• Although the verbs in a past closed condition are normally aorist, other past indicative tenses can be used according to sense (thus a repeated action would be expressed by the imperfect, which could be differentiated from a present closed condition only by sense and context).

• Note that because the verb *to be* has no aorist, its imperfect form has to be used where an aorist would strictly be required. Again you need to look at the whole sentence before trying to translate:

present closed (imperfect)
εἰ σοφὸς ἦν, σοφῶς ἂν ἔλεγεν.
If he were wise, he would be speaking wisely.

past closed (imperfect acting as aorist)
εἰ σοφὸς ἦν, σοφῶς ἂν εἶπεν.
If he had been wise, he would have spoken wisely.

• The protasis of a conditional sentence can be replaced by a participle phrase or genitive absolute (these normally express *circumstances*, here hypothetical ones). The apodosis should still make clear what kind of condition is involved, and if there is a negative with the participle, it will be μή rather than the usual οὐ:

τῶν συμμάχων μὴ ἀφικομένων, οὐκ ἂν ἐνικήσαμεν.
If the allies had not arrived, we would not have won.

Summary table of conditionals

	Open (or unknown)	Unfulfilled (closed or remote)
Future		
protasis	ἐάν + subjunctive*	εἰ + optative
apodosis	future indicative	optative + ἄν
Present		
protasis	εἰ + present indicative	εἰ + imperfect indicative
apodosis	present indicative	imperfect indicative + ἄν
Past		
protasis	εἰ + any past indicative	εἰ + aorist indicative
apodosis	any past indicative	aorist indicative + ἄν

*or εἰ + future indicative

Note:
(1) Only in future conditionals is a subjunctive or optative involved.
(2) All unfulfilled/closed/remote conditions have ἄν in the apodosis.
(3) In any type of conditional, the negative in the protasis is μή and the negative in the apodosis is οὐ.

For conditional clauses within indirect speech, see page 95.

Exercise 1.17 (Remote/closed conditionals)

Translate into English:
1   εἰ λέξειας, ἀκούσαιμι ἄν.
2   εἰ αἱ γυναῖκες ὑπὸ νύκτα ἀφίκοντο, εἴδομεν ἂν αὐτάς.
3   εἰ ὁ Σωκράτης νῦν παρῆν, τί ἐδίδασκεν ἄν;
4   εἰ οἱ πολῖται μὴ ἐφύλαξαν τὰς πύλας, ἐλήφθη ἂν ἡ πόλις.
5   εἰ τὸν ἄγγελον ἀπεπέμψατε, οὐδὲν ἂν ἠκούσατε περὶ τούτων.
6   δεινότατα ἂν ἔπαθες εἰ τὸν ἄρχοντα ἠδίκησας.
7   εἰ περὶ τῆς βουλῆς ἤκουσας, ἐν τῇ ἐκκλησίᾳ νῦν ἂν παρῆσθα.
8   εἰ εἰρήνη γένοιτο, πάντες ἂν ἐπαινέσειαν τοὺς ῥήτορας.
9   εἰ μὴ ἐζήτησα τὴν διὰ τῶν ὀρῶν ὁδόν, οὔποτε ἂν ηὗρον.
10 τοὺς λόγους μαθόντες, ἐνομίζετε ἂν τὸ ἔργον ῥᾷον εἶναι.

Exercise 1.18

Translate into Greek:
1   If you had not obeyed the king, slave, you would have been punished.
2   If the Athenians were to send an army, they would defeat the Spartans.
3   If our friends were here now, we would be eating and drinking.
4   If the poet had not died, he would be winning many prizes.
5   If I had been present myself, these things would not have happened.

Potential optative or indicative with ἄν

The optative with ἄν is quite often found on its own (i.e. without a condition attached):

> εἴποι τις ἂν ὅτι δεῖ ἀμύνεσθαι.
> Someone might say that it is necessary to resist.

This usage is in effect the same as the apodosis of a future remote condition: it implies e.g. *if the situation were to arise*. The optative with ἄν can also be a polite request:

> σιγήσειας ἄν.
> You might (be good enough to) be silent.

An aorist indicative with ἄν can also stand alone, this time as equivalent to the apodosis of a past closed condition:

> δεινὰ ἂν εἶδες.
> You would have seen strange things (i.e. if you had been there).

Exercise 1.19

Translate into English:
1   εἴποι τις ἂν ὅτι ἁμαρτάνω.
2   λέγοις ἄν μοι τί ἐγένετο;
3   ἀποκρίνοιτο ἂν ὁ δοῦλος ὅτι οὐδὲν ἤκουσεν.
4   πολὺν χρόνον ἐμείναμεν ἄν.
5   ὁ γέρων οὐκ ἂν αὖθις παῖς γένοιτο.

Chapter 2

Perfect tense

As we saw in *Greek to GCSE (1)*, the aorist is the normal tense in Greek for a single action in the past. There is however also a *perfect* tense, used only as a 'true' perfect, i.e. to stress that *the effects of a past event still continue*. It is virtually equivalent to a present tense. The distinction is shown by comparing:

aorist   The allies arrived on the third day. (*saying nothing about whether they stayed*)

perfect   The allies have arrived.   (*implying and are still here*)

The perfect predictably counts as a *primary* tense, categorised with the present and future, rather than with other past tenses (which are *historic*). Thus the perfect is followed by the subjunctive in a purpose clause: see page 148 on this principle of *sequence*.

In Latin the so-called perfect tense has to do the job of a simple past tense (regarded as historic) as well as the less common job of a true perfect (regarded as primary).

The perfect active uses endings similar to those of the first (weak) aorist. These are put onto a distinctive stem: kappa (rather than sigma) is added just before the ending, and if the verb begins with a consonant it is *reduplicated* (i.e. repeated, after inserting epsilon).

Latin has a few reduplicated perfects, e.g. *cecidi* from *cado* (I fall), *tetigi* from *tango* (I touch).

perfect active

sg	*1*	πέπαυκ-α	I have stopped
	2	πέπαυκ-ας	you (*sg*) have stopped
	3	πέπαυκ-ε(ν)	he/she/it has stopped
pl	*1*	πεπαύκ-αμεν	we have stopped
	2	πεπαύκ-ατε	you (*pl*) have stopped
	3	πεπαύκ-ασι(ν)	they have stopped

Note that the endings after kappa are like those of the first (weak) aorist except in the third person plural.

Contracted verbs use the same lengthened vowel before the kappa as they do before the sigma in the first aorist, hence for example τετίμηκα *I have honoured*.

As in the present and imperfect, the middle and passive of the perfect have the same form:

perfect middle/passive

sg	*1*	πέπαυ-μαι	I have ceased *or* been stopped
	2	πέπαυ-σαι	you (*sg*) have ceased *or* been stopped
	3	πέπαυ-ται	he/she/it has ceased *or* been stopped
pl	*1*	πεπαύ-μεθα	we have ceased *or* been stopped
	2	πέπαυ-σθε	you (*pl*) have ceased *or* been stopped
	3	πέπαυ-νται	they have ceased *or* been stopped

Most of these endings are like the normal primary middle/passive ones (-ομαι etc) without the initial vowel.

• A few of the verbs which insert a sigma before the aorist passive endings insert it also in the perfect middle/passive (e.g. κεκέλευσμαι *I have been ordered*).

• Because the perfect middle/passive endings begin with a consonant, adjustments to ease pronunciation need to be made when they are added to a verb stem ending in a consonant. Study of two typical examples illustrates what happens. (Because the changes are predictable, and because the perfect middle/passive is relatively uncommon anyway, there is no need to learn every example.)

perfect middle/passives of λείπω and διώκω:

sg	1	λέλειμμαι	δεδίωγμαι
	2	λέλειψαι	δεδίωξαι
	3	λέλειπται	δεδίωκται
pl	1	λελείμμεθα	δεδιώγμεθα
	2	λέλειφθε	δεδίωχθε
	3	λελειμμένοι εἰσί(ν)	δεδιωγμένοι εἰσί(ν)

The third person plural circumvents the problem of adding an unpronounceable -νται to a consonant stem by using the participle (agreeing with the subject) with an auxiliary verb. This corresponds to the Latin form of *all* perfect passives (e.g. *portatus sum* I have been carried [*lit* I am in a state of having been carried]).

• Verbs that begin with an *aspirated* consonant (e.g. theta, phi) reduplicate with the unaspirated equivalent (tau, pi). Hence:

θαυμάζω	I am amazed	*perfect*	τεθαύμακα
θύω	I sacrifice		τέθυκα
φιλέω	I like, I love		πεφίληκα
φοβέομαι	I fear		πεφόβημαι

Also in this category but with the peculiarity of dropping the prefix used in other tenses is:

ἀποθνήσκω	I die	τέθνηκα

Perfect participles are predictable: the perfect active (like other active participles) is 3-1-3 in declension (with the neuter as usual a variant of the masculine, and the feminine adding another syllable, in this case -υι-). The middle/passive is (like for example the present middle/passive participle) 2-1-2 in declension, and completely predictable. Note that the reduplication (unlike the augment in the aorist) is retained by the participle.

perfect active participle: πεπαυκώς -υῖα -ός (stem for masculine/neuter πεπαυκοτ-)

		masculine	feminine	neuter	
sg	nom	πεπαυκώς	πεπαυκυῖ-α	πεπαυκός	having stopped
	acc	πεπαυκότ-α	πεπαυκυῖ-αν	πεπαυκός	
	gen	πεπαυκότ-ος	πεπαυκυί-ας	πεπαυκότ-ος	
	dat	πεπαυκότ-ι	πεπαυκυί-ᾳ	πεπαυκότ-ι	
pl	nom	πεπαυκότ-ες	πεπαυκυῖ-αι	πεπαυκότ-α	
	acc	πεπαυκότ-ας	πεπαυκυί-ας	πεπαυκότ-α	
	gen	πεπαυκότ-ων	πεπαυκυι-ῶν	πεπαυκότ-ων	
	dat	πεπαυκόσι(ν)	πεπαυκυί-αις	πεπαυκόσι(ν)	

perfect middle/passive participle: πεπαυμένος -η -ον (normal 2-1-2)

perfect active infinitive: πεπαυκέναι

perfect middle/passive infinitive: πεπαύσθαι

26

• Verbs that begin with a vowel cannot reduplicate (i.e. double the opening sound) in the obvious way those with consonants can. The reduplication of verbs beginning with a vowel is like adding the augment, except that because with a perfect tense the process technically counts as reduplication (rather than augmentation), the reduplicated form is retained in the participle and infinitive. This can be seen by comparing relevant parts of ἐρωτάω (*I ask*):

	indicative	*participle*	*infinitive*
aorist (with augment)	ἠρώτησα	ἐρωτήσας	ἐρωτῆσαι
perfect (with reduplication)	ἠρώτηκα	ἠρωτηκώς	ἠρωτηκέναι

• This reduplication with epsilon is also used for verbs beginning with two consonants or a consonant that counts as double, e.g. ζητέω (*I seek*), perfect ἐζήτηκα.

• Any kind of reduplication in compounds comes (like the augment) after the prefix:
    ἀποβέβληκα   I have thrown away (*perfect of* ἀποβάλλω)

• Note the following word, which declines like the neuter of a perfect active participle:
    εἰκός -ότος τό   possibility, what is likely

• Because the present and perfect tenses are so close in meaning, it is not surprising that there is some overlap in form. The irregular verb οἶδα (*I know*) is, as we noted in *Greek to GCSE (2)*, in origin a perfect tense (*I have seen*): Latin verbs such as *odi* (*I hate*), are roughly comparable, with the form of a perfect tense but the meaning of a present. In Greek there is one important example the other way round: ἥκω *I have come* is present tense in form but perfect in meaning, often used instead of ἐλήλυθα (see below) as the perfect of ἔρχομαι.

Exercise 2.1

Translate into English:
1   ὁ χειμὼν πέπαυκε τὴν ναυμαχίαν.
2   ἆρα λελύκατε πάντας τοὺς αἰχμαλώτους;
3   πολλὰ ἔτη πεφόβημαι τὸν σκότον.
4   τιμῶμεν τοὺς ὑπὲρ τῆς πόλεως τεθνηκότας.
5   τὴν σὴν σοφίαν πολὺν χρόνον τεθαύμακα.
6   οἱ στρατιῶται πᾶσαν τὴν ἡμέραν ἐνθάδε τεταγμένοι εἰσίν.
7   αἱ παῖδες τοὺς νέους λόγους μεμαθήκασιν.
8   ὁ ἱερεὺς τέθυκε πᾶσι τοῖς θεοῖς.
9   δικαίως τετίμηκας τὸν ταῦτα πράξαντα.
10   καίπερ πολλάκις ἠδικηκότες, τὸ ἀληθὲς ἀεὶ ἐζητήκαμεν.

Exercise 2.2

Translate into Greek:
1   The old man has released all the animals.
2   The woman who has asked these things is very wise.
3   The messenger says that the king has died.
4   Night has stopped the assembly.
5   I think that these horses have been chased into the field.

27

Irregular perfect tenses

Irregular perfect tenses can be checked in the Reference Grammar (pages 188-91), but here are twenty common ones which will quickly become familiar:

ἀγγέλλω	I announce	*perfect*	ἤγγελκα
αἱρέω	I take		ᾕρηκα
ἀκούω	I hear		ἀκήκοα
ἀποθνῄσκω	I die		τέθνηκα
ἀφικνέομαι	I arrive		ἀφῖγμαι
βαίνω	I go		βέβηκα
γίγνομαι	I become, I happen		γέγονα
γιγνώσκω	I get to know		ἔγνωκα
δέχομαι	I receive		δέδεγμαι
ἔρχομαι	I come, I go		ἐλήλυθα
εὑρίσκω	I find		ηὕρηκα
λαμβάνω	I take		εἴληφα
λέγω	I say, I speak		εἴρηκα
λείπω	I leave		λέλοιπα
ὁράω	I see		ἑώρακα
πάσχω	I suffer		πέπονθα
πέμπω	I send		πέπομφα
πίπτω	I fall		πέπτωκα
σῴζω	I save		σέσωκα
φεύγω	I run away		πέφευγα

• The perfect tense of εὑρίσκω gives us (with loss of its rough breathing) the English *eureka*, by tradition the cry with which the third-century BC scientist Archimedes leapt from his bath when observation of the displacement of water by his body suggested to him the idea of testing (by specific gravity) whether the gold crown of the tyrant Hieron of Syracuse had been adulterated by base metal.

Exercise 2.3

Translate into English:
1 ὁ ἄγγελος ὁ παρὼν τὰ περὶ τῆς συμφορᾶς ἡμῖν ἤγγελκεν.
2 ἆρ᾽ οὐ περὶ τῆς ἡμετέρας νίκης ἀκηκόατε, ὦ σύμμαχοι;
3 διὰ τὴν ἀρετὴν τοὺς πολίτας σεσώκατε, ὦ στρατιῶται.
4 πολλά ἐστι τὰ δεινὰ ἃ ἐνθάδε ἑώρακα.
5 χρήματα πεπόμφαμεν τοῖς πρὸς βαρβάρων πεπόνθοσιν.*

*Note that, because the perfect is virtually a present tense, a perfect or aorist participle in a sentence with a perfect main verb does not 'move back a tense' in translation (as it would with an aorist main verb).

Exercise 2.4

The Infancy of Cyrus (2)

ὁ οὖν βουκόλος τῇ γυναικὶ διετέλει λέγων, "ὁ δὲ Ἅρπαγος ἐκέλευσέ με
ὡς τάχιστα τὸ παιδίον ἀναλαβόντα φέρειν πρὸς τὸ ἐρημότατον τῶν ὀρῶν,
ἵνα ἐκεῖ ἀποθάνῃ. καὶ κακὰ πολλὰ ἠπείλησεν εἰ μὴ ταῦτα ποιήσω. ἐγὼ
δ' ἀναλαβὼν ἔφερον, καὶ κατὰ τὴν ὁδὸν πάντα τὸν λόγον ἐπυθόμην παρὰ
5   δούλου τινός, ὅτι τῆς Μανδάνης ἐστὶ τὸ παιδίον καὶ τοῦ Καμβύσου, καὶ
ὁ Ἀστυάγης κελεύει ἀποκτεῖναι αὐτόν. καὶ νῦν ὅδε ἐστίν." ἅμα δὲ ταῦτα
ἔλεγεν ὁ βουκόλος καὶ τὸ παιδίον ἐξεκάλυψεν.

ἡ δὲ γυνή, ἐπεὶ εἶδε τὸ παιδίον μέγα τε καὶ καλὸν ὄν, δακρύσασα καὶ
τῶν τοῦ ἀνδρὸς γονάτων λαβομένη, ᾔτησε μηδαμῶς ἐν τοῖς ὄρεσιν λιπεῖν
10 αὐτό. ὁ δὲ οὐκ ἔφη οἷός τ' εἶναι ἄλλως ποιεῖν· ἀφίξεσθαι γὰρ
κατασκόπους τοῦ Ἀστυάγους ὡς ἐποψομένους· καὶ ἑαυτῷ μετὰ ταῦτα
θάνατον κάκιστον ἔσεσθαι. ἡ δὲ γυνή, ἐπεὶ οὐκ ἔπεισε τὸν ἄνδρα, εἶπε
τάδε· "ἐπεὶ οὖν οὐχ οἷά τ' εἰμὶ πεῖσαί σε, ὧδε ποίησον, εἰ χρὴ παιδίον τι
ἐν τῷ ὄρει ὀφθῆναι. ἐγὼ γὰρ σήμερον τέτοκα, τὸ δὲ παιδίον τέθνηκε.
15 τοῦτο δὲ φέρων ἐν τῷ ὄρει λιπέ, τὸν δὲ παῖδα τὸν τῆς τοῦ Ἀστυάγους
θυγατρὸς ὡς τὸν ἡμέτερον τρέφωμεν. καὶ οὕτως οὔθ' εὑρεθήσῃ ἀδικῶν τὸν
δεσπότην οὔτε κίνδυνος ἡμῖν ἔσται. πρὸς δὲ τούτοις, ὅ τε παῖς ὁ
τεθνηκὼς τάφον βασιλικὸν ἕξει, ὁ δὲ περιὼν οὐκ ἀποθανεῖται."

ὁ δὲ βουκόλος, νομίζων τὴν γυναῖκα εὖ εἰπεῖν, εὐθὺς ἐποίησε ταῦτα.
20 μετὰ γὰρ τῆς γυναικὸς ἔλιπε τὸν παῖδα ὃν ἔφερεν ὡς ἀποκτενῶν· τὸν δὲ

	βουκόλος -ου ὁ	herdsman
	διατελέω	I continue, I carry on
	Ἅρπαγος -ου ὁ	Harpagus
	παιδίον -ου τό	baby
2	ἀναλαμβάνω ἀνέλαβον	I pick up
	ἔρημος -η -ον	lonely, deserted
	ἀπειλέω ἠπείλησα	I threaten
	Μανδάνη -ης ἡ	Mandane
	Καμβύσης -ου ὁ	Cambyses
6	Ἀστυάγης -ους ὁ	Astyages
	ἐκκαλύπτω ἐξεκάλυψα	I uncover
	γόνυ -ατος τό	knee
	μηδαμῶς	in no way
	κατάσκοπος -ου ὁ	spy, scout
11	ἐφοράω *fut* ἐπόψομαι	I oversee, I inspect
	σήμερον	today
	τίκτω *pf* τέτοκα	I give birth
	τρέφω	I bring up
	πρός	(+ *dat*) in addition to
18	τάφος -ου ὁ	burial, tomb
	βασιλικός -ή -όν	royal
	περίειμι	I survive

29

ἑαυτοῦ, *νέκρον* ὄντα, ἐπεὶ τῷ τε χρυσῷ καὶ τῇ <u>ἐσθῆτι</u> τοῦ <u>ἑτέρου</u> παιδὸς <u>ἐκόσμησεν</u>, ἐν τῷ <u>ἀγγείῳ</u> (ἐν ᾧ πρότερον ἔφερε τὸν ἕτερον) πρὸς τὸ <u>ἐρημότατον</u> τῶν ὀρῶν ἐνέγκας ἐκεῖ ἔλιπεν.

τῇ δὲ τρίτῃ ἡμέρᾳ μετὰ ταῦτα, ὁ βουκόλος <u>παρὰ</u> τὸν Ἅρπαγον ἐλθὼν
25 ἔφη <u>ἑτοῖμος</u> εἶναι <u>δηλῶσαι</u> τὸν τοῦ παιδίου *νέκρον*. πέμψας δὲ ὁ Ἅρπαγος τῶν ἑαυτοῦ <u>δορυφόρων</u> τοὺς <u>πιστοτάτους</u>, εἶδε διὰ τούτων καὶ ἔθαψε τὸ τοῦ βουκόλου παιδίον. τὸν δὲ Κῦρον <u>ἔτρεφεν</u> ἡ τοῦ βουκόλου γυνή.

	ἐσθής -ῆτος ἡ	clothing
	ἕτερος -α -ον	(*first time*) one ... (*second time*) the other (*of two*)
	κοσμέω	I dress (someone) up
	ἀγγεῖον -ου τό	container
23	ἔρημος -η -ον	lonely, deserted
	παρά	(+ *acc*) before, into the presence of
	ἑτοῖμος -η -ον	ready
	δηλόω* ἐδήλωσα	I show
	δορυφόρος -ου ὁ	bodyguard
26	πιστός -ή -όν	faithful, reliable
	τρέφω	I bring up

* This is an example of a verb with omicron contraction, explained later in this chapter.

Pluperfect tense

The pluperfect (literally *more than* the *completed* perfect) refers, as in other languages, to something two stages back in the past (e.g. *they <u>had</u> done X*). But it is much rarer in Greek even than the perfect. As so often, the explanation for this is the amount of work done both by participles, and by the aorist. The normal Greek for a sentence involving an English pluperfect uses an aorist participle:

οἱ σύμμαχοι ἀφικόμενοι εὐθὺς ἐστρατοπεδεύσαντο.
When the allies had arrived, they immediately set up camp.

Even if a *when* clause is used, the verb in it is still normally aorist:

ἐπεὶ οἱ σύμμαχοι ἀφίκοντο, εὐθὺς ἐστρατοπεδεύσαντο.

Here the two aorist verbs naturally imply one single action followed by another. The pluperfect tense is not normally used in subordinate clauses such as this (where Latin *does* use a pluperfect subjunctive with *cum*, but a perfect indicative with e.g. *ubi* or *postquam*). The Greek pluperfect is more likely to be met in a main clause, indicating that *at a given point in the past the effect of a previous action was still continuing*. It is relatively rare, but you need to be able to recognise it. This is easy, because it has *both* the augment *and* reduplication (and the same stem as the perfect):

pluperfect

		active *I had stopped*	middle/passive *I had ceased/been stopped*
sg	1	ἐπεπαύκ-η	ἐπεπαύ-μην
	2	ἐπεπαύκ-ης	ἐπέπαυ-σο
	3	ἐπεπαύκ-ει(ν)	ἐπέπαυ-το
pl	1	ἐπεπαύκ-εμεν	ἐπεπαύ-μεθα
	2	ἐπεπαύκ-ετε	ἐπέπαυ-σθε
	3	ἐπεπαύκ-εσαν	ἐπέπαυ-ντο

Note the similarity of the middle/passive endings to the normal historic middle/passive ones.

Exercise 2.5

Translate into English:

1   ἐπεπαιδεύκεμεν τοὺς νέους δούλους πρὸ τοῦ πολέμου.

2   ὁ διδάσκαλος πρότερον μὲν ἐπεπαύκει τὸν ἀγῶνα, ὕστερον δὲ εἴασεν.

3   ἐπεὶ εἰς τὸν ἀγρὸν ἀφικόμην, οἱ δοῦλοι ἤδη ἐλελύκεσαν τοὺς ἵππους.

4   πρὸ τῆς νυκτὸς ἡ μάχη ὑπο τοῦ στρατηγοῦ ἐπέπαυτο.

5   ἆρα τὴν βουλὴν ἤδη ἐκεκωλύκης, καίπερ τὴν ἐμὴν ἐπιστολὴν οὐ δεξάμενος;

Exercise 2.6

Translate into Greek (using the pluperfect tense where appropriate):

1   The allies had been hindered by the storm.

2   You had released some of the prisoners, friends, but others were still waiting.

3   The women had trained their daughters well.

4   Many soldiers had been pursued into the sea.

5   When we saw the city, the battle had already been stopped.

Deponent verbs conjugated like perfect middle

There are several middle/deponent verbs whose present tense is like a perfect middle/passive, and whose imperfect is like a pluperfect:

present			I am able	I know (how to)	I lie (down)	I remember (+ *gen*)*
sg	1		δύναμαι	ἐπίσταμαι	κεῖμαι	μέμνημαι
	2		δύνασαι	ἐπίστασαι	κεῖσαι	μέμνησαι
	3		δύναται	ἐπίσταται	κεῖται	μέμνηται
pl	1		δυνάμεθα	ἐπιστάμεθα	κείμεθα	μεμνήμεθα
	2		δύνασθε	ἐπίστασθε	κεῖσθε	μέμνησθε
	3		δύνανται	ἐπίστανται	κεῖνται	μέμνηνται
imperfect	1		ἐδυνάμην	ἠπιστάμην	ἐκείμην	ἐμεμνήμην
	2		ἐδύνασο	ἠπίστασο	ἔκεισο	ἐμέμνησο
			etc	*etc*	*etc*	*etc*
participles			δυνάμενος	ἐπιστάμενος	κείμενος	μεμνήμενος
infinitives			δύνασθαι	ἐπίστασθαι	κεῖσθαι	μεμνῆσθαι

* In origin perfect middle/passive of μιμνήσκω *I remind*.

• Both δύναμαι and ἐπίσταμαι have similar meanings to other verbs we have met already, but δύναμαι (as distinct from οἷός τ᾽ εἰμί) is particularly used for *have the physical strength to*, and ἐπίσταμαι (as distinct from οἶδα) is particularly used for *know how to* (hence both are often found with the infinitive).

Exercise 2.7

Translate into English:
1   δύνασαι φέρειν τοῦτον τὸν λίθον;
2   πολλοὺς νεκροὺς ἐκεῖ κειμένους εἶδον.
3   πᾶσαν τὴν ἡμέραν ὑπὸ τῷ δένδρῳ ἐκείμην.
4   ὁ γέρων σαφῶς μέμνηται τῶν πάλαι μάχων.
5   ἀρ᾽ ἐπίστασαι τὴν ὁδὸν ἐν σκότῳ εὑρίσκειν;

Exercise 2.8

Translate into English:
1   I remember the king's father.
2   The boy was lying in the boat.
3   Not being able to release the chains, I was forced to remain there.
4   These women remembered the words of the god.
5   Do you know how to escape secretly, soldiers?

Exercise 2.9

The Boyhood of Cyrus (1)

Ancient authors often told stories about the childhood of great men which in some way indicated their character or foreshadowed their later achievements. This is seen here, along with the assumption that kingliness is an inborn characteristic which will inevitably reveal itself. The stage is thus set for the recognition of Cyrus and his true identity.

ὁ δὲ Κῦρος ὅτε <u>δεκαέτης</u> ἦν καὶ ἔτι ἐνομίζετο υἱὸς τοῦ <u>βουκόλου</u> εἶναι,
<u>ἔπαιζεν</u> ἐν τῇ κώμῃ μετ᾽ ἄλλων τινῶν παίδων. καὶ οἱ παῖδες παίζοντες
<u>εἵλοντο</u> τοῦτον ἑαυτῶν βασιλέα εἶναι. ὁ δὲ τοὺς μὲν ἐκέλευσεν οἰκίας
<u>οἰκοδομεῖν</u>, τοὺς δὲ <u>δορυφόρους</u> εἶναι, τοὺς δὲ ἄλλα ἔργα ποιεῖν. εἷς
5   μέντοι τούτων τῶν παίδων <u>συμπαιζόντων</u>, υἱὸς ὢν τοῦ Ἀρτεμβάρους
ἀνδρὸς <u>δοκίμου</u> ἐν τοῖς <u>Μήδοις</u>, οὐκ ἐποίησε τὸ ὑπὸ τοῦ Κύρου
<u>προσταχθέν</u>. ὁ οὖν Κῦρος ἐκέλευσε τοὺς ἄλλους παῖδας λαβεῖν αὐτόν.
πιθομένων δὲ τῶν παίδων ὁ Κῦρος τὸν παῖδα <u>ἐμαστίγωσεν</u>. ὁ δέ, <u>ἐπεὶ</u>
<u>τάχιστα</u> ἐλύθη, ὡς οὐκ ἄξια παθὼν μάλιστα ὀργιζόμενος ἤγγειλε τῷ πατρὶ
10 τὰ γενόμενα. ὁ δ᾽ Ἀρτεμβάρης, ἐλθὼν <u>παρὰ</u> τὸν <u>Ἀστυάγη</u> καὶ ἅμα τὸν
παῖδα ἄγων εἶπεν, "ὦ βασιλεῦ, ὑπὸ τοῦ σοῦ δούλου, ὃς βουκόλου τινὸς
υἱός ἐστιν, ὧδε ἐπάθομεν". καὶ <u>ἔφηνε</u> τοὺς τοῦ παῖδος <u>ὤμους</u>.

ἀκούσας δὲ καὶ ἰδών, ὁ Ἀστυάγης <u>μετεπέμψατο</u> τόν τε βουκόλον καὶ τὸν
παῖδα. ἐπεὶ δὲ παρῆσαν <u>ἀμφότεροι</u>, <u>βλέψας</u> πρὸς τὸν Κῦρον ἔφη, "ἆρα δὴ
15 σύ, βουκόλου παῖς ὤν, <u>ἐτόλμησας</u> τὸν παῖδα τοῦδε, ὄντος ἀνδρὸς
<u>εὐγενοῦς</u> τε καὶ δοκίμου, ὧδε <u>ὑβρίζειν</u>;"

	δεκαέτης -ες	ten years old
	βουκόλος -ου ὁ	herdsman
	παίζω	I play
	αἱρέομαι εἱλόμην	I choose
4	οἰκοδομέω	I build
	δορύφορος -ου ὁ	bodyguard (*literally* spear-carrier)
	συμπαίζω	I play together
	Ἀρτεμβάρης -ους ὁ	Artembares
	δόκιμος -ον	distinguished
6	Μῆδοι -ων οἱ	Medes
	προστάσσω	
	aor pass προσετάχθην	I assign, I instruct
	μαστιγόω ἐμαστίγωσα	I whip
	ἐπεὶ τάχιστα	as soon as
10	παρά	(+ *acc*) before, into the presence of
	Ἀστυάγης -ους ὁ	Astyages
	φαίνω ἔφηνα	I show
	ὦμος -ου ὁ	shoulder
	μεταπέμπομαι μετεπεμψάμην	I send for
14	ἀμφότεροι -αι -α	both
	βλέπω ἔβλεψα	I look
	τολμάω ἐτόλμησα	I dare
	εὐγενής -ές	noble
	ὑβρίζω	I treat (someone) violently

ὁ δὲ Κῦρος ἀπεκρίνατο, "ὦ δέσποτα, ἐγὼ ταῦτα δικαιότατα ἐποίησα. οἱ
γὰρ τῆς κώμης παῖδες, ὧν καὶ ὅδε ἦν, παίζοντες ἐμὲ εἵλοντο βασιλέα
ἑαυτῶν· ἐδόκουν γὰρ αὐτοῖς εἶναι εἰς τοῦτο ἐπιτηδειότατος. οἱ μέν νυν
20 ἄλλοι παῖδες τὰ κελευσθέντα ἔπρασσον· οὗτος δ' ἀνηκούστει τε καὶ
οὐδένα λόγον εἶχεν. τούτων οὖν ἔδει αὐτὸν δίκην δοῦναι. εἰ δὲ διὰ
ταῦτα ἄξιός εἰμι κολάζεσθαι, ὧδέ σοι πάρειμι."

τοῦ δὲ παιδὸς ταῦτα λέγοντος, ἀναγνώρισις ἔλαβε τὸν Ἀστυάγη. ὅ τε γὰρ
τοῦ προσώπου χαρακτὴρ ἐδόκει προσφέρεσθαι τῷ ἑαυτοῦ, καὶ ὁ παῖς
25 ἐλευθερώτατα ἀπεκρίνατο. πρὸς δὲ τούτοις, ὁ τῆς ἐκθέσεως χρόνος ἐδόκει
συμβαίνειν τῇ τοῦ παιδὸς ἡλικίᾳ. ταῦτα οὖν θαυμάζων, πολὺν χρόνον
ἄφθογγος ἦν.

ἔπειτα δέ, βουλόμενος ἐκπέμψαι τὸν Ἀρτεμβάρη, ἵνα τὸν βουκόλον μόνον
λαβὼν βασανίσῃ, "'Ἀρτέμβαρες," ἔφη, "πάντα ποιήσω ἵνα σύ τε καὶ ὁ
30 υἱὸς μὴ ἐπιμέμψησθε". καὶ ἀπέπεμψε τόν τε Ἀρτεμβάρη καὶ τὸν παῖδα.
καὶ οἱ δοῦλοι τὸν Κῦρον εἰς ἄλλο δωμάτιον ἤγαγον. ἐπεὶ δὲ ὁ βουκόλος
ἐλείφθη μόνος, ὁ Ἀστυάγης ἤρετο αὐτὸν ὁπόθεν λάβοι τὸν παῖδα, καὶ τίς
εἴη ὁ παραδούς. ὁ δὲ βουκόλος ἔφη τὸν παῖδα ἑαυτοῦ εἶναι, καὶ τὴν
γυναῖκα τεκεῖν αὐτόν. ὁ δ' Ἀστυάγης ὀργιζόμενος ἐκέλευσε τοὺς
35 δορυφόρους λαβεῖν αὐτόν. ἀπορῶν οὖν ὁ βουκόλος ἀληθῶς πάντα
ἐξηγήσατο, καὶ ᾔτησε τὸν βασιλέα ἑαυτῷ συγγιγνώσκειν.

	παίζω	I play
	αἱρέομαι εἱλόμην	I choose
	δοκέω	I seem
	ἐπιτήδειος -α -ον	suitable
20	ἀνηκουστέω	I disobey
	δίκην δίδωμι (aor inf δοῦναι)	I pay the penalty (for, + gen)
	ἀναγνώρισις -εως ἡ	recognition
	πρόσωπον -ου τό	face
	χαρακτήρ -ῆρος ὁ	character, appearance
24	προσφέρομαι	I resemble (+ dat)
	ἔκθεσις -εως ἡ	exposure
	συμβαίνω	(here) I am consistent with, I match (+ dat)
	ἡλικία -ας ἡ	age
	ἄφθογγος -ον	silent
29	βασανίζω ἐβασάνισα	I test, I examine
	ἐπιμέμφομαι ἐπεμεμψάμην	I have cause to complain
	δωμάτιον -ου τό	room
	παραδίδωμι aor pple παραδούς	I hand over
	τίκτω ἔτεκον	I give birth to
35	δορυφόρος -ου ὁ	bodyguard
	ἐξηγέομαι ἐξηγησάμην	I explain
	συγγιγνώσκω	I forgive (+ dat)

34

Numerals

cardinal		ordinal	
1	εἷς μία ἕν	first	πρῶτος -η -ον
2	δύο	second	δεύτερος -α -ον
3	τρεῖς τρία	third	τρίτος -η -ον
4	τέσσαρες -α	fourth	τέταρτος -η -ον
5	πέντε	fifth	πέμπτος -η -ον
6	ἕξ	sixth	ἕκτος -η -ον
7	ἑπτά	seventh	ἕβδομος -η -ον
8	ὀκτώ	eighth	ὄγδοος -η -ον
9	ἐννέα	ninth	ἔνατος -η -ον
10	δέκα	tenth	δέκατος -η -ον
11	ἕνδεκα		
12	δώδεκα		
13	τρεῖς καὶ δέκα		
14	τέσσαρες καὶ δέκα		
15	πεντεκαίδεκα		
16	ἑκκαίδεκα		
17	ἑπτακαίδεκα		
18	ὀκτωκαίδεκα	- - - - - - - - - - - - - - - - -	
19	ἐννεακαίδεκα	cardinal, continued:	
20	εἴκοσι(ν)	200	διακόσιοι -αι -α
30	τριάκοντα	300	τριακόσιοι -αι -α
40	τεσσαράκοντα	400	τετρακόσιοι -αι -α
50	πεντήκοντα	500	πεντακόσιοι -αι -α
60	ἑξήκοντα	600	ἑξακόσιοι -αι -α
70	ἑβδομήκοντα	700	ἑπτακόσιοι -αι -α
80	ὀγδοήκοντα	800	ὀκτακόσιοι -αι -α
90	ἐνενήκοντα	900	ἐνακόσιοι -αι -α
100	ἑκατόν	1000	χίλιοι -αι -α

• Small cardinal numbers (1-4) decline: see page 170. Hundreds 200-1000 are normal 2-1-2 (like the plural of σοφός). Ordinal numbers are adjectives and decline like σοφός (δεύτερος like φίλιος).

• Compounds can be done either way round with καί, or big number first without it, hence *25* can be:

> εἴκοσι καὶ πέντε
>
> *or* πέντε καὶ εἴκοσι (compare old-fashioned English *five and twenty*)
>
> *or* εἴκοσι πέντε

• In expressions of time, cardinal numbers go naturally with use of the accusative for *time how long* and the genitive for *time within which*; ordinals likewise with the use of the dative for *time when*:

> ἕξ μὲν ἡμέρας ἐπορευόμεθα, τῇ δὲ ἑβδόμῃ ἀφικόμεθα.
> We travelled for six days, and on the seventh we arrived.

• Note the use with numbers of two words for *about* or *approximately*: μάλιστα (lit *especially*, i.e. more that number than any other, like a scatter graph) and ὡς (lit *as*, i.e. *as it were, roughly* indicating that the stated figure is to be taken as a round number).

Exercise 2.10

Translate into English:
1   ὡς χίλιαι νῆες ἀπὸ τῆς Ἑλλάδος πάλαι ἔπλευσαν.
2   οἱ Ἀθηναῖοι πεντήκοντα ἔτη δυνατώτατοι ἦσαν.
3   τέσσαρες καὶ εἴκοσι ὄρνιθες ἠδέσθησαν.
4   τρεῖς ἡμέρας ἐπορευόμην, τῇ δὲ τετάρτῃ ἀφικόμην.
5   οἱ τριακόσιοι ἀνδρειότατα ἐμάχοντο.

Exercise 2.11

Translate into Greek:
1   Nine magistrates arrange the affairs of the city.
2   We have one country and one king.
3   For seven days we waited, but on the eighth we saw a ship.
4   In the council are 500 citizens.
5   The Greeks were besieging that city for ten years.

Prepositions

The following points about the use of prepositions should be familiar from *Greek to GCSE*:
   (a) prepositions take the accusative, genitive, or dative case (and some can take more
       than one of these)
   (b) prepositions make more specific a meaning or flavour which the case has already:
   with the accusative - motion towards or through
   with the genitive   - separation, going away from
   with the dative   - rest, staying put
   (not every example fits this pattern neatly or obviously, but it is a good general guide)
   (c) many prepositions are also found as prefixes in compound verbs (see below)

The fuller table on the next page enables all this to be appreciated more clearly. A
particularly good illustration is provided by παρά, the basic meaning of which is *beside*:

παρά + acc   - literally *to beside*, i.e. *into the presence of* (or *before* in the
                    sense *he was brought before the king*); but also *to a position*
                    beside (rather than hitting the target itself), hence *contrary to*
παρά + gen   - literally *from beside*, used particularly for *from* a person
παρά + dat   - literally *(resting) beside*, used for *position*
παραβαίνω   - literally *I go beside*, i.e. I pass, go beyond, hence *transgress*

Note the following special points:

(1) ἕνεκα *on account of* normally comes after rather than before the genitive noun it takes, and is thus
strictly a *postposition* rather than a preposition.

(2) πρός with the genitive (*at the hands of*) is particularly used for the agent with verbs which are not
actually passive, but express an equivalent meaning, e.g. *suffer at the hands of* (equivalent to *be badly
treated by*).

(3) Some words can be either adverbs (with a verb, and telling you for example where or when something
happens) or prepositions (with a noun). In this category are ἐγγύς *near* and ἅμα *at the same time (as)*.

Table of prepositions

preposition	+ acc	+ gen	+ dat
ἅμα			at the same time as
ἀμφί	around, about		
ἀνά	up		
ἄνευ		without	
ἀντί		opposite, instead of	
ἀπό		from, away from	
διά	on account of, because of	through	
εἰς, ἐς	into, onto, to		
ἐκ, ἐξ		out of	
ἐν			in, on, among
ἕνεκα		on account of (*follows noun*)	
ἐπί	against, to, over, for	on; in the time of	on, on condition of
κατά	down, according to, throughout, by	down from	
μετά	after	with	
παρά	along, into the presence of; contrary to	from (a person)	beside
περί	around	about, concerning	
πλήν		except	
πρό		in front of, before	
πρός	towards, to	from, at the hands of; in the name of	in addition to
σύν			with, with the help of
ὑπέρ	beyond, to beyond	above; on behalf of	
ὑπό	under, to under, along under	by (a person)	under
ὡς	to (a person)		

Note also the following common idiomatic prepositional phrases:

ἅμ' ἡμέρᾳ	at daybreak, at first light
δι' ὀλίγου	after a short time
διὰ πολλοῦ	after a long time
διὰ πέντε ἐτῶν	every five years
εἰς καιρόν	at the right time
ἐκ τούτου	after this, as a result
ἐξ ἴσου	equally
ἐν τούτῳ	meanwhile (*understand* χρόνῳ)
ἐπὶ τούτοις	on these terms
καθ' ἡμέραν	daily
κατὰ γήν	by land
κατὰ θάλασσαν	by sea
κατὰ τοὺς νόμους	according to the laws
μετὰ ταῦτα	after this (*lit* after these things)
οἱ περὶ Ξενοφῶντα	Xenophon and his men (*i.e. including him*)
περὶ πολλοῦ ποιεῖσθαι	to regard as important
ὑπὸ νύκτα	just before nightfall

Exercise 2.12

Translate into English:
1   ἡ ἑορτὴ διὰ τεσσάρων ἐτῶν γίγνεται.
2   ὁ διδάσκαλος νόσου ἕνεκα ἀπῆν.
3   αὕτη ἡ παῖς πάντα ἄνευ φόβου πράσσει.
4   ἡ νίκη ὑπὲρ ἐλπίδα ἐγένετο.
5   οἱ περὶ τὸν Κῦρον εἰς καιρὸν ἀφίκοντο.
6   ἐπὶ τῶν προγόνων ἡ θεὰ κατὰ τοῦ ὄρους ὑπὸ νύκτα κατέβαινεν.
7   οἱ δοῦλοι δεινὰ ἔπασχον πρὸς ἐκείνου τοῦ δεσπότου.
8   οἱ ἐν τῇ ἐκκλησίᾳ περὶ πολλοῦ ἐποιοῦντο ἑκάστην γνώμην ἀκούειν.
9   ἡ εἰρήνη ἐπὶ τούτοις ἐποιήθη.
10   οἱ μὲν Λακεδαιμόνιοι κατὰ γῆν ἐκράτουν, οἱ Ἀθηναῖοι κατὰ θάλασσαν.

Exercise 2.13

Translate into Greek:
1   The old man was sitting in front of the house.
2   The girl set out at daybreak, in order to arrive just before nightfall.
3   Those soldiers acted unjustly, contrary to the law.
4   All our friends have gone away except one.
5   The people there use bows instead of swords.

Compound verbs

As at GCSE, you are expected to be able to work out the meaning of compounds using common prefixes (equating to some of the prepositions listed above). In particular look out for the following:

ἀνα-	up
ἀπο-	from, away
δια-	through
εἰσ-	into
ἐκ-	out, out of
ἐν-	in
κατα-	down
περι-	around
προ-	forward
προσ-	to, towards

Remember that the augment in compound verbs comes after the prefix. It usually displaces a vowel on the prefix (hence the aorist of ἀποβάλλω is ἀπέβαλον, and compounds with ἀνα-, δια-, ἐπι- and κατα- behave similarly; this also normally happens if the verb stem itself begins with a vowel, hence e.g. ἐπέρχομαι), but περί keeps its iota (hence περιέρχομαι).

Note also that προ- is a special case: its omicron, somehow more assertive than that of ἀπο-, blends with the epsilon of the augment to produce -ου-. This is an example of *crasis*

38

(literally *mixing*) of vowels, which is usually marked with a *coronis* (like a smooth breathing: see page 91), so the aorist of προβαίνω is προὔβην.

As in other contexts, small adjustments are made in the interest of pronunciation: hence ἐν + βαίνω becomes ἐμβαίνω *I go in* (but ἐνέβην in the aorist, where the change is not needed).

• Remember too that the prefix of a compound may simply repeat for emphasis something also expressed by an adjacent preposition:

ἐκβαίνομεν ἐκ τῆς ἀγορᾶς.   We go out of the marketplace.

Or it may give further information:

ἐκβαίνομεν εἰς τὴν ὁδόν.   We go out (*implying e.g.* of our house) into the road.

• There are a few double compounds, e.g. ἐπανέρχομαι *I return* (ἐπι- plus ἀνα-), with the augment put after the second prefix (hence aorist ἐπανῆλθον): ἀνα- here means *back to base*, as in ἀναχωρέω *I retreat*, or the old-fashioned English expression *an up train*.

• Sometimes the Greeks seem to have forgotten that a word was a compound (hence the aorist of καθίζω [*I sit*] is ἐκάθισα), or to have forgotten some of the time (hence both ἐκάθευδον and καθηῦδον are found as the imperfect of καθεύδω *I sleep*).

• Some prefixes have further special uses: e.g. ἐκ- can mean *to a successful conclusion* (like English work <u>out</u> a problem), so ἐκφεύγω means *escape* (i.e. flee successfully, get away); μετα- often indicates *change* (e.g. μεταγιγνώσκω *I change my mind*, and compare Greek-derived words like *metamorphosis*), and ὑπο- often implies *secretly* or *surreptitiously* (e.g. ὑποπέμπω *I send secretly*).

Exercise 2.14

Translate into English:

1   τίνες εἰσὶν αἱ εἰς τὸ ἱερὸν εἰσελθοῦσαι;
2   κίνδυνος ἦν, ἀλλ᾽ οὐδεὶς ἀπεχώρησεν.
3   οἱ παρὰ τοῦ βασιλέως κατάσκοποι λάθρᾳ προὐχώρησαν.
4   νομίζω πάντας τοὺς στρατιώτας ἀνὰ τὸ ὄρος ἀναβῆναι.
5   αἱ παῖδες ὑπὸ τοῖς δένδροις περιέτρεχον.
6   μετὰ δύο ὥρας ἐξῆν ἡμῖν τὰς ναῦς προσπλεούσας ἰδεῖν.
7   ὁ γέρων ἀπέθανε, σίτου ἐν τῇ οἰκίᾳ οὐκ ἐνόντος.
8   πάντες οἱ πολῖται εἰς τὰς ὁδοὺς ἐξῆλθον.
9   ὁ ἄγγελος διεξῆλθε πάντα τὰ ἐκεῖ πράγματα.
10   ἆρα ὁ δεσμώτης ἐξέφυγεν;

Exercise 2.15

Translate into Greek:

1   Many women went out of their houses into the marketplace.
2   Our soldiers advanced into the land of the enemy just before nightfall.
3   The poet went down to save his wife.
4   I saw that boy leading the horse towards the field.
5   Having gone up the mountain, I was afraid to return.

Verbs with omicron contraction

In *Greek to GCSE (2)* we met contracted verbs with stems ending in alpha (e.g. τιμάω *I honour*) and the more common ones ending in epsilon (e.g. φιλέω *I like/love*). A third, much rarer type are those whose stem ends in omicron: we have met a couple of examples in this chapter. Here the rules of contraction are:

> o followed by a long vowel becomes ω
> o followed by a short vowel becomes ου
> any combination with ι becomes οι

Hence:
δηλόω I show

present		active		middle/passive	
sg	1	δηλῶ	[δηλο-ω]	δηλοῦμαι	[δηλο-ομαι]
	2	δηλοῖς	[δηλο-εις]	δηλοῖ	[δηλο-η]
	3	δηλοῖ	[δηλο-ει]	δηλοῦται	[δηλο-εται]
pl	1	δηλοῦμεν	[δηλο-ομεν]	δηλούμεθα	[δηλο-ομεθα]
	2	δηλοῦτε	[δηλο-ετε]	δηλοῦσθε	[δηλο-εσθε]
	3	δηλοῦσι(ν)	[δηλο-ουσι(ν)]	δηλοῦνται	[δηλο-ονται]

participle	δηλῶν -οῦσα -οῦν (stem δηλουντ-)	δηλούμενος -η -ον
	[δηλο-ων -ουσα -ον (δηλο-οντ-)]	[δηλο-ομενος]
infinitive	δηλοῦν	δηλοῦσθαι
	[δηλο-ειν: iota disappears here]	[δηλο-εσθαι]
imperative	sg δήλου pl δηλοῦτε	sg δηλοῦ pl δηλοῦσθε
	[δηλο-ε, -ετε]	[δηλο-ου, -εσθε]

imperfect		active		middle/passive	
sg	1	ἐδήλουν	[ἐδηλο-ον]	ἐδηλούμην	[ἐδηλο-ομην]
	2	ἐδήλους	[ἐδηλο-ες]	ἐδηλοῦ	[ἐδηλο-ου]
	3	ἐδήλου	[ἐδηλο-ε]	ἐδηλοῦτο	[ἐδηλο-ετο]
pl	1	ἐδηλοῦμεν	[ἐδηλο-ομεν]	ἐδηλούμεθα	[ἐδηλο-ομεθα]
	2	ἐδηλοῦτε	[ἐδηλο-ετε]	ἐδηλοῦσθε	[ἐδηλο-εσθε]
	3	ἐδήλουν	[ἐδηλο-ον]	ἐδηλοῦντο	[ἐδηλο-οντο]

For the first (weak) aorist and future, the omicron is lengthened to omega before adding the sigma, but the endings after the sigma are normal. Hence:

aorist active	ἐδήλωσα
aorist middle	ἐδηλωσάμην
aorist passive	ἐδηλώθην
future active	δηλώσω
future middle	δηλώσομαι
future passive	δηλωθήσομαι

Other forms should be deducible, but note that (as with epsilon and alpha verbs) there is a distinctive form of the singular of the present active optative:

1 δηλοίην
2 δηλοίης
3 δηλοίη

A few indicative forms of omicron verbs look at first sight (because of the diphthong οι) like the optative of an ordinary verb, but because there are so few omicron verbs there is little risk of confusion.

• Omicron verbs like δηλόω:

ἀξιόω	I think worthy; I urge, I demand*
δουλόω	I enslave (*contrast* δουλεύω I am a slave)
ἐλευθερόω	I set free
πληρόω	I fill

* The apparently unrelated senses of ἀξιόω come about because the basic meaning *consider something worthy* (ἄξιος) develops (rather high-handedly) into *think it worthy that someone else should do something*, and so *urge* or even *demand* that they do it.

The several Greek words for *show* have different shades of meaning: δηλόω means *make clear* (δῆλος), φαίνω means *reveal*, and in Chapter 3 we shall meet δείκνυμι, which means *point out*.

Exercise 2.16

Translate into English:
1   βουλόμεθα τοὺς δούλους τοὺς ναυμαχήσαντας ἐλευθερῶσαι.
2   ὁ τῶν συμμάχων ἄγγελος τὴν βουλὴν ἡμῖν νῦν δηλοῖ.
3   οἱ Ἕλληνες οὐδέποτε δουλωθήσονται.
4   οἱ πολῖται ἐπλήρουν τὰς ὁδούς.
5   ἀεὶ ἐλευθέρου τοὺς ἀδίκως δουλωθέντας, ὦ νεανία.
6   ἆρ’ οὐκ ἀξιοῖς ὑπὲρ τῆς πατρίδος μαχέσθαι;
7   πότε δηλωθήσεται τοῖς πολίταις τὰ ζῷα τὰ ἀπὸ τῆς νήσου ληφθέντα;
8   διὰ τί ὁ ἄρχων ἠξίωσεν ἡμᾶς ἐν τῇ ἀγορᾷ παρεῖναι;
9   ἡ ἡμέτερα οἰκία ὕδατι πεπλήρωται.
10 εἰ δηλοίης μοι τὴν τῆς ὁδοῦ βουλήν, οἷός τ’ ἂν εἴην βοηθεῖν σοι.

Exercise 2.17

Translate into Greek:
1   Enslave this boy now, master!
2   The citizens filled the agora.
3   It is easy to set such women free.
4   We are being urged by the children to provide more food.
5   The horse now being shown to the general is excellent.

The Boyhood of Cyrus (2)

ὁ δ᾽ ᾿Αστυάγης τὸν μὲν βουκόλον ὡς τὸ ἀληθὲς λέξαντα οὐκέτι ᾐτιᾶτο·
τὸν δὲ ῞Αρπαγον μάλιστα ὀργιζόμενος μετεπέμψατο. καὶ τοῦτον
ἀφικόμενον ἠρώτησεν, "῞Αρπαγε, τίνι τρόπῳ ἀπέκτεινας τὸν παῖδα ὃν
ἔδωκά σοι, τὸν τῆς ἐμῆς θυγατρὸς υἱόν;" ὁ δὲ ῞Αρπαγος, ὡς εἶδε τὸν
5 βουκόλον παρόντα, οὐκ ἐψεύσατο ἀλλ᾽ εὐθὺς ἐξηγήσατο τὰ ἐξ ἀρχῆς
γενόμενα.

ὁ δ᾽ ᾿Αστυάγης, κρύπτων τὴν ὀργήν, εἶπε, "περίεστί τε ὁ παῖς, καὶ τὸ
πρᾶγμα ἔχει καλῶς· ἐπεὶ γὰρ ἐκέλευσά σε τὸν παῖδα ἀποκτεῖναι,
οὐδαμῶς ἡδόμην, καὶ περὶ πολλοῦ ἐποιούμην τὴν τῆς θυγατρὸς ὀργήν.
10 νῦν δὲ πάντα εὐτυχῶς ἀπέβη. πέμψον οὖν τὸν σὸν παῖδα ὡς φίλον τῷ
παιδὶ τῷ περιόντι. ἔπειτα δὲ (σῶστρα γὰρ τοῦ παιδὸς τοῖς θεοῖς μέλλω
θύσειν) πάρισθί μοι ἐπὶ δεῖπνον."

ὁ δὲ ῞Αρπαγος ταῦτα ἀκούσας προσεκύνησεν. ἔπειτα δὲ οἴκαδε ἀπελθὼν
τὸν παῖδα τὸν μονογενῆ ἔτη τρία καὶ δέκα γεγονότα ὡς τὸν ᾿Αστυάγη
15 ἔπεμψεν. καὶ ὁ ᾿Αστυάγης, ἐπειδὴ ἀφίκετο ὁ τοῦ ῞Αρπάγου παῖς, σφάξας
αὐτὸν καὶ κατὰ μέλη διελών, τὰ μὲν τῶν κρεῶν ὤπτησε, τὰ δὲ ἥψησεν.
ἐπεὶ δὲ ἡ τοῦ δείπνου ὥρα ἐγένετο, παρέθηκε ταῦτα τῷ ῞Αρπάγῳ, πλὴν

	᾿Αστυάγης -ους ὁ	Astyages
	βουκόλος -ου ὁ	herdsman
	οὐκέτι	no longer
	αἰτιάομαι	I blame
5	῞Αρπαγος -ου ὁ	Harpagus
	μεταπέμπομαι μετεπεμψάμην	I send for
	τρόπος -ου ὁ	way
	ψεύδομαι ἐψευσάμην	I lie
	ἐξηγέομαι ἐξηγησάμην	I explain
7	περίειμι	I survive
	πρᾶγμα -ατος τό	matter, business
	ἔχω	(+ adv) I am
	οὐδαμῶς	in no way
	ἥδομαι	I am pleased
10	ἀποβαίνω ἀπέβην	(of events) turn out
	σῶστρα -ων τά	thank-offerings
	ἐπί	(+ acc) (here) for
	προσκυνέω προσεκύνησα	I bow
	οἴκαδε	home, homewards
14	μονογενής -ές	only (child)
	ἐπειδή	when, since
	σφάζω ἔσφαξα	slaughter
	μέλος -ους τό	limb
	διαιρέω διεῖλον	I cut up
16	κρέα -ων τά	flesh
	ὀπτάω ὤπτησα	I roast
	ἕψω ἥψησα	I boil
	ὥρα -ας ἡ	hour, time
	παρέθηκα	(irreg aor) I placed X (acc) in front of Y (dat)

τῆς τε κεφαλῆς καὶ τῶν χειρῶν καὶ τῶν ποδῶν· ταῦτα δὲ χωρὶς ἦν ἐν
ἀγγείῳ κατακαλυμμένα. ὡς δὲ ὁ Ἅρπαγος ἐδόκει ἅλις ἔχειν τοῦ δείπνου,
20 ὁ Ἀστυάγης ἤρετο αὐτὸν εἰ ἥδοιτο τῇ θοίνῃ. τοῦ δὲ Ἁρπάγου εἰπόντος
μάλιστα ἤδεσθαι, δοῦλοί τινες ἐνέφερον τὴν τοῦ παιδὸς κεφαλὴν
κατακαλυμμένην καὶ τὰς χεῖρας καὶ τοὺς πόδας. τὸν δὲ Ἅρπαγον
ἐκέλευσεν ὁ βασιλεὺς ἀποκαλύψαι τε καὶ λαβεῖν ὃ βούλεται. πιθόμενος
δὲ ὁ Ἅρπαγος καὶ ἀποκαλύψας, εἶδε τὰ τοῦ παιδὸς λοιπά. ἰδὼν δὲ οὐκ
25 ἀνεβόησεν ἀλλ' ἐν ἑαυτῷ ἐγένετο. ἤρετο δὲ αὐτὸν ὁ Ἀστυάγης εἰ
γιγνώσκει οὗτινος θηρίου κρέα ἔφαγεν. ὁ δὲ καὶ γιγνώσκειν ἔφη καὶ
ἥδεσθαι πᾶσι τοῖς ὑπὸ τοῦ βασιλέως πεπραγμένοις. οὕτω δ'
ἀποκρινάμενος καὶ ἀναλαβὼν τὰ λοιπὰ τῶν κρεῶν οἴκαδε ἀπῆλθεν. ἐκεῖ
γὰρ ἔμελλε θάψειν πάντα.

30 ὁ οὖν Ἀστυάγης τὸν Ἅρπαγον οὕτως ἐκόλασεν. περὶ δὲ τοῦ Κύρου
βουλευόμενος αὖθις ἐκάλεσε τοὺς τῶν Μάγων ὀνειροπόλους. καὶ αὖθις
εἶπον ὅτι χρὴ τὸν παῖδα βασιλεύειν εἰ μὴ ἤδη ἀπέθανεν. ὁ δὲ
Ἀστυάγης ἔφη, "περίεστιν ὁ παῖς. καὶ οἰκοῦντα αὐτὸν ἐν τοῖς ἀγροῖς οἱ
τῆς κώμης παῖδες εἵλοντο βασιλέα. καὶ ἐποίησε πάντα ὅσα οἱ ἀληθεῖς
35 βασιλῆς· καὶ γὰρ δορυφόρους εἶχε, καὶ κατὰ πάντα εὐκόσμως
ἐβασίλευεν. πῶς οὖν ταῦτα κρίνετε;" οἱ δὲ Μάγοι εἶπον, "εἰ περίεστιν ὁ
παῖς καὶ ἤδη ἐβασίλευσεν ἄνευ προνοίας, θυμὸν ἔχε ἀγαθόν· οὐ γὰρ ἔτι

	χωρίς	apart, separate
	ἀγγεῖον -ου τό	vessel, pot
19	κατακαλύπτω	
	pf pass pple κατακελυμμένος	I cover over
	δοκέω	I seem
	ἅλις	enough
	ἥδομαι	I enjoy (+ dat)
20	θοίνη -ης ἡ	feast
	ἀποκαλύπτω ἀπεκάλυψα	I uncover
	λοιπός -ή -όν	left, remaining, n pl as noun remains
	ἀναβοάω ἀνεβόησα	I shout out
	θηρίον -ου τό	animal
26	κρέα -ων τά	flesh
	ἀναλαμβάνω ἀνέλαβον	I pick up
	Μάγοι -ων οἱ	Magi (caste of wise/holy men)
	ὀνειροπόλος -ου ὁ	dream-interpreter
	βασιλεύω ἐβασίλευσα	I am king, I rule
33	περίειμι	I survive
	οἰκέω	I live
	δορυφόρος -ου ὁ	bodyguard
	κατὰ πάντα	in all respects
	εὐκόσμως	in a well-ordered way
36	κρίνω	I judge
	πρόνοια -ας ἡ	forethought, deliberate planning
	θυμός -οῦ ὁ	heart, spirit

43

δεύτερον ἄρξει". ὁ οὖν Ἀστυάγης, τοῖς λόγοις ἡσθείς, τὸν Κῦρον πρὸς τὴν <u>Περσικὴν</u> ἀπέπεμψεν. καὶ <u>νοστήσαντα</u> αὐτὸν ὅ τε πατὴρ καὶ ἡ μήτηρ
40 μάλιστα <u>χαίροντες</u> ἐδέξαντο.

ἥδομαι ἥσθην	I am pleased by (+ *dat*)
Περσική -ῆς ἡ	Persia
νοστέω	I return home
χαίρω	I rejoice, I am happy

The Magi were however proved wrong: Cyrus, as we have seen, grew up to be the founder of the Persian empire. He ousted Astyages from his throne and by 547 BC had extended Persian rule as far west as the river Halys. This was the point at which he overthrew and captured Croesus. Cyrus administered a vast empire with wisdom and tolerance: we shall see in Chapter 5 that to Xenophon (writing in the fourth century BC) he was an example of the ideal ruler, despite the intervening history of conflict between Greece and Persia.

Subordination and the complex sentence

Greek depends heavily on the principle of *subordination*. In continuous narrative most sentences (except the very simplest) consist of a main, finite verb and one or more subordinate elements:
- participles and participle phrases (with or without an introductory word such as ὡς or καίπερ, signalling how the participle is to be taken), including genitive absolute
- temporal and causal clauses (introduced by ἐπεί, ὅτε, ὡς, ὅτι, διότι)
- relative clauses (introduced by ὅς, or one of the more specialised relative pronouns from the table of correlatives, such as οἷος)
- purpose clauses (introduced by ἵνα or ὅπως, or ὡς with future participle)
- result clauses (introduced by ὥστε)
- conditional clauses (introduced by εἰ or ἐάν; the apodosis counts as the main clause)
- indirect statement (with ὅτι clause, or infinitive, or participle)
- indirect command (with infinitive)
- indirect question (introduced by εἰ or by one of the interrogative words from the table of correlatives, often in the form beginning ὁ-)

Greek builds up sentences not by just piling up the various elements (saying *X happened; Y happened; Z happened*) but by expressing their relation to each other, saying for example *Because X had happened, Y happened, with the result that Z then happened.*

Central to this is the use of participles, perhaps the single most important element in Greek sentence construction (and certainly one of the distinguishing features of the language, being far more central than in Latin). We saw at an early stage that Greek does not like to pile up main verbs. On the same principle, it avoids piling up imperatives, or infinitives in indirect speech (which themselves stand for main verbs in the original direct speech). Hence *Go and get* would be translated as ἐλθὼν λαβέ (rather than ἐλθὲ καὶ λαβέ). Similarly
The general ordered us to leave our homes and (then) run away
would be translated as
ὁ στρατηγὸς ἐκέλευσεν ἡμᾶς τὰς οἰκίας λιπόντας φυγεῖν.
(rather than ... λιπεῖν καὶ φυγεῖν). The participle in these examples is read as part of the

command: *He ordered us having done X to do Y* naturally means *He ordered us, after doing X (which we have not done yet), to do Y* rather than *He ordered us, as we had (already) done X, to do Y*. The aorist participle in this idiom expresses something (that will be) past in relation to the time the command expressed by the infinitive (φυγεῖν) is carried out, rather than something past in relation to the main verb of the sentence (ἐκέλευσεν).

Exercise 2.19

Translate into English:

1   ὁ διδάσκαλος ἐκέλευσε τοὺς παῖδας τὰς βίβλους λιπόντας ἐξελθεῖν.
2   ἕως* ὁ τῶν συμμάχων ἄγγελος ἔλεγεν, οἱ πολῖται σιγῇ ἐκάθιζον ὡς μάλιστα θαυμάζοντες.
3   αἱ θεαί, καίπερ οὐδαμῶς ὁμολογοῦσαι, ὑπὸ τοῦ ποιητοῦ ἐτιμῶντο.
4   τῶν ἐν τῇ νήσῳ ὑπὸ τῶν στρατιωτῶν ἐλευθερωθέντων, οἱ ἐκεῖ φύλακες ἠπόρουν ἕως* ἄλλοι τινὲς προσήχθησαν.
5   ἆρα οἷαί τ᾿ ἐστὲ λέγειν ἡμῖν ὅπου ὁ βασιλεὺς ἀπέθανεν, ὦ γυναῖκες;
6   μωρότατοί εἰσιν ὅσοι ταῦτα τὰ ἔργα ἐπαινοῦσιν.
7   τῆς μάχης τοιαύτης οὔσης, οὐδεὶς οὕτως ἰσχυρός ἐστιν ὥστε αὖθις μάχεσθαι.
8   ἡ τοῦ νεανίου μήτηρ ἔφη τοὺς φίλους δύο ὥρας μείναντας ἀπελθεῖν.
9   ἐκεῖνος ὁ γέρων περὶ τοῦ πολέμου οὔποτε εἶπεν ἅτε δεινότατα παθών.
10   ἡμέρας γενομένης, αἰτήσω τοὺς πολίτας τὸν χρυσὸν κρύψαντας πρὸς τὰ ὄρη φυγεῖν.

* ἕως (referring to the past) means *while* (of two actions happening simultaneously) or *until* (of one action following another): word order and context should make clear which sense is appropriate

Flexibility in translation

Inevitably you tend to learn a single meaning for a Greek word, but it is important to be flexible in translation and aim at good, natural English. Because languages conceptualise (that is, think about the world) differently, there is frequently not a simple one-to-one correspondence of meaning between words in different languages. This may initially make things difficult for the learner, but in fact it is a major source of fascination in learning any language, and thus learning about the culture that produced it. This is particularly true with Greek. Both the language and the culture are immensely rich. They belong to a world distant in time, which is simultaneously very alien to us in some respects and uncannily familiar in others.

If you look up a Greek word that appears to have a list of meanings, at first sight unrelated, this is not (of course) because the Greeks just put up with an unavoidable inconvenience, but because to them the meanings were importantly related. Thus for example ξένος may according to context need to be translated as *stranger, foreigner, host* or *guest*: various facets or stages of a person interacting outside his immediate community, and forming a relationship of reciprocal obligation.

Conversely several Greek words may be conventionally translated by the same English word. Sometimes they are synonyms in Greek too (thus στρατιά, στρατός or στράτευμα for *army*). More often there is some difference of meaning or emphasis. Words that are virtually synonymous most of the time can acquire idiomatic distinctions in a particular context: we saw in *Greek to GCSE (2)* the difference between εἶπε ταῦτα *he said this (already quoted)* and εἶπε τάδε *he said this (about to be quoted)*. Although ποιέω often means *I make*, it is in many contexts interchangeable with πράσσω as *I do*. Yet if these verbs are used with an adverb, there is an important distinction: εὖ ποιέω means *I treat (someone) well*, whereas εὖ πράσσω means *I fare well (i.e. come off well myself)*.

Often the meaning required for a word in a sentence or passage is an intelligible extension of the basic meaning. Thus νέος *new* can also mean *young*. The same applies to phrases. The idiom ὡς τάχιστα normally means *as quickly as possible*. But if it introduces a subordinate clause (ὡς τάχιστα *X happened, Y happened*), it clearly needs to be translated *as soon as*.

Often words can be built into sentences in ways that in English require different translations. Thus some adjectives can be active or passive in flavour: δυνατός can mean *capable* (able to do) or *possible* (able to be done). In a similar way some verbs can have sentences constructed around them in more than one way. The classic example here is βάλλω:

ὁ παῖς λίθους εἰς τὸν ποταμὸν ἔβαλλεν.
The boy was throwing stones into the river.

ὁ παῖς τὸν λέοντα λίθοις ἔβαλλεν.
The boy was pelting the lion with stones.

Note also the distinction between βάλλω *I pelt* (typically from a distance) and τύπτω *I hit, I strike* (successfully/at close quarters). However βάλλω is an extremely common, versatile and flexible word: often neither *I throw* nor *I pelt* is appropriate, and the meaning is no stronger than *I put*. This flexibility in the meaning of very common verbs is particularly evident in compounds. A compound of βάλλω frequently met is προσβάλλω *I attack*. This (like other Greek verbs with similar meaning) takes the dative. But εἰσβάλλω (*I invade*) normally takes εἰς + accusative. The prefixes of compounds behave like the prepositions which in origin they are; and with εἰσβάλλω there is also an understood object (*I hurl myself/an army into ...*). Particular grammatical cases taken by verbs cannot always be predicted, but all have some explanation. The middle λαμβάνομαι *I take hold of* takes the genitive, as do other verbs (such as ἅπτομαι *I grasp*, or just *I touch*) implying getting *part* of something (this is the *partitive* genitive, as in phrases like *some of*).

Finally there are idioms with particular cultural or historical resonance. The singular βασιλεύς (no article, no following phrase *of X*, yet not a proper name needing a capital letter) in classical authors invariably means *the king of Persia*, because the power of Persia was a major fact of political life, and the Persian king was the only one that people in the republican city-states of Greece would normally have occasion to talk about. *The Persian* (ὁ Πέρσης) can be a collective singular (*when we fought the Persian*, like English *the Hun*), as can (anybody's) cavalry: the feminine ἡ ἵππος usually means that, rather than an individual mare (as in English *a regiment of horse*).

46

Exercise 2.20

Translate into English:

1   εἴθε οἱ ξένοι ἡμᾶς ἀεὶ οὕτω ποίοιεν.
2   ὁ παῖς πίπτων δένδρου εὐτυχῶς ἥψατο.
3   βούλομαι γνῶναι ὅ τι εἶπεν ὁ ἄγγελος ὁ ὑπὸ βασιλέως πεμφθείς.
4   αἱ ἐγγὺς τοῦ ὄρους οἰκοῦσαι ἐδήλωσαν ἡμῖν τὴν ὁδόν.
5   ἆρ' οὐ οἱ τοιούτους νόμους ἐπαινοῦντες ἀσθενεῖς εἰσιν;
6   ὡς τάχιστα δεῦρο ἀφίκομην, οἴκαδε ἐπανελθεῖν ἐβουλόμην.
7   ἆρα φοβεῖσθε τὴν βασιλέως ἵππον;
8   εἰ ἡ γυνὴ ἴδοι με κακῶς πράσσοντα, εὐθὺς ἂν βοηθήσειεν.
9   οἱ ἡμέτεροι σύμμαχοι εἰς τὴν τῶν πολεμίων χώραν εἰσέβαλον.
10   πάντα πέπρακται ἵνα ῥᾳδίως μανθάνητε.

Exercise 2.21

Translate into Greek:

1   As soon as we heard what had happened, we all set out.
2   I punished the boys who were pelting the door with stones.
3   The girl was treated well by those who had captured her.
4   The barbarians at last invaded Athens.
5   I pity the women who are faring badly here.

Four important idioms

(1) Use of ἔχω with an adverb

The verb ἔχω (*have*) when used with an adverb instead means *be* (i.e. the same as part of εἰμί with the equivalent adjective). This is in origin an intransitive version of the normal alternative meaning *hold*: something *holds itself* in a certain way, so *is* in a certain state.

> τὰ ἐνθάδε ἔχει καλῶς.
literally   Things here hold themselves finely.
i.e.   Things here are fine.

This idiom is often used to describe situations, but it can also be used of people:

> οἱ πολιορκούμενοι κακῶς εἶχον.
> The people being besieged were in a bad way.

(2) Use of ἄγε or φέρε with a command

The singular imperatives ἄγε and φέρε (literally *lead!* and *carry!*) are often used with another imperative or jussive subjunctive (whether singular or plural) to mean *come on ...* :

> ἄγε, σκεψώμεθα πάντα ταῦτα.
> Come on, let's examine all these things!

> φέρε, παῦσαι βοῶν.
> Come on, stop shouting!

(3) Use of κινδυνεύει and φιλεῖ with an infinitive

As an extension of its normal meaning *be in danger* or *run a risk*, κινδυνεύω with an infinitive means *be likely to*. The thought in origin is that something *runs a risk* of happening, but the idiom loses any implication that the thing in question is necessarily dangerous or undesirable, and simply refers to probability.

> κινδυνεύεις τὸ ἀληθὲς λέγειν.
literally You run the risk of speaking the truth.
i.e. You are likely to be speaking the truth.

Similarly as an extension of its normal meaning *like*, the verb φιλέω with an infinitive often means *tends to do X* or *usually does X* (again without any particular emotional colouring).

> τοιαῦτα φιλεῖ γίγνεσθαι.
literally Such things like to happen.
i.e. Such things usually happen.

(4) Double statements with ἄλλος

For *one ... another* (plural *some ... others*), Greek normally uses the article with μέν and δέ (e.g. οἱ μέν ... οἱ δέ ...). But it is also possible to use parts of ἄλλος (sometimes with μέν and δέ as well), like Latin *alii ... alii*. This is particularly common with two *different* parts of ἄλλος, as an abbreviated double statement.

> ἄλλοι ἄλλα λέγουσιν.
> Some people say some things, other people say other things.
or Different people say different things.

(This is shorthand for
> ἄλλοι [1] ἄλλα [1] λέγουσιν, ἄλλοι [2] ἄλλα [2]
where [1] means *some people/things* and [2] means *other people/things*.)

Exercise 2.22

Translate into Greek:
1   ἄγε, δότε ἡμῖν σῖτον, ὦ πολῖται.
2   τὰ ἐν ταῖς Ἀθήναις ἔχει κακῶς.
3   ἆρα ἃ ἔπαθον φιλεῖ γίγνεσθαι;
4   ἄλλος ἄλλο ἐπαινεῖ.
5   κινδυνεύομεν ἀγαθὰ τάχα ἀκούειν.

Exercise 2.23

Translate into Greek (using the idioms described above):
1   I am likely to be making a mistake.
2   Different people like different things.
3   Come on, help me, friends!
4   Things in the city were bad.
5   What has happened tends to happen again.

Chapter 3

Verbs ending in -μι

We met in *Greek to GCSE* the very irregular verbs εἰμί (*I am*), εἶμι (*I shall go*) and φημί (*I say*). We also met some parts of δίδωμι (*I give*), which as we shall see below conforms to a more regular pattern. These and other verbs ending in -μι represent an older stratum of the language than the ordinary verbs ending in -ω. Excluding the very irregular ones, they largely follow a common pattern (though with different vowels), so it is convenient to show them together:

present		I place	I send	I make stand	I give	I show
sg	*1*	τίθημι	ἵημι	ἵστημι	δίδωμι	δείκνυμι
	2	τίθης	ἵης	ἵστης	δίδως	δείκνυς
	3	τίθησι(ν)	ἵησι(ν)	ἵστησι(ν)	δίδωσι(ν)	δείκνυσι(ν)
pl	*1*	τίθεμεν	ἵεμεν	ἵσταμεν	δίδομεν	δείκνυμεν
	2	τίθετε	ἵετε	ἵστατε	δίδοτε	δείκνυτε
	3	τιθέασι(ν)	ἵασι	ἵστασι	διδόασι(ν)	δεικνύασι(ν)

• Note the shared endings (-μι, -ς, σι, -μεν, -τε, -ασι). Several of these recall familiar patterns of ordinary verbs: thus -ς in the second person singular, -μεν and -τε in the first and second person plural are common to all active forms, whilst -ασι in the third person plural recalls the perfect tense.

• Note that the long vowel in the singular endings of each verb shortens in the plural. This is seen most obviously with τίθημι, ἵημι and δίδωμι. The eta of ἵστημι shortens to alpha rather than epsilon. The shortening applies to the upsilon of δείκνυμι as well, but here is a difference only of pronunciation, not of spelling. A further small variation is that τίθημι, δίδωμι and δείκνυμι keep their own vowel as well as alpha in the third person plural.

• Note that ἵημι (in origin a causative form of εἶμι, so *I make go*) has a wide range of meanings, e.g. *hurl* a missile, *utter* a sound. The slightly unnatural active sense of ἵστημι is explained below.

The imperfects are also broadly similar, and also have the vowel shortening in the plural (but here sometimes with a diphthong rather than a long vowel in the singular):

imperfect						
sg	*1*	ἐτίθην	ἵην	ἵστην	ἐδίδουν	ἐδείκνυν
	2	ἐτίθεις	ἵεις	ἵστης	ἐδίδους	ἐδείκνυς
	3	ἐτίθει	ἵει	ἵστη	ἐδίδου	ἐδείκνυ
pl	*1*	ἐτίθεμεν	ἵεμεν	ἵσταμεν	ἐδίδομεν	ἐδείκνυμεν
	2	ἐτίθετε	ἵετε	ἵστατε	ἐδίδοτε	ἐδείκνυτε
	3	ἐτίθεσαν	ἵεσαν	ἵστασαν	ἐδίδοσαν	ἐδείκνυσαν

In the aorist, τίθημι and δίδωμι follow a pattern similar to each other, yet again with the vowel shortening. Greater irregularity is seen with ἵημι (and the hyphens indicate parts found only in compounds), but ἵστημι and δείκνυμι have regular first (weak) aorist forms:

aorist

sg	1	ἔθηκα	-ἧκα	ἔστησα	ἔδωκα	ἔδειξα
	2	ἔθηκας	-ἧκας	etc (reg aor 1)	ἔδωκας	etc (reg aor 1)
	3	ἔθηκε(ν)	-ἧκε(ν)		ἔδωκε(ν)	
pl	1	ἔθεμεν	εἷμεν		ἔδομεν	
	2	ἔθετε	εἷτε		ἔδοτε	
	3	ἔθεσαν	εἷσαν		ἔδοσαν	

Alternative third person plurals ἔθηκαν, ἔδωκαν (on the model of the singular) are also found. Note how the ordinary plurals of these two verbs are shortened forms of the imperfect (their present and imperfect involving a form of reduplication).

Note that the aorist stem of δείκνυμι is δειξ-. Care needs to be taken to avoid confusing parts of this verb with parts of δέχομαι (*I receive*), whose aorist stem is δεξ-.

Note that δίδωμι has two important compounds:

present		*aorist*
παραδίδωμι	I hand over	παρέδωκα
προδίδωμι	I betray	προὔδωκα

Other parts of these verbs are set out in the Reference Grammar (pages 184-6), but here is a summary of the most important:

Like the equivalent tenses of ordinary verbs:

future	θήσω	-ἥσω	στήσω	δώσω	δείξω
perfect	τέθηκα	-εἷκα	ἔστηκα	δέδωκα	δέδειχα

infinitives

present	τιθέναι	ἱέναι	ἱστάναι	διδόναι	δεικνύναι
aorist	θεῖναι	εἷναι	στῆσαι	δοῦναι	δεῖξαι

present participles

τιθείς -εῖσα -έν (*stem* τιθεντ-)
ἱείς ἱεῖσα ἱέν (*stem* ἱεντ-)
ἱστάς -ᾶσα -άν (*stem* ἱσταντ-)
διδούς -οῦσα -όν (*stem* διδοντ-)
δεικνύς -ῦσα -ύν (*stem* δεικνυντ-)

aorist participles

θείς, θεῖσα, θέν (*stem* θεντ-)
εἵς εἵσα ἕν (*stem* ἑντ-)
στήσας -ᾶσα -αν (*stem* στησαντ-)
δούς, δοῦσα, δόν (*stem* δοντ-)
δείξας -ασα -αν (*stem* δειξαντ-)

present middle/passive (like perfect middle/passive forms)

sg	1	τίθεμαι	ἵεμαι	ἵσταμαι	δίδομαι	δείκνυμαι
	2	τίθεσαι	ἵεσαι	ἵστασαι	δίδοσαι	δείκνυσαι
	3	τίθεται	ἵεται	ἵσταται	δίδοται	δείκνυται
pl	1	τιθέμεθα	ἱέμεθα	ἱστάμεθα	διδόμεθα	δεικνύμεθα
	2	τίθεσθε	ἵεσθε	ἵστασθε	δίδοσθε	δείκνυσθε
	3	τίθενται	ἵενται	ἵστανται	δίδονται	δείκνυνται

The use of ἵστημι

The aorist active shown above for ἵστημι is transitive and means *I made something stand* or *I set something up* (e.g. *I stood the clock on the mantlepiece* or *Telemachus set up the axes for the contest*). For the intransitive (commoner and more useful) *I stood* (e.g. *I stood outside the door*), it might be expected that the middle ἐστησάμην would be used, but in fact this has the more specialised sense *I (did) set up _for myself_*. Instead, there is a separate intransitive aorist active ἔστην, which conjugates like ἔβην (the root aorist of βαίνω). Here are the two aorists in full, for comparison:

aorists			I made (something) stand	I stood (myself)
sg	1		ἔστησ-α	ἔστ-ην
	2		ἔστησ-ας	ἔστ-ης
	3		ἔστησ-ε(ν)	ἔστ-η
pl	1		ἐστήσ-αμεν	ἔστ-ημεν
	2		ἐστήσ-ατε	ἔστ-ητε
	3		ἔστησ-αν	ἔστ-ησαν

It will be seen that the two third person plurals (ἔστησ-αν and ἔστ-ησαν) end up the same, so the meaning has to be determined from context. Each of the two aorists has participle, infinitive, etc of predictable formation:

participle	στήσας - ασα -αν (στησαντ-)	στάς στᾶσα στάν (σταντ-)
infinitive	στῆσαι	στῆναι

In the present tense something similar happens. The active ἵστημι is transitive and means *I make something stand*. The middle ἵσταμαι *can* here have a reflexive/intransitive sense, but with the implication *I am in the process of standing up*. For the commoner *I stand*, once again an alternative intransitive active form is used, this time ἔστηκα (strictly a perfect tense meaning *I have taken up a stance*):

perfect as present		I stand
sg	1	ἔστηκα
	2	ἔστηκας
	3	ἔστηκε(ν)
pl	1	ἔσταμεν
	2	ἔστατε
	3	ἔστασαν

Notice the shorter forms in the plural (rather than ἐστήκαμεν etc), analogous to what happens in the aorist active of -μι verbs. This shorter stem also provides the participle and infinitive:

participle	ἑστώς -ῶσα -ός (ἑστωτ-)
infinitive	ἑστάναι

Note also that ἵστημι has two important compounds: ἀφίστημι *I make to revolt* (lit *I make to stand away*) and καθίστημι *I put in a certain state* or *I appoint*. These produce the more common intransitive forms (*I revolt* and *I am in a certain state*) in the present tense by becoming middle, and in the aorist by using the intransitive active -εστην form. Hence:

present		aorist
ἀφίστημι	I make someone revolt	ἀπέστησα
ἀφίσταμαι	I revolt	ἀπέστην
καθίστημι	I put someone in a certain state	κατέστησα
καθίσταμαι	I am in a certain state	κατέστην

Finally note two other common -μι verbs (similar in formation to δείκνυμι):

(1)   ὄμνυμι   I swear   ὤμοσα

This verb is usually followed by a future infinitive, which simply reinforces its meaning: *swear that you will do X* (like the construction with ἐλπίζω, μέλλω and ὑπισχνέομαι).

(2)   ἀπόλλυμι   I lose, I destroy   ἀπώλεσα

The two senses of this verb may seem far apart, but share the idea of *losing possession of*. In the middle it has the reflexive/intransitive sense *I perish* (i.e. lose possession of myself), with a second aorist middle form (in contrast to the first aorist of the active), and a perfect active form with this same meaning (*I have perished*):

ἀπόλλυμαι   I perish   ἀπωλόμην, *perfect* ἀπόλωλα

Exercise 3.1

Translate into English:
1   ποῦ ἔθηκας τὴν ἐμὴν βίβλον;
2   οἱ παῖδες τὰ ἆθλα πρὸ τοῦ ἱεροῦ ἔστησαν.
3   ὁ χειμὼν ἀπώλεσε τὰ δένδρα.
4   τίνα φωνὴν ἵασιν οἱ βάρβαροι;
5   οἱ παῖδες ὤμοσαν μηδέποτε τοὺς ἵππους λύσειν.
6   τίνες εἰσὶν οἱ ἐκεῖ ἑστηκότες;
7   διότι ὁ κακὸς πολίτης προὔδωκε τὴν πατρίδα, οἱ ἄλλοι ἀπώλοντο.
8   παραδός μοι ἐκεῖνο τὸ ἀργύριον, ὦ δοῦλε.
9   κατέστησα φύλακας, καὶ ἐκέλευσα αὐτοὺς τὴν ὁδὸν ἡμῖν δεῖξαι.
10   οἱ πολέμιοι ἔπεισαν πάντας τοὺς ἡμετέρους συμμάχους ἀφίστασθαι.

Exercise 3.2

Translate into Greek:
1   The gods gave many gifts to the Athenians.
2   I stood in the agora in order to hear the speaker.
3   The people living there often used to show our soldiers the road.
4   On account of the wound I lost much blood.
5   The wine given to the giant was very good.

Exercise 3.3
The Fallen of Chaeronea

The fourth-century Athenian statesman and orator Lycurgus pays tribute to the men of Athens and Thebes who died fighting Philip II of Macedon at Chaeronea in central Greece in 338 BC. Philip was at this time steadily taking over mainland Greece: his son Alexander the Great would carry Macedonian ambition further afield. Chaeronea was a defeat for Athens and Thebes, and a symbolic end to the era of the independent city-states - but a heroic defeat, and a doomed stand for freedom. Commemoration of those who had died in battle was a familiar theme of public speeches, and within works of literature. Here it forms part of a lawcourt speech, in which the orator aims to shame by contrast the man he is prosecuting (the otherwise unknown Leocrates), who allegedly fled from Athens at the news of the defeat at Chaeronea, instead of remaining to help his city in its hour of need, when Lycurgus himself took a major role in restoring political and financial stability in a changed world.

περὶ δὲ τούτων τῶν ἀνδρῶν μικρῷ πλέον βούλομαι λέγειν, καὶ ὑμῶν
ἀκοῦσαι δέομαι καὶ μὴ νομίζειν τοιοῦτον <u>ἔπαινον</u> <u>ἀλλότριον</u> εἶναι τῆς
δίκης. ὁ γὰρ τῶν ἀγαθῶν ἔπαινος <u>ἔλεγχόν</u> τε σαφῆ ποιεῖ τῶν ἐναντία
πρασσόντων καὶ ἆθλον μόνος δίδωσι τοῖς ὑπὲρ τῆς κοινῆς σωτηρίας
5   ἀπολωλόσιν. ἐκεῖνοι γὰρ τοῖς πολεμίοις ἀντέστησαν ὑπὲρ τῆς τῶν
Ἑλλήνων ἐλευθερίας μαχόμενοι, οὐ τὰς τῆς σωτηρίας ἐλπίδας ἐν τοῖς
τείχεσιν ἔχοντες, οὐδὲ τὴν χώραν παραδόντες τοῖς ἐχθροῖς κακῶς ποιεῖν·
ἀλλὰ τὴν μὲν ἑαυτῶν ἀνδρείαν ἀσφαλεστέραν <u>φυλακὴν</u> εἶναι ἐνόμιζον
τῶν λιθίνων τειχῶν, τὴν δε <u>θρέψασαν</u> ἑαυτοὺς χώραν ᾐσχύνοντο
10 ἀπολλυμένην ἰδεῖν. τελευτήσαντες δὲ τὴν δόξαν <u>καταλελοίπασιν</u>, οὐ
νικηθέντες ἀλλὰ ἀποθανόντες ὅπου ἐτάχθησαν ὑπὲρ τῆς ἐλευθερίας
πολεμοῦντες. εἰ δ᾽ ἔξεστί μοι <u>παράδοξον</u> μὲν εἰπεῖν, ἀληθὲς δέ, ἐκεῖνοι
νικῶντες ἀπέθανον. ἃ γὰρ ἆθλα τοῦ πολέμου τοῖς ἀγαθοῖς ἐστίν,
ἐλευθερία καὶ ἀρετή, ταῦτ᾽ ἀμφότερα τοῖς τελευτήσασιν ἐδόθη. μόνους
15 γὰρ τοὺς ἐν τοῖς πολέμοις καλῶς ἀποθνήσκοντας οὐδεὶς νικηθῆναι λέγοι
ἄν. ὥστε οὐκ ἂν αἰσχυνθείην εἰπὼν τὰς ἐκείνων <u>ψυχὰς</u> <u>στέφανον</u> τῆς
πατρίδος εἶναι.

	ἔπαινος -ου ὁ	praise
	ἀλλότριος -α -ον	alien to, out of keeping with (+ *gen*)
	ἔλεγχος -ου ὁ	refutation
	φυλακή -ῆς ἡ	protection
9	λίθινος -η -ον	made of stone
	τρέφω ἔθρεψα	I rear, I bring up
	καταλείπω *pf* καταλέλοιπα	I leave behind
	παράδοξος -ον	paradoxical
	ψυχή -ῆς ἡ	life
16	στέφανος -ου ὁ	wreath, crown

Time clauses

Time or *temporal* clauses referring to the past or present (telling us *when* something happened) have an indicative verb (tense by sense), unless they are indefinite (e.g. *whenever*, for which the *indefinite construction* is used: page 83). See below for the special rule about πρίν.

Various words (most of them conjunctions) can introduce time clauses. They can be divided up according to whether the action in the clause takes place *before*, *at the same time as*, or *after* the main verb.

(1) Referring to a time before that of the main verb (could often alternatively be expressed by an aorist or perfect participle):

ἐπεί	when, since, after	(*compare the adverb* ἔπειτα then, next)

ἐπεὶ ἀφικόμεθα, ἐστρατοπεδευσάμεθα.
When we (had) arrived, we set up camp.

> Greek does not use a pluperfect here (see page 30), but simply one aorist followed by another.

> Note the idiom ἐπεὶ τάχιστα *as soon as* (lit *when fastest/soonest*):
> ἐπεὶ τάχιστα σῖτον παρέχω, ἐσθίεται.
> As soon as I prepare food, it is eaten.
> ὡς τάχιστα (in other contexts *as quickly as possible*) can also be used like this.

ἐξ οὗ	since, since the time (*understand* χρόνου) when

ἐξ οὗ ταύτην τὴν βίβλον ἐκτησάμην, σοφώτερος γέγονα.
Since I acquired this book, I have become wiser.

ὅτε	when	(*compare the adverb* τότε then, at that time)

ὅτε χρυσὸς εὑρέθη, ἥ τε ἀδικία καὶ ὁ φθόνος καὶ ἐγένοντο.
When gold was found, both injustice and greed also came into being.

ὡς	when, as, because

ὡς τοῦτο ἤκουσα, μάλιστα ὠργίσθην.
When I heard this, I became very angry.

> Here (and sometimes also with ἐπεί) the *when* is virtually a *because*.

(2) Referring to the same time as that of the main verb (could often alternatively be expressed by a present participle):

ἐν ᾧ	while, *lit* in which time (*understand* χρόνῳ - *compare* ἐν τούτῳ meanwhile)

ἐν ᾧ ὑμεῖς ἐκαθεύδετε, ὁ δεσπότης ἀφίκετο.
While you were sleeping, the master arrived.

ἕως	while

ἕως ὑμεῖς ἐκαθεύδετε, ἡμεῖς ἐπονοῦμεν.
While you were sleeping, we were toiling.

(3) Referring to a time after that of the main verb (could sometimes alternatively be expressed by a future participle):

ἕως   until

> ἐκάθευδον ἕως τὴν βοὴν ἤκουσα.
> I slept until I heard the shout.

μέχρι   until

> ἐπορευόμεθα μέχρι σκότος ἐγένετο.
> We marched until darkness fell.

> Note that μέχρι can also be a preposition, referring either to time (*until*) or space (*as far as*):
> ἐπορευόμεθα μέχρι νυκτός / μέχρι τῶν ὀρῶν
> We marched until night / as far as the mountains.

A special rule applies to πρίν. With the *infinitive* it means *before*:

πρίν   before

> πρὶν τὸν πόλεμον ἄρξασθαι εὐδαίμονες ἦμεν.
> Before the war began we were happy.

> This use of *before* as a conjunction must be distinguished from the preposition πρό (*before*), e.g. πρὸ τοῦ πολέμου *before the war*.

As in indirect statements and other infinitive constructions, the subject of the infinitive is normally *accusative*, but if it is the same as the subject of the main verb it (or a complement/adjective agreeing with it) is *nominative*:

> ἐφονεύθη πρὶν βασιλεὺς γενέσθαι.
> He was murdered before becoming king.

Otherwise πρίν usually means *until*, and is normally found with a negative main verb:

πρίν   until

> ἐγὼ οὐχ οἷός τ' ἦν καθεύδειν πρὶν οἰκάδε ἦλθες.
> I was not able to sleep until you came home.

(See also page 83 on the use of πρίν in the *indefinite* construction.)

πρότερον ... ἤ   before/until, *lit* sooner ... than

Here the πρότερον is often brought forward into the main clause:

> οὐ πρότερον ἐπαύσαντο βοῶντες ἢ ὁ ῥήτωρ ἐκάθισεν.
> *lit*   They did not any sooner stop shouting than the speaker sat down.
> *i.e.*   They did not stop shouting until the speaker sat down.

Time clauses referring to the future in Greek are thought of as intrinsically indefinite, and so the indefinite construction (in primary sequence, i.e. subjunctive with ἄν) is used for them (again see page 83). If the sense is purely temporal (without a suggestion of *if*), a word like ὅταν is better translated simply *when* (rather than *whenever*):

> ὅταν χειμὼν γενήται, παυσόμεθα πλέοντες.
> When winter comes, we shall stop sailing.

• The section above describes various types of time *clause* (i.e. a group of words containing a finite verb). For simple *expressions* of time, conveyed by the use of particular cases of a noun, remember that the rules are:

time how long	e.g.	*for three days*	accusative
time within which		*within three days*	genitive
time when		*on the third day*	dative

Exercise 3.4

Translate into English:

1 ἐπεὶ ἤκουσά σε προσιόντα, οἶνον παρέσχον.
2 ἐξ οὗ οἱ βάρβαροι ἔφυγον, πλουσιώτατοι γεγόναμεν.
3 ὁ πατήρ ἔδωκέ μοι τοῦτο πρὶν ἀπελθεῖν.
4 ὡς τάχιστα τὴν ἐπιστολὴν ἐδεξάμην, ἔγνων τὸν δόλον.
5 ἡ πόλις ἐλήφθη ἐν ᾧ οἱ πολῖται ἔχαιρον.
6 αἱ παῖδες ἔμενον μέχρι νὺξ ἐγένετο.
7 πρὶν τοὺς Ἀθηναίους τὴν ἀρχὴν κτήσασθαι, ἡμεῖς ἐλεύθεροι ἦμεν.
8 δεῖ πονεῖν ἕως ἔξεστιν.
9 ὅτε ἄνθρωποι ἐγένοντο, οἱ θεοὶ ἤδη ἦσαν.
10 οὐκ ἡσύχασα πρὶν τοὺς τοῦ μαντείου λόγους ἔμαθον.

Exercise 3.5

Translate into Greek (using time clauses):

1 While we were sailing to the island, a storm arose.
2 When the women had seen the house, they were despondent.
3 I went home before the messenger arrived.
4 As soon as she read the book, my sister wanted to go to Greece.
5 We did not rejoice until we heard the whole story.

Exercise 3.6 (Revision)

Translate into English:

1 ἐπεὶ ταῦτα ἤκουσαν, οὐκέτι ἤθελον ὁμολογεῖν.
2 οἱ πολῖται ὤμοσαν ἀεὶ τοῖς νόμοις πείσεσθαι.
3 ἆρα σῖτον τῷ γέροντι πολλάκις ἐδίδους;
4 ἐὰν τὴν χεῖρα εἰς τὸ πῦρ θῇς, δεινότατα πείσῃ.
5 δός μοι ἐκείνην τὴν βίβλον, ὦ παῖ.
6 ὁ φύλαξ τὸ ξίφος ἐγγὺς τῆς θύρας ἔθηκεν.
7 πρὶν ἀποθανεῖν ὁ γέρων πάντα τὸν λόγον ἐδήλωσεν.
8 ἐκέλευσα τὸν δοῦλον τὴν ὁδὸν ἡμῖν δεῖξαι.
9 εἰ ἡ ἐπιστολὴ δειχθείη μοι, οἷός τ' ἂν εἴην τὴν βουλὴν μαθεῖν.
10 οἱ Ἕλληνες τοῖς τῶν βαρβάρων θεοῖς ὀνόματα ἔδοσαν.

Exercise 3.7
Timolaus and the Spartans

Before being taken over by Macedon, the Greek city-states in the fourth century BC had been weakened by constantly fighting among themselves. Here the Corinthians are preparing to fight the Spartans (whose strong ally they had been a century earlier), and their commander Timolaus uses two striking analogies in attempting to describe how to deal with Spartan armies.

ἐν δὲ τούτῳ οἱ Λακεδαιμόνιοι, ἕως Ἀγησίπολις ἔτι παῖς ἦν, ἐκέλευον
Ἀριστόδημον, τοῦ αὐτοῦ γένους ὄντα καὶ πρόδικον τοῦ παιδός, ἡγεῖσθαι
τῇ στρατιᾷ. ἐπεὶ δ᾽ ἐξῆλθον οἱ Λακεδαιμόνιοι, οἱ Κορίνθιοι ἐβουλεύοντο
ὅπως ἂν τὴν μάχην συμφορώτατα σφίσιν αὐτοῖς ποιήσαιντο. Τιμόλαος
5   μὲν δὴ Κορίνθιος ἔλεξεν· "ἔμοιγε δοκοῦσιν, ὦ ἄνδρες, ὅμοιοι εἶναι
οἱ Λακεδαιμόνιοι τοῖς ποταμοῖς. οἱ γὰρ ποταμοὶ πρὸς μὲν ταῖς πηγαῖς οὐ
μεγάλοι εἰσὶν ἀλλ᾽ εὐδιάβατοι, χρόνῳ δ᾽ ἕτεροι ποταμοὶ εἰσρέοντες
ἰσχυρότερον ποιοῦσι τὸ ῥεῦμα αὐτῶν, καὶ οἱ Λακεδαιμόνιοι ἐν τῷ αὐτῷ
τρόπῳ. ὅτε μὲν τὸ πρῶτον ἐξέρχονται, αὐτοὶ μόνοι εἰσί, ἐν ᾧ δε
10   προϊόντες προσλαμβάνουσι καὶ τοὺς ἑαυτῶν συμμάχους, πλείονές τε καὶ
δυσμαχώτεροι γίγνονται. καὶ ὁρῶ," ἔφη, "τοὺς βουλομένους σφῆκας
διαφθείρειν, ἐὰν μὲν ἤδη ἐξελθόντας τοὺς σφῆκας βούλωνται ἀποκτείνειν,
ὑπὸ πολλῶν βλαπτομένους· ἐὰν δέ, πρὶν τοὺς σφῆκας τὴν σφηκιὰν λιπεῖν,
προσφέρωσι πῦρ, τότε δὴ ὁρῶ τοὺς μὲν ἀνθρώπους οὐδὲν πάσχοντας, τοὺς
15   δὲ σφῆκας διαφθειρομένους. διὰ ταῦτα οὖν νομίζω βέλτιστον εἶναι τοῖς
Λακεδαιμονίοις ἢ ἐν αὐτῇ τῇ Λακεδαίμονι ἢ ὡς ἐγγύτατα προσβάλλειν."

	Ἀγησίπολις -ιδος ὁ	Agesipolis
	Ἀριστόδημος -ου ὁ	Aristodemus
	πρόδικος -ου ὁ	guardian
	Κορίνθιοι -ων οἱ	Corinthians
4	σύμφορος -ον	advantageous
	Τιμόλαος -ου ὁ	Timolaus
	ὅμοιος -α -ον	like, similar to (+ *dat*)
	πηγή -ῆς ἡ	spring
	εὐδιάβατος -ον	easy to ford
7	εἰσρέω	I flow into
	ῥεῦμα -ατος τό	flow
	προσλαμβάνω	I acquire in addition
	δύσμαχος -ον	hard to fight
	σφήξ σφηκός ὁ	wasp
13	σφηκιά -ᾶς ἡ	wasps' nest
	Λακεδαίμων -ονος ἡ	Sparta

More middles

In *Greek to GCSE (2)* we saw that the *middle* voice of the verb is so called because it is midway between active and passive, though often in practice it is easier to think of it as both active and passive at the same time. We saw various kinds of middle usage:

(1)	reflexive	ἡ κόρη ἐκρύψατο.	The girl hid (herself).
(2)	intransitive	ἡ μάχη ἐπαύσατο.	The battle ceased.
(3)	causative	διδάσκομαι τὸν παῖδα.	I get the boy taught.
(4)	deponent	ἡ συμφορὰ ἐγένετο.	The disaster happened.

Often the middle sense is deducible from the active:

παύω	I stop (*trans*)	παύομαι	I cease
φαίνω	I show	φαίνομαι	I appear

We saw too that some verbs have a special idiomatic meaning in the middle:

αἱρέω	I take	αἱρέομαι	I choose	(take for myself)
ἄρχω	I rule (+ *gen*)	ἄρχομαι	I begin	(be first in a different sense)
λύω	I release	λύομαι	I ransom	(get someone released)
πείθω	I persuade	πείθομαι	I obey (+ *dat*)	(persuade myself to comply)
φέρω	I carry	φέρομαι	I win	(carry off for myself)

Some verbs are purely deponent (no active form exists):

γίγνομαι	I become
ἔρχομαι	I come, I go
κτάομαι	I obtain
μάχομαι	I fight

Others, regarded in practice as deponent, do have an underlying but less common active form:

(ὀργίζω	I anger)	ὀργίζομαι	I get angry
(πορεύω	I convey)	πορεύομαι	I march
(φοβέω	I frighten)	φοβέομαι	I fear

We also saw that some active verbs use middle forms for some tenses (e.g. ἀκούω, future ἀκούσομαι), and that some middle verbs use passive forms for some tenses (e.g. πορεύομαι, aorist ἐπορεύθην).

Here are some more verbs, study of which should help you to understand the use of the middle:

αἰσχύνω	I disgrace	αἰσχύνομαι	I am ashamed
ἀμύνω*	I ward off	ἀμύνομαι	I defend myself; I resist (+ *gen*)
ἀνάγω	I lead up	ἀνάγομαι	I put out to sea (*thought of as a plateau*)
ἅπτω	I join	ἅπτομαι	I touch, I lay hold of (+ *gen*)
γαμέω	I (*m*) marry	γαμέομαι	I (*f*) marry
δέω	I lack	δέομαι	I ask for, I need (+ *gen*)
διαλέγω	I pick out	διαλέγομαι	I converse (*picking out words to use*)
		εὔχομαι	I pray
		ἡγέομαι	I lead (+ *dat*); I think (*lead a train of thought*)
		θεάομαι	I watch
μηχανάω	I contrive	μηχανάομαι	I devise, I construct
ὁρμάω	I set in motion	ὁρμάομαι	I set out
ψεύδω	I deceive	ψεύδομαι	I tell lies; I am mistaken

* The use of the active and middle of ἀμύνω needs some explanation. The active verb in origin means *I ward off* (with an enemy or source of danger as the direct object). Often though such an accusative is understood rather than stated, and the verb is followed by a dative:

ἀμύνω τῇ πόλει

lit   I ward off (unstated opposition) for the city.

i.e.   I defend the city.

The middle on its own means *I defend myself* (I ward off opposition for my own benefit). Followed by an accusative it means *I defend myself against*, and followed by a genitive *I resist* (though in practice these last two are much the same).

With some verbs there seems little difference between the active and middle senses. The middle of βουλεύω *I discuss, I deliberate* in origin means *I deliberate with myself*, but in practice both are used for e.g. *I consider* or *I plan*. The reason why a Greek author uses the middle form of a verb is not always obvious. As a development of the reflexive/causative senses, the middle often implies little more than *I do something for my own advantage*, and many human actions come into that category.

Note also the verb σκοπέω *I look at, I examine* forms its other tenses as if from the middle σκέπτομαι (hence future σκέψομαι, aorist ἐσκεψάμην).

Exercise 3.8

Translate into English:

1   τίνι ἐγήματο ἡ τοῦ κριτοῦ θυγάτηρ;
2   οἱ τοῦ ἀποθανουμένου φίλοι ἐν τῷ δεσμωτηρίῳ διελέγοντο.
3   αὕτη ἡ παῖς πάντα τὰ ἆθλα ἐφέρετο.
4   ὁ ναύτης εἰς τὴν θάλασσαν πεσὼν ἐπειρᾶτο ἅψασθαι τῆς νέως.
5   οἱ πολῖται πολὺν χρόνον ἠμύναντο τῶν τῇ πόλει προσβαλόντων.
6   χρή σε τῇ θεᾷ εὔχεσθαι.
7   οἱ ἐν τῇ νήσῳ εἵλοντο ἐκεῖ μένειν.
8   ἅμ᾽ ἡμέρᾳ κατὰ τῶν ὀρῶν ὁρμησάμενοι, μετὰ δύο ὥρας ἀνηγαγόμεθα.
9   ταῦτα ἀκούσας ᾐσχύνθην.
10   οἱ Ἀθηναῖοι ἀεὶ βούλονται νέον τι θεᾶσθαι καὶ ἀκουέιν.

Exercise 3.9

Translate into Greek:

1   The man leading the expedition is never afraid.
2   Surely the women in the city were not telling lies?
3   These men defended themselves for three days.
4   Who contrived the death of the giant?
5   That old man is asking for food.

Verbs with dependent participle

We have seen repeatedly that Greek makes very full use of participles. The following important verbs are commonly followed by a *dependent participle*:

	aorist	literal meaning
τυγχάνω	ἔτυχον	I happen (to be)
λανθάνω	ἔλαθον	I escape (the) notice (of)
φθάνω	ἔφθασα	I anticipate, I do something first

The use of each needs some explanation (as the literal sense may be misleading), but they have it in common that <u>the important idea is expressed by the following participle</u>.

Hence to take the simplest example:

> ἔτυχεν ἀφικόμενη.
>
> *literally* She happened having arrived.
>
> *i.e.* She happened to have arrived.

Here Greek uses a participle where we might expect an infinitive, and the minimum change to achieve acceptable English requires this substitution. But in fact we might alternatively say something like *She had arrived, as it happened* or *By chance she had arrived* (τύγχανω is closely related to the noun τύχη *chance* or *luck,* as should be clear from its aorist stem), making the Greek participle into the main verb and translating ἔτυχεν by a phrase equivalent to an adverb.

The use of λανθάνω is similar:

> ἔλαθον εἰσελθόντες.
>
> *literally* They escaped notice having gone in.

Here there is no temptation to use an infinitive in English, but it is even more natural to recast the sentence as something like:

> They went in secretly (*or* surreptitiously).

It is thus the equivalent of:

> λάθρᾳ εἰσῆλθον.

Again the Greek participle has become the main verb, and ἔλαθον has been represented by a related adverb. Another possibility would be:

> They went in without anyone seeing them.

If we want to specify *who* did not see them (i.e. whose notice they escaped), this can be put in as the direct object of ἔλαθον:

> ἔλαθον τοὺς φύλακας εἰσελθόντες.
>
> *literally* They escaped the notice of the guards in having gone in.
>
> *i.e.* They went in without the guards seeing them.

The construction with φθάνω is similar again, and here the use with a direct object is the norm:

ἔφθασε τὸν ἀδελφὸν ἀφικομένη.
literally She anticipated her brother in arriving.

Here an obvious problem in English is that this is an old-fashioned sense of *anticipate* (as *forestall*, rather than the normal modern sense *expect*), so it is even more necessary to turn the sentence round into something like:

She arrived before her brother did.

Once again the Greek participle has been made into the main verb in English.

• We saw that τυγχάνω is followed by a participle where we might expect an infinitive. One Greek verb we have met already - φαίνομαι *I appear* - can be followed by either, with an important distinction in meaning. As we have seen already, it is commonly followed by an infinitive, as in English:

φαίνεται μῶρος εἶναι.
He appears to be stupid (*often implying* but may not be really).

But it may also be followed by a participle:

φαίνεται μῶρος ὤν.

In this case the meaning is:

literally	He appears (before us as) being stupid.
or	He shows himself as ...
i.e.	He clearly is stupid.

Again the participle has become the main verb, and the main verb is translated by an adverb.

The same meaning is given (with equal or greater emphasis) by using the adjective δῆλος *clear* with the verb *to be* and a participle:

δῆλός ἐστιν ὀργιζόμενος.
| *literally* | He is clear as getting angry. |
| *i.e.* | He is clearly getting angry. |

• Other verbs are commonly followed by a participle, in a way that is natural in English too:

ἄρχομαι	I begin
παύομαι	I cease
ἥδομαι	I enjoy
χαίρω	I rejoice (in doing)

The participle again simply follows on in the nominative: ἥδομαι ἐσθίων *I enjoy eating*. The grammar is *in/while eating I take pleasure*, not *I enjoy the act of eating*. But although these verbs cannot take an accusative direct object (they are intransitive), they can express a similar meaning in other ways, for example with an articular infinitive (see page 79) in an appropriate case: ἥδομαι τῷ ἐσθίειν *I enjoy* lit *I take pleasure in eating* (ἥδομαι + dat). Similarly παύομαι μαχόμενος (lit *in/while fighting I cease*) and παύομαι τοῦ μαχέσθαι (lit *I cease from the act of fighting* - παύομαι + gen) both simply mean *I cease fighting*.

61

• Note that τυγχάνω has another important meaning and use, in addition to this participle construction. When followed by a genitive, it means *hit upon, get, attain* (the underlying idea is of *hitting a target*, and it is thus the opposite of ἁμαρτάνω *make a mistake* or *miss* a target). Being followed by the genitive is in line with other verbs suggesting *getting hold of* something. Also however note the compound ἐντυγχάνω *meet, come upon* (compare colloquial English *bump into*), which because of its prefix is followed by a dative.

• Note that λανθάνω can be used reflexively - e.g. ἔλαθον ἐμαυτὸν ἁμαρτών (active, with the reflexive pronoun as object) *I escaped the notice of myself in making a mistake* i.e. *I made a mistake without realising it*. As a development of this idea note the middle compound ἐπιλανθάνομαι *I let something escape my notice*, i.e. *forget*, followed by the genitive.

Exercise 3.10

Translate into English:

1   ἆρα ἔτυχες παρὼν τοῦ ἀγγέλου λέγοντος;
2   ὁ λέων ἔλαθε τὸν φύλακα ἐξελθών.
3   ὁ φεύγων ἔφθασε τοὺς διώκοντας πρὸς τὸ ἱερὸν ἀφικόμενος.
4   αὕτη ἡ κόρη ἐφαίνετο σοφωτάτη εἶναι.
5   ἔλαθον ἐμαυτὸν τοῦτο ποιήσας.
6   ὁ γέρων ἥδετο τοὺς τῶν πάλαι Ἑλλήνων μύθους ἀκούων.
7   αἱ γυναῖκες ἔφθασαν τοὺς ἄνδρας τὸ ἀληθές πυθόμεναι.
8   ἆρα μὴ λανθάνει σε ἡ βασίλεια ταῦτα βαρέως φέρουσα;
9   ὁ παῖς τέλος ἐπαύσατο βοῶν.
10   οἱ ἐκεῖ θανάτου κακίστου πάντες ἔτυχον.

Exercise 3.11

Translate into Greek:

1   I happened to be in the agora on the previous day.
2   The prisoners ran away without the guard seeing them.
3   Did you find the road before we did, friends?
4   The reward is clearly going to be very useful.
5   The citizens never ceased praising the king.

Exercise 3.12

The Flight of Themistocles

*We return here to the second Persian invasion of Greece under Xerxes in the early fifth century BC, which
we looked at in* Greek to GCSE (2). *The Athenian statesman and general Themistocles took a major part in
bringing about Greek victory, by persuading the Athenians to build up their navy beforehand and by
ensuring that the sea-battle of Salamis in September 480 BC was fought in a narrow channel to suit Greek
tactics. In this campaign, Athens and Sparta (together with most of the other city-states) had rather uneasily
co-operated against a common enemy. In the following years however Themistocles fell from favour, and
Athens and Sparta became enemies, eventually fighting each other in the Peloponnesian War (431-404 BC).
The historian of that war is Thucydides: he traces this growing enmity, and here describes what happened
when in about 468 BC Sparta claimed to have evidence that Themistocles was plotting with the Persians.*

οἱ δὲ Λακεδαιμόνιοι πρέσβεις πέμψαντες παρὰ τοὺς Ἀθηναίους τὸν
Θεμιστοκλέα ᾐτιῶντο τοῦ μηδισμοῦ, καὶ ἠξίουν κολάζειν αὐτόν. οἱ δὲ
πεισθέντες (ἔτυχε γὰρ ὠστρακισμένος καὶ ἐν τῇ Πελοποννήσῳ ὤν)
πέμπουσιν ἄνδρας αὐτὸν ἄξοντας. ὁ δὲ Θεμιστοκλῆς ἔφθασεν αὐτοὺς εἰς
5 τὴν Κέρκυραν φυγών, εὐεργέτης τῶν ἐκεῖ ὤν. τῶν μέντοι Κερκυραίων
λεγόντων φοβεῖσθαι σῴζειν αὐτόν, ἔλαθε πρὸς τὴν ἤπειρον κομιζόμενος.
καὶ διωκόμενος ὑπὸ τῶν ἐχθρῶν ἀναγκάζεται καταλῦσαι παρὰ τὸν
Ἄδμητον τὸν τῶν Μολοσσῶν βασιλέα, ὄντα αὐτῷ οὐ φίλον. καὶ ὁ μὲν
οὐκ ἔτυχεν ἐπιδημῶν, ὁ δὲ Θεμιστοκλῆς ἱκέτης τῆς γυναικὸς γενόμενος
10 διδάσκεται ὑπ᾽ αὐτῆς τὸν παῖδα σφῶν λαβὼν καθέζεσθαι ἐπὶ τὴν ἑστίαν.
καὶ ἐπανελθόντος οὐ πολὺ ὕστερον τοῦ Ἀδμήτου δηλοῖ ὅς ἐστιν, εἰπὼν
ὑφ᾽ ὧν διώκεται. ὁ δὲ ἀκούσας ἀνίστησί τε αὐτὸν μετὰ τοῦ παιδός (καὶ
μέγιστον ἦν ἱκέτευμα τοῦτο) καὶ ὕστερον οὐ πολλῷ τοῖς ἐχθροῖς ἐλθοῦσιν
καὶ πολλὰ εἰποῦσιν οὐκ ἐκδίδωσιν, ἀλλ᾽ ἀποστέλλει βουλόμενον ὡς
15 βασιλέα πορευθῆναι ἐπὶ τὴν ἑτέραν θάλασσαν. ἐν ᾗ ὁλκάδος τυχὼν καὶ
ἐπιβὰς καταφέρεται χειμῶνι ἐς τὸ τῶν Ἀθηναίων στρατόπεδον ὃ

	Θεμιστοκλῆς -έους ὁ	Themistocles
	αἰτιάομαι	I accuse
	μηδισμός -οῦ ὁ	siding with Persia
	ὀστρακίζω	
3	pf pass ὠστράκισμαι	I ostracize (*banish for ten years, by vote on potsherds*)
	Πελοπόννησος -ου ἡ	Peloponnese
	Κέρκυρα -ας ἡ	Corcyra (*modern Corfu*)
	εὐεργέτης -ου ὁ	benefactor
	Κερκυραῖοι -ων οἱ	Corcyreans
8	καταλύω κατέλυσα	I rest
	Ἄδμητος -ου ὁ	Admetus
	Μολοσσοί -ῶν οἱ	Molossians
	ἐπιδημέω	I am at home
	ἱκέτης -ου ὁ	suppliant
10	καθέζομαι	I sit
	ἑστία -ας ἡ	hearth
	ἱκέτευμα -ατος τό	means of persuasion
	ἀποστέλλω	I send someone on their way
	ἕτερος -α -ον	the other, *here* on the other side (*i.e. the Aegean*)
15	ὁλκάς -άδος ἡ	merchant ship
	ἐπιβαίνω ἐπέβην	I get on board

ἐπολιόρκει <u>Νάξον</u>. καί (ἦν γὰρ <u>ἀγνὼς</u> τοῖς ἐν τῇ νηί) <u>φράζει</u> τῷ <u>ναυκλήρῳ</u> ὅστις ἐστί, καὶ εἰ μὴ σώσει αὐτόν, ἔφη ἐρεῖν ὅτι χρήμασι πεισθεὶς αὐτὸν ἄγει. ὁ δὲ ναύκληρος <u>ἀποσαλεύσας</u> ἡμέραν καὶ νύκτα
20 ὕστερον ἀφικνεῖται ἐς <u>Ἔφεσον</u>. καὶ ὁ Θεμιστοκλῆς ἐκείνῳ τε χρήματα ἔδωκε καὶ <u>ἄνω</u> πορευθεὶς πέμπει <u>γράμματα</u> πρὸς <u>Ἀρταξέρξην</u> τὸν <u>Ξέρξου</u> ἄρτι <u>βασιλεύοντα</u>.

	Νάξος -ου ἡ	Naxos (*island in the central Aegean*)
	ἀγνώς -ῶτος	unknown
	φράζω	I tell, I inform (+ *dat*)
	ναύκληρος -ου ὁ	captain
19	ἀποσαλεύω ἀπεσάλευσα	I anchor in open sea
	Ἔφεσος -ου ἡ	Ephesus
	ἄνω	(*here*) inland
	γράμματα, -ων τά	letter
	Ἀρταξέρξης -ου ὁ	Artaxerxes
21	Ξέρξης -ου ὁ	Xerxes (*gen here* indicates son of)
	βασίλευω	I am king, *here* I have become king

Verbs of fearing

As in English, φοβέομαι *I fear/I am afraid (of)* can be followed by a direct object, or by an infinitive:

τίς φοβεῖται τὸν σκότον;
Who is afraid of the dark?

πάντες εἰς τὴν ὕλην εἰσιέναι ἐφοβούμεθα.
We all feared to go into the forest.

A fear *that* something may happen is expressed by μή and the subjunctive or optative. The word μή here corresponds to the old-fashioned word *lest* (which however is now not very natural, and better avoided), but the important point is that in modern English it is *not really a negative*, and should be translated *that*:

φοβοῦμαι μὴ τοιοῦτό τι γενήται.
I fear that something of this sort may happen.

The thought behind this is that you are afraid, hoping that it may *not* happen, therefore you fear that it *may* happen.

If you are afraid that something may *not* happen (i.e. you hope it *will* happen), this *negative* fear is expressed by μὴ οὐ and the same construction (one of the few places in Greek where the two negative words are found together):

ἐφοβούμην μὴ οὐ σήμερον ἀφίκοισθε.
I was afraid that you would not arrive today.

The use of μή and μὴ οὐ corresponds exactly to the use of *ne* and *ne non* with verbs of fearing in Latin.

The use of the subjunctive or optative is exactly the same as in a purpose clause, i.e. subjunctive in primary sequence, and normally optative in historic (except that the

subjunctive may be used here too for 'vividness'), the use of present or aorist subjunctive/
optative determined as usual by aspect (see page 147).

The same construction is used with expressions such as **φόβος ἐστί** *there is fear (that)*, **φόβον ἔχω** *I have fear (that)*, **κίνδυνός ἐστι** *there is danger (that)*, and in other contexts where fearing is implied.

The construction described above expresses fear *for the future*. The much less common fear that something (currently unknown) will prove to be true about the *present or past* (compare the equivalent open/unknown conditionals - see pages 18-19) is expressed by **μή** (neg **μή οὐ**, as above) and a verb in the appropriate indicative tense, according to sense:

> φοβοῦμαι μὴ οἱ τοῦ μαντείου λόγοι ἀληθεῖς ἦσαν.
> I fear that the words of the oracle were true.

Exercise 3.13

Translate into English:

1   οἱ πολῖται ἐφοβοῦντο μὴ ἡ πόλις ληφθείη.
2   οὗτος ὁ παῖς οὐδένα κίνδυνον φοβεῖται.
3   φοβούμεθα μὴ οὐ ἀκουσθῶμεν.
4   ὁ δοῦλος τῷ δεσπότῃ ἐπείθετο, φοβούμενος μὴ κολάζηται.
5   οἱ στρατιῶται ἐφοβοῦντο μὴ οὐκ οἴκαδε ἐπανέλθοιεν.
6   φοβοῦμαι ἀναγνῶναι τὴν ἐπιστολήν.
7   ἆρα φόβον ἔχεις μὴ ἀληθῶς εἶπεν ὁ θεός;
8   πάντες οἱ αἰχμάλωτοι φοβοῦνται μη δουλωθῶσιν.
9   ἔγραψα τοὺς λόγους, μὴ ἐπιλαθοίμην.
10   φόβος ἦν μὴ οὐκ ἀφικοίντο οἱ σύμμαχοι.

Exercise 3.14

Translate into Greek:

1   We fear that the summer may soon end.
2   The old man was afraid to send for the doctor.
3   The people on the island feared they might not be saved.
4   Were you afraid that the enemy would return, citizens?
5   I am afraid that we were seen by the teacher.

Exercise 3.15
Themistocles in Persia (1)

The subsequent adventures of Themistocles are recounted by the historian and biographer Plutarch, writing long afterwards (about 100 AD), but using sources now lost. Here he receives an omen about his future fortunes and is helped on his way into the Persian heartland, wanting to remain anonymous until he can speak to the king in person. Note that Plutarch uses -ττ- instead of -σσ-.

ἐπεὶ δὲ εἰσέπλευσεν εἰς Κύμην καὶ πολλοὺς ἥσθετο τῶν ἐπὶ θαλάττῃ
παραφυλάττοντας αὐτὸν λαβεῖν (ἦν γὰρ ἡ θήρα λυσιτελὴς τοῖς γε τὸ
κερδαίνειν ἀπὸ παντὸς φιλοῦσι, διακοσίων κηρυχθέντων αὐτῷ ταλάντων
ὑπὸ βασιλέως) ἔφυγεν εἰς Αἰγάς, οὗ ἀγνὼς ἦν πᾶσι πλὴν τοῦ ξένου
5   Νικογένους. παρὰ τούτῳ κρυπτόμενος ἡμέρας ὀλίγας ἔμενεν. ἔπειτα δὲ
μετὰ δεῖπνον ὁ τῶν παίδων παιδαγωγὸς θεοφόρητος γενόμενος εἶπεν ἐν
μέτρῳ τάδε· "νυκτὶ φωνήν, νυκτὶ βουλήν, νυκτὶ τὴν νίκην δίδου."

καὶ μετὰ ταῦτα ὁ Θεμιστοκλῆς καθεύδων ἔδοξεν ἰδεῖν δράκοντα, ὃς ἀετὸς
ἐξαίφνης γενόμενος καὶ τὰς πτέρυγας περιβαλὼν ἐκόμιζεν αὐτὸν πολλὴν
10 ὁδόν· ἔπειτα χρυσοῦ τινος κηρυκείου φανέντος, ἐπὶ τούτῳ ἔστησε βεβαίως
αὐτόν, φόβου καὶ ἀπορίας λυθέντα. ἐκ τούτου πέμπεται ὑπὸ τοῦ
Νικογένους μηχανησαμένου τάδε. οἱ Πέρσαι τὰς γυναῖκας ἰσχυρῶς
φυλάττουσι, ἐῶντες αὐτὰς ὑπ᾽ οὐδενὸς ὁρᾶσθαι, καὶ ἐν ὁδοιπορίαις δεῖ
ὑπὸ σκηναῖς ἐπὶ τῶν ἁμάξων ὀχεῖσθαι. τοιαύτης ἀπήνης τῷ Θεμιστοκλεῖ
15 παρασκευασθείσης, οὕτως ἐκομίζετο, τῶν περὶ αὐτὸν ἀεὶ τοῖς
ἐντυγχάνουσι καὶ πυνθανομένοις λεγόντων ὅτι γυναῖκα Ἑλληνικὴν ἄγουσι
πρὸς ὑπηρέτην τινὰ βασιλέως.

	Κύμη -ης ἡ	Cyme (*coastal city in Asia Minor, modern Turkey*)
	παραφυλάττω	I look out for a chance to
	θήρα -ας ἡ	hunt
	λυσιτελής -ές	profitable
3	κερδαίνω	I make money
	τάλαντον -ου τό	talent (*large unit of currency, worth 6000 drachmas*)
	Αἰγαί -ῶν αἱ	Aegae (*another city in Asia Minor*)
	ἀγνώς -ῶτος	unknown
	Νικογένης -ους ὁ	Nicogenes
6	παιδαγωγός -οῦ ὁ	tutor (*elderly male slave looking after children*)
	θεοφόρητος -ον	divinely possessed
	μέτρον -ου τό	verse
	Θεμιστοκλῆς -έους ὁ	Themistocles
	δράκων -οντος ὁ	snake
8	ἀετός -οῦ ὁ	eagle
	πτέρυξ -υγος ἡ	wing
	κηρύκειον -ου τό	herald's staff
	Πέρσαι -ῶν οἱ	Persians
	ὁδοιπορία -ας ἡ	journey
14	ἅμαξα -ης ἡ	wagon
	ὀχέομαι	I am carried, I travel
	ἀπήνη -ης ἡ	covered wagon
	Ἑλληνικός -ή -όν	Greek
	ὑπηρέτης -ου ὁ	servant

Nouns and adjectives with epsilon contraction

In *Greek to GCSE (2)* we met some nouns and adjectives which, because their stems end in epsilon, undergo contraction when endings are added according to the same rules as contracted -εω verbs: third declension neuter nouns like γένος (*type, family, race*) and 3-3 adjectives like ἀληθής (*true*). Note also the feminine noun τριήρης *trireme* (fast warship with three banks of oars), shown here alongside γένος for comparison.

		type, family, race (n)		trireme (f)	
sg	nom	γέν-ος		τριήρ-ης	
	acc	γέν-ος		τριήρ-η	[ε-α]
	gen	γέν-ους	[ε-ος]	τριήρ-ους	[ε-ος]
	dat	γέν-ει	[ε-ι]	τριήρ-ει	[ε-ι]
pl	nom	γέν-η	[ε-α]	τριήρ-εις	[ε-ε]
	acc	γέν-η	[ε-α]	τριήρ-εις	[ε-α, *but assimilated to nom*]
	gen	γεν-ῶν	[ε-ω]	τριήρ-ων	[ε-ω]
	dat	γέν-εσι(ν)		τριήρ-εσι(ν)	

Nouns like γένος pose an obvious risk of confusion with second declension (mostly masculine) ones like λόγος. With both types of epsilon contraction noun and with the equivalent adjectives, note in particular endings that look like other parts of other declensions, e.g. genitive singular -ους confusable with second declension accusative plural; accusative singular or neuter plural -η confusable with first declension nominative singular.

Latin also has neuter third declension nouns that look like masculine second, for example *corpus* (*body*), *genus* (*type* - the same word as Greek), and *opus* (*work*).

Note the following third declension neuter nouns with epsilon contraction:

γένος	type, family, race	μῖσος	hatred
ἔθνος	tribe, race, nation	ξίφος	sword
ἔτος	year	ὄρος	hill, mountain
θέρος	summer	πλῆθος	crowd, large number
κράτος	might, authority	τεῖχος	wall
μέρος	part, share	τέλος	end, result, fulfilment

Note the following 3-3 adjectives with epsilon contraction (see page 180):

ἀληθής	true	εὐσεβής	pious
ἀσεβής	impious	εὐτυχής	fortunate, lucky
ἀσθενής	weak	σαφής	clear
ἀσφαλής	safe	συγγενής	related, kin
δυστυχής	unfortunate		

See also the next section on the nature of most of these as *compounds*.

Note also two 2-1-2 adjectives with epsilon contraction (ε-ος becomes -οῦς, etc):

ἀργυροῦς -ῆ -οῦν	(made of) silver
χρυσοῦς -ῆ -οῦν	(made of) gold

Exercise 3.16

Translate into English:

1. ἆρα πάντα τὰ ἔθνη συγγενῆ ἦν;
2. νομίζω τὸ θέρος ἄριστον μέρος τοῦ ἔτους εἶναι.
3. ποῦ ηὗρες τοὺς τοῦ τείχους λίθους;
4. οἱ εὐσεβεῖς οὐκ ἀεὶ εὐτυχεῖς εἰσίν.
5. τὸ ἀργυροῦν ξίφος καλὸν μέν ἐστι, χρήσιμον δ' οὔ.

Privative alpha and compound adjectives

Almost all the third declension adjectives (e.g. ἀληθής *true*) discussed in the previous section are *compounds*. This accounts for why they are 3-3 in declension (rather than 3-1-3 like for example βαρύς *heavy*), i.e. have no separate feminine (though there is no obvious explanation of this rule itself). The same applies to 2-2 (rather than 2-1-2) compounds like ἄδικος *unjust* - often referred to as *two-termination* adjectives. Compound adjectives (like compound verbs) can have various prefixes. The pair εὐτυχής and δυστυχής mean respectively *well* and *badly* provided with τύχη (*luck*). The σύν of συγγενής means that one person or group belongs *with* another in γένος. Several of them however simply use the *privative alpha* (ἀ- as a prefix), which makes a negative by *depriving* the word of its usual sense. The following examples should make this clear:

ἄδικος -ον	unjust	(lacking δίκη)
ἀδύνατος -ον	impossible; unable	(not δύνατος)
ἀληθής -ές	true	(lit *unconcealed* - cf λανθάνω, Lethe)
ἀπροσδόκητος -ον	unexpected	(not as προσδοκάω *I expect*)
ἀσεβής -ές	impious	(opposite of εὐσεβής lit *well pious*)
ἀσθενής -ές	weak	(lacking σθένος *strength*)
ἀσφαλής -ές	safe	(does not σφάλλω *cause to slip*)

The privative alpha is also used as a verb prefix:

ἀγνοέω	I do not know	(cf γιγνώσκω)
ἀθυμέω	I am despondent	(I lack θυμός *spirit*)
ἀπορέω	I am at a loss	(I lack πόρος *way of coping*)

Note also the pair of adjectives:

ἑκών -οῦσα -όν (ἑκοντ-)	(being) willing
ἄκων -ουσα -ον (ἀκοντ-)	(being) unwilling

These behave in effect as participles, though no verb exists (and with ἄκων the rule about not having a separate feminine does not apply). They are often best translated as adverbs: *(un)willingly*.

Finally as a 2-2 compound adjective note βάρβαρος -ον *foreign, barbarian* (making *bar bar* noises instead of speaking Greek), often made into a noun οἱ βάρβαροι *non-Greeks, foreigners*.

Exercise 3.17

Translate into English:

1. ἀγνοῶ τὴν τῶν βαρβάρων φωνήν.
2. ὁ ἡγεμὼν ᾔδει τὴν γέφυραν ἀσθενῆ ἀλλὰ ἀσφαλῆ οὖσαν.
3. διότι ἀδύνατον ἦν τὸν ποταμὸν διαβῆναι, πολὺν χρόνον ἠποροῦμεν.
4. τὴν τῶν ἀδίκων καὶ ἀσεβῶν βουλὴν ἄκοντες ἐδεξάμεθα.
5. ἆρ' ἀθυμεῖς διὰ τὰ ἀπροσδοκήτως γενόμενα;

Exercise 3.18

Themistocles in Persia (2)

Themistocles here learns of the requirement for bodily prostration before the king. His adaptable compliance seems justified by the unexpected (though self-interested) goodwill of the king, Artaxerxes I, who subsequently made him governor of the important Asia Minor city of Magnesia.

ἀφικόμενος δὲ πρὸς τὰ <u>βασίλεια</u> ὁ Θεμιστοκλῆς ἐντυγχάνει πρῶτον
<u>Ἀρταβάνῳ</u>, φάσκων Ἕλλην μὲν εἶναι, βούλεσθαι δ᾽ ἐντυχεῖν βασιλεῖ περὶ
πραγμάτων μεγάλων. ὁ δέ φησιν· "ὦ ξένε, νόμοι ἀνθρώπων <u>διαφέρουσιν</u>·
ἄλλα δ᾽ ἄλλοις καλά. ἡμῖν δὲ πολλῶν νόμων καὶ καλῶν ὄντων κάλλιστος
5 οὗτός ἐστι, τιμᾶν βασιλέα καὶ <u>προσκυνεῖν</u> ὡς <u>εἰκόνα</u> θεοῦ τοῦ τὰ πάντα
σῴζοντος. εἰ μὲν τὰ ἡμέτερα ἐπαινῶν προσκυνήσεις, ἔξεστί σοι καὶ
θεάσθαι βασιλέα καὶ προσεῖπειν· εἰ δ᾽ ἄλλο τι <u>φρονεῖς</u>, ἀγγέλοις χρήσῃ."
ταῦθ᾽ ὁ Θεμιστοκλῆς ἀκούσας, λέγει πρὸς αὐτόν· "ἀλλ᾽ ἐγὼ τὴν βασιλέως
δύναμιν, ὦ Ἀρτάβανε, τιμήσων ἀφῖγμαι, καὶ αὐτός τε πείσομαι τοῖς
10 ὑμετέροις νόμοις, καὶ δι᾽ ἐμὲ πλείονες τῶν νῦν βασιλέα προσκυνήσουσιν."

ἐπεὶ δ᾽ οὖν εἰσήχθη πρὸς βασιλέα καὶ προσκυνήσας ἔστη σιγῇ, καὶ
βασιλέως διὰ τοῦ <u>ἑρμηνέως</u> ἐρωτήσαντος τίς ἐστιν, εἶπε τάδε· "ἥκω σοι
βασιλεῦ Θεμιστοκλῆς ὁ Ἀθηναῖος ἐγὼ φυγάς, ὑφ᾽ Ἑλλήνων διωχθείς, ᾧ
πολλὰ μὲν <u>ὀφείλουσι</u> Πέρσαι κακά, πλείω δ᾽ ἀγαθὰ κωλύσαντι τὴν δίωξιν,
15 ὅτε τῆς Ἑλλάδος ἐν ἀσφαλεῖ γεγενημένης παρέσχε τὰ <u>οἰκεῖα</u> σῳζόμενα
<u>χαρίσασθαί</u> τι καὶ ὑμῖν. αἰτῶ σε σῴζειν τὸν σὸν <u>ἱκέτην</u>, τοῖς Ἕλλησι
πολέμιον γενόμενον." ἀκούσας δὲ βασιλεὺς οὐδὲν εὐθὺς ἀπεκρίνατο,
καίπερ θαυμάσας τήν τε τόλμαν καὶ τὴν ἀρετὴν αὐτοῦ. λέγεται δὴ ὅτι
μετὰ ταῦτα σὺν τοῖς φίλοις ἔπιεν, καὶ καθευδὼν ὑπὸ <u>χαρᾶς</u> <u>τρὶς</u> ἐβόησεν·
20 "ἔχω Θεμιστοκλέα τὸν Ἀθηναῖον." τῇ δ᾽ ὑστεραίᾳ, τοῦ Θεμιστοκλέους
αὖθις παρελθόντος καὶ προσκυνήσαντος, <u>φιλοφρόνως</u> βασιλεὺς ἔφησεν ἤδη
μὲν ὀφείλειν αὐτῷ διακόσια <u>τάλαντα</u>· κομίσαντα γὰρ ἑαυτὸν τὸ κηρυχθὲν
τῷ παραδιδόντι δικαίως δέξεσθαι. πολλὰ δὲ πλείω τούτων ὑπισχνεῖτο εἰ
λέξει περὶ τῶν Ἑλληνικῶν πραγμάτων <u>παρρησιάζων</u>.

	βασίλεια -ων τά	palace
	Ἀρτάβανος -ου ὁ	Artabanus
	διαφέρω	I differ
	προσκυνέω προσεκύνησα	I prostrate myself (before)
5	εἰκών -όνος ἡ	image
	φρονέω	I think
	ἑρμηνεύς -έως ὁ	interpreter
	ὀφείλω	I owe
	οἰκεῖος -α -ον	of one's home or homeland
16	χαρίζομαι ἐχαρισάμην	I do a favour (to, + *dat*)
	ἱκέτης -ου ὁ	suppliant
	χαρά -ᾶς ἡ	joy
	τρίς	three times
	φιλοφρόνως	in a kindly way
22	τάλαντον -ου τό	talent
	παρρησιάζω	I speak frankly

Particles

Particles are short indeclinable words that connect groups of words together, or qualify or colour other words (often where English would achieve the effect by emphasis or tone of voice). They are important in Greek both for giving emphasis within sentences, and for indicating how sentences are linked (indicating for example whether a new sentence reinforces, explains or contradicts a previous one). Words conventionally listed as particles include conjunctions and adverbs, as well as some not so easily categorised:

ἀλλά	but
οὐ μόνον ... ἀλλὰ καί	not only ... but also
ἄρα	so then, in that case (*drawing an inference*)
ἆρα;	is it the case that ... ?
αὖ*	again, then again, in turn
γάρ*	for (*giving an explanation*)
γε*	at least, at any rate
γοῦν*	at least, at any rate (*crasis of* γε οὖν, *emphatic*)
δέ*	but, and (*sometimes better omitted in English*)
δή*	indeed (*emphasises preceding word*)
δῆτα*	certainly, to be sure (*strengthened form of* δή)
δήπου*	of course, surely, I presume (*can be ironic*)
εἴτε ... εἴτε	whether ... or
ἤ	or; than
ἤ ... ἤ	either ... or
ἴσως	perhaps, probably (*lit* equally)
καί	and; even, also, actually
καί ... καί	both ... and
καίτοι	and yet
μέν* ... δέ*	on the one hand ... but on the other hand, whilst (*put between the contrasted items*)
μέντοι*	however; certainly
ὅμως	nevertheless (*lit* samely, *i.e.* all the same)
οὐδέ (*also* μηδέ)	and not, not even
οὔτε ... οὔτε (*also* μήτε ... μήτε)	neither ... nor
οὔκουν	not ... therefore
οὐκοῦν	therefore
οὖν*	therefore
που*	I suppose (*lit* somewhere)
τε*	and (*translated in front of word it follows*)
τε* ... καί	both ... and (τε *comes after first or only word of first item,* καί *before second item*)
τοι*	in truth, I assure you
ὡς	as, when, since because; that (*introducing indirect statement, alternative to* ὅτι); how ... ! (exclamation)

* indicates a word that cannot come first in a sentence or clause

Note the following points:

(1) ἤ The senses *or* and *than* may seem very distinct, but the similarity of thought may be seen in an ambiguous sentence like *I wonder if A is better ἤ B*, naturally meaning *I wonder if A is better than B*, but which can also be read as *I wonder whether A is better, or B.*

(2) ἴσως The literal meaning *equally* produces the sense *perhaps, probably* because the thought is that the thing in question has an equal chance of happening and not happening (there is not an exact English equivalent, as *perhaps* suggests less than 50% likelihood, and *probably* suggests more).

(3) καί If it is not required/does not make sense as a *copulative* (joining two things together), it *must* be translated e.g. *even, also.*

(4) μέν ... δέ They co-ordinate (i.e. contrast two things grammatically parallel or of equal weight); they do not *subordinate* (so they cannot contrast e.g. a participle phrase or *when* clause with a main clause).

(5) ὅμως As with ἴσως, the literal sense (*samely*) has produced the idiom, exactly like *all the same* in English.

(6) που Here again the literal sense (*somewhere*, the indefinite from the table of correlatives) has produced the idiom, because if you *suppose* something, you assume it is *somewhere near being the case.*

(7) τε ... καί The placing of τε needs care when translating into Greek. First isolate the two elements of the sentence which are to be joined; τε comes second word within the first bit, and καί before the second bit. They will end up next to each other only if the first element consists of a single word.

Exercise 3.19

Translate into English:

1   τὸν σῖτον ἤδη ἔχω· ζητῶ καὶ οἶνον.
2   τοσαῦτα κλέψας, θρασὺς δὴ ἐγένετο.
3   ἐγώ τε καὶ σύ εὐτυχεῖς ἐσμεν.
4   ἀπέπεμψα τὸν ἄγγελον· μῶρος γὰρ ἦν.
5   ἓν ἆθλον χθὲς ἠνεγκάμην, καὶ ἄλλο αὔριον ἴσως δέξομαι.
6   εἰ αἰσχρόν ἐστι τοιαῦτα πράσσειν, αἰσχρόν ἐστι καὶ λέγειν.
7   οἱ πολῖται ἔχαιρόν που περὶ τῆς νίκης ἀκούσαντες;
8   λέγεις ὅτι αἰχμάλωτος ἦσθα· πῶς δῆτα ὕστερον ἐλύθης;
9   ἀπώλεσα τὸ ἀργύριον· τήν γε τιμὴν ἔσωσα.
10 ἐκείνη ταράσσει τὴν οἰκίαν· φιλῶ δ' αὐτὴν ὅμως.

Themistocles in Persia (3)

Here Themistocles while travelling in Asia receives a divine warning about an impending attack, and so escapes with his life. He subsequently expresses his gratitude.

καταβαίνοντι δ' αὐτῷ πρὸς τὴν θάλατταν ὁ τῆς <u>ἄνω</u> Φρυγίας σατράπης
ἐπεβούλευσε, πρότερον παρεσκευακὼς Πισίδας τινὰς ἀποκτενοῦντας, ὅταν
ἐν τῇ κώμῃ <u>Λεοντοκεφάλῳ</u> καλουμένῃ <u>καταυλισθῇ</u>. λέγεται μέντοι ὅτι ἡ
τῶν θεῶν Μήτηρ αὐτῷ καθεύδοντι φανεῖσα εἶπεν· "ὦ Θεμιστόκλεις,
5   <u>ὑστέρει</u> κεφαλῆς λέοντος, ἵνα μὴ λέοντι <u>περιπέσῃς</u>. ἐγὼ δ' ἀντὶ τούτου σε
αἰτῶ <u>θεράπαιναν Μνησιπτολέμαν</u>." διαταραχθεὶς οὖν ὁ Θεμιστοκλῆς
προσευξάμενος τῇ θεῷ τὴν μὲν ὁδὸν ἔλιπεν, ἑτέρᾳ δὲ περιελθὼν καὶ
<u>παραλλάξας</u> τὸν τόπον ἐκεῖνον ἤδη νυκτὸς οὔσης κατηυλίσατο.

τῶν δὲ τὴν σκηνὴν κομιζόντων <u>ὑποζυγίων</u> ἑνὸς εἰς τὸν ποταμὸν
10   ἐμπεσόντος, οἱ τοῦ Θεμιστοκλέους <u>οἰκέται</u> τὰς <u>αὐλαίας διαβρόχους</u>
γενομένας <u>ἐκπετάσαντες ἀνέψυχον</u>. οἱ δὲ Πισίδαι τὰ ξίφη λαβόντες ἐν
τούτῳ προσέβαινον, καὶ τὰ ἀναψυχόμενα <u>πρὸς τὴν σελήνην</u> οὐ σαφῶς
ἰδόντες ἐνομίζοντο εἶναι τὴν τοῦ Θεμιστοκλέους σκηνὴν καὶ ἐκεῖνον
ἔνδον εὑρήσειν καθεύδοντα. ὡς δ' ἐγγὺς γενόμενοι τὴν αὐλαίαν
15   <u>ἀνέστελλον</u>, ἐπιπίπτουσιν αὐτοῖς οἱ φυλάττοντες καὶ <u>συλλαμβάνουσιν</u>.
διαφυγὼν δὲ τὸν κίνδυνον οὕτω καὶ θαυμάσας τὴν <u>ἐπιφάνειαν</u> τῆς θεοῦ,
ὁ Θεμιστοκλῆς ἱερόν τε <u>κατεσκεύασεν</u> τῆς <u>Κύβελης</u> καὶ τὴν θυγατέρα
Μνησιπτολέμαν <u>ἱέρειαν</u> ἔδωκεν.

	ἄνω	(*here*) upper
	Φρυγία -ας ἡ	Phrygia (*region of Asia Minor, modern Turkey*)
	σατράπης -ου ὁ	satrap (*Persian provincial governor*)
	Πισίδαι -ῶν οἱ	Pisidians, people of Pisidia (*area south of Phrygia*)
3	Λεοντοκέφαλος -ου ὁ	Lion's Head (*name of a village*)
	καταυλίζομαι κατηυλίσθην	I camp for the night
	ὑστερέω	I avoid (+ *gen*)
	περιπίπτω περιέπεσον	I fall prey to (+ *dat*)
	θεράπαινα -ης ἡ	(female) servant
6	Μνησιπτολέμα -ης ἡ	Mnesiptolema (*daughter of Themistocles*)
	παραλλάσσω παρήλλαξα	I bypass
	ὑποζύγιον -ου τό	baggage animal
	οἰκέτης -ου ὁ	attendant
	αὐλαία -ας ἡ	curtain
10	διάβροχος -ον	soaked
	ἐκπετάννυμι ἐξεπάτασα	I spread (something) out
	ἀναψύχω	I dry (something)
	πρός	(+ *acc*) (*here*) in the light of
	σελήνη -ης ἡ	moon
15	ἀναστέλλω	I lift
	συλλαμβάνω	I seize, I arrest
	ἐπιφάνεια -ας ἡ	epiphany, appearance
	κατακευάζω κατεσκεύασα	(*here*) I build
	Κύβελη -ης ἡ	Cybele (*Asiatic mother goddess*)
18	ἱέρεια -ας ἡ	priestess

Chapter 4

Impersonal verbs

In *Greek to GCSE (2)* we met several *impersonal* verbs (whose built-in subject is *it*):

		imperfect	infinitive
δεῖ	it is necessary	ἔδει	δεῖν
χρή	it is necessary	(ἐ)χρῆν	χρῆναι

These two hardly differ in meaning, though χρή often implies *moral* obligation. They are followed by an *accusative* (rather than the dative that might be expected from English):

> δεῖ με τοῦτο ποιεῖν.
> It is necessary for me to do this.

The thought and construction are similar to an indirect statement (*It is necessary that I should do this*). The sentence can alternatively be turned round to make the person the subject:

> I have to do this.

• Note carefully that the negative οὐ with δεῖ means *it is necessary not to* (rather than the weaker *it is not necessary to*):

> οὐ δεῖ με τοῦτο ποιεῖν
> It is necessary for me not to do this.
> *or*   I must not do this.

This can be compared with the use of οὐ φημί with an indirect statement, meaning *I say that ... not* (rather than *I do not say*).

• Note further that reference to the past is expressed by the impersonal verb rather than the infinitive (whereas English says *I ought to have done this*). The Greek construction is reflected by the very old-fashioned English word *behove*:

> ἐχρῆν με τοῦτο ποιεῖν.
> It behoved me to do this.   (*correct but obsolete*)
> *or*   I oughted (*at the time*) to do this.   (*not English idiom*)
> *i.e.*   I ought to have done this.

The phrase ἀνάγκη ἐστί (literally *there is compulsion*) is yet another way of saying *it is necessary*, and takes the same accusative and infinitive construction.

We also met:

		imperfect	infinitive
ἔξεστι	it is possible	ἐξῆν	ἐξεῖναι

This and other impersonal verbs *do* take a dative, as in English:

> ἐξῆν μοι τοῦτο ποιεῖν.
> It was possible for me to do this.

73

We also saw that impersonal verbs can be formed from a neuter adjective with the verb *to be*, for example:

> ἀγαθόν ἐστι
> it is good

> ἀδύνατον ἦν ἡμῖν ἀκοῦσαι.
> It was impossible for us to hear.

There are in fact several different ways of saying *it is possible*:

> πάρεστι (*imperfect* παρῆν)
> οἷόν τ' ἐστί
> δυνατόν ἐστι

πάρεστι is a synonym of ἔξεστι, and is an impersonal version of πάρειμι *I am present* (the thought is *the opportunity is present*, whilst ἔξεστι implies *the opportunity is out there*); οἷόν τ' ἐστί is an impersonal version of οἷός τ' εἰμί *I am able*.

• Note the important verb δοκέω, which has a range of uses but whose basic meaning is *I seem*. We met at GCSE its common impersonal form:

	aorist	
δοκεῖ	ἔδοξε	*literally* it seems (a good idea) to X (*dat*)
		i.e. X decides

The thought behind this is that something *commends itself* (it *seems* attractive/a good idea). The Greek idiom however implies the consequent stage, of *making a positive decision*. So for example:

> δοκεῖ μοι τοῦτο ποιεῖν.
> *literally* It seems to me (a good idea) to do this.
> *i.e.* I decide to do this.

> ἔδοξε τῷ δήμῳ προσβαλεῖν τοῖς Λακεδαιμονίοις.
> *literally* It seemed a good idea to the people to attack the Spartans.
> *i.e.* The people decided to attack the Spartans.

(The phrase in the second example is the standard expression for decisions of the democratic Assembly in Athens, for example in decrees recorded on stone inscriptions.) Note that in English it is natural to turn the expression round, making the person in the dative the subject of an ordinary active verb. If however no person is indicated, it is better to translate the impersonal verb as a passive:

> ἔδοξε ἀναχωρῆσαι.
> It was decided (*or* a decision was made) to retreat.

This idiom needs to be distinguished from the impersonal use of δοκεῖ *with an adjective*:

> ἔδοξε χαλεπὸν τὸν ποταμὸν διαβῆναι.
> It seemed difficult to cross the river.

Things can seem anything, but (by optimistic default) an unspecified δοκεῖ implies *seem good*.

74

Accusative absolute

We saw in *Greek to GCSE (2)* that a participle phrase grammatically separate from the rest of the sentence (and describing 'attendant circumstances', i.e. a situation applying at the time) is expressed as a *genitive absolute* (using *absolute* in its old Latinate sense *cut off* or *independent*):

ταῦτα ἐγένετο τοῦ Περικλέους στρατηγοῦντος.

literally	These things happened with Pericles being general
i.e.	... while Pericles was general.
or	... during the generalship of Pericles.

An impersonal verb instead of a genitive uses its neuter participle (because the subject is *it*) alone (because the *it* is built in) as an *accusative absolute*. Hence:

δέον	*literally*	with it being necessary
ἐξόν		with it being possible
παρόν		with it being possible
ἀδύνατον ὄν		with it being impossible

Because δοκεῖ usually describes a momentary decision (and does so after the event) it uses as its accusative absolute the *aorist* participle:

δόξαν	*literally*	with it having seemed good
	i.e.	with it having been decided, *or (if a person is expressed in the dative)* with X having decided

If the stress is on the continuing effects of the decision, the perfect participle δεδογμένον can be used in a similar way.

Words normally used to focus the sense of participles - καίπερ (*although, despite*), ἅτε (*since, inasmuch as*) and ὡς (*on the grounds that*) - can also be used with the accusative absolute:

καίπερ ἔξον ἀπιέναι, ἐνθάδε μένομεν.
Although it is possible to go away, we are staying here.

Exercise 4.1

Translate into English:

1	πάρεστί μοι πρὸς τὸ ἄκρον ὄρος ἀφικέσθαι.
2	καίπερ ἐξὸν φυγεῖν αἱρούμεθα μένειν.
3	ἔδοξεν ἡμῖν βοηθῆσαι τοῖς αἰχμαλώτοις.
4	διὰ τί σιγᾷς, δέον ἀποκρίνασθαι;
5	χρὴ ὑμᾶς θεραπεύειν τοῦτον τὸν γερόντα.
6	δέον λαβεῖν τὴν πόλιν, πολὺν χρόνον ἀποροῦμεν.
7	ἐξῆν τοῖς παῖσι ἐκεῖ τρέχειν.
8	δόξαν πολεμῆσαι, τῇ ὑστεραίᾳ πρῲ ὡρμησάμεθα.
9	ἀνάγκη ἐστί με τὸ ἔργον τελευτῆσαι.
10	ἅτε ἀδύνατον ὂν ἄλλον σῖτον εὑρεῖν, ἐφάγομεν τὸν ἵππον.

Exercise 4.2

Translate into Greek:

1   It being possible to go out, we all went out.
2   The women in the city decided to punish the men.
3   Is it necessary for us to wait here?
4   It was not possible to hear all the words.
5   Although it is necessary to be silent, I enjoy being in the temple.

Exercise 4.3

Astyochus and the Chians

At a late stage in the Peloponnesian War (as described by Thucydides), Athens has suffered a crushing defeat in Sicily and the main theatre of war has shifted to Ionia (the coast of modern Turkey and the islands off it). Here in 411 BC the people of Chios, hard-pressed by the Athenians (from whose empire they and others have taken the opportunity to revolt) ask for help from the Spartan admiral Astyochus. He is prevented from giving it by the need to meet up with other Peloponnesian ships, in order to establish Spartan naval supremacy.

ἐν δὲ τῷ αὐτῷ χειμῶνι οἱ <u>Χῖοι</u> ἀγγέλους ἔπεμπον πρὸς τὸν <u>Ἀστύοχον</u>.
καὶ ἠξίουν ἐκεῖνον σφίσι πολιορκουμένοις βοηθῆσαι πάσαις ταῖς ναυσίν.
ἔλεγον δὲ ὅτι οὐ δεῖ αὐτὸν <u>περιιδεῖν</u> τὴν μεγίστην τῶν ἐν Ἰωνίᾳ
συμμάχων <u>εἴργεσθαί</u> τε ἀπὸ τῆς θαλάσσης ὑπὸ τῶν Ἀθηναίων καὶ κατὰ
5   γῆν <u>πορθεῖσθαι</u>. πρὸς δὲ τούτοις οἱ δοῦλοι αὐτοὺς ἔβλαπτον. πλείονες γὰρ
τοῖς Χίοις ἦσαν ἢ ἐν ἄλλῃ τινὶ πόλει πλὴν Λακεδαιμονίων. ἐπεὶ οὖν ἡ
τῶν Ἀθηναίων στρατιὰ ἔδοξε βεβαίως <u>ἱδρῦσθαι</u> ἐν τῷ τειχίσματι, εὐθὺς
πλεῖστοι τῶν δούλων ἀπεχώρησαν πρὸς αὐτούς· καί, ἅτε τὴν χώραν
ἐπιστάμενοι, τοὺς Χίους οὕτω κάκιστα ἐποίουν.

10   ἔφασαν οὖν οἱ Χῖοι χρῆναι τὸν Ἀστύοχον ὡς τάχιστα σφίσι βοηθῆσαι,
ἔτι παρὸν τοὺς πολεμίους κωλῦσαι· τὸ γὰρ τεῖχος, ὃ οἱ Ἀθηναῖοι
περιέβαλλον τῷ τε στρατοπέδῳ καὶ ταῖς ναυσίν, οὔπω <u>περανθῆναι</u>. ὁ δὲ
Ἀστύοχος, καίπερ πρῶτον οὐκ ἐθέλων αὐτοὺς ὠφελῆσαι, τότε δὴ ὡρμήθη
ἵνα βοηθήσειε· ἑώρα γὰρ καὶ τοὺς ἄλλους συμμάχους προθύμους ὄντας.
15   ἔπειτα μέντοι ἠγγέλθη αὐτῷ ὅτι ἑπτὰ καὶ εἴκοσι νῆες τοῦ τῶν
Λακεδαιμονίων ναυτικοῦ προσέρχονται. καὶ νομίσας μέγιστον εἶναι τὰς
μεθ' αὐτοῦ ναῦς ταύταις <u>συμμῖξαι</u>, ὅπως οἱ Λακεδαιμόνιοι ῥᾷον

	Χῖοι -ων οἱ	Chians, people of Chios
	Ἀστύοχος -ου ὁ	Astyochus (*Spartan admiral*)
	περιοράω περιεῖδον	I ignore the fact that (+ *acc* + *inf*)
	Ἰωνία -ας ἡ	Ionia
4	εἴργω	I exclude
	πορθέω	I lay waste
	ἱδρύομαι	I am established, I am settled
	περαίνω *aor pass* ἐπεράνθην	I complete
	συμμίγνυμι *aor inf* συμμῖξαι	I join X (*acc*) together with Y (*dat*)

θαλασσοκρατοῖεν, ἀφεὶς τὰ τῶν Χίων, ἔπλει πρὸς τὴν <u>Κνίδον</u>. ἐν δὲ τῷ
στόλῳ πορθήσας πόλιν τινὰ <u>ἀτείχιστον</u> καὶ νικήσας ναῦς ὀλίγας τῶν
20 Ἀθηναίων, εἰς τὴν Κνίδον ἀφίκετο, οὗ πᾶσαι αἱ τῶν Πελοποννησίων νῆες
ἤδη συλλεγμέναι ἦσαν.

θαλασσοκρατέω	I have command of the sea
ἀφίημι *aor pple* ἀφείς	I neglect
Κνίδος -ου ἡ	Cnidus (*city in Asia Minor, modern Turkey*)
ἀτείχιστος -ον	unwalled

More complex relative clauses

We saw in *Greek to GCSE (2)* that the relative pronoun (ὅς ἥ ὅ) agrees with its *antecedent*
(the noun in the main clause that it refers back to) in number and gender, but takes its case
from the job it does in its own clause:

κολάσω τὸν δοῦλον ὃς ἐψεύσατο.
I shall punish the slave who lied.

Here the relative pronoun ὅς agrees with the antecedent δοῦλον in number and gender
(singular and masculine), but each has its own case: δοῦλον accusative as object in the main
clause, ὅς nominative as subject in the relative clause.

In Chapter 1 of this book we met in the table of correlatives more specialised relative
pronouns (e.g. οἷος *of the sort which*, and the indefinite relative ὅστις *whoever*), as well as
relative adverbs (e.g. οὗ *where*): see pages 4-7.

Note now the following further possibilities which are often found in a relative clause:

(1) Relative attraction

The rule above is broken when a relative pronoun in the accusative is induced by the
magnetic force of a genitive or dative antecedent to forget its grammar and simply
follow suit:

χρῶμαι ταῖς βίβλοις αἷς ἔχω.   (*for* ἃς ἔχω)
I use the books which I have.

(2) Antecedent missed out

ὃν οἱ θεοὶ φιλοῦσιν ἀποθνῄσκει νέος.
He whom the gods love dies young.

Here the nominative word *he* or *the man* is left to be understood (from the masculine
singular relative pronoun); it would also be correct to say that *the whole relative clause*
(ὃν οἱ θεοὶ φιλοῦσιν) is regarded as the subject of the sentence.

77

(3) Antecedent and relative pronoun telescoped into one

> ἐρωτήσω τὸν στρατιώτην περὶ ὧν ἔπραξεν.   (*for* περὶ τούτων ἅ)
> I shall ask the soldier about the things he did.

(1) and (2) combined: ἅ is attracted into the case τούτων, which is then omitted. This is the norm where the antecedent would be a demonstrative pronoun (in English often *that/those*, though Greek uses οὗτος rather than ἐκεῖνος when it *is* put in).

(4) Antecedent sucked into relative clause

> πρὸς ἣν ἀφίκοντο κώμην μεγάλη ἦν.   (*for* ἡ κώμη πρὸς ἣν)
> The village at which they arrived was big.

Here *village* (object in the relative clause, literally *at which village they arrived*) has to be taken out and understood as the subject of ἦν, agreeing with μεγάλη.

(5) Relative in apposition to whole main clause

> οὗτος ἔσωσε τὴν πόλιν, ὃ ἀεὶ θαυμάζεται.
> This man saved his city, (a thing) which is always admired.

Here the neuter ὃ refers back to the whole main clause rather than to one word within it.

Exercise 4.4

Translate into English:
1   πιστεύω τῇ ἐπιστολῇ ᾗ δέδεγμαι.
2   ὃν ἔλαβες δεσμώτην ξένος ἐστίν.
3   ἆρα ἆθλα ζητεῖς πρὸς οἷς ἔχεις;
4   οὓς ὁ βασιλεὺς ἐπαινεῖ εὐτυχεῖς εἰσίν.
5   ἥδομαι τῇ τύχῃ ᾗ ἔχω.
6   χώρων ὅσων ἑώρακα ἡ Ἑλλὰς καλλίστη ἐστίν.
7   δυστυχὴς ὅστις ὑπὸ τῶν θεῶν μισεῖται.
8   ἠρόμην τὴν γυναῖκα περὶ ὧν ἤκουσεν.
9   ἣν ηὗρον βίβλον χρησίμη ἔσται.
10 ἡ γέφυρα διέφθαρται, ὃ πολλάκις γίγνεται.

Exercise 4.5

Translate into Greek (using relative attraction and telescoping where appropriate):
1   I use the words which I have learned.
2   Whoever has both money and wisdom is fortunate.
3   This is the most reliable of all the slaves I have seen.
4   The girl obeyed the voice which she heard.
5   The man whom the goddess loved died nonetheless.

Articular infinitive (gerund)

Sometimes also referred to as a *verbal noun*, this is a way of making a verb into a noun by putting the neuter article in front of the infinitive:

τὸ τρέχειν
literally the to-run
i.e. (the act of) running

(This use of the *-ing* ending needs to be distinguished in English from the present participle, as in *I fell while running* or *the running boy fell.*)

• The infinitive is regarded as neuter because this idiom resembles an impersonal verb, with the subject *it*. Consider how similar are:

ἀγαθόν ἐστι θαυμάζεσθαι.
It is good to be admired.

and τὸ θαυμάζεσθαι ἀγαθόν ἐστι.
Being admired is good.

Any infinitive can be used in this way. Present and aorist are distinguished by aspect, e.g.

τὸ ἀποθανεῖν
death, the act of dying (*momentary, and so expressed by the aorist infinitive*)

The infinitive itself cannot of course change its endings, but the neuter article declines (in the singular) to show the job the verbal noun is doing in the sentence. It can be used in the nominative, accusative, genitive or dative, and with prepositions (taking the appropriate case). Hence for example:

διὰ τὸ νενικῆσθαι
on account of having been conquered

ἡ τοῦ γράφειν τέχνη
the art of writing

ἀντὶ τοῦ ἰέναι
instead of going

τῷ σοφῶς λέγειν
by speaking wisely (*instrumental dative*)

Although it has in effect become a noun, the infinitive also continues to behave as a verb: for example, a subject can be expressed. This is normally accusative (as in indirect statement and other infinitive constructions), and sandwiched between article and infinitive:

οὐ θαυμάζω τὸ τοὺς ἀνθρώπους ἁμαρτάνειν.
I am not surprised at the fact that human beings make mistakes.

But if it is the same as the subject of the main verb, the subject of the infinitive or any adjective agreeing with it is nominative (again exactly as in indirect statement and other infinitive constructions):

οὗτος ὁ ῥήτωρ ἐπαινεῖται διὰ τὸ σοφὸς εἶναι.
This speaker is praised on account of being wise.

Because the infinitive can also have an object, there is potential confusion between an accusative subject and an accusative object. This is avoided by not sandwiching the object:

ἐβουλευσάμεθα περὶ τοῦ κολάζειν τοὺς ἀδικοῦντας.
We had a discussion about punishing those acting unjustly.

If however the verb takes a case other than the accusative, that can be sandwiched:

τὸ τοῖς πολεμίοις προσβαλεῖν
the act of attacking the enemy

The negative version of an articular infinitive is expressed by μή (sandwiched):

τῷ μὴ βλέπειν
by not looking

Greek often has several different ways of expressing the same idea:

ἐπαύσαντο τοῦ μαχέσθαι.
ἐπαύσαντο τῆς μάχης.
ἐπαύσαντο μαχόμενοι.
are all equally valid ways of saying
They stopped fighting.

Exercise 4.6

Translate into English:
1   φιλῶ τὸ τρέχειν.
2   ἆρα θαυμάζεις τὸ εὖ λέγειν, ἢ τὸ εὖ πράσσειν;
3   οὗτος οὐκ ἐβλάβη διὰ τὸ γέρων εἶναι.
4   ἡ τέχνη ἡ τοῦ δήλως γράφειν χρήσιμόν ἐστι.
5   τῷ ἀνδρείως μάχεσθαι ἀεὶ νικῶμεν.
6   οἱ νεανίαι πάρεισι τοῦ διαλέγεσθαι ἕνεκα.
7   τί φῇς περὶ τοῦ ἐνθάδε μένειν;
8   τὸ διδόναι βέλτιόν ἐστι τοῦ δέχεσθαι.
9   τῷ μὴ τοῦτο πράσσειν μᾶλλον θαυμαζόμεθα.
10   οὐκ οἶδα ὅ τι ἐγένετο διὰ τὸ μὴ παρεῖναι.

Exercise 4.7

Translate into Greek (using articular infinitives):
1   By speaking well, he won many prizes.
2   This girl is admired on account of being reliable.
3   These men were honoured for not acting unjustly.
4   Our allies have learned the art of fighting.
5   Being silent is wise.

Exercise 4.8

Xenophon on Agesilaus (1)

The Athenian historian and general Xenophon wrote on a great variety of subjects. He took up the account of the Peloponnesian War where the unfinished work of Thucydides left off (in 411 BC, soon after the Astyochus passage) and continued the story of the Greek city-states and their involvement with Persia down to the mid-fourth century. Later we shall read extracts from his autobiographical account of an expedition attempting to effect regime change in Persia. He also wrote a number of shorter works. A recurrent preoccupation is the nature of leadership. As a military man of conservative views Xenophon was out of sympathy with the radical democracy and liberal culture of his native Athens, and admired and befriended many Spartans, including the king Agesilaus about whom he wrote the biographical essay from which the following passage is taken. Here he describes (with a marvellous sense of bustling activity) preparations early in 395 BC for Agesilaus' campaign against the Persian satrap Tissaphernes. Note that the passage (Agesilaus 1. 25-8) and all subsequent ones in this book are completely unadapted.

ἐπειδὴ δὲ <u>ἔαρ</u> <u>ὑπέφαινε</u>, συνήγαγε πᾶν τὸ στράτευμα εἰς Ἔφεσον·
<u>ἀσκῆσαι</u> δ᾿ αὐτὸ βουλόμενος ἆθλα <u>προὔθηκε</u> καὶ ταῖς <u>ἱππικαῖς</u> <u>τάξεσιν</u>,
ἥτις <u>κράτιστα</u> ἱππεύοι, καὶ ταῖς <u>ὁπλιτικαῖς</u>, ἥτις ἄριστα σωμάτων ἔχοι·
καὶ πελτασταῖς δὲ καὶ τοξόταις ἆθλα προὔθηκεν, οἵτινες κράτιστοι τὰ
5 <u>προσήκοντα</u> ἔργα φαίνοιντο. ἐκ τούτου δὲ παρῆν ὁρᾶν τὰ μὲν <u>γυμνάσια</u>
<u>μεστὰ</u> τῶν ἀνδρῶν <u>γυμναζομένων</u>, τὸν δὲ <u>ἱππόδρομον</u> ἱππέων <u>ἱππαζομένων</u>,
τοὺς δὲ <u>ἀκοντιστὰς</u> καὶ τοὺς τοξότας ἐπὶ <u>στόχον</u> ἱέντας. ἀξίαν δὲ καὶ
<u>ὅλην</u> τὴν πόλιν, ἐν ᾗ ἦν, <u>θέας</u> ἐποίησεν. ἥ τε γὰρ ἀγορὰ μεστὴ ἦν
<u>παντοδαπῶν</u> καὶ ὅπλων καὶ ἵππων <u>ὠνίων</u> οἵ τε <u>χαλκοτύποι</u> καὶ οἱ
10 <u>τέκτονες</u> καὶ οἱ <u>σιδηρεῖς</u> καὶ οἱ <u>σκυτεῖς</u> καὶ οἱ <u>γραφεῖς</u> πάντες <u>πολεμικὰ</u>

	ἔαρ ἔαρος τό	spring
	ὑπόφαινω	I begin to appear
	Ἔφεσος -ου ἡ	Ephesus (*city in Asia Minor, modern Turkey*)
	ἀσκέω ἤσκησα	I train
2	προτίθημι προὔθηκα	I offer
	ἱππικός -ή -όν	(of) cavalry
	τάξις -εως ἡ	division, squadron
	κράτιστος -η -ον	best
	ὁπλιτικός -ή -όν	(of) heavy infantry
5	προσήκων -ουσα -ον	applicable, appropriate
	γυμνάσιον -ου τό	gymnasium
	μεστός -ή -όν	full, crowded
	γυμνάζομαι	I exercise
	ἱππόδρομος	racecourse
6	ἱππάζομαι	I ride
	ἀκοντιστής -οῦ ὁ	javelin-man
	στόχος -ου ὁ	mark, target
	ὅλος -η -ον	whole
	θέα -ας ἡ	seeing, looking at
9	παντοδαπός -ή -όν	of all sorts
	ὤνιος -α -ον	for sale
	χαλκοτύπος -ου ὁ	copper-smith
	τέκτων -ονος ὁ	carpenter
	σιδηρεύς -έως ὁ	worker in iron
10	σκυτεύς -έως ὁ	cobbler
	γραφεύς -έως ὁ	painter
	πολεμικός -ή -όν	of war

ὅπλα <u>κατεσκεύαζον</u>· ὥστε τὴν πόλιν <u>ὄντως</u> ἂν ἡγήσω πολέμου
<u>ἐργαστήριον</u> εἶναι. <u>ἐπερρώσθη</u> δ' ἄν τις <u>κἀκεῖνο</u> ἰδών, ᾿Αγησίλαον μὲν
πρῶτον, ἔπειτα δὲ καὶ τοὺς ἄλλους στρατιώτας <u>ἐστεφανωμένους</u> τε, ὅπου
ἀπὸ τῶν γυμνασίων ἴοιεν, καὶ <u>ἀνατιθέντας</u> τοὺς στεφάνους τῇ ᾿Αρτέμιδι.
15 ὅπου γὰρ ἄνδρες θεοὺς μὲν <u>σέβοιεν</u>, πολεμικὰ δὲ ἀσκοῖεν, <u>πειθαρχίαν</u> δὲ
<u>μελετῷεν</u>, πῶς οὐκ εἰκὸς ἐνταῦθα πάντα μεστὰ ἐλπίδων ἀγαθῶν εἶναι;
ἡγούμενος δὲ καὶ τὸ καταφρονεῖν τῶν πολεμίων <u>ῥώμην</u> τινὰ ἐμβαλεῖν
πρὸς τὸ μάχεσθαι <u>προεῖπε</u> τοῖς κήρυξι τοὺς ὑπὸ τῶν <u>ληστῶν</u>
<u>ἁλισκομένους</u> βαρβάρους γυμνοὺς <u>πωλεῖν</u>. ὁρῶντες οὖν οἱ στρατιῶται
20 <u>λευκοὺς</u> μὲν διὰ τὸ μηδέποτε <u>ἐκδύεσθαι</u>, <u>πίονας</u> δὲ καὶ <u>ἀπόνους</u> διὰ τὸ
ἀεὶ ἐπ' <u>ὀχημάτων</u> εἶναι ἐνόμισαν μηδὲν <u>διοίσειν</u> τὸν πόλεμον ἢ εἰ γυναιξὶ
δέοι μάχεσθαι.

	κατασκευάζω	I make
	ὄντως	really
	ἐργαστήριον -ου τό	workshop
	ἐπιρρώνυμι	
12	aor pass ἐπερρώσθην	I encourage
	κἀκεῖνο	(crasis of καὶ ἐκεῖνο)
	᾿Αγησίλαος -ου ὁ	Agesilaus
	στεφανόω pf pass ἐστεφάνωμαι	I wreathe, I garland
	ἀνατίθημι	I dedicate
14	στέφανος -ου ὁ	garland
	῎Αρτεμις -ιδος ἡ	Artemis (patron goddess of Ephesus)
	σέβω	I revere
	πειθαρχία -ας ἡ	obedience to authority
	μελετάω	I practise
17	ῥώμη -ης ἡ	fighting spirit
	προεῖπον (aor with no pres)	I gave instructions
	λῃστής -οῦ ὁ	raider
	ἁλίσκομαι	I am captured
	πωλέω	I sell
20	λευκός -ή -όν	white
	ἐκδύομαι	I strip, I undress
	πίων -ον	fat
	ἄπονος -ον	lazy
	ὄχημα -ατος τό	carriage
21	διαφέρω fut διοίσω	I differ

Indefinite construction

The *indefinite construction* is used for a subordinate clause (relative or temporal) referring to something general or uncertain, rather than a specific known fact. It is typically marked in English by adding *-ever* to the introductory word, for example:

> whoever
> whatever
> whenever

In Greek this affects the mood of the verb:

primary sequence	subjunctive + ἄν
historic sequence	optative (without ἄν)

The distinction between subjunctive and optative (both used, as usual, by *aspect*) is in line with other constructions (e.g. purpose clauses), but the use of ἄν is unusual (more often, e.g. in conditionals, it is used with the optative or indicative). The negative with either is μή.

Various words can introduce indefinite clauses. We have seen already the indefinite relative pronoun ὅστις *whoever*; the ordinary relative ὅς (and more specialised ones from the table of correlatives [page 5], e.g. ὅσοι) in the indefinite construction have the same effect. (The word ὅστις itself is indefinite enough already, because of its meaning, and so usually takes an indicative; but it can also take the indefinite construction for good measure.)

> ὃς ἂν ἐκεῖσε βαίνῃ ἀνδρεῖός ἐστιν.
> Whoever goes there is brave.

> ἐποίουν ὅσα ὁ βασιλεύς βούλοιτο.
> I used to do whatever (*lit* as many things as) the king wanted.

For *whenever*, in primary sequence ὅτε combines with ἄν to make ὅταν (or ἐπειδή with ἄν to make ἐπειδάν):

> ὅταν τοιαῦτα ἀκούωμεν, φοβούμεθα.
> Whenever we hear such things, we are afraid.

In historic sequence ὁπότε is preferred (as with ὅστις and other words from the table of correlatives, the indirect question form is used also for the indefinite):

> ὁπότε τοιαῦτα ἀκούοιμεν, ἐφοβούμεθα.
> Whenever we heard such things, we were afraid.

An indefinite *until* (meaning *until such time as*, without implying the thing necesarily happens at all) is particularly common in primary sequence, using ἕως or (particularly after a negative main clause) πρίν:

> μέλλομεν μενεῖν ἕως ἂν ὁ δεσπότης ἐπανέλθῃ.
> We intend to wait until (such time as) the master returns.

> οὐκ ἄπειμι πρὶν ἂν ἀποκρίνῃ.
> I shall not go away until you reply.

This is possible in historic sequence too, so long as the meaning is still indefinite:

> ἐμείναμεν ἕως ὁ δεσπότης ἐπανέλθοι.
> We waited until (such time as) the master might return.
>
> *or* We waited for the master to return (*without implying he ever did*).

Contrast: ἐμείναμεν ἕως ὁ δεσπότης ἐπανῆλθεν.
We waited until the master returned (*indicative for a known fact*).

See also pages 54-5 on time clauses, and other uses of ἕως and πρίν.

Finally, note that the use of ἐάν (εἰ combined with ἄν) and the subjunctive in the protasis of a future open condition is another example of the indefinite which we have met already. In a similar way εἰ can be used in a historic indefinite (meaning *if ever/whenever*):

> εἴ τι ἀγαθὸν πράσσοιεν, ἐπηνοῦντο.
> If ever they did something good, they were praised.

This counts as a *past unknown* condition: the use of the optative here must be carefully distinguished from that in a *future remote condition* (where the optative occurs in both protasis and apodosis, the latter with ἄν).

Exercise 4.9

Translate into English:

1 ὅσα ἔχοιμι, ἔδωκά σοι.
2 αὕτη ποιήσει ἃ ἂν βούληται.
3 ὁπότε μαχοίμεθα, ἐνικῶμεν.
4 δεῖ σε ἐσθίειν ὅ τι ἂν παρεχήται.
5 ὅταν περὶ τούτων ἀκούσητε, ἀγγείλατε ἡμῖν.
6 εἰ ἴδοι με ἀποροῦντα, ὁ πατὴρ ὠφέλει.
7 φιλῶ ἅστινας ἂν βίβλους γράφῃς.
8 εἱπόμεθα ὅποι οὗτος ἡγοῖτο.
9 οὐ σιγήσομεν πρὶν ἂν τὸ ἀληθὲς λέγῃς.
10 ἀεὶ ζητοῦμεν ἕως ἂν εὑρίσκωμεν.

Exercise 4.10

Translate into Greek:

1 Whoever trusts this letter is foolish.
2 We always do whatever our leader orders.
3 Whenever a stranger arrived, the people on the island ate him.
4 I shall not write this until you (*sg*) say why it is necessary.
5 If my mother had any food, she always used to give it to us.

Xenophon on Agesilaus (2)

Towards the end of his biography, Xenophon sums up the king's patriotism (Agesilaus 7.1-3):

ὥς γε μὴν φιλόπολις ἦν, καθ᾽ ἓν μὲν ἕκαστον μακρὸν ἂν εἴη γράφειν·
οἴομαι γὰρ οὐδὲν εἶναι τῶν πεπραγμένων αὐτῷ, ὅ τι οὐκ εἰς τοῦτο
συντείνει. ὡς δ᾽ ἐν βραχεῖ εἰπεῖν, ἅπαντες ἐπιστάμεθα, ὅτι Ἀγησίλαος
ὅπου ᾤετο τὴν πατρίδα τί ὠφελήσειν, οὐ πόνων ὑφίετο, οὐ κινδύνων
5   ἀφίστατο, οὐ χρημάτων ἐφείδετο, οὐ σῶμα, οὐ γῆρας προὐφασίζετο, ἀλλὰ
καὶ βασιλέως ἀγαθοῦ τοῦτο ἔργον ἐνόμιζε, τὸ τοὺς ἀρχομένους ὡς
πλεῖστα ἀγαθὰ ποιεῖν. ἐν τοῖς μεγίστοις δὲ ὠφελήμασι τῆς πατρίδος καὶ
τόδε ἐγὼ τίθημι αὐτοῦ, ὅτι δυνατώτατος ὢν ἐν τῇ πόλει φανερὸς ἦν
μάλιστα τοῖς νόμοις λατρεύων. τίς γὰρ ἂν ἠθέλησεν ἀπειθεῖν ὁρῶν τὸν
10 βασιλέα πειθόμενον; τίς δ᾽ ἂν ἡγούμενος μειονεκτεῖν νεώτερόν τι
ἐπεχείρησε ποιεῖν εἰδὼς τὸν βασιλέα νομίμως καὶ τὸ κρατεῖσθαι φέροντα;
ὃς καὶ πρὸς τοὺς διαφόρους ἐν τῇ πόλει ὥσπερ πατὴρ πρὸς παῖδας
προσεφέρετο. ἐλοιδορεῖτο μὲν γὰρ ἐπὶ τοῖς ἁμαρτήμασιν, ἐτίμα δ᾽ εἴ τι
καλὸν πράττοιεν, παρίστατο δ᾽ εἴ τις συμφορὰ συμβαίνοι, ἐχθρὸν μὲν
15 οὐδένα ἡγούμενος πολίτην, ἐπαινεῖν δὲ πάντας ἐθέλων, σῴζεσθαι δὲ
πάντας κέρδος νομίζων, ζημίαν δὲ τιθείς, εἰ καὶ ὁ μικροῦ ἄξιος ἀπόλοιτο·

	μήν	truly
	φιλόπολις -ιδος	patriotic
	οἴομαι *impf* ᾠόμην	I think
	συντείνω	I tend towards
3	βραχύς -εῖα -ύ	brief
	ὑφίεμαι	I shirk (+ *gen*)
	φείδομαι	I spare (+ *gen*)
	γῆρας -ως τό	old age
	προφασίζομαι	I make X (*acc*) an excuse
7	ὠφέλημα -ατος τό	service, benefit
	φανερός -ά -όν	conspicuous
	λατρεύω	I serve, I am the servant of (+ *dat*)
	ἀπειθέω	I disobey (+ *dat*)
	μειονεκτέω	I am at a disadvantage
10	νέος -α -ον	(*here*) revolutionary
	ἐπιχειρέω ἐπεχείρησα	I try
	νομίμως	lawfully, in accordance with the law
	διάφορος -ον	at odds, disagreeing
	προσφέρομαι	I behave towards
13	λοιδορέομαι	I reproach, I criticise
	ἁμάρτημα -ατος τό	error
	παρίσταμαι	I stand by
	συμβαίνω	(*of events*) happen
	κέρδος -ους τό	gain
16	ζημία -ας ἡ	loss

εἰ δ' ἐν τοῖς νόμοις <u>ἠρεμοῦντες</u> <u>διαμένοιεν</u>, δῆλος ἦν εὐδαίμονα ἀεὶ
ἔσεσθαι τὴν πατρίδα <u>λογιζόμενος</u>, ἰσχυρὰν δὲ τότε, ὅταν οἱ Ἕλληνες
<u>σωφρονῶσιν</u>.

ἠρεμέω	I live peacefully
διαμένω	I continue
λογίζομαι	I reckon
σωφρονέω	I am prudent

Verbal adjective (gerundive)

As its name implies, the verbal adjective or *gerundive* is an adjective formed from a verb
(thus rather like a participle, but not classed as one): it is *passive*, and means *(needing) to be
X-ed* (as in *many mountains are to be climbed* or *much work remains to be done*; this needs
to be distinguished in English from a passive infinitive, e.g. *he wants to be praised*). It
behaves like the gerundive in Latin. It is easily recognised by its distinctive endings:

-τεος -τεα -τεον   (2-1-2 in declension, like φίλιος)

These are added to a stem of the verb found by removing -θην from the aorist passive (and
converting φ or χ left on the end to their unaspirated form π or κ. Hence for example:

	aorist passive	*gerundive*
παύω	ἐπαύσθην	παυστέος -α -ον
λαμβάνω	ἐλήφθην	ληπτέος -α -ον
διώκω	ἐδιώχθην	διωκτέος -α -ον
πείθω	ἐπείσθην	πειστέος -α -ον
πράσσω	ἐπράχην	πρακτέος -α -ον

The agent (the person *by* whom the action is to be done) is put in the *dative* without a
preposition.

This is exactly as with a Latin gerundive: the thought behind it is that *for you* or *as far as you are concerned*
the action is *needing to be done* - the duty of doing it comes *to you*.

In English it is usually better turned round into an active verb:

σωστέα μοι ἡ πόλις ἐστίν.
literally   The city is needing to be saved by me.
i.e.   I must save the city.

ὁ φεύγων σοι διωκτέος.
literally   The fugitive is needing to be pursued by you.
i.e.   You must pursue the fugitive.

Note in the second example that the verb *to be* is often omitted in a gerundive construction.
This passive adjectival use is only possible with *transitive* verbs (ones which take an
accusative direct object, which becomes the subject in passive forms of the verb). For verbs
which take other cases, or intransitive verbs of motion, an *impersonal neuter* version of the
gerundive must be used (literally *an act of X-ing which needs to be done*):

βοηθητέον μοι τοῖς αἰχμαλώτοις.

literally An act of giving help to the prisoners needs to be done by me.

or It needs to be helped by me to the prisoners.

i.e. I must help the prisoners.

(Word order and context here distinguish the dative agent from the dative after βοηθέω.)

The neuter plural form of this impersonal neuter gerundive (e.g. βοηθητέα) can alternatively be used, with no difference of meaning.

Note the irregular but common impersonal neuter gerundive of 'the other εἶμι (= *go*)':

ἰτέον + *dat*   *lit* there is for X an act of going (to be done), *i.e.* X must go

So for example:

ἡμῖν πᾶσιν ἐκεῖσε ἰτέον ἐστίν.
We all have to go there.

• The impersonal neuter use of the gerundive for intransitive verbs is again closely parallel to Latin:
    festinandum est nobis.
    We must hurry.

• The gerundive is relatively uncommon in Greek. Any of the examples above could equally be expressed in other (and often simpler) ways, e.g. by using δεῖ or χρή:
    δεῖ με σῶσαι τὴν πόλιν.
    δεῖ σε διῶξαι τὸν φεύγοντα.
    χρή με βοηθεῖν τοῖς αἰχμαλώτοις.
    δεῖ ἡμᾶς πάντας ἐκεῖσε ἰέναι.

• The impersonal neuter form *can* be used also (where not strictly necessary) with transitive verbs; and because *the act of X-ing* is in effect active, it can take an object. But in practice the impersonal ποιητέον ἡμῖν ταῦτα (where ταῦτα is the direct object) is virtually the same as the passive and adjectival ταῦτα ἡμῖν ποιητέα for *we must do these things*.

• The use of the dative without a preposition for the agent (rather than the more usual ὑπό with the genitive) is the norm with a gerundive, and an optional alternative with the perfect and pluperfect passive. (In Latin similarly the gerundive must, and the perfect and pluperfect passive can, use the dative alone for agent rather than the more usual *a/ab* with the ablative.)

Exercise 4.12

Translate into English:
1   ἡ θεὰ τιμητέα ἡμῖν ἐστίν.
2   ὁ στρατηγὸς ἔφη πολλὰς ναῦς πεμπτέας εἶναι.
3   ἡ ἐπιστολὴ γραπτέα τῇ γυναικὶ ἦν.
4   πειστέοι οἱ φίλοι ὑμῖν εἰσίν.
5   ἆρα ἰτέον μοι εἰς τὴν ὕλην;
6   ληπτέα ἡμῖν ἡ τῶν πολεμίων κώμη.
7   τί νῦν πρακτέον μοι ἐστίν;
8   πιστεύτεον τοῖς τοῦ θεοῦ λόγοις.
9   πολλὰ ἔτι ποιητέα τοῖς παισίν ἐστίν.
10   ἆρα νῦν φεύκτεον ἡμῖν;

Exercise 4.13

Translate into Greek (using gerundives):
1   The girls must chase the horses into the field.
2   The king must be honoured by everyone.
3   The messenger needs to persuade the men in the assembly.
4   The sea-battle must be stopped by the generals.
5   We had to go into the temple.

Exercise 4.14

Listening to the Cicadas

*Beside the river Ilissus outside Athens on a very hot day, Socrates and Phaedrus (in Plato's dialogue
Phaedrus) begin a discussion about the enchanting power of song (before moving on to the grand Platonist
topics of beauty and the immortality of the soul). Socrates illustrates his points by appeal to popular belief
about the cicadas which were (and are) a familiar feature of the Greek countryside (Phaedrus 258e-259d).*

ΣΩ. σχολὴ μὲν δή, ὡς ἔοικε. καὶ ἅμα μοι δοκοῦσιν ὡς ἐν τῷ πνίγει ὑπὲρ
κεφαλῆς ἡμῶν οἱ τέττιγες ᾄδοντες καὶ ἀλλήλοις διαλεγόμενοι
καθορᾶν. εἰ οὖν ἴδοιεν καὶ νὼ καθάπερ τοὺς πολλοὺς ἐν μεσημβρίᾳ
μὴ διαλεγομένους, ἀλλὰ νυστάζοντας καὶ κηλουμένους ὑφ' αὑτῶν
5   δι' ἀργίαν τῆς διανοίας, δικαίως ἂν καταγελῷεν, ἡγούμενοι
ἀνδράποδα ἄττα σφίσιν ἐλθόντα εἰς τὸ καταγώγιον ὥσπερ προβάτια
μεσημβριάζοντα περὶ τὴν κρήνην εὕδειν. ἐὰν δὲ ὁρῶσι διαλεγομένους
καὶ παραπλέοντάς σφας ὥσπερ Σειρῆνας ἀκηλήτους, ὃ γέρας παρὰ
θεῶν ἔχουσιν ἀνθρώποις διδόναι, τάχ' ἂν δοῖεν ἀγασθέντες.

	σχολή -ῆς ἡ	leisure
	ἔοικε	it seems
	πνῖγος -ους τό	stifling heat
	τέττιξ -ῖγος ὁ	cicada (*loud-chirping insect, similar to grasshopper*)
3	καθοράω	I look down on
	νώ	us two (*dual form*)
	καθάπερ	just as
	μεσημβρία -ας ἡ	midday
	νυστάζω	I doze
4	κηλέω	I charm
	ἀργία -ας ἡ	indolence, laziness
	διάνοια -ας ἡ	mind
	καταγελάω	I laugh at
	ἀνδράποδον -ου τό	slave
6	ἄττα	(= τινά)
	καταγώγιον -ου τό	resort, place to stay
	προβάτια -ων τά	sheep
	μεσημβριάζω	I rest at noon
	κρήνη -ης ἡ	spring, fountain
7	εὕδω	I sleep
	Σειρήν -ῆνος ἡ	Siren (*creature drawing men to destruction by song*)
	ἀκήλητος -ον	not charmed
	γέρας -ως τό	gift
	ἄγαμαι ἠγάσθην	I am pleased

10 ΦΑ. ἔχουσι δὲ δὴ τί τοῦτο; <u>ἀνήκοος</u> γάρ, ὡς ἔοικε, τυγχάνω ὤν.

ΣΩ. οὐ μὲν δὴ <u>πρέπει</u> γε <u>φιλόμουσον</u> ἄνδρα τῶν τοιούτων ἀνήκοον εἶναι·
λέγεται δ' ὥς ποτ' ἦσαν οὗτοι ἄνθρωποι τῶν πρὶν τὰς Μούσας
γεγονέναι, γενομένων δὲ Μουσῶν καὶ φανείσης <u>ᾠδῆς</u> οὕτως ἄρα τινὲς
τῶν τότε <u>ἐξεπλάγησαν</u> ὑφ' <u>ἡδονῆς</u>, ὥστε <u>ᾄδοντες ἠμέλησαν</u> σίτων τε
15 καὶ <u>ποτῶν</u>, καὶ ἔλαθον τελευτήσαντες αὑτούς· ἐξ ὧν τὸ τεττίγων
γένος μετ' ἐκεῖνο <u>φύεται</u>, γέρας τοῦτο παρὰ Μουσῶν λαβόν, μηδὲν
<u>τροφῆς</u> δεῖσθαι, ἀλλ' <u>ἄσιτόν</u> τε καὶ <u>ἄποτον</u> εὐθὺς γενόμενον <u>ᾄδειν</u>,
ἕως ἂν τελευτήσῃ, καὶ μετὰ ταῦτα ἐλθὸν παρὰ Μούσας <u>ἀπαγγέλλειν</u>,
τίς τίνα αὐτῶν τιμᾷ τῶν ἐνθάδε. <u>Τερψιχόρᾳ</u> μὲν οὖν τοὺς ἐν τοῖς
20 <u>χοροῖς</u> τετιμηκότας αὐτὴν ἀπαγγέλλοντες ποιοῦσι <u>προσφιλεστέρους</u>, τῇ
δὲ <u>Ἐρατοῖ</u> τοὺς ἐν τοῖς <u>ἐρωτικοῖς</u>, καὶ ταῖς ἄλλαις οὕτω, κατὰ τὸ
<u>εἶδος</u> ἑκάστης τιμῆς· τῇ δὲ <u>πρεσβυτάτῃ Καλλιόπῃ</u> καὶ τῇ μετ' αὐτὴν
<u>Οὐρανίᾳ</u> τοὺς ἐν <u>φιλοσοφίᾳ διάγοντάς</u> τε καὶ τιμῶντας τὴν ἐκείνων
<u>μουσικὴν</u> ἀγγέλλουσιν, αἳ δὴ μάλιστα τῶν Μουσῶν περί τε οὐρανὸν
25 καὶ λόγους οὖσαι <u>θείους</u> τε καὶ <u>ἀνθρωπίνους</u> ἱᾶσι καλλίστην φωνήν.
πολλῶν δὴ οὖν ἕνεκα λεκτέον τι καὶ οὐ καθευδητέον ἐν τῇ
μεσημβρίᾳ.

ΦΑ. λεκτέον γὰρ οὖν.

	ἀνήκοος -ον	not in the know, not having heard
	πρέπει	it is fitting
	φιλόμουσος -ον	loving the Muses (*goddesses of music and the arts*)
	ᾠδή -ῆς ἡ	song
14	ἐκπλήσσω *aor pass* ἐξεπλάγην	I strike, I overcome
	ἡδονή -ῆς ἡ	pleasure
	ᾄδω	I sing
	ἀμελέω ἠμέλησα	I forget about (+ *gen*)
	πότος -ου ὁ	drinking
16	φύομαι	I grow
	τροφή -ῆς ἡ	nourishment
	ἄσιτος -ον	without food
	ἄποτος-ον	without drink
	ἀπαγγέλλω	I report
19	Τερψιχόρα -ας ἡ	Terpsichore (*Muse of choral dance and song*)
	χορός -οῦ ὁ	dance
	προσφιλής -ές	dear
	Ἐρατώ -οῦς ἡ	Erato (*Muse of lyric poetry, often erotic*)
	ἐρωτικός -ή -όν	of love
23	εἶδος -ους τό	form
	πρεσβύτατος -η -ον	eldest
	Καλλιόπη -ης ἡ	Calliope (*Muse of epic poetry*)
	Οὐρανία -ας ἡ	Urania (*Muse of astronomy*)
	φιλοσοφία -ας ἡ	philosophy
24	διάγω	I spend my time
	μουσική -ῆς ἡ	music, the pursuits of the Muses, the arts
	θεῖος -α -ον	divine
	ἀνθρώπινος -η -ον	human

89

Dual forms

The Greek *plural* seems originally to have implied three or more, with special separate *dual* endings to refer to two (people or things, or subjects of a verb). The dual is a linguistic fossil: it has almost died out in classical Greek, but dual forms are sometimes met and you need to be able to recognise them. We saw an example in the last passage: νώ *us two*, and you have already met the distinctive genitive/dative δυοῖν of the numeral *two*.

Dual endings for nouns and adjectives according to declension are:

	first	*second*	*third*
nom/acc	-α	-ω	-ε
gen/dat	-αιν	-οιν	-οιν

The article has dual forms:

nom/acc	τώ
gen/dat	τοῖν

(usually the same for all three genders, though feminine forms τά, ταῖν are also found)

Hence: τὼ νεανία τὼ τρέχοντε   the two young men who are running

• Duals are particularly found referring to things that naturally occur as a pair, e.g.

τὼ ὀφθαλμώ	the two eyes
τοῖν χειροῖν	of/with the two hands

Dual forms for verbs (normally only second and third person) use a very limited range of endings, added to the stem and characteristic vowel of the relevant tense and mood (ε for present of παύω):

	active	*middle/passive*
2nd person, and 3rd person of primary tenses	-τον	-σθον
3rd person of historic tenses	-την	-σθην

Hence for example (showing plural, then equivalent dual each time):

plural		*dual*	
παύετε	you (*pl*) stop	παύετον	you both stop
ἔπλευσαν	they sailed	ἐπλευσάτην	the two of them sailed
γένοιντο	they might become	γενοίσθην	they both might become

Note the following dual forms of the verb *to be*:

present	ἐστόν	you/they both are
imperfect	ἦστον	you both were
	ἤστην	they both were

Exercise 4.15

Translate into English:

1   διὰ τί οὐχ ἑτοίμω ἐστόν, ὦ παῖδε;
2   ποτέραν ταῖν καλαῖν γυναικοῖν φιλεῖς;
3   τούτω τὼ φύλακε πιστὼ ἤστην.
4   τὼ ἵππω εὐθὺς ἐφύγετον.
5   εἴθε τὼ ἡμετέρω συμμάχω ἀφικοίσθην.

Crasis and elision

Crasis (κρᾶσις *mixing*, from κεράννυμι *I mix*) occurs when one word ending with (or consisting of) a vowel or diphthong coalesces with another starting in the same way, to form one single word. This can be hard to spot, but it can often be identified by the apparent presence of a breathing in the middle of a word; and it tends to occur with certain common combinations of words (which therefore become familiar):

κἀγώ	and I	(καὶ ἐγώ)
καλοὶ κἀγαθοί	the fine and good	(καλοὶ καὶ ἀγαθοί)
κἄν	even if	(καὶ ἐάν)
κἄπειτα	and then	(καὶ ἔπειτα)
τἀγαθά	good things	(τὰ ἀγαθά)
τἀμά	my things	(τὰ ἐμά)
ταὐτά	the same things	(τὰ αὐτά)
τοὔνομα	the name	(τὸ ὄνομα)
ὦνδρες	O men	(ὦ ἄνδρες)

The consonants kappa, pi and tau before crasis where the second word starts with a rough breathing turn into their aspirated forms chi, phi and theta:

χὠ	and the	(καὶ ὁ)

It may appear that the aspiration has *transferred*, but in fact the breathing mark is here simply a sign that crasis has occurred (technically called a *coronis*), rather than smooth as opposed to rough.

See page 38 for crasis in compound verbs beginning προ-.

Crasis should be distinguished from *elision*, where a (usually short) vowel ending a word is simply left off (and its absence indicated by an apostrophe) before another word beginning with a vowel:

δεῦρ' ἐλθέ	come here!	(δεῦρο ἐλθέ)

Again the consonants kappa, pi and tau if left exposed at the end of a word by elision before a rough breathing turn into their aspirated forms chi, phi and theta (in this case the aspiration *spreads*):

ἐφ' ἵππου	on a horse	(ἐπὶ ἵππου)
μεθ' ἑταίρου	with a companion	(μετὰ ἑταίρου)

Note that elision routinely occurs in certain idioms:

ἆρ' οὐ;	surely it is the case?	(ἆρα οὐ)
οἷός τ' εἰμί	I am able	(οἷός τε εἰμί)

Exercise 4.16

Translate into English:

1   οὐ θαυμάζω, διότι κἀκεῖνο πρότερον ἀκήκοα.
2   αὕτη ἐστὶν ἡ χώρα ἀφ' ἧς ὁ ἡμέτερος σῖτος πορίζεται.
3   κἂν χρήματα παρέχῃς, οὐκ ἐκεῖσε εἰμι.
4   οὗτος ὁ γέρων ταὐτὰ ἀεὶ λέγει.
5   ὁ Ξενοφῶν τοὺς καλοὺς κἀγαθοὺς πολλάκις ἐπαινεῖ.

Exercise 4.17

Timon of Athens

Timon was a semi-legendary Athenian famous for his misanthropy and avoidance of society, an attitude supposedly brought about by the ingratitude of his friends. His only associates were Apemantus (said to have been a similar character) and the brilliantly erratic politician and general Alcibiades (because Timon sensed rightly that he would bring about his city's downfall). Plutarch (whose account of Themistocles in Persia we read in Chapter 3) tells this story as a digression in his biography of the Roman Mark Antony, who during a period of unpopularity and exile claimed to be emulating the lifestyle of Timon. This was the source Shakespeare used for his play Timon of Athens. *As usual, Plutarch himself draws on a range of literary sources both familiar and unfamiliar* (Antony 70).

ὁ δὲ <u>Τίμων</u> ἦν Ἀθηναῖος καὶ γέγονεν <u>ἡλικίᾳ</u> <u>μάλιστα</u> <u>κατὰ</u> τὸν
<u>Πελοποννησιακὸν</u> πόλεμον, ὡς ἐκ τῶν <u>Ἀριστοφάνους</u> καὶ <u>Πλάτωνος</u>
<u>δραμάτων</u> λαβεῖν <u>ἔστι·</u> <u>κωμῳδεῖται</u> γὰρ ἐν ἐκείνοις ὡς <u>δυσμενὴς</u> καὶ
<u>μισάνθρωπος.</u> <u>ἐκκλίνων</u> δὲ καὶ <u>διωθούμενος</u> ἅπασαν <u>ἔντευξιν,</u> <u>Ἀλκιβιάδην</u>
5 νέον ὄντα καὶ θρασὺν <u>ἠσπάζετο</u> καὶ <u>κατεφίλει</u> προθύμως. <u>Ἀπημάντου</u> δὲ
θαυμάσαντος καὶ πυθομένου τὴν <u>αἰτίαν,</u> φιλεῖν ἔφη τὸν <u>νεανίσκον</u> εἰδὼς
ὅτι πολλῶν Ἀθηναίοις κακῶν αἴτιος ἔσοιτο. τὸν δ᾽ <u>Ἀπήμαντον</u> μόνον ὡς
ὅμοιον αὐτῷ καὶ <u>ζηλοῦντα</u> τὴν <u>δίαιταν</u> <u>ἔστιν ὅτε</u> <u>προσίετο·</u> καί ποτε τῆς
τῶν <u>Χοῶν</u> οὔσης ἑορτῆς <u>εἱστιῶντο</u> καθ᾽ αὑτοὺς οἱ δύο. τοῦ δ᾽ Ἀπημάντου
10 φήσαντος "ὡς καλὸν ὦ Τίμων τὸ <u>συμπόσιον</u> ἡμῶν," "εἴ γε σύ" ἔφη "μὴ
παρῇς."

	Τίμων -ωνος ὁ	Timon
	ἡλικία -ας ἡ	age, life-span
	μάλιστα	(*with number/time*) about, approximately
	κατά	in the time of
2	Πελοποννησιακός -ή -όν	Peloponnesian (*Peloponnesian War, 431-404 BC*)
	Ἀριστοφάνης -ους ὁ	Aristophanes
	Πλάτων -ωνος ὁ	Plato
	δρᾶμα -ατος τό	play, dramatic dialogue
	ἔστι	(= ἔξεστι)
3	κωμῳδέω	I satirise, I make fun of
	δυσμενής -ές	malevolent, full of ill will
	μισάνθρωπος -ον	hating one's fellow human beings
	ἐκκλίνω	I avoid
	διωθέομαι	I refuse
4	ἔντευξις -εως ἡ	social intercourse
	Ἀλκιβιάδης -ου ὁ	Alcibiades (*brilliant but treacherous Athenian leader*)
	ἀσπάζομαι	I greet
	καταφιλέω	I embrace
	Ἀπήμαντος -ου ὁ	Apemantus
6	αἰτία -ας ἡ	cause, reason
	νεανίσκος -ου ὁ	young man
	ζηλόω	I rival, I emulate
	δίαιτα -ης ἡ	way of life, lifestyle
	ἔστι ὅτε	(*lit* there is when, *i.e.*) sometimes
8	προσίημι	I admit, *mid* I admit to my company
	Χοαί -ῶν αἱ	Pitchers (*Athenian wine festival*)
	ἑστιάω	I entertain
	συμπόσιον -ου τό	symposium, drinking party

λέγεται δ' Ἀθηναίων ἐκκλησιαζόντων ἀναβὰς ἐπὶ τὸ βῆμα ποιῆσαι
σιωπὴν καὶ προσδοκίαν μεγάλην διὰ τὸ παράδοξον, εἶτ' εἰπεῖν "ἔστι μοι
μικρὸν οἰκόπεδον ὦ ἄνδρες Ἀθηναῖοι, καὶ συκῆ τις ἐν αὐτῷ πέφυκεν, ἐξ
ἧς ἤδη συχνοὶ τῶν πολιτῶν ἀπήγξαντο. μέλλων οὖν οἰκοδομεῖν τὸν
15   τόπον, ἐβουλήθην δημοσίᾳ προειπεῖν, ἵν', ἂν ἄρα τινὲς ἐθέλωσιν ὑμῶν,
πρὶν ἐκκοπῆναι τὴν συκῆν ἀπάγξωνται." τελευτήσαντος δ' αὐτοῦ καὶ
ταφέντος Ἁλῆσι παρὰ τὴν θάλασσαν, ὤλισθε τὰ προὔχοντα τοῦ αἰγιαλοῦ,
καὶ τὸ κῦμα περιελθὸν ἄβατον καὶ ἀπροσπέλαστον ἀνθρώπῳ πεποίηκε
τὸν τάφον. ἦν δ' ἐπιγεγραμμένον·

20   ἐνθάδ' ἀπορρήξας ψυχὴν βαρυδαίμονα κεῖμαι.
τοὔνομα δ' οὐ πεύσεσθε, κακοὶ δὲ κακῶς ἀπόλοισθε.

καὶ τοῦτο μὲν αὐτὸν ἔτι ζῶντα πεποιηκέναι λέγουσι, τὸ δὲ περιφερόμενον
Καλλιμάχειόν ἐστι·

Τίμων μισάνθρωπος ἐνοικέω. ἀλλὰ πάρελθε,
25   οἰμώζειν εἶπας πολλά, πάρελθε μόνον.

	ἐκκλησιάζω	I hold an assembly
	βῆμα -ατος τό	platform
	σιωπή -ῆς ἡ	silence
	προσδοκία -ας ἡ	expectation
12	παράδοξος -ον	strange, surprising
	οἰκόπεδον -ου τό	building plot
	συκῆ -ῆς ἡ	fig tree
	φύω pf πέφυκα	I grow
	συχνός -ή -όν	numerous
14	ἀπάγχομαι ἀπηγξάμην	I hang myself
	οἰκοδομέω	I build (on)
	δημοσίᾳ	in public
	προεῖπον	(aor with no pres) I announce
	ἐκκόπτω aor pass ἐξεκόπην	I fell (a tree), I cut down
17	Ἁλαί -ῶν αἱ	Halae (coastal district of Attica)
	ὀλισθάνω ὤλισθον	I slip away, I subside
	προέχω	I project
	αἰγιαλός -οῦ ὁ	beach, shore
	κῦμα -ατος τό	surge, sea-water
18	ἄβατος -ον	inaccessible
	ἀπροσπέλαστος -ον	hard to approach
	ἀπορρήγνυμι ἀπέρρηξα	I break off
	ψυχή -ῆς ἡ	life
	βαρυδαίμων -ον (-ονος)	luckless, ill-starred
21	τοὔνομα	(crasis of τὸ ὄνομα)
	περιφερόμενος -η -ον	(lit carried around, i.e.) in general circulation
	Καλλιμάχειος -ον	of Callimachus (third century BC poet)
	οἰμώζω	(lit I lament, in command as curse) go to hell!
	εἶπας	(= εἰπών) here telling him to

Third person imperatives

We saw in *Greek to GCSE (2)* that direct commands are normally expressed by the present or aorist imperative (implied to be second person unless stated), except that negative commands for one occasion are expressed by μή with the (second person) aorist subjunctive. We saw earlier in this book (see page 11) that first person plural commands or exhortations (*let us do X*, urging others to join you) are expressed by the jussive subjunctive (first person). The same idiom could be used in the third person (*let them/may they do X*, expressing something you want a third party to do), but Greek verbs do have third person imperative forms. These are not very common, but you need to be able to recognise them when they occur in texts.

The basic endings for third person imperatives are:

	active	middle/passive
sg	-ετω	-εσθω
pl	-οντων	-εσθων

These are used (on the appropriate stem) for the present and for the second aorist (active and middle). The first aorist (active and middle) uses predictable alpha variants:

	active	middle/passive
sg	-σατω	-σασθω
pl	-σαντων	-σασθων

The aorist passive uses (as in its other forms) endings which are versions of the active ones:

sg	-θητω
pl	-θητων

Common very irregular verbs have third person imperatives as follows:

	εἰμί I am	εἶμι I (shall) go	οἶδα I know
sg	ἔστω	ἴτω	ἴστω
pl	ἔστων	ἰόντων	ἴστων

Contracted verbs contract the present endings according to the usual rules.

As with other imperatives, the distinction between present and aorist is by aspect. The negative is μή and (unlike the restriction in the second person) this can here be used with the aorist imperative.

Examples:

μανθανόντων	let them learn!	μὴ νικηθήτων	let them be conquered!
προσελθέτω	let him approach!	ἀκουσάτω	let him listen!
πορευέσθων	let them march!	ἀνδρεῖα ἔστω	let her be brave!
νικησάντων	let them conquer!	ἴστω Ζεύς	may Zeus know! (*i.e.* be my witness)

The present and aorist active plural forms risk being confused with the masculine/neuter genitive plural of the equivalent participles, a problem most easily solved by consideration of context.

Exercise 4.18

Translate into English:

1   παυσάσθων βοῶντες.
2   διωξάντων πάντες τὸν φεύγοντα.
3   οἴκαδε ἴτω ἡ παῖς, καὶ μὴ περὶ τῶν ἐνθάδε ἴστω.
4   εἰ ὁ ξένος πάρεστιν, ἐλθέτω δεῦρο.
5   ἀποβαλόντων πάντα ταῦτα.

Subordinate (especially conditional) clauses in indirect speech

Any subordinate clause *within* indirect speech (usually indirect statement, but can also be question or command) follows a similar *sequence* rule (see page 148) to the ὅτι version of indirect statement, or to indirect question:

primary   no change (keeps whatever form it had in the original direct speech)
historic   verb of subordinate clause can become optative, but is often left unchanged

As well as the vividness principle, there are two further possible reasons why the verb here may be left unchanged: (i) historic tenses of the indicative are not changed; (ii) if the subordinate clause did not actually form part of what was said at the time, but is information supplied by the narrator.

Although the change to the optative is therefore relatively uncommon, you need to be aware of it, in particular because of the misleading appearance it may give to conditional clauses. Consider the following examples:

    ἐάν ταῦτα μάθῃς, μίσθον εὑρήσεις.   *future open condition*
    If you learn these things, you will find a reward.

If this is put into indirect statement with a ὅτι clause, and following the above rule, it comes out as:

    εἶπεν ὅτι εἰ ἡ κόρη ταῦτα μάθοι, μίσθον εὑρήσοι.
    He said that if the girl learned these things, she would find a reward.

Because we see two optatives (and in changing subjunctive to optative, ἐάν automatically becomes εἰ), this sentence has the misleading appearance of a future remote condition - but it is not, most obviously because there is no ἄν.* Conversely if there was an ἄν in the original, it is retained even if the infinitive or participle construction is used for indirect statement:

    εἰ ταῦτα μάθοι, μίσθον εὕροι ἄν.   *future remote condition*
    If you were to learn these things, you would find a reward.

If this is put into indirect statement with the infinitive, it comes out as:

    ἔφη τὴν κόρην, εἰ ταῦτα μάθοι, μίσθον εὑρεῖν ἄν.
    He said that the girl, if she were to learn these things, would find a reward.

Note that here the aorist infinitive with ἄν is used by aspect (*to do X once*), because it represents an original optative used by aspect, whereas normally in indirect statement it is used by tense (*to have done X*), representing an original indicative used by tense: in either case it *behaves like what it is replacing*.

    εἰ ταῦτα ἔμαθες, μίσθον ηὗρες ἄν.   *past closed condition*
    If you had learned these things, you would have found a reward.

If this is put into indirect statement with the infinitive, it comes out as:

    ἔφη τὴν κόρην, εἰ ταῦτα ἔμαθε, μίσθον εὑρεῖν ἄν.
    He said that the girl, if she had learned these things, would have found a reward.

Here the protasis remains unchanged (because it is a historic indicative, not put into the optative), and the aorist infinitive with ἄν represents a sort of potential/hypothetical version of its use by tense.

* Also because the optative in the apodosis is future (keeping the tense of the original), whereas in a future remote condition it would be present or aorist by aspect.

Exercise 4.19

Translate into English:

1   ἔφη τὸν δοῦλον, ὃς οὐδέποτε πιστὸς εἴη, φυγεῖν.
2   ἔφη τὸν δοῦλον, ὃς ὕστερον ηὑρέθη, φυγεῖν.
3   ὁ διδάσκαλος εἶπεν ὅτι ἡ παῖς, εἰ ἀκούοι, ῥᾳδίως μαθήσοιτο.
4   ὁ διδάσκαλος ἔφη τὴν παῖδα, εἰ ἤκουσεν, ῥᾳδίως ἂν μαθεῖν.
5   ὁ διδάσκαλος ἔφη τὴν παῖδα, εἰ ἀκούοι, ῥᾳδίως ἂν μαθεῖν.

Exercise 4.20 (Revision)

Translate into English:

1   ὁ φίλος πειστέος σοι ἐστίν.
2   ἆρ᾽ ἐλπίζεις μὴ ἀδικηθήσεσθαι διὰ τὸ ξένος εἶναι;
3   οἱ πάλαι ἐπολέμουν ὁπότε δέοι.
4   ἡ γυνὴ ἔφη τὸν υἱόν, εἰ τοῦτο ποιήσειεν, εὐθὺς κολασθήσεσθαι.
5   ὅποι ἂν ἔλθῃς, τοιαῦτα εὑρήσεις.
6   ἆρα τοῖν χειροῖν ἤνεγκας πάντα ταῦτα;
7   τοῦτο τὸ πρᾶγμα νῦν ἔχει καλῶς.
8   ἐσθιέτω ὅ τι ὁ ἰατρὸς κελεύει.
9   εἰ τὸν μίσθον ζητεῖς, προσελθὼν λαβέ.
10   πάντα τἀγαθὰ ἐνθάδε εὑρίσκεται.

Chapter 5: Readings

Reading 1:

The Choice of Xenophon

Xenophon's Anabasis *('March up-country') describes the expedition of the Persian prince Cyrus against his brother, king Artaxerxes II. Cyrus was satrap of Lydia and was disappointed that, as the favourite son, he had not been chosen to succeed their father Darius II. His resentment fuelled when Artaxerxes accused him of conspiracy, Cyrus recruited an auxiliary force of 10,000 Greeks. Xenophon describes their long march, which he accompanied at the invitation of his friend Proxenus. At the battle of Cunaxa near Babylon, Cyrus was defeated and killed. This left the Greeks in a tricky situation, but Xenophon (who speaks of himself in the third person) stepped in to take a major role in organizing a safe retreat. Here he describes the moment when he first came under the spotlight, and looks back to events before he left Athens (3.1.4-14).*

ἦν δέ τις ἐν τῇ στρατιᾷ <u>Ξενοφῶν</u> Ἀθηναῖος, ὃς οὔτε στρατηγὸς οὔτε
λοχαγὸς οὔτε στρατιώτης ὢν <u>συνηκολούθει</u>, ἀλλὰ <u>Πρόξενος</u> αὐτὸν
μετεπέμψατο οἴκοθεν ξένος ὢν ἀρχαῖος· ὑπισχνεῖτο δὲ αὐτῷ, εἰ ἔλθοι,
φίλον αὐτὸν <u>Κύρῳ</u> ποιήσειν, ὃν αὐτὸς ἔφη <u>κρείττω</u> ἑαυτῷ νομίζειν τῆς
5 πατρίδος. ὁ μέντοι Ξενοφῶν ἀναγνοὺς τὴν ἐπιστολὴν <u>ἀνακοινοῦται</u>
<u>Σωκράτει</u> τῷ Ἀθηναίῳ περὶ τῆς <u>πορείας</u>. καὶ ὁ Σωκράτης <u>ὑποπτεύσας</u> μή
τι πρὸς τῆς πόλεως <u>ὑπαίτιον</u> εἴη Κύρῳ φίλον γενέσθαι, ὅτι ἐδόκει ὁ
Κῦρος προθύμως τοῖς Λακεδαιμονίοις ἐπὶ τὰς Ἀθήνας συμπολεμῆσαι,
συμβουλεύει τῷ Ξενοφῶντι ἐλθόντα εἰς Δελφοὺς ἀνακοινῶσαι τῷ θεῷ περὶ
10 τῆς πορείας. ἐλθὼν δ᾽ ὁ Ξενοφῶν <u>ἐπήρετο</u> τὸν <u>Ἀπόλλω</u> τίνι ἂν θεῶν θύων
καὶ εὐχόμενος κάλλιστα καὶ ἄριστα ἔλθοι τὴν ὁδὸν ἣν <u>ἐπινοεῖ</u> καὶ καλῶς
πράξας σωθείη. καὶ <u>ἀνεῖλεν</u> αὐτῷ ὁ Ἀπόλλων θεοῖς οἷς ἔδει θύειν. ἐπεὶ
δὲ πάλιν ἦλθε, λέγει τὴν <u>μαντείαν</u> τῷ Σωκράτει. ὁ δ᾽ ἀκούσας <u>ᾐτιᾶτο</u>
αὐτὸν ὅτι οὐ τοῦτο πρῶτον ἠρώτα πότερον <u>λῷον</u> εἴη αὐτῷ πορεύεσθαι ἢ
15 μένειν, ἀλλ᾽ αὐτὸς κρίνας ἰτέον εἶναι τοῦτ᾽ ἐπυνθάνετο ὅπως ἂν κάλλιστα
πορευθείη. "ἐπεὶ μέντοι οὕτως ἤρου, ταῦτ᾽," ἔφη, "χρὴ ποιεῖν ὅσα ὁ θεὸς
ἐκέλευσεν."

	Ξενοφῶν -ῶντος ὁ	Xenophon
	συνακολουθέω	I follow along
	Πρόξενος -ου ὁ	Proxenus
	Κῦρος -ου ὁ	Cyrus
4	κρείττων -ον	better, more valuable (*contracted acc sg* -ω *for* -ονα)
	ἀνακοινόω	I consult (+ *dat*), *mid* I confer with (+ *dat*)
	Σωκράτης -ους ὁ	Socrates
	πορεία -ας ἡ	march, expedition
	ὑποπτεύω ὑπώπτευσα	I suspect
7	ὑπαίτιος -ον	open to accusation
	ἐπερωτάω ἐπήρομην	I ask
	Ἀπόλλων -ωνος ὁ	Apollo (*acc* -ω *for* -ωνα)
	ἐπινοέω	I have in mind
	ἀναιρέω ἀνεῖλον	I reply
13	μαντεία -ας ἡ	oracle, oracular response
	αἰτιάομαι	I find fault with
	λῷων -ον	better

ὁ μὲν δὴ Ξενοφῶν οὕτω θυσάμενος οἷς <u>ἀνεῖλεν</u> ὁ θεὸς ἐξέπλει, καὶ <u>καταλαμβάνει</u> ἐν <u>Σάρδεσι</u> Πρόξενον καὶ Κῦρον μέλλοντας ἤδη <u>ὁρμᾶν</u> τὴν
20 <u>ἄνω</u> ὁδόν, καὶ <u>συνεστάθη</u> Κύρῳ. <u>προθυμουμένου</u> δὲ τοῦ Προξένου καὶ ὁ Κῦρος συμπρούθυμεῖτο μεῖναι αὐτόν, εἶπε δὲ ὅτι ἐπειδὰν τάχιστα ἡ στρατεία <u>λήξῃ</u>, εὐθὺς ἀποπέμψει αὐτόν. ἐλέγετο δὲ στόλος εἶναι εἰς <u>Πισίδας</u>. ἐστρατεύετο μὲν δὴ οὕτως ἐξαπατηθείς - οὐχ ὑπὸ Προξένου· οὐ γὰρ ᾔδει τὴν ἐπὶ βασιλέα <u>ὁρμὴν</u> οὐδὲ ἄλλος οὐδεὶς τῶν Ἑλλήνων πλὴν
25 <u>Κλεάρχου</u>· ἐπεὶ μέντοι εἰς <u>Κιλικίαν</u> ἦλθον, σαφὲς πᾶσιν ἤδη ἐδόκει εἶναι ὅτι στόλος εἴη ἐπὶ βασιλέα. φοβούμενοι δὲ τὴν ὁδὸν καὶ ἄκοντες ὅμως οἱ πολλοὶ δι' <u>αἰσχύνην</u> καὶ ἀλλήλων καὶ Κύρου <u>συνηκολούθησαν</u>· ὧν δὲ εἷς καὶ Ξενοφῶν ἦν.

ἐπεὶ δὲ ἀπορία ἦν, <u>ἐλυπεῖτο</u> μὲν σὺν τοῖς ἄλλοις καὶ οὐκ ἐδύνατο
30 καθεύδειν· μικρὸν δ' ὕπνου <u>λαχὼν</u> εἶδεν ὄναρ. ἔδοξεν αὐτῷ βροντῆς γενομένης <u>σκηπτὸς</u> πεσεῖν εἰς τὴν πατρῴαν οἰκίαν, καὶ ἐκ τούτου <u>λάμπεσθαι</u> πᾶσα. περίφοβος δ' εὐθὺς <u>ἀνηγέρθη</u>, καὶ τὸ ὄναρ <u>τῇ μὲν</u> ἔκρινεν ἀγαθόν, ὅτι ἐν πόνοις ὢν καὶ κινδυνοίς <u>φῶς</u> μέγα ἐκ Διὸς ἰδεῖν ἔδοξε· <u>τῇ δὲ</u> καὶ ἐφοβεῖτο, ὅτι ἀπὸ Διὸς μὲν βασιλέως τὸ ὄναρ ἐδόκει
35 αὐτῷ εἶναι, κύκλῳ δὲ ἐδόκει λάμπεσθαι τὸ πῦρ, μὴ οὐ δύναιτο ἐκ τῆς χώρας ἐξελθεῖν τῆς βασιλέως, ἀλλ' <u>εἴργοντο</u> <u>πάντοθεν</u> ὑπό τινων ἀποριῶν. ὁποῖόν τι μὲν δή ἐστι τὸ τοιοῦτον ὄναρ ἰδεῖν ἔξεστι σκοπεῖν ἐκ τῶν <u>συμβάντων</u> μετὰ τὸ ὄναρ. γίγνεται γὰρ τάδε. εὐθὺς ἐπειδὴ ἀνηγέρθη

	ἀναιρέω ἀνεῖλον	I reply
	καταλαμβάνω	I find, I met
	Σάρδεις -εων αἱ	Sardis (*city in Asia Minor, old Lydian capital*)
	ὁρμάω	I set out on, I begin
20	ἄνω	(*here*) up-country, inland
	συνίστημι *aor pass* συνεστάθην	I bring together, *pass* I am introduced (to, + *dat*)
	προθυμέομαι	I am eager (that X should happen, + *acc* + *inf*)
	λήγω ἔληξα	I come to an end
	Πισίδαι -ων οἱ	Pisidians
24	ὁρμή -ῆς ἡ	march, attack
	Κλέαρχος -ου ὁ	Clearchus
	Κιλικία -ας ἡ	Cilicia (*area of southern Asia Minor*)
	αἰσχύνη -ης ἡ	shame
	συνακολουθέω	I follow along
29	λυπέομαι	I am grieved
	λαγχάνω ἔλαχον	I get
	ὄναρ τό	dream
	βροντή -ῆς ἡ	thunder
	σκηπτός -οῦ ὁ	thunderbolt
32	λάμπομαι	I am ablaze
	περίφοβος -ον	terrified
	ἀνεγείρω *aor pass* ἀνηγέρθην	I wake (someone) up, *pass* I waken up
	τῇ μέν ... τῇ δέ	in one way ... in another way
	φῶς φωτός τό	light
36	εἴργω	I shut in
	πάντοθεν	on all sides
	συμβαίνω *aor pple* συμβάς	(*of events*) happen

πρῶτον μὲν ἔννοια αὐτῷ ἐμπίπτει· τί κατάκειμαι; ἡ δὲ νὺξ προβαίνει·
40 ἅμα δὲ τῇ ἡμέρᾳ εἰκὸς τοὺς πολεμίους ἥξειν. εἰ δὲ γενησόμεθα ἐπὶ
βασιλεῖ, τί ἐμποδὼν μὴ οὐχὶ πάντα μὲν τὰ χαλεπώτατα ἐπιδόντας, πάντα
δὲ τὰ δεινότατα παθόντας ὑβριζομένους ἀποθανεῖν; ὅπως δ' ἀμυνούμεθα
οὐδεὶς παρασκευάζεται οὐδὲ ἐπιμελεῖται, ἀλλὰ κατακείμεθα ὥσπερ ἐξὸν
ἡσυχίαν ἄγειν. ἐγὼ οὖν τὸν ἐκ ποίας πόλεως στρατηγὸν προσδοκῶ ταῦτα
45 πράξειν; ποίαν δ' ἡλικίαν ἐμαυτῷ ἐλθεῖν ἀναμείνω; οὐ γὰρ ἔγωγ' ἔτι
πρεσβύτερος ἔσομαι, ἐὰν τήμερον προδῶ ἐμαυτὸν τοῖς πολεμίοις.

	ἔννοια -ας ἡ	thought
	προβαίνω	(of time) wear on
	ἐμποδών	in the way, to prevent
	ὑβρίζω	I insult, I treat outrageously
43	ἐπιμελέομαι	I take thought
	ἡσυχία -ας ἡ	ease, leisure
	προσδοκάω	I expect
	ἡλικία -ας ἡ	age
	ἀναμείνω	I wait for
46	πρεσβύτερος -α -ον	older

Reading 2:

The Sea, the Sea

*The Ten Thousand marched northwards through inhospitable lands towards the Black Sea coast. Here
Xenophon describes the famous moment when the Greeks, climbing Mount Theches, at last catch sight of
the sea. Although this is by no means the end of the story of the* Anabasis, *it is a symbolic turning point as
they have reached comparative safety. Meanwhile there is an unexpected bit of good luck as they pass
though the territory of the Macronians. (4.7.19 - 4.8.7)*

ἐντεῦθεν διῆλθον σταθμοὺς τέτταρας παρασάγγας εἴκοσι πρὸς πόλιν
μεγάλην καὶ εὐδαίμονα καὶ οἰκουμένην ἣ ἐκαλεῖτο Γυμνιάς. ἐκ ταύτης ὁ
τῆς χώρας ἄρχων τοῖς Ἕλλησιν ἡγεμόνα πέμπει, ὅπως διὰ τῆς ἑαυτῶν
πολεμίας χώρας ἄγοι αὐτούς. ἐλθὼν δ' ἐκεῖνος λέγει ὅτι ἄξει αὐτοὺς πέντε
5 ἡμερῶν εἰς χωρίον ὅθεν ὄψονται θάλατταν· εἰ δὲ μή, τεθνάναι
ἐπηγγείλατο. καὶ ἡγούμενος ἐπειδὴ ἐνέβαλεν εἰς τὴν πολεμίαν,
παρεκελεύετο αἴθειν καὶ φθείρειν τὴν χώραν· ᾧ καὶ δῆλον ἐγένετο ὅτι
τούτου ἕνεκα ἔλθοι, οὐ τῆς τῶν Ἑλλήνων εὐνοίας. καὶ ἀφικνοῦνται ἐπὶ
τὸ ὄρος τῇ πέμπτῃ ἡμέρᾳ· ὄνομα δὲ τῷ ὄρει ἦν Θήχης. ἐπεὶ δὲ οἱ πρῶτοι
10 ἐγένοντο ἐπὶ τοῦ ὄρους καὶ κατεῖδον τὴν θάλατταν, κραυγὴ πολλὴ

	σταθμός -οῦ ὁ	day's march
	παρασάγγης -ου ὁ	parasang (= 30 stades, i.e. just under six kilometres)
	Γυμνιάς -άδος ἡ	Gymnias (city in northern Asia Minor)
	ἀπαγγέλλομαι	I offer, I promise
6	ἐμβάλλω ἐνέβαλον	I make an inroad
	αἴθω	I burn
	φθείρω	I lay waste, I destroy
	εὔνοια -ας ἡ	goodwill
	Θήχης ὁ	Theches
10	κραυγή -ῆς ἡ	cry

99

ἐγένετο. ἀκούσας δὲ ὁ Ξενοφῶν καὶ οἱ <u>ὀπισθοφύλακες</u> <u>ᾠήθησαν</u> καὶ <u>ἔμπροσθεν</u> ἄλλους <u>ἐπιτίθεσθαι</u> πολεμίους· εἵποντο γὰρ καὶ ὄπισθεν ἐκ τῆς καιομένης χώρας, καὶ αὐτῶν οἱ ὀπισθοφύλακες ἀπέκτεινάν τέ τινας καὶ <u>ἐζώγρησαν</u> <u>ἐνέδραν</u> ποιησάμενοι, καὶ <u>γέρρα</u> ἔλαβον <u>δασεῖων</u> <u>βοῶν</u>
15 <u>ὠμοβόινα</u> ἀμφὶ τὰ εἴκοσιν.

ἐπειδὴ δὲ ἡ βοὴ πλείων τε ἐγίγνετο καὶ <u>ἐγγύτερον</u> καὶ οἱ ἀεὶ <u>ἐπίοντες</u> <u>ἔθεον</u> δρόμῳ ἐπὶ τοὺς ἀεὶ βοῶντας καὶ πολλῷ μείζων ἐγίγνετο ἡ βοὴ ὅσῳ δὴ πλείους ἐγίγνοντο, ἐδόκει δὴ μεῖζόν τι εἶναι τῷ Ξενοφῶντι, καὶ ἀναβὰς ἐφ' ἵππον καὶ <u>Λύκιον</u> καὶ τοὺς ἱππέας ἀναλαβὼν <u>παρεβοήθει·</u> καὶ τάχα δὴ
20 ἀκούουσι βοώντων τῶν στρατιωτῶν "θάλαττα θάλαττα" καὶ <u>περεγγυώντων.</u> ἔνθα δὴ ἔθεον ἅπαντες καὶ οἱ ὀπισθοφύλακες, καὶ τὰ <u>ὑποζύγια</u> ἠλαύνετο καὶ οἱ ἵπποι. ἐπεὶ δὲ ἀφίκοντο πάντες ἐπὶ τὸ ἄκρον, ἐνταῦθα δὴ <u>περιέβαλλον</u> ἀλλήλους καὶ στρατηγοὺς καὶ λοχαγοὺς δακρύοντες. καὶ <u>ἐξαπίνης</u> <u>ὅτου</u> δὴ παρεγγυήσαντος οἱ στρατιῶται φέρουσι λίθους καὶ
25 ποιοῦσι <u>κολωνὸν</u> μέγαν. ἐνταῦθα <u>ἀνετίθεσαν</u> <u>δερμάτων</u> πλῆθος <u>ὠμοβοείων</u> καὶ <u>βακτηρίας</u> καὶ τὰ <u>αἰχμάλωτα</u> γέρρα, καὶ ὁ ἡγεμὼν αὐτός τε <u>κατέτεμνε</u> τὰ γέρρα καὶ τοῖς ἄλλοις <u>διεκελεύετο</u>. μετὰ ταῦτα τὸν ἡγεμόνα οἱ Ἕλληνες ἀποπέμπουσι δῶρα δόντες <u>ἀπὸ κοινοῦ</u> ἵππον καὶ <u>φιάλην</u>

	ὀπισθοφύλακες -ων οἱ	rearguard
	οἴομαι ᾠήθην	I think
	ἔμπροσθεν	in front
	ἐπιτίθεμαι	I attack
14	ζωγρέω ἐζώγρησα	I capture, I take prisoner
	ἐνέδρα -ας ἡ	ambush
	γέρρον -ου τό	wicker shield
	δασύς -εῖα -ύ	shaggy
	βοῦς βοός ὁ	ox
15	ὠμοβόινος -η -ον	covered with raw hide
	ἐγγύτερον	nearer
	ἔπειμι	I come up, I approach
	θέω	I rush
	Λύκιος -ου ὁ	Lycius
19	παραβοηθέω	I come to help
	παρεγγυάω	I pass the word along
	ὑποζύγιον -ου τό	baggage animal
	περιβάλλω	I embrace
	ἐξαπίνης	suddenly
24	ὅστις *gen* ὅτου	(*here*) someone or other
	κολωνός -οῦ ὁ	cairn, mound
	ἀνατίθημι	I dedicate, I place as an offering
	δέρμα -ατος τό	hide, animal skin
	ὠμοβόειος -α -ον	raw
26	βακτηρία -ας ἡ	walking-stick
	αἰχμάλωτος -ον	captured
	κατατέμνω	I cut into pieces (*i.e. to make useless to enemies*)
	διακελεύομαι	I urge
	ἀπὸ κοινοῦ	from the common stock
28	φιάλη -ης ἡ	cup

ἀργυρᾶν καὶ σκευὴν Περσικὴν καὶ δαρεικούς δέκα· ᾔτει δὲ μάλιστα τοὺς
30 δακτυλίους, καὶ ἔλαβε πολλοὺς παρὰ τῶν στρατιωτῶν. κώμην δὲ δείξας
αὐτοῖς οὗ σκηνήσουσι καὶ τὴν ὁδὸν ἣν πορεύσονται εἰς Μάκρωνας, ἐπεὶ
ἑσπέρα ἐγένετο, ᾤχετο τῆς νυκτὸς ἀπιών.

ἐντεῦθεν δ' ἐπορεύθησαν οἱ Ἕλληνες διὰ Μακρώνων σταθμοὺς τρεῖς
παρασάγγας δέκα. τῇ πρώτῃ δὲ ἡμέρᾳ ἀφίκοντο ἐπὶ τὸν ποταμὸν ὃς ὥριζε
35 τήν τε τῶν Μακρώνων καὶ τὴν τῶν Σκυθηνῶν. εἶχον δ' ὑπὲρ δεξιῶν
χωρίον οἷον χαλεπώτατον καὶ ἐξ ἀριστερᾶς ἄλλον ποταμόν, εἰς ὃν
ἐνέβαλλεν ὁ ὁρίζων, δι' οὗ ἔδει διαβῆναι. ἦν δὲ οὗτος δασὺς δένδρεσι
παχέσι μὲν οὔ, πυκνοῖς δέ. ταῦτα ἐπεὶ προσῆλθον οἱ Ἕλληνες ἔκοπτον,
σπεύδοντες ἐκ τοῦ χωρίου ὡς τάχιστα ἐξελθεῖν. οἱ δὲ Μάκρωνες ἔχοντες
40 γέρρα καὶ λόγχας καὶ τριχίνους χιτῶνας κατ' ἀντιπέρας τῆς διαβάσεως
παρατεταγμένοι ἦσαν καὶ ἀλλήλοις διεκελεύοντο καὶ λίθους εἰς τὸν
ποταμὸν ἔρριπτον· ἐξικνοῦντο δὲ οὗ οὐδ' ἔβλαπτον οὐδέν.

ἔνθα δὴ προσέρχεται Ξενοφῶντι τῶν πελταστῶν ἀνὴρ Ἀθήνησι φάσκων
δεδουλευκέναι, λέγων ὅτι γιγνώσκοι τὴν φωνὴν τῶν ἀνθρώπων. "καὶ
45 οἶμαι," ἔφη, "ἐμὴν ταύτην πατρίδα εἶναι· καὶ εἰ μη τι κωλύει, ἐθέλω
αὐτοῖς διαλεχθῆναι." "ἀλλ' οὐδὲν κωλύει," ἔφη ὁ Ξενοφῶν, "ἀλλὰ διαλέγου
καὶ μάθε πρῶτον τίνες εἰσίν." οἱ δ' εἶπον ἐρωτήσαντος ὅτι Μάκρωνες.
"ἐρώτα τοίνυν," ἔφη, "αὐτοὺς τί ἀντιτετάχαται καὶ χρήζουσιν ἡμῖν
πολέμιοι εἶναι." οἱ δ' ἐπεκρίναντο· "ὅτι ὑμεῖς ἐπὶ τὴν ἡμετέραν χώραν
50 ἔρχεσθε." λέγειν ἐκέλευον οἱ στρατηγοὶ ὅτι "οὐ κακῶς γε ποιήσοντες,

	Περσικός -ή -όν	Persian
	δαρεικός -οῦ ὁ	daric (Persian gold coin, named after king Darius)
	δακτύλιος -ου ὁ	ring
	σκηνέω	I camp
31	Μάκρωνες -ων οἱ	Macronians
	οἴχομαι	I am gone
	σταθμός -οῦ ὁ	day's march
	παρασάγγης -ου ὁ	parasang
	ὁρίζω	I separate, I form a boundary (between)
35	Σκυθηνοί -ῶν οἱ	Scytheni
	δασύς -εῖα -ύ	(here) fringed
	δένδρος -ους τό	tree
	παχύς -εῖα -ύ	large
	πυκνός -ή -όν	thickly-growing
39	σπεύδω	I hurry
	γέρρον -ου τό	wicker shield
	τρίχινος -η -ον	made of (animal) hair
	χιτών -ῶνος ὁ	tunic
	κατ' ἀντιπέρας	opposite
40	διάβασις -εως ἡ	crossing-place
	ἐξικνέομαι	I reach my target
	Ἀθήνησι	in Athens
	οἶμαι	I think
	ἀντιτάσσω	
48	pf pass 3 pl ἀντιτετάχαται	I draw up against
	χρήζω	I want

101

ἀλλὰ βασιλεῖ πολεμήσαντες ἀπερχόμεθα εἰς τὴν Ἑλλάδα, καὶ ἐπὶ
θάλατταν βουλόμεθα ἀφικέσθαι." ἠρώτων ἐκεῖνοι εἰ δοῖεν ἂν τούτων τὰ
<u>πιστά</u>. οἱ δ' ἔφασαν καὶ δοῦναι καὶ λαβεῖν ἐθέλειν. ἐντεῦθεν διδόασιν οἱ
Μάκρωνες <u>βαρβαρικὴν</u> λόγχην τοῖς Ἕλλησι, οἱ δὲ Ἕλληνες ἐκείνοις
55 <u>Ἑλληνικήν</u>· ταῦτα γὰρ ἔφασαν πιστὰ εἶναι· θεοὺς δ' <u>ἐπεμαρτύραντο</u>
ἀμφότεροι.

πιστόν -οῦ τό	pledge
βαρβαρικός -ή -όν	barbarian, foreign, non-Greek
Ἑλληνικός -ή -όν	Greek
ἐπιμαρτύρομαι	
ἐπεμαρτυράμην	I call to witness

Reading 3:

Gobryas the Assyrian

*The prince Cyrus whose unsuccessful coup the Ten Thousand had gone to support was the descendant and
namesake of Cyrus the Great, founder of the Persian empire. This earlier Cyrus is a major character in
Herodotus: we read in Greek to GCSE (2) of his conquest of the Lydian kingdom ruled by Croesus, and we
traced his early life in the opening chapters of this book. Xenophon also wrote about him, in his remarkable
Cyropaedia ('The Education of Cyrus'), a semi-fictional biography which is also the first historical novel.
Xenophon's concerns with training and leadership emerge here too, and he sees in the early history of
Persia ideals similar to those of Sparta. In this passage Cyrus is approached by the Assyrian Gobryas, who
has a sad story to tell but becomes a grateful and useful ally (4.6.1-10).*

<u>Γωβρύας</u> δ' ἐν τούτῳ παρῆν <u>Ἀσσύριος</u> πρεσβύτης ἀνὴρ ἐφ' ἵππου σὺν
ἱππικῇ <u>θεραπείᾳ</u>· εἶχον δὲ πάντες τὰ <u>ἐφίππων</u> ὅπλα. καὶ οἱ μὲν ἐπὶ τῷ τὰ
ὅπλα <u>παραλαμβάνειν</u> τεταγμένοι ἐκέλευον παραδιδόναι τὰ <u>ξυστά</u>, ὅπως
<u>κατακάοιεν</u> ὥσπερ τἆλλα. ὁ δὲ Γωβρύας εἶπεν ὅτι <u>Κῦρον</u> πρῶτον
5 βούλοιτο ἰδεῖν· καὶ οἱ <u>ὑπηρέται</u> τοὺς μὲν ἄλλους ἱππέας αὐτοῦ <u>κατέλιπον</u>,
τὸν δὲ Γωβρύαν ἄγουσι πρὸς τὸν Κῦρον. ὁ δ' ὡς εἶδε τὸν Κῦρον, ἔλεξεν
ὧδε· "ὦ δέσποτα, ἐγώ εἰμι τὸ μὲν γένος Ἀσσύριος· ἔχω δὲ καὶ τεῖχος
ἰσχυρὸν καὶ χώρας <u>ἐπάρχω</u> πολλῆς· καὶ ἵππον ἔχω εἰς χιλίαν, ἣν τῷ τῶν
Ἀσσυρίων βασιλεῖ παρειχόμην καὶ φίλος ἦν ἐκείνῳ ὡς μάλιστα· ἐπεὶ δὲ
10 ἐκεῖνος τέθνηκεν ὑφ' ὑμῶν ἀνὴρ ἀγαθὸς ὤν, ὁ δὲ παῖς ἐκείνου τὴν ἀρχὴν
ἔχει ἔχθιστος ὢν ἐμοί, ἥκω πρὸς σὲ καὶ <u>ἱκέτης</u> προσπίπτω καὶ δίδωμί σοι

	Γωβρύας ὁ	Gobryas
	Ἀσσύριος -α -ον	Assyrian
	πρέσβυτης -ου ὁ	old (man)
	ἱππικός -ή -όν	of horses/cavalry
2	θεραπεία -ας ἡ	escort
	ἔφιππος -ον	of cavalry
	παραλαμβάνω	I receive, I take possession of
	ξυστόν -οῦ τό	spear
	κατακάω	I burn
4	Κῦρος -ου ὁ	Cyrus
	ὑπηρέτης -ου ὁ	(*here*) officer
	καταλείπω κατέλιπον	I leave behind
	ἐπάρχω	I govern (+ *gen*)
	ἱκέτης -ου ὁ	suppliant

ἐμαυτὸν δοῦλον καὶ σύμμαχον, σὲ δὲ <u>τιμωρὸν</u> αἰτοῦμαι ἐμοὶ γενέσθαι·
καὶ παῖδα οὕτως ὡς δυνατόν σε ποιοῦμαι· <u>ἄπαις</u> δ' εἰμὶ <u>ἀρρένων</u> παίδων.
ὃς γὰρ ἦν μοι μόνος καὶ καλὸς κἀγαθός, ὦ δέσποτα, καὶ ἐμὲ φιλῶν καὶ
15 τιμῶν ὥσπερ ἂν εὐδαίμονα πατέρα παῖς τιμῶν τιθείη, τοῦτον ὁ νῦν
βασιλεὺς οὗτος ... * καλέσαντος τοῦ τότε βασιλέως, πατρὸς δὲ τοῦ νῦν, ὡς
δώσοντος τὴν θυγατέρα τῷ ἐμῷ παιδί, ἐγὼ μὲν ἀπεπεμψάμην <u>μέγα φρονῶν</u>
ὅτι <u>δῆθεν</u> τῆς βασιλέως θυγατρὸς ὀψοίμην τὸν ἐμὸν υἱὸν <u>γαμέτην</u>· ὁ δὲ
νῦν βασιλεὺς εἰς <u>θήραν</u> αὐτὸν <u>παρακαλέσας</u> καὶ <u>ἀνεὶς</u> αὐτῷ <u>θηρᾶν</u> <u>ἀνὰ</u>
20 <u>κράτος</u>, ὡς πολὺ <u>κρείττων</u> αὐτοῦ ἱππεὺς ἡγούμενος εἶναι, ὁ μὲν ὡς φίλῳ
συνεθήρα, φανείσης δὲ <u>ἄρκτου</u> διώκοντες ἀμφότεροι, ὁ μὲν νῦν ἄρχων
οὗτος <u>ἀκοντίσας</u> ἥμαρτεν, ὡς μήποτε <u>ὤφελεν</u>, ὁ δ' ἐμὸς παῖς βαλών,
οὐδὲν δέον, καταβάλλει τὴν ἄρκτον.

"καὶ τότε μὲν δὴ <u>ἀνιαθεὶς</u> ἄρ' οὗτος <u>κατέσχεν</u> ὑπὸ σκότου τὸν φθόνον· ὡς
25 δὲ πάλιν λέοντος <u>παρατυχόντος</u> ὁ μὲν αὖ ἥμαρτεν, οὐδὲν <u>θαυμαστὸν</u>
οἶμαι παθών, ὁ δ' αὖ ἐμὸς παῖς αὖθις τυχὼν <u>κατειργάσατό</u> τε τὸν λέοντα
καὶ εἶπεν· 'ἆρα βέβληκα <u>δὶς</u> <u>ἐφεξῆς</u> καὶ καταβέβληκα <u>θῆρα</u> <u>ἑκατεράκις</u>.'
ἐν τούτῳ δὴ οὐκέτι <u>κατίσχει</u> ὁ <u>ἀνόσιος</u> τὸν φθόνον, ἀλλ' <u>αἰχμὴν</u> παρά
τινος τῶν ἑπομένων ἁρπάσας, <u>παίσας</u> εἰς τὰ <u>στέρνα</u> τὸν μόνον μοι καὶ

	τιμωρός -οῦ ὁ	avenger
	ἄπαις -αιδος	childless
	ἄρρην -εν	male
	* the broken syntax, with this clause unfinished, seems to reflect Gobryas' sobs	
17	μέγα φρονέω	I am proud (lit I think big)
	δῆθεν	no doubt, as I thought
	γαμέτης -ου ὁ	husband
	θήρα -ας ἡ	hunt
	παρακαλέω παρακάλεσα	I invite
19	ἀνίημι aor pple ἀνείς	I allow
	θηράω	I hunt
	ἀνὰ κράτος	to the best of one's power
	κρείττων -ον	better, stronger
	ἄρκτος -ου ἡ	bear
22	ἀκοντίζω ἠκόντισα	I throw a javelin
	ὀφείλω ὤφελον	(lit I owe, I ought) aor ought to have
	ἀνιάω aor pass ἠνιάθην	I anger
	κατέχω κατέσχον	I restrain, I conceal
	παρατυγχάνω περέτυχον	I appear
25	θαυμαστός -ή -όν	remarkable
	κατεργάζομαι κατειργασάμην	I kill
	δίς	twice
	ἐφεξῆς	in succession
	θήρ θηρός ὁ	wild beast
27	ἑκατεράκις	both times
	κατίσχω	I restrain
	ἀνόσιος -ον	unholy, wicked
	αἰχμή -ῆς ἡ	spear
	παίω ἔπαισα	I strike, I hit
29	στέρνα -ων τά	chest

30 φίλον παῖδα ἀφείλετο τὴν <u>ψυχήν</u>. κἀγὼ μὲν ὁ <u>τάλας</u> νεκρὸν ἀντὶ <u>νυμφίου</u>
ἐκομισάμην καὶ ἔθαψα <u>τηλικοῦτος</u> ὢν ἄρτι <u>γενειάσκοντα</u> τὸν ἄριστον
παῖδα τὸν <u>ἀγαπητόν</u>· ὁ δὲ <u>κατακτανὼν</u> ὥσπερ ἐχθρὸν ἀπολέσας οὔτε
<u>μεταμελόμενος</u> πώποτε <u>φανερὸς</u> ἐγένετο οὔτε ἀντὶ τοῦ κακοῦ ἔργου τιμῆς
τινος ἠξίωσε τὸν κατὰ γῆς. ὅ γε <u>μὴν</u> πατὴρ αὐτοῦ καὶ <u>συνῴκτισέ</u> με καὶ
35 δῆλος ἦν <u>συναχθόμενός</u> μοι τῇ συμφορᾷ. ἐγὼ οὖν, εἰ μὲν ἔζη ἐκεῖνος,
οὐκ ἄν ποτε ἦλθον πρὸς σὲ ἐπὶ τῷ ἐκείνου κακῷ· πολλὰ γὰρ <u>φιλικὰ</u>
ἔπαθον ὑπ' ἐκείνου καὶ <u>ὑπηρέτησα</u> ἐκείνῳ· ἐπεὶ δ' εἰς τὸν τοῦ ἐμοῦ παιδὸς
<u>φονέα</u> ἡ ἀρχὴ <u>περιήκει</u>, οὐκ ἄν ποτε τούτῳ ἐγὼ δυναίμην <u>εὔνους</u>
γενέσθαι, οὐδὲ οὗτος ἐμὲ εὖ οἶδ' ὅτι φίλον ἄν ποτε ἡγήσαιτο. οἶδε γὰρ ὡς
40 ἐγὼ πρὸς αὐτὸν ἔχω καὶ ὡς πρόσθεν <u>φαιδρῶς βιοτεύων</u> νῦν <u>διάκειμαι</u>,
<u>ἔρημος</u> ὢν καὶ διὰ <u>πένθους</u> τὸ <u>γῆρας διάγων</u>. εἰ οὖν σύ με δέχει καὶ
ἐλπίδα τινὰ λάβοιμι τῷ φίλῳ παιδὶ <u>τιμωρίας</u> ἄν τινος μετὰ σοῦ τυχεῖν,
καὶ <u>ἀνηβῆσαι</u> ἂν πάλιν δοκῶ μοι καὶ οὔτε ζῶν ἄν ἔτι αἰσχυνοίμην οὔτε
ἀποθνῄσκων <u>ἀνιώμενος</u> ἂν τελευτᾶν δοκῶ."
45 ὁ μὲν οὕτως εἶπε· Κῦρος δ' ἀπεκρίνατο, "ἀλλ' ἥπερ, ὦ Γωβρύα, καὶ
<u>φρονῶν</u> φαίνῃ <u>ὅσαπερ</u> λέγεις πρὸς ἡμᾶς, δέχομαί τε <u>ἱκέτην</u> σε καὶ
τιμωρήσειν σοι τοῦ παιδὸς σὺν θεοῖς ὑπισχνοῦμαι. λέξον δέ μοι, ἔφη, ἐὰν
σοι ταῦτα ποιῶμεν καὶ τὰ τείχη σε ἔχειν ἐῶμεν καὶ τὴν χώραν καὶ τὰ

	ψυχή -ῆς ἡ	life
	τάλας -αινα -αν	wretched
	νυμφίος -ου ὁ	bridegroom
	τηλικοῦτος -αύτη -οῦτο	at such an age
31	γενειάσκω	I have down on my cheeks, I begin to grow a beard
	ἀγαπητός -ή -όν	beloved
	κατακτείνω κατέκτανον	I kill
	μεταμέλομαι	I repent
	φανερός -ά -όν	(*lit* visible), *here* showing signs of
34	μήν	indeed
	συνοικτίζω συνῴκτισα	I express sorry for
	συνάχθομαι	I sympathise with (+ *dat*)
	φιλικός -ή -όν	friendly
	ὑπηρέτεω ὑπηρέτησα	I serve (+ *dat*)
38	φονεύς -έως ὁ	murderer
	περιήκω	I pass, I come in turn
	εὔνους -ουν	loyal
	φαιδρός -ά -όν	joyful
	βιοτεύω	I live my life
40	διάκειμαι	I am affected
	ἔρημος -η -ον	deserted, lonely
	πένθος -ους τό	grief
	γῆρας -ως τό	old age
	διάγω	I spend (time)
42	τιμωρία -ας ἡ	vengeance
	ἀνηβάω ἀνήβησα	I grow young again
	ἀνιάω	I anger, I grieve (someone)
	φρονέω	(*lit* I think), *here* I mean
	ὅσαπερ	all the things which (-περ *is emphatic suffix*)
46	ἱκέτης -ου ὁ	suppliant (*person seeking refuge or sanctuary*)

ὅπλα καὶ τὴν δύναμιν ἥνπερ πρόσθεν εἶχες, σὺ ἡμῖν τί ἀντὶ τούτων
50 ὑπηρετήσεις;"

ὁ δὲ εἶπε· "τὰ μὲν τείχη, ὅταν ἔλθῃς, οἰκόν σοι παρέχω· δασμὸν δὲ τῆς
χώρας ὅνπερ ἔφερον ἐκείνῳ σοὶ ἀποίσω καὶ ὅποι ἂν στρατεύῃ,
συστρατεύσομαι τὴν ἐκ τῆς χώρας δύναμιν ἔχων. ἔστι δέ μοι," ἔφη, "καὶ
θυγάτηρ παρθένος ἀγαπητὴ γάμου ἤδη ὡραία, ἥν ἐγὼ πρόσθεν μὲν ᾤμην
55 τῷ νῦν βασιλεύοντι γυναῖκα τρέφειν· νῦν δὲ αὐτή τέ μοι ἡ θυγάτηρ
πολλὰ γοωμένη ἱκέτευσε μὴ δοῦναι αὐτὴν τῷ τοῦ ἀδελφοῦ φονεῖ, ἐγώ τε
ὡσαύτως γιγνώσκω. νῦν δέ σοι δίδωμι βουλεύσασθαι καὶ περὶ ταύτης
οὕτως ὥσπερ ἂν καὶ ἐγὼ βουλεύων περὶ σὲ φαίνωμαι."

οὕτω δὴ ὁ Κῦρος εἶπεν· "ἐπὶ τούτοις." ἔφη, "ἐγὼ ἀληθευομένοις δίδωμί
60 σοι τὴν ἐμὴν καὶ λαμβάνω τὴν σὴν δεξιάν· θεοὶ δ' ὑμῖν μάρτυρες ἔστων."

	ὑπηρέτεω	I serve
	δασμός -οῦ ὁ	tribute, taxation
	ἀγαπητός -ή -όν	beloved
	ὡραῖος -α -ον	of an age for, ripe for (+ gen)
54	οἴμαι impf ᾤμην	I think
	τρέφω	I rear, I bring up
	γοάομαι	I wail
	ἱκετεύω ἱκέτευσα	I beseech
	φονεύς -έως ὁ	murderer
57	ὡσαύτως	in the same way
	γιγνώσκω	(here) I think, I hold an opinion
	ἀληθεύω	I speak truthfully
	μάρτυς -υρος ὁ	witness

Reading 4:

An Adulterer Apprehended

The orator Lysias was the son of a rich businessman from Syracuse who had settled in Athens. When the family lost their wealth in the upheavals at the end of the Peloponnesian War, he became a professional speech-writer. People involved in court cases in Athens spoke on their own behalf, but could have their speeches written for them. This passage comes from On the murder of Eratosthenes, *a speech of self-defence by a husband who had killed his wife's lover: it gives a good insight into everyday life in Athens (1.6-27).*

ἐγὼ γάρ, ὦ Ἀθηναῖοι, ἐπειδὴ ἔδοξέ μοι γῆμαι καὶ γυναῖκα ἠγαγόμην εἰς
τὴν οἰκίαν, τὸν μὲν ἄλλον χρόνον οὕτω διεκείμην ὥστε μήτε λυπεῖν μήτε
λίαν ἐπ' ἐκείνῃ εἶναι ὅ τι ἂν ἐθέλῃ ποιεῖν, ἐφύλαττόν τε ὡς οἷόν τε ἦν,
καὶ προσεῖχον τὸν νοῦν ὥσπερ εἰκὸς ἦν· ἐπειδὴ δέ μοι παιδίον γίγνεται,
5 ἐπίστευον ἤδη καὶ πάντα τὰ ἐμαυτοῦ ἐκείνῃ παρέδωκα, ἡγούμενος ταύτην
οἰκειότητα μεγίστην εἶναι. ἐν μὲν οὖν τῷ πρώτῳ χρόνῳ, ὦ Ἀθηναῖοι,

	διακεῖμαι	I am disposed, I am inclined
	λυπέω	I cause grief to
	λίαν	excessively
	ἐπ' ἐκείνῃ	on her own terms, left to her own devices
4	προσέχω	I apply
	παιδίον -ου τό	baby
	οἰκειότης -ητος ἡ	intimacy

105

πασῶν ἦν βελτίστη, καὶ γὰρ <u>οἰκονόμος</u> δεινὴ καὶ <u>φειδωλὸς</u> καὶ <u>ἀκριβῶς</u>
πάντα <u>διοικοῦσα</u>· ἐπειδὴ δέ μοι ἡ μήτηρ ἐτελεύτησεν, ἣ πάντων τῶν
κακῶν ἀποθανοῦσα αἰτία μοι γεγένηται· ἐπ' <u>ἐκφορὰν</u> γὰρ αὐτῇ
10 <u>ἀκολουθήσασα</u> ἡ ἐμὴ γυνὴ ὑπὸ τούτου τοῦ ἀνθρώπου ὀφθεῖσα, χρόνῳ
διαφθείρεται· <u>ἐπιτηρῶν</u> γὰρ τὴν <u>θεράπαιναν</u> τὴν εἰς τὴν ἀγορὰν
βαδίζουσαν καὶ λόγους <u>προσφέρων</u> ἀπώλεσεν αὐτήν.

πρῶτον μὲν οὖν, ὦ ἄνδρες (δεῖ γὰρ ταῦθ' ὑμῖν <u>διηγήσασθαι</u>), <u>οἰκίδιον</u> ἔστι
μοι <u>διπλοῦν</u>, ἴσα ἔχον τὰ <u>ἄνω</u> τοῖς <u>κάτω</u> κατὰ τὴν <u>γυναικωνῖτιν</u> καὶ κατὰ
15 τὴν <u>ἀνδρωνῖτιν</u>. ἐπειδὴ δὲ τὸ παιδίον ἐγένετο ἡμῖν, ἡ μήτηρ αὐτὸ
<u>ἐθήλαζεν</u>· ἵνα δὲ μή, ὁπότε <u>λοῦσθαι</u> δέοι, κινδυνεύῃ κατὰ τῆς <u>κλίμακος</u>
καταβαίνουσα, ἐγὼ μὲν ἄνω <u>διῃτώμην</u>, αἱ δὲ γυναῖκες κάτω. καὶ οὕτως
ἤδη <u>συνειθισμένον</u> ἦν, ὥστε πολλάκις ἡ γυνὴ ἀπῄει κάτω καθευδήσουσα
ὡς τὸ παιδίον, ἵνα τὸν <u>τιτθὸν</u> αὐτῷ διδῷ καὶ μὴ βοᾷ. καὶ ταῦτα πολὺν
20 χρόνον οὕτως ἐγίγνετο, καὶ ἐγὼ οὐδέποτε <u>ὑπώπτευσα</u>, ἀλλ' οὕτως <u>ἠλιθίως</u>
<u>διεκείμην</u>, ὥστε <u>ᾤμην</u> τὴν <u>ἑαυτοῦ</u> γυναῖκα πασῶν σωφρονεστάτην εἶναι
τῶν ἐν τῇ πόλει.

<u>προϊόντος</u> δὲ τοῦ χρόνου, ὦ ἄνδρες, ἧκον μὲν <u>ἀπροσδοκήτως</u> ἐξ
ἀγροῦ, μετὰ δὲ τὸ δεῖπνον τὸ παιδίον ἐβόα καὶ <u>ἐδυσκόλαινεν</u> ὑπὸ τῆς

	οἰκονόμος -ου ὁ/ἡ	housekeeper
	φειδωλός -ή -όν	economical
	ἀκριβῶς	exactly, in precise order
	διοικέω	I organize
9	ἐκφορά -ᾶς ἡ	funeral
	ἀκολουθέω	I follow (+ *dat*)
	ἐπιτηρέω	I look out for
	θεράπαινα -ης ἡ	maidservant
	προσφέρω	I apply, I use
13	διηγέομαι διηγησάμην	I explain
	οἰκίδιον -ου τό	house
	διπλοῦς -ῆ -οῦν	*lit* double, *here* on two floors
	ἄνω	upstairs
	κάτω	downstairs
14	γυναικωνῖτις *acc* -ιν ἡ	women's quarters
	ἀνδρωνῖτις *acc* -ιν ἡ	men's quarters
	θηλάζω	I breast feed
	λούω	I wash
	κλῖμαξ -ακος ἡ	staircase
17	διαιτάομαι	I live
	συνειθισμένον ἦν	it was the custom (*impsnl plpf pass of* συνεθίζω I accustom)
	τιτθός -οῦ ὁ	teat, nipple
	ὑποπτεύω ὑπώπτευσα	I suspect
20	ἠλιθίως	foolishly
	διακείμαι	I am disposed, I am inclined
	οἶμαι *impf* ᾤμην	I think
	ἑαυτοῦ	(= ἐμαυτοῦ)
	πρόειμι	(*of time*) elapse, go on
23	ἀπροσδοκήτως	unexpectedly
	δυσκολαίνω	I am discontented

106

θεραπαίνης ἐπίτηδες λυπούμενον, ἵνα ταῦτα ποιῇ· ὁ γὰρ ἄνθρωπος ἔνδον
25 ἦν· ὕστερον γὰρ ἅπαντα ἐπυθόμην. καὶ ἐγὼ τὴν γυναῖκα ἀπιέναι
ἐκέλευον καὶ δοῦναι τῷ παιδίῳ τὸν τιτθόν, ἵνα παύσηται κλᾶον. ἡ δὲ τὸ
μὲν πρῶτον οὐκ ἤθελεν, ὡς ἂν ἀσμένη με ἑορακυῖα ἥκοντα διὰ χρόνου·
ἐπειδὴ δὲ ἐγὼ ὠργιζόμην καὶ ἐκέλευον αὐτὴν ἀπιέναι, "ἵνα σύ γε," ἔφη,
"πειρᾷς ἐνταῦθα τὴν παιδίσκην· καὶ πρότερον δὲ μεθύων εἷλκες αὐτήν."
30 κἀγὼ μὲν ἐγέλων, ἐκείνη δὲ ἀναστᾶσα καὶ ἀπιοῦσα προστίθησι τὴν
θύραν, προσποιουμένη παίζειν, καὶ τὴν κλεῖν ἐφέλκεται. κἀγὼ τούτων
οὐδὲν ἐνθυμούμενος οὐδ' ὑπονοῶν ἐκάθευδον ἄσμενος, ἥκων ἐξ ἀγροῦ.
ἐπειδὴ δὲ ἦν πρὸς ἡμέραν, ἧκεν ἐκείνη καὶ τὴν θύραν ἀνέῳξεν. ἐρομένου
δέ μου τί αἱ θύραι νύκτωρ ψοφοῖεν, ἔφασκε τὸν λύχνον ἀποσβεσθῆναι
35 τὸν παρὰ τῷ παιδίῳ, εἶτα ἐκ τῶν γειτόνων ἐνάψασθαι. ἐσιώπων ἐγὼ καὶ
ταῦτα οὕτως ἔχειν ἡγούμην. ἔδοξε δέ μοι, ὦ ἄνδρες, τὸ πρόσωπον
ἐψιμυθιῶσθαι, τοῦ ἀδελφοῦ τεθνεῶτος οὔπω τριάκονθ' ἡμέρας· ὅμως δ'
οὐδ' οὕτως οὐδὲν εἰπὼν περὶ τοῦ πράγματος ἐξελθὼν ᾠχόμην ἔξω σιωπῇ.

μετὰ δὲ ταῦτα, ὦ ἄνδρες, χρόνου μεταξὺ διαγενομένου καὶ ἐμοῦ πολὺ
40 ἀπολελειμμένου τῶν ἐμαυτοῦ κακῶν, προσέρχεταί μοί τις πρεσβῦτις

	ἐπίτηδες	deliberately, on purpose
	λυπέω	I cause grief to
	ἔνδον	inside, *here* in the house
	κλάω	I cry
29	πειράω	(*lit* I try) *here* I (try to) seduce (+ *gen*)
	παιδίσκη -ης ἡ	young girl, maid
	μεθύω	I am drunk
	προσποιέομαι	I pretend
	παίζω	I play, I act in fun
31	κλείς κλειδός ἡ	bolt (on door)
	ἐφέλκομαι	I draw, I fasten
	ἐνθυμέομαι	I take to heart
	ὑπονοέω	I suspect
	ἀνοίγνυμι ἀνέῳξα	I open
34	νύκτωρ	during the night
	ψοφέω	I make a noise
	φάσκω	I say
	λύχνος -ου ὁ	lamp
	ἀποσβέννυμι	
34	*aor pass* ἀπεσβέσθην	I extinguish
	γείτων -ονος ὁ/ἡ	neighbour
	ἐνάπτομαι ἐνηψάμην	I light
	σιωπάω	I am silent
	πρόσωπον -ου τό	face
37	ψιμυθιόω	
	pf mid inf ἐψιμυθιῶσθαι	I paint with white lead (*as cosmetic*)
	οὔπω	not yet
	οἴχομαι	I am gone
	σιωπῇ	in silence
39	μεταξύ	meanwhile
	διαγίγνομαι διεγενόμην	(*of time*) pass, elapse
	ἀπολείπομαι *pf* ἀπολέλειμαι	I am left unaware (of, + *gen*)
	πρεσβῦτις -ιδος ἡ	old (woman)

107

ἄνθρωπος, ὑπὸ γυναικὸς <u>ὑποπεμφθεῖσα</u> ἣν ἐκεῖνος <u>ἐμοίχευεν</u>, ὡς ἐγὼ
ὕστερον ἤκουον· αὕτη δὲ ὀργιζομένη καὶ ἀδικεῖσθαι νομίζουσα, ὅτι
οὐκέτι ὁμοίως <u>ἐφοίτα</u> παρ' αὐτήν, ἐφύλαττεν ἕως ἐξηῦρεν ὅ τι εἴη τὸ
αἴτιον. προσελθοῦσα οὖν μοι ἐγγὺς ἡ ἄνθρωπος τῆς οἰκίας τῆς ἐμῆς
45 <u>ἐπιτηροῦσα</u>, "Εὐφίλητε," ἔφη, "μηδεμιᾷ <u>πολυπραγμοσύνῃ</u> προσεληλυθέναι
με νόμιζε πρὸς σέ· ὁ γὰρ ἀνὴρ ὁ ὑβρίζων εἰς σὲ καὶ τὴν σὴν γυναῖκα
ἐχθρὸς ὢν ἡμῖν τυγχάνει. ἐὰν οὖν λάβῃς τὴν <u>θεράπαιναν</u> τὴν εἰς ἀγορὰν
βαδίζουσαν καὶ <u>διακονοῦσαν</u> ὑμῖν καὶ <u>βασανίσῃς</u>, ἅπαντα πεύσει. ἔστι
δ'," ἔφη, "<u>Ἐρατοσθένης Ὀῆθεν</u> ὁ ταῦτα πράττων, ὃς οὐ μόνον τὴν σὴν
50 γυναῖκα διέφθαρκεν ἀλλὰ καὶ ἄλλας πολλάς· ταύτην γὰρ τὴν τέχνην
ἔχει." ταῦτα εἰποῦσα, ὦ ἄνδρες, ἐκείνη μὲν <u>ἀπηλλάγη</u>, ἐγὼ δ' <u>εὐθέως</u>
ἐταραττόμην, καὶ πάντα μου εἰς τὴν γνώμην εἰσῄει, καὶ <u>μεστὸς</u> ἦν
<u>ὑποψίας</u>, <u>ἐνθυμούμενος</u> μὲν ὡς <u>ἀπεκλήσθην</u> ἐν τῷ <u>δωματίῳ</u>,
<u>ἀναμιμνησκόμενος</u> δὲ ὅτι ἐν ἐκείνῃ τῇ νυκτὶ <u>ἐψόφει</u> ἡ <u>μέταυλος</u> θύρα καὶ
55 ἡ <u>αὔλειος</u>, ὃ οὐδέποτε ἐγένετο, ἔδοξέ τέ μοι ἡ γυνὴ <u>ἐψιμυθιῶσθαι</u>. ταῦτά
μου πάντα εἰς τὴν γνώμην εἰσῄει, καὶ μεστὸς ἦ ὑποψίας.

ἐλθὼν δὲ οἴκαδε ἐκέλευον <u>ἀκολουθεῖν</u> μοι τὴν θεράπαιναν εἰς τὴν
ἀγοράν, ἀγαγὼν δ' αὐτὴν ὡς τῶν <u>ἐπιτηδείων</u> τινὰ ἔλεγον ὅτι ἐγὼ πάντα
εἴην πεπυσμένος τὰ γιγνόμενα ἐν τῇ οἰκίᾳ· "σοὶ οὖν," ἔφη, "ἔξεστι δυοῖν
60 ὁπότερον βούλει ἑλέσθαι, ἢ <u>μαστιγωθεῖσαν</u> εἰς <u>μύλωνα</u> ἐμπεσεῖν καὶ

	ὑποπέμπω *aor pass* ὑπεπέμφθην	I send secretly
	μοιχεύω	I commit adultery with
	φοιτάω	I visit frequently
	ἐπιτηρέω	I watch out for
45	πολυπραγμοσύνη -ης ἡ	interference, meddlesomeness
	θεράπαινα -ης ἡ	maidservant
	διακονέω	I serve, I wait on (+ *dat*)
	βασανίζω ἐβασάνισα	I torture (*to get evidence - routinely done to slaves*)
	Ἐρατοσθένης -ους ὁ	Eratosthenes
49	Ὀῆθεν	from Oe (*district of Athens*)
	ἀπαλάσσομαι ἀπηλλάγην	I go away
	εὐθέως	(= εὐθύς)
	μεστός -ή -όν	full
	ὑποψία -ας ἡ	suspicion
53	ἐνθυμέομαι	I bear in mind
	ἀποκλήω *aor pass* ἀπεκλήσθην	I shut in
	δωμάτιον -ου τό	room
	ἀναμιμνήσκομαι	I remember
	ψοφέω	I make a noise
54	μέταυλος -ον	inner
	αὔλειος -ον	of the courtyard
	ψιμυθιόω	
	pf mid inf ἐψιμυθιῶσθαι	I paint with white lead
	ἀκολουθέω	I follow, I accompany (+ *dat*)
58	ἐπιτήδειος -ου ὁ	companion
	μαστιγόω	
	aor pass ἐμαστιγώθην	I whip
	μυλών -ῶνος ὁ	mill-house

μηδέποτε παύσασθαι κακοῖς τοιούτοις <u>συνεχομένην</u>, ἢ <u>κατειποῦσαν</u>
ἅπαντα τἀληθῆ μηδὲν παθεῖν κακόν, ἀλλὰ <u>συγγνώμης</u> παρ᾽ ἐμοῦ τυχεῖν
τῶν ἡμαρτημένων. ψεύση δὲ μηδέν, ἀλλὰ πάντα τἀληθῆ λέγε." κἀκείνη τὸ
μὲν πρῶτον <u>ἔξαρνος</u> ἦν, καὶ ποιεῖν ἐκέλευεν ὅ τι βούλομαι· οὐδὲν γὰρ
65 εἰδέναι· ἐπειδὴ δὲ ἐγὼ <u>ἐμνήσθην</u> Ἐρατοσθένους πρὸς αὐτήν, καὶ εἶπον ὅτι
οὗτος ὁ <u>φοιτῶν</u> εἴη πρὸς τὴν γυναῖκα, <u>ἐξεπλάγη</u> ἡγησαμένη με πάντα
<u>ἀκριβῶς</u> ἐγνωκέναι. καὶ τότε ἤδη πρὸς τὰ <u>γόνατά</u> μου πεσοῦσα, καὶ
<u>πίστιν</u> παρ᾽ ἐμοῦ λαβοῦσα μηδὲν πείσεσθαι κακόν, κατηγόρει πρῶτον μὲν
ὡς μετὰ τὴν <u>ἐκφορὰν</u> αὐτῇ προσίοι, ἔπειτα ὡς αὐτὴ τελευτῶσα
70 <u>εἰσαγγείλειε</u> καὶ ὡς ἐκείνη τῷ χρόνῳ πεισθείη, καὶ τὰς <u>εἰσόδους</u> οἷς
τρόποις προσίοιτο, καὶ ὡς <u>Θεσμοφορίοις</u> ἐμοῦ ἐν ἀγρῷ ὄντος <u>ᾤχετο</u> εἰς τὸ
ἱερὸν μετὰ τῆς μητρὸς τῆς ἐκείνου· καὶ τἆλλα τὰ γενόμενα πάντα
ἀκριβῶς <u>διηγήσατο</u>.

ἐπειδὴ δὲ πάντα εἴρητο αὐτῇ, εἶπον ἐγώ, "<u>ὅπως</u> τοίνυν ταῦτα μηδεὶς
75 ἀνθρώπων πεύσεται· εἰ δὲ μή, οὐδέν σοι <u>κύριον</u> ἔσται τῶν πρὸς ἔμ᾽
ὡμολογημένων. ἀξιῶ δὲ σε <u>ἐπ᾽ αὐτοφώρῳ</u> ταῦτά μοι ἐπιδεῖξαι· ἐγὼ γὰρ
οὐδὲν δέομαι λόγων, ἀλλὰ τὸ ἔργον <u>φανερὸν</u> γενέσθαι, <u>εἴπερ</u> οὕτως ἔχει."
ὡμολόγει ταῦτα ποιήσειν. καὶ μετὰ ταῦτα <u>διεγένοντο</u> ἡμέραι τέτταρες ἢ
πέντε καὶ ἐπ᾽ αὐτοφώρῳ τὸν <u>μοιχὸν</u> ἔνδον ἔλαβον, ὡς ἐγὼ μεγάλοις ὑμῖν
80 <u>τεκμηρίοις</u> ἐπιδείξω. πρῶτον δὲ διηγήσασθαι βούλομαι τὰ πραχθέντα τῇ
<u>τελευταίᾳ</u> ἡμέρᾳ. <u>Σώστρατος</u> ἦν μοι <u>ἐπιτήδειος</u> καὶ φίλος. τούτῳ ἡλίου

	συνέχομαι	I am afflicted
	καταλέγω κατεῖπον	I relate, I list
	συγγνώμη -ης ἡ	pardon
	ἔξαρνος -ον	denying
65	μιμνήσκομαι ἐμνήσθην	I mention (+ gen)
	φοιτάω	I visit frequently
	ἐκπλήσσω aor pass ἐξεπλάγην	I strike with terror
	ἀκριβῶς	exactly, in detail
	γόνυ -ατος τό	knee
68	πίστις -εως ἡ	pledge
	ἐκφορά -ᾶς ἡ	funeral
	εἰσαγγέλλω	I act as a messenger
	εἴσοδος -ου ἡ	entrance
	Θεσμοφόρια -ων τά	Thesmophoria (Athenian festival for women only)
71	οἴχομαι impf ᾠχόμην	I am gone
	διηγέομαι διηγησάμην	I explain
	ὅπως	(+ fut) make sure that ...
	κύριος -α -ον	valid
	ἐπ᾽ αὐτοφώρῳ	caught in the act
77	φανερός -ά -όν	manifest, clearly known
	εἴπερ	if ... really
	διαγίγνομαι διεγενόμην	(of time) pass, elapse
	μοιχός -οῦ ὁ	adulterer
	τεκμήριον -ου τό	proof
81	τελευταῖος -α -ον	final, last
	Σώστρατος -ου ὁ	Sostratus
	ἐπιτήδειος -ου ὁ	companion

δεδυκότος ἰόντι ἐξ ἀγροῦ <u>ἀπήντησα</u>. εἰδὼς δ᾽ ἐγὼ ὅτι <u>τηνικαῦτα</u> ἀφιγμένος
οὐδένα <u>καταλήψοιτο</u> οἴκοι τῶν ἐπιτηδείων, ἐκέλευον <u>συνδειπνεῖν</u>· καὶ
ἐλθόντες οἴκαδε ὡς ἐμέ, ἀναβάντες εἰς τὸ <u>ὑπερῷον</u> ἐδειπνοῦμεν. ἐπειδὴ δὲ
85 καλῶς αὐτῷ εἶχεν, ἐκεῖνος μὲν ἀπιὼν ᾤχετο, ἐγὼ δ᾽ ἐκάθευδον.

ὁ δ᾽ Ἐρατοσθένης, ὦ ἄνδρες, εἰσέρχεται, καὶ ἡ θεράπαινα <u>ἐπεγείρασά</u> με
εὐθὺς <u>φράζει</u> ὅτι <u>ἔνδον</u> ἐστί. κἀγὼ εἰπὼν ἐκείνῃ <u>ἐπιμελεῖσθαι</u> τῆς θύρας,
καταβὰς σιωπῇ ἐξέρχομαι, καὶ ἀφικνοῦμαι ὡς <u>τὸν καὶ τόν</u>, καὶ τοὺς μὲν
οὐκ ἔνδον κατέλαβον, τοὺς δὲ οὐδ᾽ <u>ἐπιδημοῦντας</u> ηὗρον. <u>παραλαβὼν</u> δ᾽ ὡς
90 οἷον τ᾽ ἦν πλείστους ἐκ τῶν παρόντων ἐβάδιζον. καὶ <u>δᾷδας</u> λαβόντες ἐκ
τοῦ <u>ἐγγύτατα καπηλείου</u> εἰσερχόμεθα, <u>ἀνεῳγμένης</u> τῆς θύρας καὶ ὑπὸ τῆς
ἀνθρώπου παρεσκευασμένης. <u>ὤσαντες</u> δὲ τὴν θύραν τοῦ <u>δωματίου</u> οἱ μὲν
πρῶτοι εἰσιόντες ἔτι εἴδομεν αὐτὸν κατακείμενον παρὰ τῇ γυναικί, οἱ δ᾽
ὕστερον ἐν τῇ <u>κλίνῃ</u> γυμνὸν ἑστηκότα. ἐγὼ δ᾽, ὦ ἄνδρες, <u>πατάξας</u>
95 καταβάλλω αὐτόν, καὶ <u>τὼ χεῖρε</u> περιαγαγὼν εἰς <u>τοὐπισθεν</u> καὶ <u>δήσας</u>
ἠρώτων διὰ τί ὑβρίζει εἰς τὴν οἰκίαν τὴν ἐμὴν εἰσιών. κἀκεῖνος ἀδικεῖν
μὲν ὡμολόγει, <u>ἠντεβόλει</u> δὲ καὶ <u>ἱκέτευε</u> μὴ ἀποκτεῖναι ἀλλ᾽ ἀργύριον
πράξασθαι. ἐγὼ δ᾽ εἶπον <u>ὅτι</u> "οὐκ ἐγώ σε ἀποκτενῶ, ἀλλ᾽ ὁ τῆς πόλεως
νόμος, ὃν σὺ <u>παραβαίνων περὶ ἐλάττονος</u> τῶν <u>ἡδονῶν</u> ἐποιήσω, καὶ

	δύω *pf* δέδυκα	(*of the sun*) set
	ἀπαντάω ἀπήντησα	I meet (+ *dat*)
	τηνικαῦτα	at that hour
	καταλαμβάνω	I find
83	συνδειπνέω	I dine with
	ὑπερῷον -ου τό	upper room
	ἐπεγείρω ἐπήγειρα	I waken (someone) up
	φράζω	I say, I tell
	ἔνδον	inside, in the house
87	ἐπιμελέομαι	I keep a watch on (+ *gen*)
	σιωπῇ	in silence
	τὸν καὶ τόν	this man and that
	ἐπιδημέω	I am in town
	παραλαμβάνω παρέλαβον	I take with me
90	δᾷς δᾳδός ἡ	torch
	ἐγγύτατα	very nearby
	καπηλεῖον -ου τό	shop, tavern
	ἀνοιγνύμι *pf pass* ἀνέῳγμαι	I open
	ὠθέω ὦσα	I push
87	δωμάτιον -ου τό	room
	κλίνη -ης ἡ	bed
	πατάσσω ἐπάταξα	I strike
	τὼ χεῖρε	(*dual form*)
	τοὐπισθεν	(*crasis of* τὸ ὄπισθεν), *i.e.* behind his back
85	δέω ἔδησα	I bind, I tie up
	ἀντιβολέω	I entreat
	ἱκετεύω	I beg
	ὅτι	(*here redundant, introducing direct speech*)
	παραβαίνω	I transgress
99	περὶ ἐλάττονος ποιέομαι	I regard as less important (than, + *gen*)
	ἡδονή -ῆς ἡ	pleasure

100 μᾶλλον εἵλου τοιοῦτον <u>ἁμάρτημα</u> ἐξαμαρτάνειν εἰς τὴν γυναῖκα τὴν ἐμὴν καὶ εἰς τοὺς παῖδας τοὺς ἐμοὺς ἢ τοῖς νόμοις πείθεσθαι καὶ <u>κόσμιος</u> εἶναι." οὕτως, ὦ ἄνδρες, ἐκεῖνος τούτων ἔτυχεν ὧνπερ οἱ νόμοι κελεύουσι τοὺς τὰ τοιαῦτα πράττοντας.

ἁμάρτημα -ατος τό	offence
κόσμιος -α -ον	decent, orderly

Reading 5:

The Curse of Cylon

Cylon was an Athenian aristocrat who in 632 BC attempted to establish a tyranny. (Solon's reforms aimed to forestall further attemps, but we saw in the story of Peisistratus that Athens did in due course have a tyrant). With the help of his father-in-law Theagenes, tyrant of neighbouring Megara, Cylon seized the Acropolis. The Athenians under the archon (chief magistrate) Megacles besieged it: Cylon and his brother escaped, but their associates were killed despite taking refuge as suppliants at the altar of Athene. Because of this sacrilege Megacles' family the Alcmaeonids were thenceforth under a curse (hence Peisistratus was unwilling to have children by the daughter of Megacles' grandson and namesake). Thucydides in his History of the Peloponnesian War *here (in his account of the build-up to the outbreak of hostilities in 431 BC) describes how the Spartans tried to use the curse as a propaganda weapon against the Athenian leader Pericles, whose mother Agariste was an Alcmaeonid. Note that Thucydides writes* ξύν *for* σύν *(1.126-7).*

ἐν τούτῳ δὲ <u>ἐπρεσβεύοντο</u> τῷ χρονῷ πρὸς τοὺς Ἀθηναίους <u>ἐγκλήματα</u> ποιούμενοι, ὅπως σφίσιν ὅτι μεγίστη <u>πρόφασις</u> εἴη πολεμεῖν, ἢν μή τι <u>ἐσακούωσιν</u>. καὶ πρῶτον μὲν πρέσβεις πέμψαντες οἱ Λακεδαιμόνιοι ἐκέλευον τοὺς Ἀθηναίους τὸ <u>ἄγος</u> ἐλαύνειν τῆς θεοῦ· τὸ δὲ ἄγος ἦν
5 τοιόνδε. <u>Κύλων</u> ἦν Ἀθηναῖος ἀνὴρ <u>Ὀλυμπιονίκης</u> τῶν πάλαι εὐγενής τε καὶ δυνατός, ἐγεγαμήκει δὲ θυγατέρα <u>Θεαγένους Μεγαρέως</u> ἀνδρός, ὃς <u>κατ'</u> ἐκεῖνον τὸν χρόνον <u>ἐτυράννει Μεγάρων</u>. χρωμένῳ δὲ τῷ Κύλωνι ἐν <u>Δελφοῖς ἀνεῖλεν</u> ὁ θεὸς ἐν τοῦ Διὸς τῇ μεγίστῃ ἑορτῇ <u>καταλαβεῖν</u> τὴν Ἀθηναίων <u>ἀκρόπολιν</u>. ὁ δὲ παρά τε τοῦ Θεαγένους <u>δύναμιν</u> λαβὼν καὶ

	πρεσβεύομαι	I send ambassadors (*subject here is* the Spartans)
	ἔγκλημα -ατος τό	complaint
	πρόφασις -εως ἡ	pretext
	ἐσακούω	I pay attention
4	ἄγος -ους τό	curse
	Κύλων -ωνος ὁ	Cylon
	Ὀλυμπιονίκης -ου ὁ	Olympic victor
	Θεαγένης -ους ὁ	Theagenes
	Μεγαρεύς -εως	of Megara
7	κατά (+ *acc*)	(*here*) at
	τυραννέω	I am tyrant
	Μέγαρα -ων τά	Megara
	χράομαι	(*here*) I consult an oracle
	Δελφοί -ῶν οἱ	Delphi
8	ἀναιρέω ἀνεῖλον	I reply
	καταλαμβάνω κατέλαβον	I seize
	ἀκρόπολις -εως ἡ	acropolis, citadel
	δύναμις -εως ἡ	(*here*) force, troops

111

10 τοὺς φίλους ἀναπείσας, ἐπειδὴ ἐπῆλθεν Ὀλύμπια τὰ ἐν Πελοποννήσῳ,
    κατέλαβε τὴν ἀκρόπολιν ὡς ἐπὶ τυραννίδι, νομίσας ἑορτήν τε τοῦ Διὸς
    μεγίστην εἶναι καὶ ἑαυτῷ τι προσήκειν Ὀλύμπια νενικήκοτι. εἰ δὲ ἐν τῇ
    Ἀττικῇ ἢ ἄλλοθί που ἡ μεγίστη ἑορτὴ εἴρητο, οὔτε ἐκεῖνος ἔτι κατενόησε
    τό τε μαντεῖον οὐκ ἐδήλου (ἔστι γὰρ καὶ Ἀθηναίοις Διάσια ἃ καλεῖται
15 Διὸς ἑορτὴ Μειλιχίου μεγίστη ἔξω τῆς πόλεως, ἐν ᾗ πανδημεὶ θύουσι
    πολλὰ οὐχ ἱερεῖα, ἀλλ' ἁγνὰ θύματα ἐπιχώρια), δοκῶν δὲ ὀρθῶς
    γιγνώσκειν ἐπεχείρησε τῷ ἔργῳ.

    οἱ δὲ Ἀθηναῖοι αἰσθόμενοι ἐβοήθησάν τε πανδημεὶ ἐκ τῶν ἀγρῶν ἐπ'
    αὐτοὺς καὶ προσκαθεζόμενοι ἐπολιόρκουν. χρόνου δὲ ἐπιγιγνομένου οἱ
20 Ἀθηναῖοι τρυχόμενοι τῇ προσεδρίᾳ ἀπῆλθον οἱ πολλοί, ἐπιτρέψαντες τοῖς
    ἐννέα ἄρχουσι τήν τε φυλακὴν καὶ τὸ πᾶν αὐτοκράτορσι διαθεῖναι ᾗ ἂν
    ἄριστα διαγιγνώσκωσιν· τότε δὲ τὰ πολλὰ τῶν πολιτικῶν οἱ ἐννέα
    ἄρχοντες ἔπρασσον. οἱ δὲ μετὰ τοῦ Κύλωνος πολιορκούμενοι φλαύρως
    εἶχον σίτου τε καὶ ὕδατος ἀπορίᾳ. ὁ μὲν οὖν Κύλων καὶ ὁ ἀδελφὸς
25 αὐτοῦ ἐκδιδράσκουσιν· οἱ δ' ἄλλοι ὡς ἐπιέζοντο καί τινες καὶ

	ἀναπείθω ἀνέπεισα	I win over, I persuade
	ἐπέρχομαι ἐπῆλθον	(of events) come round, occur
	Ὀλύμπια -ων τά	Olympic festival
	Πελοπόννησος -ου ἡ	Peloponnese
11	ἐπί (+ dat)	(here) for the purpose of, to try to gain
	τυραννίς -ίδος ἡ	tyranny, tyrannical power
	προσήκει	it is fitting
	Ἀττική -ῆς ἡ	Attica
	ἄλλοθι	somewhere else
13	εἴρητο	(plpf pass 3 sg of λέγω)
	κατανοέω	I consider
	Διάσια -ων τά	Diasia (Athenian festival of Zeus)
	μειλίχιος -α -ον	gracious (as proper name, a title of Zeus)
	πανδημεί	with all the people
16	ἱερεῖον -ου τό	blood sacrifice
	ἁγνός -ή -όν	pure
	θῦμα -ατος τό	offering
	ἐπιχώριος -ον	of the country, local
	ἐπιχειρέω	I attempt (+ dat)
19	προσκαθέζομαι	I blockade
	ἐπιγίγνομαι	(of time) pass, elapse
	τρυχόομαι	I become wearied
	προσεδρία -ας ἡ	blockade
	ἄρχων -οντος ὁ	(here) Archon (one of nine annual magistrates)
21	φυλακή -ῆς ἡ	keeping guard
	αὐτοκράτωρ -ορος	with full power
	διατίθημι aor inf διαθεῖναι	I arrange, I settle (something)
	διαγιγνώσκω	I decide
	πολιτικά -ῶν τά	politics, political affairs
23	φλαύρως ἔχω	I am in a bad way
	ἐκδιδράσκω	I escape
	πιέζω	I crush, I oppress

ἀπέθνησκον ὑπὸ τοῦ λιμοῦ, καθίζουσιν ἐπὶ τὸν βωμὸν ἱκέται τὸν ἐν τῇ ἀκροπόλει. ἀναστήσαντες δὲ αὐτοὺς οἱ τῶν Ἀθηναίων ἐπιτετραμμένοι τὴν φυλακήν, ὡς ἑώρων ἀποθνήσκοντας ἐν τῷ ἱερῷ, ἐφ' ᾧ μηδὲν κακὸν ποιήσουσιν, ἀπαγαγόντες ἀπέκτειναν· καθεζομένους δέ τινας καὶ ἐπὶ τῶν
30 σεμνῶν θεῶν τοῖς βωμοῖς ἐν τῇ παρόδῳ ἀπεχρήσαντο. καὶ ἀπὸ τούτου ἐναγεῖς καὶ ἀλιτήριοι τῆς θεοῦ ἐκεῖνοί τε ἐκαλοῦντο καὶ τὸ γένος τὸ ἀπ' ἐκείνων. ἤλασαν μὲν οὖν καὶ οἱ Ἀθηναῖοι τοὺς ἐναγεῖς τούτους, ἤλασε δὲ καὶ Κλεομένης ὁ Λακεδαιμόνιος ὕστερον μετὰ Ἀθηναίων στασιαζόντων, τούς τε ζῶντας ἐλαύνοντες καὶ τῶν τεθνεώτων τὰ ὀστᾶ
35 ἀνελόντες ἐξέβαλον· κατῆλθον μέντοι ὕστερον, καὶ τὸ γένος αὐτῶν ἔστιν ἔτι ἐν τῇ πόλει.

τοῦτο δὴ τὸ ἄγος οἱ Λακεδαιμόνιοι ἐκέλευον ἐλαύνειν δῆθεν τοῖς θεοῖς πρῶτον τιμωροῦντες, εἰδότες δὲ Περικλέα τὸν Ξανθίππου προσεχόμενον αὐτῷ κατὰ τὴν μητέρα καὶ νομίζοντες ἐκπεσόντος αὐτοῦ ῥᾷον ἂν σφίσι
40 προχωρεῖν τὰ ἀπὸ τῶν Ἀθηναίων. οὐ μέντοι τοσοῦτον ἤλπιζον παθεῖν ἂν αὐτὸν τοῦτο ὅσον διαβολὴν οἴσειν αὐτῷ πρὸς τὴν πόλιν ὡς καὶ διὰ τὴν ἐκείνου ξυμφορὰν τὸ μέρος ἔσται ὁ πόλεμος. ὢν γὰρ δυνατώτατος τῶν καθ' ἑαυτὸν καὶ ἄγων τὴν πολιτείαν ἠναντιοῦτο πάντα τοῖς Λακεδαιμονίοις, καὶ οὐκ εἴα ὑπείκειν, ἀλλ' ἐς τὸν πόλεμον ὥρμα τοὺς
45 Ἀθηναίους.

	λιμός -οῦ ὁ	hunger
	ἱκέτης -ου ὁ	suppliant (*person claiming protection or sanctuary*)
	ἐπιτετραμμένοι	(*pf pass pple m nom pl of* ἐπιτρέπω)
	καθέζομαι	I sit
30	σεμνός -ή -όν	revered (*as proper name, euphemistic title of the Furies*)
	πάροδος -ου ἡ	passing by (ἐν τῇ ~ as they passed by)
	ἀποχράομαι ἀπεχρησάμην	I kill
	ἐναγής -ές	polluted, accursed
31	ἀλιτήριος -ον	guilty
	Κλεομένης -ους ὁ	Cleomenes
	στασιάζω	I join a faction
	τεθνεώτων	(*pf pple m gen pl of* ἀποθνήσκω)
	ὀστέον -ου τό	bone
35	κατέρχομαι κατῆλθον	I return
	ἄγος -ους τό	curse
	δῆθεν	of course *here ironic, i.e.* as they claimed
	Περικλῆς -έους ὁ	Pericles
	Ξάνθιππος -ου ὁ	Xanthippus (*gen indicates* son of)
38	προσέχομαι	I am connected
	ἐκπίπτω ἐξέπεσον	(*here*) I am exiled
	προχωρέω	I advance, I succeed
	διαβολή -ῆς ἡ	grounds for reproach, unpopularity
	κατά (+ *acc*)	(*here*) in the time of
43	πολιτεία -ας ἡ	state, government
	ἐναντιόομαι	I oppose (+ *dat*)
	ὑπείκω	I make concessions
	ὁρμάω	I urge on

113

Reading 6:
Conon and his Gang

Demosthenes (writing in the middle of the fourth century BC) was the greatest of the Athenian orators. He was prominent in politics and leader of the resistance to the encroachments of Philip II of Macedon (father of Alexander the Great). He also however (like Lysias in an earlier generation) wrote private speeches for people involved in lawsuits to read out in court. This passage comes from a speech for a case of assault, Against Conon. *The speaker Ariston describes the outrageous behaviour of the sons of his opponent Conon when they were on garrison duty together on the borders of Attica in 343 BC (young Athenians did a period of national sevice as 'ephebes'), and the continuation of the hostility (now involving Conon himself) when they were back in Athens. The court action probably took place two years later. As in Lysias' speech about Eratosthenes, we are given here a fascinating picture of everyday life in Athens. Following usual Athenian courtroom practice, a point is indicated where witness statements were read out. (3-9).*

ἐξῆλθον, ἔτος τουτὶ τρίτον, εἰς Πάνακτον φρουρᾶς ἡμῖν προγραφείσης.
ἐσκήνωσαν οὖν οἱ υἱεῖς οἱ Κόνωνος τουτουὶ ἐγγὺς ἡμῶν, ὡς οὐκ ἂν
ἐβουλόμην· ἡ γὰρ ἐξ ἀρχῆς ἔχθρα καὶ τὰ προσκρούματα ἐκεῖθεν ἡμῖν
συνέβη, ἐξ ὧν δ', ἀκούσεσθε. ἔπινον ἑκάστοτ' οὗτοι τὴν ἡμέραν, ἐπειδὴ
5 τάχιστ' ἀριστήσειαν, ὅλην, καὶ τοῦθ', ἕως περ ἦμεν ἐν τῇ φρουρᾷ,
διετέλουν ποιοῦντες. ἡμεῖς δ' ὥσπερ ἐνθάδ' εἰώθειμεν, οὕτω διήγομεν καὶ
ἔξω. ἦν οὖν δειπνοποιεῖσθαι τοῖς ἄλλοις ὥραν συμβαίνοι, ταύτην ἂν ἤδη
παρῴνουν οὗτοι, τὰ μὲν πόλλ' εἰς τοὺς παῖδας ἡμῶν τοὺς ἀκολούθους,
τελευτῶντες δὲ καὶ εἰς ἡμᾶς αὐτούς. φήσαντες γὰρ καπνίζειν αὐτοὺς
10 ὀψοποιουμένους τοὺς παῖδας ἢ κακῶς λέγειν ὅ τι τύχοιεν, ἔτυπτον καὶ

	ἔτος τουτὶ τρίτον	this (is) the third year (since), *i.e.* two years ago
	Πάνακτον -ου τό	Panactum (*Athenian fort on the border of Boeotia*)
	φρουρά -ᾶς ἡ	guard duty
	προγράφω	
1	aor pass προὐγράφην	I give public notice of
	σκηνόω ἐσκήνωσα	I pitch my tent
	υἱεῖς	(= υἱοί)
	Κόνων -ωνος ὁ	Conon
	τουτουί	(-ί *suffix points/emphasises*)
3	ἔχθρα -ας ἡ	enmity
	πρόσκρουμα -ατος τό	quarrel
	συμβαίνει συνέβη	(*of events*) happen
	ἑκάστοτε	at all times, constantly
	ἀριστάω ἠρίστησα	I have breakfast
5	ὅλος -η -ον	whole
	περ	indeed (*emphasises previous word*)
	διατελέω	I carry on
	εἴωθα (*pf as pres*)	
	εἰώθειν (*plpf as past*)	I am accustomed
6	διάγω	I conduct myself
	ἔξω	*lit* outside, *i.e. here* away from Athens
	δειπνοποιέομαι	I have dinner
	παροινέω	I am drunkenly abusive
	ἀκόλουθος -ου ὁ	servant, attendant
9	καπνίζω	I annoy with smoke
	ὀψοποιέομαι	I make a meal

τὰς ἀμίδας κατεσκεδάννυον καὶ προσεούρον, καὶ ἀσελγείας καὶ ὕβρεως
οὐδ᾿ ὁτιοῦν ἀπέλιπον.

ὁρῶντες δ᾿ ἡμεῖς ταῦτα καὶ λυπούμενοι, τὸ μὲν πρῶτον ἀπεπεμψάμεθα, ὡς
δ᾿ ἐχλεύαζον ἡμᾶς καὶ οὐκ ἐπαύοντο, τῷ στρατηγῷ τὸ πρᾶγμ᾿ εἴπομεν
15 κοινῇ πάντες οἱ σύσσιτοι προσελθόντες, οὐκ ἐγὼ τῶν ἄλλων ἔξω.
λοιδορηθέντος δ᾿ αὐτοῖς ἐκείνου καὶ κακίσαντος αὐτούς, οὐ μόνον περὶ
ὧν εἰς ἡμᾶς ἠσέλγαινον, ἀλλὰ καὶ περὶ ὧν ὅλως ἐποίουν ἐν τῷ
στρατοπέδῳ, τοσούτου ἐδέησαν παύσασθαι ἢ αἰσχυνθῆναι ὥστ᾿, ἐπειδὴ
θᾶττον συνεσκότασεν, εὐθὺς ὡς ἡμᾶς εἰσεπήδησαν ταύτῃ τῇ ἑσπέρᾳ, καὶ
20 τὸ μὲν πρῶτον κακῶς ἔλεγον, ἔπειτα δὲ καὶ πληγὰς ἐνέτειναν ἐμοί, καὶ
τοσαύτην κραυγὴν καὶ θόρυβον περὶ τὴν σκηνὴν ἐποίησαν, ὥστε καὶ τὸν
στρατηγὸν καὶ τοὺς ταξιάρχους ἐλθεῖν καὶ τῶν ἄλλων τινὰς στρατιωτῶν,
οἵπερ ἐκώλυσαν μηδὲν ἡμᾶς ἀνήκεστον παθεῖν μηδ᾿ αὐτοὺς ποιῆσαι
παροινουμένους ὑπὸ τούτων.

25 τοῦ δὲ πράγματος εἰς τοῦτο προελθόντος, ὡς δεῦρ᾿ ἐπανήλθομεν, ἦν ἡμῖν,
οἷον εἰκός, ἐκ τούτων ὀργὴ καὶ ἔχθρα πρὸς ἀλλήλους. οὐ μὴν ἔγωγε μὰ

	ἀμίς -ίδος ἡ	chamber pot
	κατασκεδαννύω	I scatter (the contents of)
	προσουρέω	I urinate on
	ἀσέλγεια -ας ἡ	shamelessness
11	ὕβρις -εως ἡ	outrageous behaviour
	ὁτιοῦν	anything at all
	ἀπολείπω ἀπέλιπον	I leave out
	λυπέομαι	I am aggrieved
	ἀποπέμπομαι ἀπεπεψάμην	I ignore
14	χλευάζω	I mock, I ridicule
	κοινῇ	together
	σύσσιτοι -ων οἱ	mess-mates
	ἔξω	(here, foll gen) apart from
	λοιδορέομαι ἐλοιδορήθην	I rebuke (+ dat)
16	κακίζω ἐκάκισα	I reproach
	ἀσελγαίνω	I treat brutally
	ὅλως	in general
	τοσούτου δέω	I am so far (from doing X, + inf)
	ἐπειδὴ θᾶττον	as soon as
19	συσκοτάζει συνεσκότασε	it grows dark
	εἰσπηδάω εἰσεπήδησα	I burst in
	πληγή -ῆς ἡ	blow
	ἐντείνω ἐνέτεινα	I deal
	κραυγή -ῆς ἡ	cry
21	θόρυβος -ου ὁ	commotion
	ταξίαρχος -ου ὁ	captain
	ἀνήκεστος -ον	incurable, irreparable
	παροινέω	I treat with drunken violence
	μήν	indeed
26	μά	by, in the name of (+ acc)

τοὺς θεοὺς <u>ᾤμην</u> δεῖν οὔτε <u>δίκην λαχεῖν</u> αὐτοῖς οὔτε <u>λόγον ποιεῖσθαι</u> τῶν <u>συμβάντων</u> οὐδένα, ἀλλ' ἐκεῖνο <u>ἁπλῶς ἐγνώκειν</u>, <u>τὸ λοιπὸν εὐλαβεῖσθαι</u> καὶ <u>φυλάττεσθαι</u> μὴ <u>πλησιάζειν</u> τοῖς τοιούτοις. πρῶτον μὲν οὖν ὧν
30 εἴρηκα τούτων βούλομαι τὰς <u>μαρτυρίας</u> παρασχόμενος, μετὰ ταῦθ' οἵ ὑπ' αὐτοῦ τούτου πέπονθ' ἐπιδεῖξαι, ἵν' εἰδῆσθ' ὅτι ᾧ <u>προσῆκε</u> τοῖς τὸ πρῶτον ἁμαρτηθεῖσιν <u>ἐπιτιμᾶν</u>, οὗτος αὐτὸς πρὸς τούτοις πολλῷ δεινότερ' <u>εἴργασται</u>.

ΜΑΡΤΥΡΙΑΙ

ὧν μὲν <u>τοίνυν</u> οὐδέν' ᾤμην δεῖν λόγον ποιεῖσθαι, ταῦτ' ἔστιν. χρόνῳ δ'
35 ὕστερον οὐ πολλῷ <u>περιπατοῦντος</u>, ὥσπερ <u>εἰώθειν</u>, ἑσπέρας ἐν ἀγορᾷ μου μετὰ <u>Φανοστράτου</u> τοῦ <u>Κηφισιέως</u>, τῶν <u>ἡλικιωτῶν</u> τινός, παρέρχεται <u>Κτησίας</u> ὁ υἱὸς ὁ τούτου, <u>μεθύων</u>, κατὰ τὸ <u>Λεωκόριον</u>, ἐγγὺς <u>τῶν Πυθοδώρου</u>. κατιδὼν δ' ἡμᾶς καὶ <u>κραυγάσας</u>, καὶ διαλεχθείς τι πρὸς αὐτὸν οὕτως ὡς ἂν μεθύων, ὥστε μὴ μαθεῖν ὅ τι λέγοι, παρῆλθε πρὸς
40 <u>Μελίτην ἄνω</u>. ἔπινον γὰρ ἐνταῦθα (ταῦτα γὰρ ὕστερον ἐπυθόμεθα) παρὰ

	οἶμαι *impf* ᾤμην	I think
	δίκην λαγχάνω (*aor* ἔλαχον)	I bring a lawsuit against (+ *dat*)
	λόγον ποιέομαι	I take account (of, + *gen*)
	συμβαίνω συνέβη	(*of events*) happen
28	ἁπλῶς	simply
	γιγνώσκω *plpf* ἐγνώκειν	(*here*) I resolve
	τὸ λοιπόν	in future
	εὐλαβέομαι	I take care
	πλησιάζω	I approach, I associate with (+ *dat*)
30	μαρτυρία -ας ἡ	testimony, witness statement
	προσήκει *impf* προσῆκε	it is appropriate
	ἐπιτιμάω	I punish
	ἐργάζομαι *pf 3 sg* εἴργασται	I do
	τοίνυν	so then
35	περιπατέω	I take a walk
	εἴωθα (*pf as pres*)	
	εἰώθειν (*plpf as past*)	I am accustomed
	Φανόστρατος -ου ὁ	Phanostratus
	Κηφισιεύς -έως	of Cephisia (*district of Athens*)
36	ἡλικιώτης -ου ὁ	contemporary, person of one's own age
	Κτησίας -ου	Ctesias
	μεθύω	I am drunk
	Λεωκόριον -ου τό	Leocorion (*shrine in memory of daughters of Leon who sacrificed them for the safety of his country*)
37	τῶν	*lit* the things/people *i.e.* house (of, + *gen*)
	Πυθόδωρος -ου ὁ	Pythodorus
	καθοράω κατεῖδον	I catch sight of
	κραυγάζω ἐκραύγασα	I utter a yell
	Μελίτη -ης ἡ	Melite (*district of Athens*)
40	ἄνω	upwards, uphill

Παμφίλῳ τῷ κναφεῖ Κόνων οὑτοσί, Θεότιμός τις, Ἀρχεβιάδης, Σπίνθαρος
ὁ Εὐβούλου, Θεογένης ὁ Ἀνδρομένους, πολλοί τινες, οὓς ἐξαναστήσας ὁ
Κτησίας ἐπορεύετ᾽ εἰς τὴν ἀγοράν. καὶ ἡμῖν συνέβαινεν ἀναστρέφουσιν
ἀπὸ τοῦ Φερσεφαττίου καὶ περιπατοῦσι πάλιν κατ᾽ αὐτό πως τὸ
45 Λεωκόριον εἶναι, καὶ τούτοις περιτυγχάνομεν. ὡς δ᾽ ἀνεμείχθημεν, εἰς μὲν
αὐτῶν, ἀγνώς τις, τῷ Φαναστράτῳ προσπίπτει καὶ κατεῖχεν ἐκεῖνον,
Κόνων δ᾽ οὑτοσὶ καὶ ὁ υἱὸς αὐτοῦ καὶ ὁ Ἀνδρομένους υἱὸς ἐμοὶ
προσπεσόντες, τὸ μὲν πρῶτον ἐξέδυσαν, εἶθ᾽ ὑποσκελίσαντες καὶ
ὠθήσαντες εἰς τὸν βόρβορον, οὕτω διέθηκαν ἐναλλόμενοι καὶ παίοντες,
50 ὥστε τὸ μὲν χεῖλος διακόψαι, τοὺς δ᾽ ὀφθαλμοὺς συγκλεῖσαι· οὕτω δὲ
κακῶς ἔχοντα κατέλιπον, ὥστε μήτ᾽ ἀναστῆναι μήτε φθέγξασθαι δύνασθαι.

κείμενος δ᾽ αὐτῶν ἤκουον πολλὰ καὶ δεινὰ λεγόντων. καὶ τὰ μὲν ἄλλα
καὶ βλασφημίαν ἔχει τινὰ καὶ λέγειν ὀκνήσαιμ᾽ ἂν ἐν ὑμῖν ἔνια, ὃ δὲ τῆς
ὕβρεώς ἐστι τῆς τούτου σημεῖον καὶ τεκμήριον τοῦ πᾶν τὸ πρᾶγμ᾽ ὑπὸ
55 τούτου γεγενῆσθαι, τοῦθ᾽ ὑμῖν ἐρῶ· ᾗδε γὰρ τοὺς ἀλεκτρυόνας

	Πάμφιλος -ου ὁ	Pamphilus
	κναφεύς -έως ὁ	fuller (*person who cleans and finishes new cloth*)
	Θεότιμος -ου ὁ	Theotimus
	Ἀρχεβιάδης -ου ὁ	Achebiades
41	Σπίνθαρος -ου ὁ	Spintharus
	Εὔβουλος -ου ὁ	Eubulus (*gen indicates* son of)
	Θεογένης -ους ὁ	Theogenes
	Ἀνδρομένης -ους ὁ	Andromenes
	ἐξανίστημι ἐξανάστησα	I make (someone) stand up
43	συμβαίνει (*impsnl*)	it happens (to, + *dat*)
	ἀναστρέφω	I turn back
	Φερσεφάττιον -ου τό	temple of Persephone
	περτυγχάνω	I meet, I bump into (+ *dat*)
	ἀναμίγνυμι	
45	*aor pass* ἀνεμείχθην	I mix together
	ἀγνώς -ῶτος ὁ	stranger
	κατέχω	I hold down
	ἐκδύω ἐξέδυσα	I strip (someone)
	ὑποσκελίζω ὑπεσκέλισα	I trip (someone) up
49	ὠθέω ὤθησα	I push
	βόρβορος -ου ὁ	mud
	διατίθημι διέθηκα	I treat
	ἐνάλλομαι	I leap on
	παίω	I beat
50	χεῖλος -ους τό	lip
	συγκλείω συνέκλεισα	I close
	φθέγγομαι ἐφθεγξάμην	I utter a sound
	βλασφημία -ας ἡ	abuse
	ὀκνέω ὤκνησα	I hesitate to, I shrink from (+ *inf*)
53	ἔνιοι -αι -α	some
	σημεῖον -ου τό	sign, indication
	τεκμήριον -ου τό	proof
	ᾄδω *impf* ᾖδον	I sing
	ἀλεκτρυών -όνος ὁ	cock

117

μιμούμενος τοὺς νενικηκότας, οἱ δὲ <u>κροτεῖν</u> τοῖς <u>ἀγκῶσιν</u> αὐτὸν ἠξίουν
ἀντὶ <u>πτερύγων</u> τὰς <u>πλευράς</u>. καὶ μετὰ ταῦτ᾽ ἐγὼ μὲν ἀπεκομίσθην ὑπὸ τῶν
<u>παρατυχόντων</u> γυμνός, οὗτοι δ᾽ <u>ᾤχοντο</u> <u>θοἰμάτιον</u> λαβόντες μου. ὡς δ᾽ ἐπὶ
τὴν θύραν ἦλθον, <u>κραυγὴ</u> καὶ βοὴ τῆς μητρὸς καὶ τῶν <u>θεραπαινίδων</u> ἦν,
60 καὶ <u>μόγις</u> ποτ᾽ εἰς <u>βαλανεῖον</u> ἐνεγκόντες με καὶ <u>περιπλύναντες</u> ἔδειξαν τοῖς
ἰατροῖς.

	μιμέομαι	I imitate
	κροτέω	I beat, I flap
	ἀγκών -ῶνος ὁ	elbow
	πτέρυξ -υγος ἡ	wing
57	πλευρά -ᾶς ἡ	side
	παρατυγχάνω παρέτυχον	I pass by
	οἴχομαι	I am gone
	ἱμάτιον -ου τό	cloak (θοἰμάτιον = *crasis of* τὸ ἱμάτιον)
	κραυγή -ῆς ἡ	cry
59	θεραπαινίς -ίδος ἡ	maidservant
	μόγις	(= μόλις)
	βαλανεῖον -ου τό	bath
	περιπλύνω περιέπλυνα	I bathe (someone)

Reading 7:

The Origins of Virtue

Plato's dialogue Protagoras *shows us Socrates in conversation with the famous Sophist Protagoras of Abdera: we read in* Greek to GCSE (2) *of his doctrine of relativism ('man is the measure of all things', implying there are no fixed or divinely-ordained truths) and the religious agnosticism that went with it. We also saw that he claimed to teach virtue or success (interpreted in wordly terms, and for a high fee). Socrates is portrayed by Plato as sceptical of all this, yet as treating Protagoras with personal and intellectual respect. Just before this passage, Socrates has questioned whether virtue is teachable. The myth of the origin of virtue is the first part of Protagoras' reply (320c-323a).*

ἦν γάρ ποτε χρόνος, ὅτε θεοὶ μὲν ἦσαν, <u>θνητὰ</u> δὲ γένη οὐκ ἦν. ἐπειδὴ δὲ
καὶ τούτοις χρόνος ἦλθεν <u>εἱμαρμένος</u> <u>γενέσεως</u>, <u>τυποῦσιν</u> αὐτὰ θεοὶ γῆς
<u>ἔνδον</u>, ἐκ γῆς καὶ πυρὸς <u>μίξαντες</u> καὶ τῶν ὅσα πυρὶ καὶ γῆ <u>κεράννυται</u>.
ἐπειδὴ δ᾽ ἄγειν αὐτὰ πρὸς <u>φῶς</u> ἔμελλον, <u>προσέταξαν</u> <u>Προμηθεῖ</u> καὶ
5 <u>Ἐπιμηθεῖ</u> <u>κοσμῆσαί</u> τε καὶ <u>νεῖμαι</u> δυνάμεις ἑκάστοις ὡς <u>πρέπει</u>. Προμηθέα

	θνητός -ή -όν	mortal
	εἱμαρμένος -η -ον	appointed, destined
	γένεσις -εως ἡ	creation, coming into being
	τυπόω	I mould
3	ἔνδον	inside (*here foll gen*)
	μίγνυμι ἔμιξα	I mix
	κεράννυμι	I blend, I compound
	φῶς φωτός τό	light
	προστάσσω προσέταξα	I appoint
4	Προμηθεύς -έως ὁ	Prometheus
	Ἐπιμηθεύς -έως ὁ	Epimetheus
	κοσμέω ἐκόσμησα	I arrange, I equip
	νέμω ἔνειμα	I distribute
	πρέπει	it is fitting

δὲ <u>παραιτεῖται</u> Ἐπιμηθεὺς αὐτὸς νεῖμαι, "νείμαντος δ' ἐμου," ἔφη,
"<u>ἐπίσκεψαι</u>"· καὶ οὕτω πείσας νέμει. νέμων δὲ τοῖς μὲν <u>ἰσχὺν</u> ἄνευ
<u>τάχους προσῆπτε</u>, τοὺς δ' ἀσθενεστέρους τάχει ἐκόσμει· τοὺς δὲ ὥπλιζε,
τοῖς δ' <u>ἄοπλον</u> διδοὺς <u>φύσιν</u> ἄλλην τιν' αὐτοῖς ἐμηχανᾶτο δύναμιν εἰς
10 σωτηρίαν. ἃ μὲν γὰρ αὐτῶν <u>σμικρότητι</u> <u>ἤμπισχε</u>, <u>πτηνὸν</u> φυγὴν ἢ
<u>κατάγειον</u> <u>οἴκησιν</u> ἔνεμεν· ἃ δὲ <u>ηὖξε</u> <u>μεγέθει</u>, τῷδε αὐτῷ αὐτὰ ἔσῳζε·
καὶ τἄλλα οὕτως <u>ἐπανισῶν</u> ἔνεμεν. ταῦτα δὲ ἐμηχανᾶτο <u>εὐλάβειαν</u> ἔχων
μή τι γένος <u>ἀϊστωθείη</u>· ἐπειδὴ δὲ αὐτοῖς <u>ἀλληλοφθοριῶν</u> διαφυγὰς
ἐπήρκεσε, πρὸς τὰς ἐκ Διὸς ὥρας <u>εὐμάρειαν</u> ἐμηχανᾶτο <u>ἀμφιεννὺς</u> αὐτὰ
15 <u>πυκναῖς</u> τε <u>θριξὶ</u> καὶ <u>στερεοῖς</u> <u>δέρμασιν</u>, ἱκανοῖς μὲν ἀμῦναι χειμῶνα,
δυνατοῖς δὲ καὶ <u>καύματα</u>, καὶ εἰς <u>εὐνὰς</u> ἰοῦσιν ὅπως <u>ὑπάρχοι</u> τὰ αὐτὰ
<u>στρωμνὴ</u> <u>οἰκεία</u> τε καὶ <u>αὐτοφυὴς</u> ἑκάστῳ· καὶ ὑπὸ ποδῶν τὰ μὲν <u>ὁπλαῖς</u>,
τὰ δὲ <u>ὄνυξι</u> καὶ δέρμασι στερεοῖς καὶ <u>ἀναίμοις</u>.

	παραιτέομαι	I ask
	ἐπισκοπέω ἐπεσεψάμην	I inspect
	ἰσχύς -ύος ἡ	strength
	τάχος -ους τό	speed
8	προσάπτω	I allocate
	ἄοπλος -ον	unarmed
	φύσις -εως ἡ	nature, condition
	σμικρότης -ητος ἡ	smallness
	ἀμπίσχω	I invest X (acc) with Y (dat)
10	πτηνός -ή -όν	winged
	κατάγειος -ον	underground
	οἴκησις -εως ἡ	dwelling, habitation
	αὔξω	I increase (something)
	μέγεθος -ους τό	great size
12	ἐπανισόω	I make equal
	εὐλάβεια -ας ἡ	care, concern
	ἀϊστόω ἀϊστώθην	I annihilate
	ἀλληλοφθορία -ας ἡ	act of mutual destruction
	διαφυγή -ῆς ἡ	way of escape (from, + gen)
14	ἐπαρκέω ἐπήρκεσα	I supply
	εὐμάρεια -ας ἡ	protection
	ἀμφιέννυμι	I clothe
	πυκνός -ή -όν	thick
	θρίξ τριχός ἡ	(usu pl) hair
15	στερεός -ά -όν	tough
	δέρμα -ατος τό	skin
	καῦμα -ατος τό	heat
	εὐνή -ῆς ἡ	rest, sleep
	ὑπάρχω	I serve as
17	στρωμνή -ῆς ἡ	bedding
	οἰκεῖος -α -ον	their own
	αὐτοφυής -ές	natural
	ὁπλή -ῆς ἡ	hoof
	ὄνυξ -υχος ὁ	claw
18	ἄναιμος -ον	bloodless

τοὐντεῦθεν τροφὰς ἄλλοις ἄλλας ἐξεπόριζε, τοῖς μὲν ἐκ γῆς βοτάνην,
20 ἄλλοις δὲ δένδρων καρπούς, τοῖς δὲ ῥίζας· ἔστι δ᾽ οἷς ἔδωκεν εἶναι
τροφὴν ζῴων ἄλλων βοράν· καὶ τοῖς μὲν ὀλιγογονίαν προσῆψε, τοῖς δ᾽
ἀναλισκομένοις ὑπὸ τούτων πολυγονίαν, σωτηρίαν τῷ γένει πορίζων. ἅτε
δὴ οὖν οὐ πάνυ τι σοφὸς ὢν ὁ Ἐπιμηθεὺς ἔλαθεν αὑτὸν καταναλώσας
τὰς δυνάμεις εἰς τὰ ἄλογα· λοιπὸν δὴ ἀκόσμητον ἔτι αὐτῷ ἦν τὸ
25 ἀνθρώπων γένος, καὶ ἠπόρει ὅ τι χρήσαιτο. ἀποροῦντι δὲ αὐτῷ ἔρχεται
Προμηθεὺς ἐπισκεψόμενος τὴν νομήν, καὶ ὁρᾷ τὰ μὲν ἄλλα ζῷα ἐμμελῶς
πάντων ἔχοντα, τὸν δὲ ἄνθρωπον γυμνόν τε καὶ ἀνυπόδητον καὶ
ἄστρωτον καὶ ἄοπλον· ἤδη δὲ καὶ ἡ εἱμαρμένη ἡμέρα παρῆν, ἐν ᾗ ἔδει
καὶ ἄνθρωπον ἐξιέναι ἐκ γῆς εἰς φῶς.

30 ἀπορίᾳ οὖν ἐχόμενος ὁ Προμηθεύς, ἥντινα σωτηρίαν τῷ ἀνθρώπῳ εὕροι,
κλέπτει Ἡφαίστου καὶ Ἀθηνᾶς τὴν ἔντεχνον σοφίαν σὺν πυρί (ἀμήχανον
γὰρ ἦν ἄνευ πυρὸς αὐτὴν κτητήν τῳ ἢ χρησίμην γενέσθαι) καὶ οὕτω δὴ
δωρεῖται ἀνθρώπῳ. τὴν μὲν οὖν περὶ τὸν βίον σοφίαν ἄνθρωπος ταύτῃ
ἔσχε, τὴν δὲ πολιτικὴν οὐκ εἶχεν· ἦν γὰρ παρὰ τῷ Διί· τῷ δὲ Προμηθεῖ

τοὐντεῦθεν		(*crasis of* τὸ ἐντεῦθεν, *lit* with respect to the thing next)
τροφή -ῆς ἡ		food
ἐκπορίζω		I provide
19	βοτάνη -ης ἡ	herbage, pasture
	καρπός -οῦ ὁ	fruit
	ῥίζα -ης ἡ	root
	ἔστι δ᾽ οἷς	(*lit* there is to whom, *i.e.*) to some
	βορά -ᾶς ἡ	prey
21	ὀλιγογονία -ας ἡ	scanty procreation, having few offspring
	προσάπτω προσῆψα	I allocate
	ἀναλίσκω	I consume
	πολυγονία -ας ἡ	plentiful procreation, having many offspring
	πάνυ	very
23	καταναλίσκω κατανήλωσα	I use up
	ἄλογος -ον	non-rational, unreasoning
	ἀκόσμητος -ον	not provided for
	ἐπισκοπέω ἐπισκέψομαι	I inspect
	νομή -ῆς ἡ	distribution
26	ἐμμελῶς	fully, properly
	ἀνυπόδητος -ον	unshod
	ἄστρωτος -ον	without bedding
	εἱμαρμένος -η -ον	appointed, destined
	φῶς φωτός τό	light
31	Ἥφαιστος -ου ὁ	Hephaestus
	Ἀθήνη -ης ἡ	Athene
	ἔντεχνος -ον	technical
	ἀμήχανος -ον	impossible
	κτητός -ή -όν	acquired
32	τῳ	(= τινί)
	δωρέομαι	I give, I present
	πολιτικός -ή -όν	political, to do with running a city

35 εἰς μὲν τὴν <u>ἀκρόπολιν</u> τὴν τοῦ Διὸς <u>οἴκησιν</u> οὐκέτι <u>ἐνεχώρει</u> εἰσελθεῖν·
    πρὸς δὲ καὶ αἱ Διὸς <u>φυλακαὶ</u> <u>φοβεραὶ</u> ἦσαν· εἰς δὲ τὸ τῆς Ἀθηνᾶς καὶ
    Ἡφαίστου <u>οἴκημα</u> τὸ κοινόν, ἐν ᾧ <u>ἐφιλοτεχνείτην</u>, λαθὼν εἰσέρχεται, καὶ
    κλέψας τήν τε <u>ἔμπυρον</u> τέχνην τὴν τοῦ Ἡφαίστου καὶ τὴν ἄλλην τὴν τῆς
    Ἀθηνᾶς δίδωσιν ἀνθρώπῳ, καὶ ἐκ τούτου <u>εὐπορία</u> μὲν ἀνθρώπῳ τοῦ βίου
40 γίγνεται, Προμηθέα δὲ δι' Ἐπιμηθέα ὕστερον, ᾗπερ λέγεται, <u>κλοπῆς</u> δίκη
    <u>μετῆλθεν</u>.

    ἐπειδὴ δὲ ὁ ἄνθρωπος <u>θείας</u> μετέσχε <u>μοίρας</u>, πρῶτον μὲν διὰ τὴν τοῦ
    θεοῦ <u>συγγένειαν</u> ζῴων μόνον θεοὺς ἐνόμισε, καὶ ἐπεχείρει βωμούς τε
    <u>ἱδρύεσθαι</u> καὶ <u>ἀγάλματα</u> θεῶν· ἔπειτα φωνὴν καὶ ὀνόματα ταχὺ
45 <u>διηρθρώσατο</u> τῇ τέχνῃ, καὶ <u>οἰκήσεις</u> καὶ <u>ἐσθῆτας</u> καὶ <u>ὑποδέσεις</u> καὶ
    <u>στρωμνὰς</u> καὶ τὰς ἐκ γῆς <u>τροφὰς</u> ηὕρετο. οὕτω δὴ παρασκευασμένοι κατ'
    ἀρχὰς ἄνθρωποι ᾤκουν <u>σποράδην</u>, πόλεις δὲ οὐκ ἦσαν· ἀπώλλυντο οὖν
    ὑπὸ τῶν <u>θηρίων</u> διὰ τὸ <u>πανταχῇ</u> αὐτῶν ἀσθενέστεροι εἶναι, καὶ ἡ
    <u>δημιουργικὴ</u> τέχνη αὐτοῖς πρὸς μὲν τροφὴν ἱκανὴ <u>βοηθὸς</u> ἦν, πρὸς δὲ τὸν
50 τῶν θηρίων πόλεμον <u>ἐνδεής</u>· <u>πολιτικὴν</u> γὰρ τέχνην οὔπω εἶχον, ἧς μέρος
    πολεμική. ἐζήτουν δὴ ἀθροίζεσθαι καὶ σῴζεσθαι <u>κτίζοντες</u> πόλεις· ὅτ' οὖν

	ἀκρόπολις -εως ἡ	citadel
	οἴκησις -εως ἡ	dwelling, habitation
	ἐγχωρεῖ	it is possible
	φυλακή -ῆς ἡ	guard, guard-force
36	φοβερός -ά -όν	terrifying
	οἴκημα -ατος τό	house
	φιλοτεχνέω	I practise an art (here impf dual)
	ἔμπυρος -ον	of fire, working with fire
	εὐπορία -ας ἡ	facility, plentiful supply
40	κλοπή -ῆς ἡ	theft
	μετέρχομαι μετῆλθον	I pursue
	θεῖος -α -ον	divine
	μοῖρα -ας ἡ	portion, something allocated
	συγγένεια -ας ἡ	kinship
44	ἱδρύομαι	I set up, I erect
	ἄγαλμα -ατος τό	statue
	διαρθρόομαι διηρθρωσάμην	I articulate, I invent in articulate form
	οἴκησις -εως ἡ	dwelling
	ἐσθής -ῆτος ἡ	clothing
45	ὑπόδεσις -εως ἡ	shoes, sandals
	στρωμνή -ῆς ἡ	bedding
	τροφή -ῆς ἡ	food
	σποράδην	scattered, here and there
	θηρίον -ου τό	wild beast
48	πανταχῇ	in every way
	δημιουργικός -ή -όν	of craftsmanship
	βοηθός -όν	helpful
	ἐνδεής -ές	deficient
	πολιτικός -ή -όν	political, to do with running a city
51	πολεμικός -ή -όν	of war
	κτίζω	I found

121

ἀθροισθεῖεν, ἠδίκουν ἀλλήλους ἅτε οὐκ ἔχοντες τὴν πολιτικὴν τέχνην,
ὥστε πάλιν σκεδαννύμενοι διεφθείροντο.

Ζεὺς οὖν δείσας περὶ τῷ γένει ἡμῶν, μὴ ἀπόλοιτο πᾶν, Ἑρμῆν πέμπει
55 ἄγοντα εἰς ἀνθρώπους αἰδῶ τε καὶ δίκην, ἵν' εἶεν πόλεων κόσμοι τε καὶ
δεσμοὶ φιλίας συναγωγοί. ἐρωτᾷ οὖν Ἑρμῆς Δία, τίνα οὖν τρόπον δοίη
δίκην καὶ αἰδῶ ἀνθρώποις· "πότερον ὡς αἱ τέχναι νενέμηνται, οὕτω καὶ
ταύτας νείμω; νενέμηνται δὲ ὧδε· εἷς ἔχων ἰατρικὴν πολλοῖς ἱκανὸς
ἰδιώταις, καὶ οἱ ἄλλοι δημιουργοί· καὶ δίκην δὴ καὶ αἰδῶ οὕτω θῶ ἐν
60 τοῖς ἀνθρώποις, ἢ ἐπὶ πάντας νείμω;" "ἐπὶ πάντας," ἔφη ὁ Ζεύς, "καὶ
πάντες μετεχόντων· οὐ γὰρ ἂν γένοιντο πόλεις, εἰ ὀλίγοι αὐτῶν μετέχοιεν
ὥσπερ ἄλλων τεχνῶν· καὶ νόμον γε θὲς παρ' ἐμοῦ, τὸν μὴ δυνάμενον
αἰδοῦς καὶ δίκης μετέχειν κτείνειν ὡς νόσον πόλεως."

οὕτω δή, ὦ Σώκρατες, καὶ διὰ ταῦτα οἵ τε ἄλλοι καὶ Ἀθηναῖοι,
65 ὅταν μὲν περὶ ἀρετῆς τεκτονικῆς ἢ λόγος ἢ ἄλλης τινὸς δημιουργικῆς,
ὀλίγοις οἴονται μετεῖναι συμβουλῆς, καὶ ἐάν τις ἐκτὸς ὢν τῶν ὀλίγων
συμβουλεύῃ, οὐκ ἀνέχονται, ὡς σὺ φής· εἰκότως, ὡς ἐγώ φημι· ὅταν δὲ
εἰς συμβουλὴν πολιτικῆς ἀρετῆς ἴωσιν, ἣν δεῖ διὰ δικαιοσύνης πᾶσαν
ἰέναι καὶ σωφροσύνης, εἰκότως ἅπαντος ἀνδρὸς ἀνέχονται, ὡς παντὶ
70 προσῆκον ταύτης γε μετέχειν τῆς ἀρετῆς, ἢ μὴ εἶναι πόλεις.

	σκεδάννυμι	I scatter
	δείδω ἔδεισα	I fear
	Ἑρμῆς -οῦ ὁ	Hermes
	αἰδώς -οῦς ἡ	respect, conscience, sense of shame
55	κόσμος -ου ὁ	regulation, means of organization
	συναγωγός -όν	bringing people together
	νέμω pf pass νενέμημαι	I distribute
	ἰατρική -ῆς ἡ	(the art of) medicine (*understand* τέχνη)
	ἰδιώτης -ου ὁ	layman, ordinary citizen
59	δημιουργός -οῦ ὁ	expert
	μετεχόντων	(*impv 3 pl of* μετέχω)
	τεκτονικός -ή -όν	to do with carpentry
	οἴομαι	I think
	συμβουλή -ῆς ἡ	advice
66	ἐκτός	outside (of, + *gen*)
	ἀνέχομαι	I tolerate, I allow
	εἰκότως	reasonably, with good reason
	σωφροσύνη -ης ἡ	good sense, prudence
	προσήκει	it is appropriate

Reading 8:
The Lost Atlantis

Plato in his dialogue Timaeus *describes the mythical lost island Atlantis, off the Straits of Gibraltar: its empire, supposedly in contact with Athens in prehistoric times, was defeated, and the island later swallowed up by great earthquakes and floods. The tradition may contain real memories of Minoan Crete (a naval power whose contact with Athens is reflected in the Theseus story) or of the volcanic island of Thera (Santorini), devastated by a major eruption about 1500 BC. Another view sees Atlantis as a gloomy allegory for Athens in the late fifth century BC when Plato was growing up. In this passage Socrates converses at a symposium with the Athenian aristocrat Critias. As in the story of Croesus, the lawgiver Solon is seen as an archetypal traveller and sage; wise Egyptian priests are also Herodotean* (20d-22d and 24d-25d).

KP. ἄκουε δή, ὦ <u>Σώκρατες</u>, λόγου μάλα μὲν <u>ἀτόπου</u>, <u>παντάπασί</u> γε <u>μὴν</u> ἀληθοῦς, ὡς ὁ τῶν ἑπτὰ σοφώτατος <u>Σόλων</u> ποτ᾽ ἔφη. ἦν γὰρ οὖν <u>οἰκεῖος</u> καὶ σφόδρα φίλος ἡμῖν <u>Δρωπίδου</u> τοῦ <u>προπάππου</u>, <u>καθάπερ</u> λέγει <u>πολλαχοῦ</u> καὶ αὐτὸς ἐν τῇ <u>ποιήσει</u>· πρὸς δὲ <u>Κριτίαν</u> τὸν

5 ἡμέτερον <u>πάππον</u> εἶπεν, ὡς <u>ἀπεμνημόνευεν</u> αὖ πρὸς ἡμᾶς ὁ γέρων, ὅτι μεγάλα καὶ <u>θαυμαστὰ</u> τῇσδ᾽ εἴη παλαιὰ ἔργα τῆς πόλεως ὑπὸ χρόνου καὶ <u>φθορᾶς</u> ἀνθρώπων <u>ἠφανισμένα</u>, πάντων δὲ ἓν μέγιστον, οὗ νῦν <u>ἐπιμνησθεῖσιν</u> <u>πρέπον</u> ἂν ἡμῖν εἴη σοί τε ἀποδοῦναι χάριν καὶ τὴν θεὸν ἅμα ἐν τῇ <u>πανηγύρει</u> δικαίως τε καὶ ἀληθῶς <u>οἱόνπερ</u>

10 <u>ὑμνοῦντας</u> <u>ἐγκωμιάζειν</u>.

ΣΩ. εὖ λέγεις. ἀλλὰ δὴ ποῖον ἔργον τοῦτο Κριτίας οὐ λεγόμενον μέν, ὡς δὲ πραχθὲν <u>ὄντως</u> ὑπὸ τῆσδε τῆς πόλεως ἀρχαῖον διηγεῖτο κατὰ τὴν Σόλωνος <u>ἀκοήν</u>;

	Σωκράτης -ους ὁ (*voc* -ες)	Socrates
	ἄτοπος -ον	strange
	παντάπασι	entirely
	μήν	however
2	Σόλων -ωνος ὁ	Solon (*regarded as one of the 'Seven Sages'*)
	οἰκεῖος -α -ον	related
	Δροπίδης -ου ὁ	Dropides
	πρόπαππος -ου ὁ	great-grandfather
	καθάπερ	just as
4	πολλαχοῦ	in many places
	ποίησις -εως ἡ	poetry
	Κριτίας -ου ὁ	Critias
	πάππος -ου ὁ	grandfather
	ἀπομνημονεύω	I repeat
6	θαυμαστός -ή -όν	wonderful
	φθορά -ᾶς ἡ	destruction
	ἀφανίζω *pf pass* ἠφάνισμαι	I obliterate
	ἐπιμιμνήσκομαι ἐπεμνήσθην	I recall
	πρέπει	it is fitting
9	πανήγυρις -εως ἡ	festival
	οἱόνπερ	as if, just like
	ὑμνέω	I sing a hymn
	ἐγκωμιάζω	I praise
	ὄντως	actually, really
13	ἀκοή -ῆς ἡ	hearing, something heard

123

ΚΡ. ἐγὼ φράσω, παλαιὸν ἀκηκοὼς λόγον οὐ νέου ἀνδρός. ἦν μὲν γὰρ δὴ
15 τότε Κρίτιας, ὡς ἔφη, σχεδὸν ἐγγὺς ἤδη τῶν ἐνενήκοντα ἐτῶν, ἐγὼ δέ
πῃ μάλιστα δεκέτης· ἡ δὲ Κουρεῶτις ἡμῖν οὖσα ἐτύγχανεν
Ἀπατουρίων. τὸ δὴ τῆς ἑορτῆς σύνηθες ἑκάστοτε καὶ τότε συνέβη
τοῖς παισίν· ἆθλα γὰρ ἡμῖν οἱ πατέρες ἔθεσαν ῥαψῳδίας. πολλῶν μὲν
οὖν δὴ καὶ πολλὰ ἐλέχθη ποιητῶν ποιήματα, ἅτε δὲ νέα κατ' ἐκεῖνον
20 τὸν χρόνον ὄντα τὰ Σόλωνος πολλοὶ τῶν παίδων ᾔσαμεν. εἶπεν οὖν
τις τῶν φρατέρων, εἴτε δὴ δοκοῦν αὐτῷ τότε εἴτε καὶ χάριν τινὰ τῷ
Κριτίᾳ φέρων, δοκεῖν οἱ τά τε ἄλλα σοφώτατον γεγονέναι Σόλωνα καὶ
κατὰ τὴν ποίησιν αὖ τῶν ποιητῶν πάντων ἐλευθεριώτατον. ὁ δὴ
γέρων (σφόδρα γὰρ οὖν μέμνημαι) μάλα τε ἥσθη καὶ διαμειδιάσας
25 εἶπεν· "εἴ γε, ὦ Ἀμύνανδρε, μὴ παρέργῳ τῇ ποιήσει κατεχρήσατο,
ἀλλ' ἐσπουδάκει καθάπερ ἄλλοι, τόν τε λόγον ὃν ἀπ' Αἰγύπτου δεῦρο
ἠνέγκατο ἀπετέλεσεν, καὶ μὴ διὰ τὰς στάσεις ὑπὸ κακῶν τε ἄλλων
ὅσα ηὗρεν ἐνθάδε ἥκων ἠναγκάσθη καταμελῆσαι, κατά γε ἐμὴν
δόξαν οὔτε Ἡσίοδος οὔτε Ὅμηρος οὔτε ἄλλος οὐδεὶς ποιητὴς
30 εὐδοκιμώτερος ἐγένετο ἄν ποτε αὐτοῦ." "τίς δ' ἦν ὁ λόγος," ἦ δ' ὅς,

	φράζω *fut* φράσω	I tell
	πῃ	somewhere
	μάλιστα	(*with numbers*) about
	δεκέτης -ες	ten years old
16	Κουρεῶτις -ιδος ἡ	Koureotis (*lit* hair-cutting: *day when young men were registered in tribes*)
	Ἀπατούρια -ων τά	Apaturia (*Athenian tribal festival*)
	συνήθης -ες	usual, customary
	ἑκάστοτε	each time
17	συμβαίνει συνέβη	(*of events*) happen, occur
	ῥαψῳδία -ας ἡ	recitation
	ποιητής -οῦ ὁ	poet
	ποίημα -ατος τό	poem
	ᾄδω ᾖσα	I sing
21	φράτηρ -ερος ὁ	clan member
	οἱ	(= αὐτῷ)
	ποίησις -εως ἡ	poetry
	ἐλευθέριος -α -ον	independent
	διαμειδιάω διεμειδίασα	I smile
25	Ἀμύνανδρος -ου ὁ	Amynander
	πάρεργον -ου τό	diversion, hobby
	καταχράομαι κατεχρησάμην	I treat as (+ *dat*)
	σπουδάζω *plpf* ἐσπούδακειν	I work seriously at
	καθάπερ	just as
26	Αἴγυπτος -ου ἡ	Egypt
	ἀποτελέω ἀπετέλεσα	I finish
	στάσις -εως ἡ	civil unrest
	καταμελέω κατημέλησα	I neglect
	Ἡσίοδος -ου ὁ	Hesiod (*second oldest Greek poet, after Homer*)
29	Ὅμηρος -ου ὁ	Homer
	εὐδόκιμος -ον	distinguished
	ἦ δ' ὅς	he said

124

"ὦ Κριτία;" "ἢ περὶ μεγίστης," ἔφη, "καὶ <u>ὀνομαστοτάτης</u> πασῶν δικαιότατ' ἂν <u>πράξεως</u> οὔσης, ἣν ἥδε ἡ πόλις ἔπραξε μέν, διὰ δὲ χρόνον καὶ <u>φθορὰν</u> τῶν <u>ἐργασμένων</u> οὐ <u>διήρκεσε</u> δεῦρο ὁ λόγος." "λέγε ἐξ ἀρχῆς," ἢ δ' ὅς, "τί τε καὶ πῶς καὶ παρὰ τίνων ὡς ἀληθῆ
35 <u>διακηκοὼς</u> ἔλεγεν ὁ Σόλων."

"<u>ἔστιν</u> τις κατ' Αἴγυπτον," ἢ δ' ὅς, "ἐν τῷ <u>Δέλτα</u>, περὶ ὃν κατὰ <u>κορυφὴν σχίζεται</u> τὸ τοῦ <u>Νείλου ῥεῦμα Σαϊτικὸς</u> ἐπικαλούμενος <u>νομός</u>, τούτου δὲ τοῦ νομοῦ μεγίστη πόλις <u>Σάις</u> (ὅθεν δὴ ᾽Ἄμασις ἦν ὁ βασιλεύς) οἷς τῆς πόλεως θεὸς <u>ἀρχηγός</u> τίς ἐστιν, <u>Αἰγυπτιστὶ</u> μὲν
40 <u>τοὔνομα Νηίθ</u>, Ἑλληνιστὶ δέ, ὡς ὁ ἐκείνων λόγος, Ἀθηνᾶ· μάλα δὲ <u>φιλαθήναιοι</u> καί τινα τρόπον <u>οἰκεῖοι</u> τῶνδ' εἶναι φασιν. οἱ δὴ Σόλων ἔφη πορευθεὶς σφόδρα τε γενέσθαι παρ' αὐτοῖς <u>ἔντιμος</u>, καὶ δὴ καὶ τὰ παλαιὰ <u>ἀνερωτῶν</u> ποτε τοὺς μάλιστα περὶ ταῦτα τῶν ἱερέων <u>ἐμπείρους</u>, σχεδὸν οὔτε αὐτὸν οὔτε ἄλλον Ἕλληνα οὐδένα οὐδὲν <u>ὡς</u>
45 <u>ἔπος εἰπεῖν</u> εἰδότα περὶ τῶν τοιούτων <u>ἀνευρεῖν</u>. καί ποτε προαγαγεῖν βουληθεὶς αὐτοὺς περὶ τῶν ἀρχαίων εἰς λόγους, τῶν τῇδε τὰ ἀρχαιότατα λέγειν ἐπιχειρεῖν, περὶ <u>Φορωνέως</u> τε τοῦ πρώτου λεχθέντος καὶ <u>Νιόβης</u>, καὶ μετὰ τὸν <u>κατακλυσμὸν</u> αὖ περὶ

	ὀνομαστός -ή -όν	famous, renowned
	πρᾶξις -εως ἡ	achievement
	φθορά -ῆς ἡ	destruction
	ἐργάζομαι *pf* εἰργάσμαι	I accomplish
33	διαρκέω διήρκεσα	I last, I endure
	διακούω *pf* διακήκοα	I hear all through
	Δέλτα τό	Delta
	κορυφή -ῆς ἡ	crown, head (*of Delta*)
	σχίζω	I split
37	Νεῖλος -ου ὁ	River Nile
	ῥεῦμα -ατος τό	stream
	Σαϊτικός -ή -όν	Saitic
	νομός -οῦ ὁ	province
	Σάις -ιος ἡ	Sais (*city in Egypt*)
38	᾽Ἄμασις -ιδος ὁ	Amasis (*sixth-century BC Egyptian king*)
	ἀρχηγός -οῦ ὁ	founder
	Αἰγυπτιστί	in Egyptian
	τοὔνομα	(*crasis of* τὸ ὄνομα)
	Νηίθ	Neith
40	Ἑλληνιστί	in Greek
	φιλαθήναιος -ον	pro-Athenian
	οἰκεῖος -α -ον	related
	ἔντιμος -ον	honoured
	ἀνερωτάω	I question
44	ἔμπειρος -ον	experienced
	ὡς ἔπος εἰπεῖν	so to speak
	ἀνευρίσκω ἀνεῦρον	I discover
	Φορωνεύς -έως ὁ	Phoroneus (*regarded here as the first man - equivalent to Adam*)
48	Νιόβη -ης ἡ	Niobe (*daughter of Phoroneus and founding mother by Zeus of the Argive race*)
	κατακλυσμός -οῦ ὁ	flood

Δευκαλίωνος καὶ Πύρρας ὡς διεγένοντο μυθολογεῖν, καὶ τοὺς ἐξ
50 αὑτῶν γενεαλογεῖν, καὶ τὰ τῶν ἐτῶν οἷς ἔλεγεν πειρᾶσθαι
διαμνημονεύων τοὺς χρόνους ἀριθμεῖν· καί τινα εἰπεῖν τῶν ἱερέων εὖ
μάλα παλαιόν· 'ὦ Σόλων, Σόλων, Ἕλληνες ἀεὶ παῖδές ἐστε, γέρων δὲ
Ἕλλην οὐκ ἔστιν.' ἀκούσας οὖν, 'πῶς τί τοῦτο λέγεις;' φάναι. 'νέοι
ἐστέ,' εἰπεῖν, 'τὰς ψυχὰς πάντες· οὐδεμίαν γὰρ ἐν αὐταῖς ἔχετε δι'
55 ἀρχαίαν ἀκοὴν παλαιὰν δόξαν οὐδὲ μάθημα χρόνῳ πολιὸν οὐδέν. τὸ
δὲ τούτων αἴτιον τόδε. πολλαὶ κατὰ πολλὰ φθοραὶ γεγόνασιν
ἀνθρώπων καὶ ἔσονται, πυρὶ μὲν καὶ ὕδατι μέγισται, μυρίοις δὲ
ἄλλοις ἕτεραι βραχύτεραι. τὸ γὰρ οὖν καὶ παρ' ὑμῖν λεγόμενον, ὥς
ποτε Φαέθων Ἡλίου παῖς τὸ τοῦ πατρὸς ἅρμα ζεύξας διὰ τὸ μὴ
60 δυνατὸς εἶναι κατὰ τὴν τοῦ πατρὸς ὁδὸν ἐλαύνειν τά τ' ἐπὶ γῆς
συνέκαυσεν καὶ αὐτὸς κεραυνωθεὶς διεφθάρη, τοῦτο μύθου μὲν
σχῆμα ἔχον λέγεται, τὸ δὲ ἀληθές ἐστι τῶν περὶ γῆν κατ' οὐρανὸν
ἰόντων παράλλαξις καὶ διὰ μακρῶν χρόνων γιγνομένη τῶν ἐπὶ γῆς
πυρὶ πολλῷ φθορά.'

	Δευκαλίων -ωνος ὁ	Deucalion (*flood survivor - the Noah of Greek myth*)
	Πύρρα -ας ἡ	Pyrrha (*wife of Deucalion*)
	διαγίγνομαι	I survive
	μυθολογέω	I tell a story
50	γενεαλογέω	I trace the genealogy (of)
	διαμνημονεύω	I mention
	ἀριθμέω	I count
	ψυχή -ῆς ἡ	mind
	ἀκοή -ῆς ἡ	(*here*) tradition
55	μάθημα -ατος τό	learning
	πολιός -ά -όν	aged by time (*lit* grey-haired)
	φθορά -ᾶς ἡ	destruction
	μυρίος -α -ον	countless
	βραχύς -εῖα -ύ	brief
59	Φαέθων -οντος ὁ	Phaethon (*son of sun god Helios*)
	ζεύγνυμι ἔζευξα	I yoke
	συγκαίω συνέκαυσα	I burn up
	κεραυνόω	
	aor pass ἐκεραυνώθην	I strike with a thunderbolt
62	σχῆμα -ατος τό	form
	παράλλαξις ἡ	deviation

The priest goes on to describe the unusual geographical conditions of Egypt, the antiquity of its traditions, and the contrasts between Egyptian and Athenian lifesyles: in effect a reworking in reverse of Herodotus, who had described Egyptian customs through Greek eyes. In the following section he returns the story of Atlantis.

65 " 'πολλὰ μὲν οὖν ὑμῶν καὶ μεγάλα ἔργα τῆς πόλεως <u>τῇδε</u> γεγραμμένα
θαυμάζεται, πάντων <u>μὴν</u> ἓν <u>ὑπερέχει</u> <u>μεγέθει</u> καὶ ἀρετῇ. λέγει γὰρ τὰ
γεγραμμένα ὅσην ἡ πόλις ὑμῶν ἔπαυσέν ποτε δύναμιν <u>ὕβρει</u>
πορευομένην ἅμα ἐπὶ πᾶσαν <u>Εὐρώπην</u> καὶ <u>'Ασίαν</u>, <u>ἔξωθεν</u>
<u>ὁρμηθεῖσαν</u> ἐκ τοῦ <u>'Ατλαντικοῦ</u> <u>πελάγους</u>. τότε γὰρ <u>πορεύσιμον</u> ἦν
70 τὸ ἐκεῖ πέλαγος. νῆσον γὰρ πρὸ τοῦ στόματος εἶχεν ὃ καλεῖτε, ὥς
φατε, ὑμεῖς <u>Ἡρακλέους</u> <u>στήλας</u>, ἡ δὲ νῆσος ἅμα <u>Λιβύης</u> ἦν καὶ
'Ασίας μείζων, ἐξ ἧς <u>ἐπιβατὸν</u> ἐπὶ τὰς ἄλλας νήσους τοῖς τότε
ἐγίγνετο πορευομένοις, ἐκ δὲ τῶν νήσων ἐπὶ τὴν <u>καταντικρὺ</u> πᾶσαν
ἤπειρον τὴν περὶ τὸν <u>ἀληθινὸν</u> ἐκεῖνον <u>πόντον</u>. τάδε μὲν γάρ, ὅσα
75 ἐντὸς τοῦ στόματος οὗ λέγομεν, φαίνεται λιμὴν στένον τινα ἔχων
<u>εἴσπλουν·</u> ἐκεῖνο δὲ πέλαγος <u>ὄντως</u> ἥ τε <u>περιέχουσα</u> αὐτὸ γῆ
<u>παντελῶς</u> ἀληθῶς ὀρθότατ' ἂν λέγοιτο ἤπειρος. ἐν δὲ δὴ τῇ
'Ατλαντίδι νήσῳ ταύτῃ μεγάλη <u>συνέστη</u> καὶ <u>θαυμαστὴ</u> δύναμις
βασιλέων, κρατοῦσα μὲν ἁπάσης τῆς νήσου, πολλῶν δὲ ἄλλων
80 νήσων καὶ μερῶν τῆς ἠπείρου· πρὸς δὲ τούτοις ἔτι τῶν <u>ἐντὸς</u> τῇδε
Λιβύης μὲν ἦρχον μέχρι πρὸς Αἴγυπτον, τῆς δὲ Εὐρώπης μέχρι
<u>Τυρρηνίας</u>. αὕτη δὴ πᾶσα <u>συναθροισθεῖσα</u> εἰς ἓν ἡ δύναμις τόν τε
παρ' ὑμῖν καὶ τὸν παρ' ἡμῖν καὶ τὸν ἐντὸς τοῦ στόματος πάντα τόπον

	τῇδε	here
	μήν	however
	ὑπερέχω	I stand out
	μέγεθος -ους τό	importance
67	ὕβρις -εως ἡ	insolence, arrogance
	Εὐρώπη -ης ἡ	Europe
	'Ασία -ας ἡ	Asia
	ἔξωθεν	from outside
	ὁρμάω *aor pass* ὡρμήθην	I send out
69	'Ατλαντικός -ή -όν	Atlantic
	πέλαγος -ους τό	ocean
	πορεύσιμος -ον	navigable
	Ἡρακλῆς -έους ὁ	Heracles
	στήλη -ης ἡ	pillar (*'Pillars of Hercules'* = Straits of Gibraltar)
71	Λιβύη -ης ἡ	Libya
	ἐπιβατός -ή -όν	giving access
	καταντικρύ	opposite
	ἀληθινός -ή -όν	genuine
	πόντος -ου ὁ	sea
76	εἴσπλους -ου ὁ	entrance
	ὄντως	truly
	περιέχω	I surround
	παντελῶς	entirely
	'Ατλαντίς -ίδος ἡ	Atlantis
78	συνίστημι συνέστην	I come together, I arise
	θαυμαστός -ή -όν	remarkable
	ἐντός	inside
	Τυρρηνία -ας ἡ	Etruria (*region of central Italy*)
	συναθροίζω	
82	*aor pass* συνηθροίσθην	I gather together

μιᾷ ποτὲ <u>ἐπεχειρησεν</u> <u>ὁρμῇ</u> δουλοῦσθαι. τότε οὖν ὑμῶν, ὦ Σόλων, τῆς
πόλεως ἡ δύναμις εἰς ἅπαντας ἀνθρώπους <u>διαφανὴς</u> ἀρετῇ τε καὶ
<u>ῥώμη</u> ἐγένετο· πάντων γὰρ <u>προστᾶσα</u> <u>εὐψυχίᾳ</u> καὶ τέχναις ὅσαι κατὰ
πόλεμον, τὰ μὲν τῶν Ἑλλήνων ἡγουμένη, τὰ δ' αὐτὴ <u>μονωθεῖσα</u> ἐξ
ἀνάγκης τῶν ἄλλων ἀποστάντων, ἐπὶ τοὺς ἐσχάτους κινδύνους,
κρατήσασα μὲν τῶν <u>ἐπιόντων</u> τρόπαιον ἔστησεν, τοὺς δὲ <u>μήπω</u>
δεδουλωμένους διεκώλυσεν δουλωθῆναι, τοὺς δ' ἄλλους, ὅσοι
<u>κατοικοῦμεν</u> ἐντὸς <u>ὅρων</u> Ἡρακλείων, <u>ἀφθόνως</u> ἅπαντας ἠλευθέρωσεν.
ὑστέρῳ δὲ χρόνῳ <u>σεισμῶν</u> <u>ἐξαισίων</u> καὶ <u>κατακλυσμῶν</u> γενομένων,
μιᾶς ἡμέρας καὶ νυκτὸς χαλεπῆς ἐπελθούσης, τό τε παρ' ὑμῖν
<u>μάχιμον</u> πᾶν <u>ἁθρόον</u> <u>ἔδυ</u> κατὰ γῆς, ἥ τε Ἀτλαντὶς νῆσος <u>ὡσαύτως</u>
κατὰ τῆς θαλάττης δῦσα <u>ἠφανίσθη</u>· <u>διὸ</u> καὶ νῦν <u>ἄπορον</u> καὶ
<u>ἀδιερεύνητον</u> γέγονεν <u>τοὐκεῖ</u> πέλαγος, <u>πηλοῦ</u> <u>κάρτα</u> <u>βραχέος</u>
<u>ἐμποδὼν</u> ὄντος, ὃν ἡ νῆσος <u>ἱζομένη</u> παρέσχετο.' "

85 (line marker)
90 (line marker)
95 (line marker)

	ἐπιχειρέω	I try
	ὁρμή -ῆς ἡ	attack, onslaught
	διαφανής -ές	plain for all to see
	ῥώμη -ης ἡ	strength
86	προΐσταμαι προὔστην	I excel
	εὐψυχία -ας ἡ	courage
	μονόω *aor pass* ἐμονώθην	I leave alone, I abandon
	ἔπειμι	I attack, I invade
	μήπω	not yet
91	κατοικέω	I live
	ὅρος -ου ὁ	boundary
	ἀφθόνως	generously, unstintingly
	σεισμός -οῦ ὁ	earthquake
	ἐξαίσιος -ον	extraordinary
92	κατακλυσμός -οῦ ὁ	flood
	μάχιμος -ον	fighting
	ἁθρόος -η -ον	altogether
	δύω ἔδυν	I sink
	ὡσαύτως	likewise
95	ἀφανίζω *aor pass* ἠφανίσθην	I obliterate
	διό	therefore
	ἄπορος -ον	impassable
	ἀδιερεύνητος -ον	unable to be explored
	τοὐκεῖ	(*crasis of* τὸ ἐκεῖ)
96	πηλός -οῦ ὁ	mud
	κάρτα	very
	βραχύς -εῖα -ύ	(*here*) close below the surface
	ἐμποδών	in the way
	ἵζομαι	(*here*) I sink down

Reading 9:

A Spartan Childhood

Plutarch in his Lycurgus *describes the founder of the political, educational and military system which made Sparta unique for its conformist efficiency and prowess. Myths abounded: few other Greeks went to Sparta, and Plutarch was writing about 100 AD, eight centuries or more after the events he describes. The system probably in fact evolved over time, but perhaps there was one influential legislator at the point when the Spartans enslaved the people of Messenia, containable only by single-minded militarism. In this passage Plutarch describes the notoriously harsh treatment to which young Spartans were subjected (16-18).*

τὸ δὲ γεννηθὲν οὐκ ἦν κύριος ὁ γεννήσας τρέφειν, ἀλλ᾽ ἔφερε λαβὼν εἰς
τόπον τινὰ λέσχην καλούμενον, ἐν ᾧ καθήμενοι τῶν φυλετῶν οἱ
πρεσβύτατοι καταμάθοντες τὸ παιδάριον, εἰ μὲν εὐπαγὲς εἴη καὶ
ῥωμαλέον, τρέφειν ἐκέλευον, κλῆρον αὐτῷ τῶν ἐνακισχιλίων
5 προσνείμαντες· εἰ δ᾽ ἀγεννὲς καὶ ἄμορφον, ἀπέπεμπον εἰς τὰς λεγομένας
Ἀποθέτας, παρὰ Ταΰγετον βαραθρώδη τόπον, ὡς οὔτε αὐτῷ ζῆν ἄμεινον
ὂν οὔτε τῇ πόλει τὸ μὴ καλῶς εὐθὺς ἐξ ἀρχῆς πρὸς εὐεξίαν καὶ ῥώμην
πεφυκός. ὅθεν οὐδὲ ὕδατι τὰ βρέφη, ἀλλ᾽ οἴνῳ περιέλουον αἱ γυναῖκες,
βάσανόν τινα ποιούμεναι τῆς κράσεως αὐτῶν. λέγεται γὰρ ἐξίστασθαι τὰ
10 ἐπιληπτικὰ καὶ νοσώδη πρὸς τὸν ἄκρατον ἀποσφακελίζοντα, τὰ δ᾽ ὑγιεινὰ

	γεννάω *aor pass* ἐγεννήθην	I beget, I father
	κύριος -α -ον	having power
	τρέφω	I rear, I bring up
	λέσχη -ης ἡ	assembly hall
2	κάθημαι	I sit
	φυλέτης -ου ὁ	tribesman
	πρεσβύτατος -η -ον	eldest
	καταμανθάνω κατεμαθον	I examine
	παιδάριον -ου τό	infant
3	εὐπαγής -ές	sturdy
	ῥωμαλέος -α -ον	strong
	κλῆρος -ου ὁ	plot of land
	ἐνακισχίλιοι -αι -α	9000 (*traditional number of Spartan citizens*)
	προσνέμω προσένειμα	I assign
5	ἀγγενής -ές	ill-born
	ἄμορφος -ον	deformed
	Ἀποθέται -ων αἱ	Apothetae (*lit* disposal place)
	Ταΰγετον -ου τό	Mount Taygetus (*range towering above Sparta*)
	βαραθρώδης -ες	full of chasms
7	εὐεξία -ας ἡ	good state, health
	ῥώμη -ης ἡ	strength
	φύω *pf* πέφυκα	I grow
	βρέφος -ους τό	baby
	περιλούω	I bathe
9	βάσανος -ου ἡ	test
	κρᾶσις -εως ἡ	constitution (*lit* mixture, *i.e. of elements in the body*)
	ἐξίσταμαι	I lose my senses (*lit* stand outside myself)
	ἐπιληπτικός -ή -όν	epileptic
	νοσώδης -ες	sickly
10	ἄκρατος -ον	strong, unmixed (*understand* wine)
	ἀποσφακελίζω	I fall into convusions
	ὑγιεινός -ή -όν	healthy

μᾶλλον στομοῦσθαι καὶ κρατύνεσθαι τὴν ἕξιν. ἦν δὲ περὶ τὰς τροφοὺς
ἐπιμέλειά τις μετὰ τέχνης, ὥστ᾽ ἄνευ σπαργάνων ἐκτρεφούσας τὰ βρέφη
τοῖς μέλεσι καὶ τοῖς εἴδεσιν ἐλευθέρια ποιεῖν, ἔτι δὲ εὔκολα ταῖς διαίταις
καὶ ἄσικχα καὶ ἀθαμβῆ σκότου καὶ πρὸς ἐρημίαν ἄφοβα καὶ ἄπειρα
15 δυσκολίας ἀγεννοὺς καὶ κλαυθμυρισμῶν. διὸ καὶ τῶν ἔξωθεν ἔνιοι τοῖς
τέκνοις Λακωνικὰς ἐωνοῦντο τίτθας.

τοὺς δὲ Σπαρτιατῶν παῖδας οὐκ ἐπὶ ὠνητοῖς οὐδὲ μισθίοις ἐποιήσατο
παιδαγωγοῖς ὁ Λυκοῦργος, οὐδ᾽ ἐξῆν ἑκάστῳ τρέφειν οὐδὲ παιδεύειν ὡς
ἐβούλετο τὸν υἱόν, ἀλλὰ πάντας εὐθὺς ἑπταετεῖς γενομένους
20 παραλαμβάνων αὐτὸς εἰς ἀγέλας κατελόχιζε, καὶ συννόμους ποιῶν καὶ
συντρόφους μετ᾽ ἀλλήλων εἴθιζε συμπαίζειν καὶ συσχολάζειν. ἄρχοντα

	στομόω	I harden
	κρατύνω	I strengthen
	ἕξις -εως ἡ	condition
	τροφός -οῦ ἡ	nurse
12	ἐπιμέλεια -ας ἡ	care, concern
	σπάργανα -ων τά	swaddling clothes
	μέλος -ους τό	limb
	εἶδος -ους τό	figure
	ἐλευθέριος -α -ον	free
13	εὔκολος -ον	contented
	δίαιτα -ης ἡ	diet, daily regime
	ἄσικχος -ον	not fussy about food
	ἀθαμβής -ές	not scared
	ἐρημία -ας ἡ	solitude, being left alone
14	ἄφοβος -ον	fearless
	ἄπειρος -ον	without experience of
	δυσκολία -ας ἡ	peevishness
	ἀγγενής -ές	ignoble
	κλαυθμυρισμός -οῦ ὁ	whining
15	διό	for that reason
	ἔξωθεν	from outside, from other states
	ἔνιοι -αι -α	some
	Λακωνικός -ή -όν	Spartan
	ὠνέομαι	I buy
16	τίτθη -ης ἡ	nurse
	Σπαρτιάτης -ου ὁ	Spartan citizen
	ὠνητός -ή -όν	bought
	μίσθιος -α -ον	hired
	παιδαγωγός -οῦ ὁ	tutor (*elderly male slave looking after children*)
18	Λυκοῦργος -ου ὁ	Lycurgus
	ἑπταετής -ές	seven years old
	παραλαμβάνω	I take over, I take with me
	ἀγέλη -ης ἡ	company
	καταλοχίζω	I enrol (someone)
20	σύννομος -ον	feeding together
	σύντροφος -ον	brought up together
	ἐθίζω	I accustom (someone)
	συμπαίζω	I play together
	συσχολάζω	I learn together

δ' αὐτοῖς <u>παρίστατο</u> τῆς ἀγέλης τὸν τῷ <u>φρονεῖν διαφέροντα</u> καὶ
<u>θυμοειδέστατον</u> ἐν τῷ μάχεσθαι· καὶ πρὸς τοῦτον <u>ἀφεώρων</u> καὶ
<u>προστάττοντος ἠκροῶντο</u> καὶ κολάζοντος <u>ἐκαρτέρουν</u>, ὥστε τὴν <u>παιδείαν</u>
25 εἶναι <u>μελέτην εὐπειθείας</u>. <u>ἐπεσκόπουν</u> δὲ οἱ <u>πρεσβύτεροι</u> παίζοντας
αὐτούς, καὶ <u>τὰ πολλὰ</u> μάχας τινὰς ἐμβάλλοντες ἀεὶ καὶ <u>φιλονεικίας</u>, οὐ
<u>παρέργως</u> κατεμάνθανον ὁποῖός ἐστι τὴν <u>φύσιν</u> ἕκαστος αὐτῶν πρὸς τὸ
τολμᾶν καὶ μὴ <u>φυγομαχεῖν</u> ταῖς <u>ἁμίλλαις</u>.

<u>γράμματα</u> μὲν οὖν ἕνεκα τῆς <u>χρείας</u> ἐμάνθανον· ἡ δ' ἄλλη πᾶσα παιδεία
30 πρὸς τὸ ἄρχεσθαι καλῶς <u>ἐγίνετο</u> καὶ καρτερεῖν <u>πονοῦντα</u> καὶ νικᾶν
μαχόμενον. διὸ καὶ τῆς <u>ἡλικίας προερχομένης ἐπέτεινον</u> αὐτῶν τὴν
<u>ἄσκησιν</u>, ἐν <u>χρῷ</u> τε <u>κείροντες</u> καὶ βαδίζειν <u>ἀνυποδήτους</u> παίζειν τε
γυμνοὺς ὡς τὰ πολλὰ <u>συνεθίζοντες</u>. γενόμενοι δὲ <u>δωδεκαετεῖς</u> ἄνευ
<u>χιτῶνος</u> ἤδη <u>διετέλουν</u>, ἓν <u>ἱμάτιον</u> εἰς τὸν <u>ἐνιαυτὸν</u> λαμβάνοντες,

	παρίσταμαι	I put X (acc) in charge of Y (dat)
	φρονέω	I am sensible, I have good judgement
	διαφέρω	I stand out
	θυμοειδής -ές	courageous
23	ἀφοράω impf ἀφεώρων	I keep my eyes on
	προστάττω	I give orders
	ἀκροάομαι	I obey
	καρτερέω	I am strong, I endure
	παιδεία -ας ἡ	training, education
25	μελέτη -ης ἡ	practice
	εὐπειθεία -ας ἡ	obedience
	ἐπισκοπέω	I watch, I oversee
	πρεσβύτερος -α -ον	older
	τὰ πολλά	often
26	φιλονεικία -ας ἡ	dispute
	παρέργως	incidentally, cursorily
	φύσις -εως ἡ	nature, disposition
	φυγομαχέω	I shun battle
	ἄμιλλα -ης ἡ	contest
29	γράμμα -ατος τό	letter (of the alphabet)
	χρεία -ας ἡ	use
	ἐγίνετο	(= ἐγίγνετο)
	πονέω	I toil, I endure hardship
	ἡλικία -ας ἡ	age
31	προέρχομαι	(of time) elapse, go forward
	ἐπιτείνω	I extend, I increase
	ἄσκησις -εως ἡ	exercise
	χρώς dat χρῷ ὁ	skin (phrase implies down to ...)
	κείρω	I cut
32	ἀνυπόδητος -ον	unshod
	συνεθίζω	I accustom (someone)
	δωδεκαετής -ές	twelve years old
	χιτών -ῶνος ὁ	cloak
	διατελέω	I continue (here implying do X from that point on)
34	ἱμάτιον -ου τό	tunic
	ἐνιαυτός -οῦ ὁ	year

35 αὐχμηροὶ τὰ σώματα καὶ λουτρῶν καὶ ἀλειμμάτων ἄπειροι· πλὴν ὀλίγας
   ἡμέρας τινὰς τοῦ ἐνιαυτοῦ τῆς τοιαύτης φιλανθρωπίας μετεῖχον.
   ἐκάθευδον δὲ ὁμοῦ κατ᾽ ἴλην καὶ ἀγέλην ἐπὶ στιβάδων, ἃς αὑτοῖς
   συνεφόρουν, τοῦ παρὰ τὸν Εὐρώταν πεφυκότος καλάμου τὰ ἄκρα ταῖς
   χερσὶν ἄνευ σιδήρου κατακλάσαντες.

40 ἤδη δὲ τοῖς τηλικούτοις ἐρασταὶ τῶν εὐδοκίμων νέων συνανεστρέφοντο·
   καὶ προσεῖχον οἱ πρεσβύτεροι, καὶ μᾶλλον ἐπιφοιτῶντες εἰς τὰ γυμνάσια,
   καὶ μαχομένοις καὶ σκώπτουσιν ἀλλήλους παρατυγχάνοντες, οὐ παρέργως,
   ἀλλὰ τρόπον τινὰ πάντες οἰόμενοι πάντων καὶ πατέρες εἶναι καὶ
   παιδαγωγοὶ καὶ ἄρχοντες, ὥστε μήτε καιρὸν ἀπολείπεσθαι μήτε χωρίον
45 ἔρημον τοῦ νουθετοῦντος τὸν ἁμαρτάνοντα καὶ κολάζοντος. οὐ μὴν ἀλλὰ
   καὶ παιδονόμος ἐκ τῶν καλῶν καὶ ἀγαθῶν ἀνδρῶν ἐτάττετο, καὶ κατ᾽
   ἀγέλας αὐτοὶ προίσταντο τῶν λεγομένων εἰρένων ἀεὶ τὸν σωφρονέστατον
   καὶ μαχιμώτατον (εἴρενας δὲ καλοῦσι τοὺς ἔτος ἤδη δεύτερον ἐκ παίδων
   γεγονότας).

	αὐχμηρός -ά -όν	hard and dry
	λουτρόν -ου τό	bath
	ἄλειμμα -ατος τό	ointment, oil
	ἄπειρος -ον	without experience
36	φιλανθρωπία -ας ἡ	indulgence, amenity
	ὁμοῦ	together
	ἴλη -ης ἡ	troop
	ἀγέλη -ης ἡ	company
	στιβάς -άδος ἡ	bed of rushes
38	συμφορέω	I gather
	Εὐρώτας -α ὁ	River Eurotas (Sparta lies in its fertile valley)
	φύω pf πέφυκα	I grow
	κάλαμος -ου ὁ	reed
	σίδηρος -ου ὁ	knife
39	κατακλάω κατέκλασα	I break off
	τηλικοῦτος -αύτη -οῦτο	at this age
	ἐραστής -οῦ ὁ	lover
	εὐδόκιμος -ον	reputable, distinguished
	συναναστρέφομαι	I associate with (+ dat)
41	προσέχω	I pay attention (lit apply, understanding τὸν νοῦν)
	ἐπιφοιτάω	I come frequently
	γυμνάσιον -ου τό	exercise ground
	σκώπτω	I make fun of
	παρατυγχάνω	I happen to be present
42	παρέργως	incidentally, cursorily
	οἴομαι	I think
	παιδαγωγός -οῦ ὁ	tutor
	ἀπολείπω	I leave
	ἔρημος -η -ον	deprived of, without (+ gen)
45	νουθετέω	I advise, I warn
	οὐ μὴν ἀλλά	and furthermore
	παιδονόμος -ου ὁ	inspector or overseer of boys
	προίσταμαι	I put myself under the command of (+ gen)
	εἰρήν -ένος ὁ	eiren (Spartan term for pack leader)
48	μάχιμος -ον	warlike, good at fighting

132

50 οὗτος οὖν ὁ εἴρην, εἴκοσι ἔτη γεγονώς, ἄρχει τε τῶν ὑποτεταγμένων ἐν
    ταῖς μάχαις, καὶ κατ' οἶκον ὑπηρέταις χρῆται πρὸς τὸ δεῖπνον. ἐπιτάσσει
    δὲ τοῖς μὲν ἁδροῖς ξύλα φέρειν, τοῖς δὲ μικροτέροις λάχανα. καὶ φέρουσι
    κλέπτοντες, οἱ μὲν ἐπὶ τοὺς κήπους βαδίζοντες, οἱ δὲ εἰς τὰ τῶν ἀνδρῶν
    συσσίτια παρεισρέοντες εὖ μάλα πανούργως καὶ πεφυλαγμένως· ἂν δ' ἁλῷ,
55 πολλὰς λαμβάνει πληγὰς τῇ μάστιγι, ῥᾳθύμως δοκῶν κλέπτειν καὶ
    ἀτέχνως. κλέπτουσι δὲ καὶ τῶν σιτίων ὅ τι ἂν δύνωνται, μανθάνοντες
    εὐφυῶς ἐπιτίθεσθαι τοῖς καθεύδουσιν ἢ ῥᾳθύμως φυλάττουσιν. τῷ δὲ
    ἁλόντι ζημία πληγαὶ καὶ τὸ πεινῆν. γλίσχρον γὰρ αὐτοῖς ἐστι δεῖπνον,
    ὅπως δι' αὑτῶν ἀμυνόμενοι τὴν ἔνδειαν ἀναγκάζωνται τολμᾶν καὶ
60 πανουργεῖν. οὕτω δὲ κλέπτουσι πεφροντισμένως οἱ παῖδες, ὥστε λέγεταί
    τις ἤδη σκύμνον ἀλώπεκος κεκλοφὼς καὶ τῷ τριβωνίῳ περιστέλλων,
    σπαρασσόμενος ὑπὸ τοῦ θηρίου τὴν γαστέρα τοῖς ὄνυξι καὶ τοῖς ὀδοῦσι,
    ὑπὲρ τοῦ λαθεῖν ἐγκαρτερῶν ἀποθανεῖν.

	ὑποτάσσω *pf pass* ὑποτέταγμαι	I put under authority
	ὑπηρέτης -ου ὁ	servant, attendant
	ἐπιτάσσω	I instruct
	ἁδρός -ά -όν	fully grown
52	ξύλον -ου τό	wood
	λάχανον -ου τό	vegetable
	κῆπος -ου ὁ	garden, orchard
	συσσίτιον -ου τό	mess, communal dining room
	παρεισρέω	I creep in secretly
54	πανούργως	cunningly
	πεφυλαγμένως	cautiously
	ἁλίσκομαι ἑάλων	
	(*here aor subj 3 sg*)	I am caught
	πληγή -ῆς ἡ	blow
55	μάστιξ -ιγος ἡ	whip
	ῥᾳθύμως	carelessly
	ἀτέχνως	without skill
	σιτίον -ου τό	food
	εὐφυῶς	cleverly
57	ἐπιτίθεμαι	I attack (+ *dat*)
	ζημία -ας ἡ	penalty
	πεινάω	I go hungry
	γλίσχρος -α -ον	scanty
	ἔνδεια	lack (*here understand* of food)
60	πανουργέω	I am cunning
	πεφροντισμένως	carefully, earnestly
	σκύμνος -ου ὁ	cub
	ἀλώπηξ -εκος ἡ	fox
	τριβώνιον -ου τό	cloak
61	περιστέλλω	I wrap, I conceal
	σπαράσσω	I tear at
	θηρίον -ου τό	beast
	γαστήρ -τρος ἡ	stomach
	ὄνυξ -υχος ὁ	claw
62	ὀδούς -όντος ὁ	tooth
	ἐγκαρτερέω	I endure, I withstand

Reading 10:

Anacharsis and Athletics

Lucian was a Syrian Greek writing about 160 AD (the latest author represented in this book), when many people looked back with nostalgia to the great days of Greek history. Anacharsis is one of his 'imaginary conversations' which involve a range of historical and mythological characters from earlier literature. As in Herodotus and Plato, the Athenian Solon has the role of wise man and interpreter. Anacharsis himself also featured in Herodotus, as a sixth-century BC Scythian prince who travelled widely and acquired a reputation for wisdom. Here he is presented as a visitor to the Lyceum gymnasium in Athens unable to comprehend the value the Greeks attach to athletics, which Solon proceeds to explain and defend. (1-10)

AN. ταῦτα δὲ ὑμῖν, ὦ <u>Σόλων</u>, τίνος ἕνεκα οἱ <u>νέοι</u> ποιοῦσιν; οἱ μὲν αὐτῶν
<u>περιπλεκόμενοι</u> ἀλλήλους <u>ὑποσκελίζουσιν</u>, οἱ δὲ <u>ἄγχουσι</u> καὶ
<u>λυγίζουσι</u> καὶ ἐν τῷ <u>πηλῷ</u> <u>συναναφύρονται</u> <u>κυλινδούμενοι</u> ὥσπερ
<u>σύες</u>. καίτοι κατ᾽ ἀρχὰς εὐθὺς <u>ἀποδυσάμενοι</u> (ἑώρων γάρ) <u>λίπα</u> τε
5 <u>ἠλείψαντο</u> καὶ <u>κατέψησε</u> μαλα <u>εἰρηνικῶς</u> <u>ἅτερος</u> τὸν ἕτερον ἐν τῷ
<u>μέρει</u>. <u>μετὰ</u> δὲ οὐκ οἶδ᾽ <u>ὅ τι παθόντες</u> <u>ὠθοῦσί</u> τε ἀλλήλους
<u>συννενευκότες</u> καὶ τὰ <u>μέτωπα</u> <u>συναράττουσιν</u> ὥσπερ οἱ <u>κριοί</u>. καὶ <u>ἦν</u>
ἰδοὺ <u>ἀράμενος</u> <u>ἐκεινοσὶ</u> τὸν ἕτερον ἐκ τοῖν <u>σκελοῖν</u> <u>ἀφῆκεν</u> εἰς τὸ
<u>ἔδαφος</u>, εἶτ᾽ ἐπικαταπεσὼν <u>ἀνακύπτειν</u> οὐκ ἐᾷ, συνωθῶν <u>κάτω</u> εἰς τὸν
10 πηλόν· τέλος δὲ ἤδη <u>περιπλέξας</u> αὐτῷ τὰ σκέλη κατὰ τὴν <u>γαστέρα</u>

	Σόλων -ωνος ὁ	Solon
	περιπλέκομαι	I wind myself round
	ὑποσκελίζω	I trip (someone) up
	ἄγχω	I throttle
3	λυγίζω	I twist (something/someone)
	πηλός -οῦ ὁ	mud
	συναναφύρομαι	I wallow together
	κυλινδέομαι	I roll around
	σῦς συός ὁ/ἡ	pig
4	ἀποδύομαι ἀπεδυσάμην	I undress
	λίπα	thickly with oil
	ἀλείφομαι ἠλειψάμην	I anoint myself
	καταψάω κατέψησα	I rub down
	εἰρηνικῶς	peacefully
5	ἅτερος	(*crasis of* ὁ ἕτερος)
	μετά	(*as adv*) afterwards
	τί παθόντες	*lit* having suffered what? *i.e.* why ever do they ... ?
	ὠθέω	I push
	συννεύω *pf* συννένευκα	I lower my head
7	μέτωπον -ου τό	forehead
	συναράττω	I strike together
	κριός -οῦ ὁ	ram
	ἦν	look!
	ἐκεινοσί	that one there (-ὶ *suffix indicates pointing*)
8	σκέλος -ους τό	leg
	ἀφίημι ἀφῆκα	I throw
	ἔδαφος -ους τό	ground
	ἀνακύπτω	I get up
	κάτω	downwards
10	περιπλέκω περιέπλεξα	I wind (something) round
	γαστήρ -τρός ἡ	stomach

τὸν πῆχυν ὑποβαλὼν τῷ λαιμῷ ἄγχει ἄθλιον, ὁ δὲ παρακροτεῖ εἰς
τὸν ὦμον, ἱκετεύων οἶμαι, ὡς μὴ τέλεον ἀποπνιγείη. καὶ οὐδὲ τοῦ
ἐλαίου ἕνεκα φείδονται μὴ μολύνεσθαι, ἀλλ᾿ ἀφανίσαντες τὸ χρίσμα
καὶ τοῦ βορβόρου ἀναπλησθέντες ἐν ἱδρῶτι ἅμα πολλῷ γέλωτα ἐμοὶ
γοῦν παρέχουσιν ὥσπερ αἱ ἐγχέλυες ἐκ τῶν χειρῶν διολισθαίνοντες.

ἕτεροι δὲ ἐν τῷ αἰθρίῳ τῆς αὐλῆς τὸ αὐτὸ τοῦτο δρῶσιν, οὐκ ἐν
πηλῷ οὗτοί γε, ἀλλὰ ψάμμον ταύτην βαθεῖαν ὑποβαλόμενοι ἐν τῷ
ὀρύγματι πάττουσίν τε ἀλλήλους καὶ αὐτοὶ ἑκόντες ἐπαμῶνται τὴν
κόνιν ἀλεκτρυόνων δίκην, ὡς ἀφυκτότεροι εἶεν ἐν ταῖς συμπλοκαῖς,
οἶμαι, τῆς ψάμμου τὸν ὄλισθον ἀφαιρούσης καὶ βεβαιοτέραν ἐν ξηρῷ
παρεχούσης τὴν ἀντίληψιν.

	πῆχυς -εως ὁ	forearm
	λαιμός -οῦ ὁ	throat
	ἄγχω	I throttle
	ἄθλιος -α -ον	poor, wretched
11	παρακροτέω	I slap
	ὦμος -ου ὁ	shoulder
	ἱκετεύω	I beg
	οἶμαι	I think
	τέλεον	completely
12	ἀποπνίγω *aor pass* ἀπεπνίγην	I strangle
	ἔλαιον -ου τό	olive oil
	φείδομαι	*lit* I spare, (+ μή + *inf*) I avoid (doing X)
	μολύνομαι	I get dirty
	ἀφανίζω ἠφάνισα	I remove
13	χρίσμα -ατος τό	oil rubbed on
	βόρβορος -ου ὁ	mud
	ἀναπίμπλημι	
	aor pass ἀνεπλήσθην	*lit* I fill up, *here* I plaster with
	ἱδρώς -ῶτος ὁ	sweat
14	γέλως -ωτος ὁ	object of laughter
	ἔγχελυς -υος ἡ	eel
	διολισθαίνω	I slip through
	αἰθρίον -ου τό	uncovered part
	αὐλή -ῆς ἡ	courtyard
17	πηλός -οῦ ὁ	mud
	ψάμμος -ου ἡ	sand
	ὄρυγμα -ατος τό	pit
	πάττω	I sprinkle
	ἐπαμάομαι	I scrape together
19	κόνις -εως ἡ	dust
	ἀλεκτρυών -όνος ὁ	cock
	δίκην	(*foll gen*) *lit* according to the just behaviour of, *i.e.* like
	ἄφυκτος -ον	unable to escape
	συμπλοκή -ῆς ἡ	close encounter
20	ὄλισθος -ου ὁ	slipperiness
	ξηρός -ά -όν	dry
	ἀντίληψις -εως ἡ	grip

οἱ δὲ ὀρθοστάδην κεκονιμένοι καὶ αὐτοὶ παίουσιν ἀλλήλους
προσπεσόντες καὶ λακτίζουσιν. οὑτοσὶ γοῦν καὶ τοὺς ὀδόντας ἔοικεν
ἀποπτύσειν ὁ κακοδαίμων, οὕτως αἵματος αὐτῷ καὶ ψάμμου
25 ἀναπέπλησται τὸ στόμα, πύξ, ὡς ὁρᾷς, παταχθέντος εἰς τὴν γνάθον.
ἀλλ᾽ οὐδὲ ὁ ἄρχων οὑτοσὶ διίστησιν αὐτοὺς καὶ λύει τὴν μάχην
(τεκμαίρομαι γὰρ τῇ πορφυρίδι τῶν ἀρχόντων τινὰ τοῦτον εἶναι) ὁ δὲ
καὶ ἐποτρύνει καὶ τὸν πατάξαντα ἐπαινεῖ.

ἄλλοι δὲ ἀλλαχόθι πάντες ἐγκονοῦσιν καὶ ἀναπηδῶσιν ὥσπερ θέοντες
30 ἐπὶ τοῦ αὐτοῦ μένοντες καὶ εἰς τὸ ἄνω συναλλόμενοι λακτίζουσιν
τὸν ἀέρα. ταῦτα οὖν ἐθέλω εἰδέναι τίνος ἀγαθοῦ ἂν εἴη ποιεῖν· ὡς
ἔμοιγε μανίᾳ μᾶλλον ἐοικέναι δοκεῖ τὸ πρᾶγμα, καὶ οὐκ ἔστιν ὅστις
ἂν ῥᾳδίως μεταπείσειέ με ὡς οὐ παραπαίουσιν οἱ ταῦτα δρῶντες.

ΣΩ. καὶ εἰκότως, ὦ Ἀνάχαρσι, τοιαῦτά σοι τὰ γιγνόμενα φαίνεται, ξένα
35 γε ὄντα καὶ πάμπολυ τῶν Σκυθικῶν ἐθῶν ἀπᾴδοντα, καθάπερ καὶ

	ὀρθοστάδην	standing upright
	κονίω *pf pass* κεκόνιμαι	I cover with dust
	παίω	I hit
	λακτίζω	I kick
23	ὀδούς -όντος ὁ	tooth
	ἔοικα (*pf with pres sense*)	I seem likely (to, + *inf*)
	ἀποπτύω	I spit out
	κακοδαίμων -ον	unlucky
	ἀναπίμπλημι	
25	*pf pass* ἀναπέπλημαι	I fill up
	πύξ	with the fist
	πατάσσω *aor pass* ἐπατάχθην	I strike
	γνάθος -ους ἡ	jaw
	ἄρχων -οντος ὁ	official
26	διίστημι	I make stand apart
	λύω	(*here*) I break up
	τεκμαίρομαι	I infer
	πορφυρίς -ίδος ἡ	purple cloak
	ἐποτρύνω	I urge on
29	ἀλλαχόθι	in other places
	ἐγκονέω	I exert myself
	θέω	I run
	ἄνω	upwards
	συνάλλομαι	I leap together
31	ἀήρ -έρος ὁ	air
	μεταπείθω μετέπεισα	I change someone's mind
	παραπαίω	I am out of my mind
	εἰκότως	reasonably
	Ἀνάχαρσις -εως ὁ	Anacharsis
35	πάμπολυ	very much
	Σκυθικός -ή -όν	Scythian (*from Scythia, roughly modern southern Russia*)
	ἔθος -ους τό	custom
	ἀπᾴδω	I am out of tune with (+ *gen*)
35	καθάπερ	just as

ὑμῖν πολλὰ εἰκὸς εἶναι <u>μαθήματα</u> καὶ <u>ἐπιτηδεύματα</u> τοῖς Ἕλλησιν
ἡμῖν <u>ἀλλόκοτα</u> εἶναι δόξαντα ἄν, εἴ τις ἡμῶν ὥσπερ σὺ νῦν <u>ἐπισταίη</u>
αὐτοῖς. πλὴν ἀλλὰ θάρρει, <u>ὦγαθέ</u>· οὐ γὰρ μανία τὰ γιγνόμενά ἐστιν

40 οὐδ᾽ ἐφ᾽ <u>ὕβρει</u> οὗτοι <u>παίουσιν</u> ἀλλήλους καὶ <u>κυλίουσιν</u> ἐν τῷ πηλῷ ἢ
<u>ἐπιπάττουσιν</u> τὴν κόνιν, ἀλλ᾽ ἔχει τινὰ <u>χρείαν</u> οὐκ <u>ἀτερπῆ</u> τὸ πρᾶγμα
καὶ <u>ἀκμὴν</u> οὐ μικρὰν ἐπάγει τοῖς σώμασιν· ἢν γοῦν <u>ἐνδιατρίψῃς</u>,
ὥσπερ οἶμαί σε ποιήσειν, τῇ Ἑλλάδι, <u>οὐκ εἰς μακρὰν</u> εἷς καὶ αὐτὸς
ἔσῃ τῶν <u>πεπηλωμένων</u> ἢ κεκονιμένων· οὕτω σοι τὸ πρᾶγμα ἡδύ τε
ἅμα καὶ <u>λυσιτελὲς</u> εἶναι δόξει.

45 ΑΝ. <u>ἄπαγε</u>, ὦ Σόλων, ὑμῖν ταῦτα γένοιτο τὰ <u>ὠφέλιμα</u> καὶ <u>τερπνά</u>, ἐμὲ δὲ
εἴ τις ὑμῶν τοιοῦτό τι <u>διαθείη</u>, εἴσεται ὡς οὐ μάτην <u>παρεζώσμεθα</u>
τὸν <u>ἀκινάκην</u>. <u>ἀτὰρ</u> εἰπέ μοι, τί ὄνομα ἔθεσθε τοῖς γιγνομένοις, ἢ τί
φῶμεν ποιεῖν αὐτούς;

ΣΩ. ὁ μὲν <u>χῶρος</u> αὐτός, ὦ Ἀνάχαρσι, <u>γυμνάσιον</u> ὑφ᾽ ἡμῶν <u>ὀνομάζεται</u>

50 καὶ ἔστιν ἱερὸν <u>Ἀπόλλωνος</u> τοῦ <u>Λυκείου</u>. καὶ τὸ <u>ἄγαλμα</u> δὲ αὐτοῦ
ὁρᾷς, τὸν ἐπὶ τῇ <u>στήλῃ</u> <u>κεκλιμένον</u>, τῇ ἀριστερᾷ μὲν τὸ τόξον

	μάθημα -ατος τό	art, doctrine
	ἐπιτήδευμα -ατος τό	practice
	ἀλλόκοτος -ον	strange
	ἐφίστημι (aor opt 3 sg ἐπισταίη)	I pause and look at (+ dat)
38	ὠγαθέ	(crasis of ὦ ἀγαθέ)
	ὕβρις -εως ἡ	violence, brutality
	παίω	I hit
	κυλίω	I wallow
	ἐπιπάττω	I sprinkle on
40	χρεία -ας ἡ	usefulness
	ἀτερπής -ές	unpleasant
	ἀκμή -ῆς ἡ	vigour, strength
	ἐνδιατρίβω ἐνδιέτριψα	I spend time in (+ dat)
	οὐκ εἰς μακράν	before long
45	πηλόομαι pf πεπήλωμαι	I wallow in the mud
	λυσιτελής -ές	profitable
	ἄπαγε	get away with you!
	ὠφέλιμος -ον	useful
	τερπνός -ή -όν	pleasant
46	διατίθημι (aor opt 3 sg διαθείη)	I treat
	παραζώννυμι	
	pf pass παρέζωσμαι	I fasten to my belt
	ἀκινάκης -ου ὁ	dagger
	ἀτάρ	but
49	γυμνάσιον -ου τό	gymnasium
	ὀνομάζω	I call
	Ἀπόλλων -ωνος ὁ	Apollo
	Λύκειος	Lyceian (title of Apollo, variously explained as wolf god/from Lycia/god of light)
50	ἄγαλμα -ατος τό	statue
	στήλη -ης ἡ	pillar
	κλίνω pf pass κέκλιμαι	I lean (something)

137

ἔχοντα, ἡ δεξιὰ δὲ ὑπὲρ τῆς κεφαλῆς <u>ἀνακεκλασμένη</u> ὥσπερ ἐκ
<u>καμάτου</u> μακροῦ <u>ἀναπαυόμενον</u> δείκνυσι τὸν θεόν. τῶν <u>γυμνασμάτων</u>
δὲ τούτων τὸ μὲν ἐν τῷ πηλῷ ἐκεῖνο <u>πάλη</u> καλεῖται, οἱ δ' ἐν τῇ κόνει
55   <u>παλαίουσι</u> καὶ αὐτοί, τὸ δὲ παίειν ἀλλήλους <u>ὀρθοστάδην</u>
<u>παγκρατιάζειν</u> λέγομεν. καὶ ἄλλα δὲ ἡμῖν ἐστι <u>γυμνάσια</u> τοιαῦτα
<u>πυγμῆς</u> καὶ <u>δίσκου</u> καὶ τοῦ <u>ὑπεράλλεσθαι</u>, ὧν ἁπάντων ἀγῶνας
<u>προτίθεμεν</u>, καὶ ὁ κρατήσας ἄριστος εἶναι δοκεῖ τῶν <u>καθ' αὐτὸν</u> καὶ
<u>ἀναιρεῖται</u> τὰ ἆθλα.

60   ΑΝ. τὰ δὲ ἆθλα τίνα ὑμῖν ταῦτά ἐστιν;

ΣΩ. Ὀλυμπίασι μὲν <u>στέφανος</u> ἐκ <u>κοτίνου</u>, <u>Ἰσθμοῖ</u> δὲ ἐκ <u>πίτυος</u>, ἐν <u>Νεμέα</u>
δὲ <u>σελίνων</u> <u>πεπλεγμένος</u>, <u>Πυθοῖ</u> δὲ <u>μῆλα</u> τῶν ἱερῶν τοῦ θεοῦ, παρ'
ἡμῖν δὲ τοῖς <u>Παναθηναίοις</u> τὸ ἔλαιον τὸ ἐκ τῆς <u>μορίας</u>. τί ἐγέλασας,
ὦ Ἀνάχαρσι· ἢ διότι μικρά σοι εἶναι ταῦτα δοκεῖ;

65   ΑΝ. οὔκ, ἀλλὰ <u>πάνσεμνα</u>, ὦ Σόλων, <u>κατέλεξας</u> τὰ ἆθλα καὶ ἄξια τοῖς τε
<u>διαθεῖσιν</u> αὐτὰ <u>φιλοτιμεῖσθαι</u> ἐπὶ τῇ <u>μεγαλοδωρεᾷ</u> καὶ τοῖς <u>ἀγωνισταῖς</u>

	ἀνακλάω	
	pf pass ἀνακέκλασμαι	I bend back
	κάματος -ου ὁ	exertion
	ἀναπαύομαι	I rest
53	γύμνασμα -ατος τό	athletic exercise
	πάλη -ης ἡ	wrestling
	παλαίω	I wrestle
	ὀρθοστάδην	standing upright
	παγκρατιάζω	I take part in the pancratium (*'all-in' boxing/wrestling*)
56	γυμνάσια -ων τά	athletic exercises
	πυγμή -ῆς ἡ	boxing
	δίσκος -ου ὁ	discus
	ὑπεράλλομαι	I jump
	προτίθημι	I hold, I arrange
58	καθ' αὑτόν	in his own time
	ἀναιρέομαι	I carry off
	Ὀλυμπίασι	at Olympia, *i.e.* at the Olympic games
	στέφανος -ου ὁ	wreath
	κότινος -ου ὁ	wild olive
61	Ἰσθμοῖ	at the Isthmus (of Corinth), *i.e.* at the Isthmian games
	πίτυς -υος ἡ	pine
	Νεμέα -ας ἡ	Nemea (*in the Peloponnese; Nemean games held there*)
	σέλινον -ου τό	parsley
	πλέκω *pf pass* πέπλεγμαι	I plait, I weave together
62	Πυθοῖ	at Delphi (*also called* Pytho), *i.e.* at the Pythian games
	μῆλον -ου τό	apple
	Παναθηναία -ων τά	Panathenaea (*Athenian festival including games*)
	μορία -ας ἡ	sacred olive
	πάνσεμνος -ον	highly impressive (*here ironic*)
65	καταλέγω κατέλεξα	I list
	διατίθημι *aor pple* διαθείς	I offer
	φιλοτιμέομαι	I take pride
	μεγαλοδωρεά -ᾶς ἡ	generous provision of gifts
	ἀγωνιστής -οῦ ὁ	competitor

138

αὐτοῖς <u>ὑπερεσπουδακέναι</u> περὶ τὴν <u>ἀναίρεσιν</u> τῶν <u>τηλικούτων</u>, ὥστε
<u>μήλων</u> ἕνεκα καὶ <u>σελίνων</u> τοσαῦτα <u>προπονεῖν</u> καὶ κινδυνεύειν
ἀγχομένους πρὸς ἀλλήλων καὶ <u>κατακλωμένους</u>, ὡς οὐκ <u>ἐνὸν</u>
70 <u>ἀπραγμόνως</u> <u>εὐπορῆσαι</u> μήλων ὅτῳ <u>ἐπιθυμία</u> ἢ σελίνῳ <u>ἐστεφανῶσθαι</u>
ἢ <u>πίτυι</u> μήτε πηλῷ <u>καταχρίομενον</u> τὸ <u>πρόσωπον</u> μήτε <u>λακτιζόμενον</u>
εἰς τὴν γαστέρα ὑπὸ <u>ἀνταγωνιστῶν</u>.

ΣΩ. ἀλλ', ὦ ἄριστε, οὐκ εἰς <u>ψιλὰ</u> τὰ διδόμενα ἡμεῖς <u>ἀποβλέπομεν</u>. ταῦτα
μὲν γάρ ἐστι <u>σημεῖα</u> τῆς <u>νίκης</u> καὶ <u>γνωρίσματα</u> οἵτινες οἱ
75 κρατήσαντες. ἡ δὲ <u>παρακολουθοῦσα</u> τούτοις δόξα τοῦ παντὸς ἀξία
τοῖς νενικηκόσιν, ὑπὲρ ἧς καὶ λακτίζεσθαι καλῶς ἔχει τοῖς
<u>θηρωμένοις</u> τὴν <u>εὔκλειαν</u> ἐκ τῶν πόνων. οὐ γὰρ <u>ἀπονητὶ</u> προσγένοιτο
ἂν αὕτη, ἀλλὰ χρὴ τὸν <u>ὀρεγόμενον</u> αὐτῆς πολλὰ τὰ <u>δυσχερῆ</u>
<u>ἀνασχόμενον</u> ἐν τῇ ἀρχῇ τότ' ἤδη τὸ <u>λυσιτελὲς</u> καὶ ἡδὺ τέλος ἐκ τῶν
80 <u>καμάτων</u> <u>περιμένειν</u>.

ΑΝ. τοῦτο φῇς, ὦ Σόλων, τὸ τέλος ἡδὺ καὶ λυσιτελές, ὅτι πάντες αὐτοὺς
ὄψονται ἐστεφανωμένους καὶ ἐπὶ τῇ νίκῃ ἐπαινέσονται πολὺ πρότερον

	ὑπερσπουδάζω	
	pf ὑπερεσπούδακα	I get very enthusiastic
	ἀναίρεσις -εως ἡ	winning, carrying off
	τηλικοῦτος -αύτη -οῦτο	such great
68	μῆλον -ου τό	apple
	σέλινον -ου τό	parsley
	προπονέω	I toil beforehand
	κατακλάω	I smash up
	ἔνεστι *acc absolute* ἐνόν	it is possible
70	ἀπραγμόνως	without any trouble
	εὐπορέω ηὐπόρησα	I get plenty
	ἐπιθυμία -ας ἡ	desire
	στεφανόω	
	pf pass inf ἐστεφανῶσθαι	I wreathe, I crown with a wreath
71	πίτυς -υος ἡ	pine
	καταχρίω	*lit* I anoint *here* I bedaub
	πρόσωπον -ου τό	face
	λακτίζω	I kick
	ἀνταγωνιστής -οῦ τό	opponent
73	ψιλός -ή -όν	bare
	ἀποβλέπω	I look at, I fix my attention on (ἀπο- *because away from everything else*)
	σημεῖον -ου τό	sign
	γνώρισμα -ατος τό	token
75	παρακολουθέω	I go along with, I accompany (+ *dat*)
	θηράω	I hunt, I pursue
	εὔκλεια -ας ἡ	reputation
	ἀπονητί	without hardship
	ὀρέγομαι	I reach out for, I aim at (+ *gen*)
78	δυσχερής -ές	unpleasant
	ἀνέχομαι ἀνεσχόμην	I bear, I put up with
	λυσιτελής -ές	profitable
	κάματος -ου ὁ	exertion
	περιμένω	I wait for, I expect

οἰκτείραντες ἐπὶ ταῖς πληγαῖς, οἱ δὲ εὐδαινονήσουσιν ἀντὶ τῶν πόνων μῆλα καὶ σέλινα ἔχοντες.

85 ΣΩ. ἄπειρος εἶ, φημί, τῶν ἡμετέρων ἔτι· μετὰ μικρὸν δὲ ἄλλα σοι δόξει περὶ αὐτῶν, ἐπειδὰν εἰς τὰς πανηγύρεις ἀπιὼν ὁρᾷς τοσοῦτο πλῆθος ἀνθρώπων συλλεγόμενον ἐπὶ τὴν θέαν τῶν τοιούτων καὶ θέατρα μυρίανδρα συμπληρούμενα καὶ τοὺς ἀγωνιστὰς ἐπαινουμένους, τὸν δὲ καὶ νικήσαντα αὐτῶν ἰσόθεον νομίζομενον.

	οἰκτείρω ᾤκτειρα	I pity
	πληγή -ῆς ἡ	blow, knock
	εὐδαιμονέω	I am fortunate
	ἄπειρος -ον	without experience (of, + *gen*)
86	πανήγυρις -εως ἡ	festival
	θέα -ας ἡ	sight, spectacle
	θέατρον -ου τό	(*here*) amphitheatre
	μυρίανδρος -ον	holding 10,000 men
	ἰσόθεος -ον	equal to a god

Chapter 6: Summaries of syntax

Use of cases

NOMINATIVE

subject	of finite verb (main or subordinate), and of infinitive whose subject is the same as that of the main verb (neuter plural subject normally takes a singular verb)
complement	another noun agreeing with the subject (*Socrates, a very wise man, said ...*)

VOCATIVE

direct address	with or without ὦ (singular often, plural always the same as nominative)

ACCUSATIVE

direct object	(verbs like *ask* and *teach* take a double accusative - *I taught her Greek*)
with prepositions	especially expressing *motion towards* or *through*
subject of infinitive	in indirect statement, generalised result clause, and articular infinitive unless the same as the subject of the main verb
time how long	(e.g. *We walked for the whole night*)
respect	(e.g. *Injured in* - lit *with respect to* - *the shoulder*) also called *part affected*
accusative absolute	neuter participle of impersonal verb, unconnected grammatically with the rest of the sentence, e.g. ἐξόν *with it being possible*

GENITIVE

possession	(e.g. *the land of the Phaeacians, the judge's house*)
partitive	(e.g. *some of the slaves*) - as an extension of this, after verbs expressing ideas like *get hold of*
with prepositions	especially expressing *motion away from*
agent	of passive verb, with ὑπό
time within which	(e.g. *We shall arrive within two hours*)
genitive absolute	noun + participle, unconnected grammatically with the rest of the sentence
comparative	in a simple comparison, instead of using ἤ (*than*)

DATIVE

indirect object	(e.g. *We gave the money to the old man/We gave the old man the money*) - as an extension of this, after verbs like *trust* (give trust *to*)
with prepositions	especially indicating *rest in* a place
time when	(e.g. *They arrived on the third day*)
possession	(e.g. *There is to me a dog* for *I have a dog*)
instrument	of passive verb (e.g. *with a sword*)
agent	of gerundive (and optionally of perfect/pluperfect passive verb)

Use of the definite article

1   With a noun:
    Like English *the* (Greek has no *a*, but can use the indefinite τις *a certain*). Also for general classes (οἱ δοῦλοι *slaves* [in general]) and abstractions (ὁ χρόνος *time*), and with proper names (ὁ Ζεύς *Zeus*), though often omitted at first mention; also see 11 and 12 below. Indicates the number/gender/case of a noun.

2   With an adjective, to make a noun:
    οἱ ἐλεύθεροι   the free, free men
    τὸ ἀληθές   (the) truth

3   With adverbs:
    οἱ ἐκεῖ   men/people there
    αἱ νῦν   women now, women of today

4   With a preposition phrase:
    οἱ ἐν τῇ νήσῳ   the men on the island
    τὰ ἐν τῇ πόλει   (the) affairs in the city

5   With a participle, often instead of relative clause:
    οἱ διώκοντες   those pursuing, the pursuers
    αἱ ἀκούσασαι   the women who heard

6   With an infinitive, to make a verbal noun:
    τὸ τρέχειν   (the act of) running

7   Sandwiched (to tell you *which one*):
    ὁ σοφὸς γέρων   the wise old man
    ἡ τοῦ ἰατροῦ οἰκία the of-the-doctor house *i.e.* the doctor's house
    (genitive sandwich marked by two forms of the article next to each other)

8   Repeated, with same effect as a sandwich (either is bound/attributive position, fastening the description to the noun, and specifying which one):
    ἡ οἰκία ἡ τοῦ ἰατροῦ   *lit* the house the (one) of the doctor, *i.e.* the doctor's house
    ὁ γέρων ὁ σοφός   the old man the wise (one), *i.e.* the wise old man
    ὁ δοῦλος ὁ φεύγων   the fleeing slave

9   With μέν ... δέ (important, and can be hard to spot):
    οἱ μὲν τῶν δούλων ἔμενον, οἱ δὲ ἔφυγον.
    Some of the slaves stayed, others fled.
    Distinguish this from the use simply of μέν ... δέ to express a contrast:
    ἀνδρείως μὲν ἐμαχέσατο, μωρῶς δὲ εἶπεν.
    He fought bravely but spoke stupidly.

10 With δέ, starting new sentence (or clause after colon), marking change of subject:
    ἐκάλεσα τὸν δοῦλον· ὁ δὲ οὐκ ἤκουσεν.
    I called the slave; but he did not hear.

11 Redundant (i.e. English would not have *the*) and sandwiching, with possessive adjectives:
    ὁ ἐμὸς ἵππος   my horse

12 Redundant and not sandwiching, with demonstratives:
    οὗτος ὁ ξένος   this stranger
    ἐκεῖναι αἱ νῆες   those ships

Exercise 6.1

Translate into English:

1   ἡ παῖς οὐκ ἔγνω ὑπὸ πάντων ἐπαινεθεῖσα.
2   ὁ Ξενοφῶν, ἡγεμὼν ἄριστος, ἔσωσε τοὺς Ἕλληνας.
3   πολλὰς ὥρας ἐπορευόμεθα, ἀλλ᾽ οὐδεμίαν κώμην ηὕρομεν.
4   ἡ σὴ βουλὴ ἀμείνων ἐστὶ τῆς ἐμῆς, ὦ βασιλεῦ.
5   ἐλπίζομεν τὴν ναῦν ὀλίγων ἡμερῶν ἀφίξεσθαι.
6   ὁ στρατιώτης ἄνευ φόβου εἰς τὴν οἰκίαν καιομένην εἰσῆλθεν.
7   τί δώσομεν τούτῳ τῷ γέροντι;
8   ἅμα τῷ σίτῳ ἐδεξάμην καὶ οἶνον.
9   τῶν πολιτῶν φυγόντων, οὐδεὶς ἐν τῇ ἀγορᾷ παρῆν.
10 ὁ ἄγγελος ξίφει ἐτραυματίσθη.

Exercise 6.2

Translate into English:

1   πόσοι τῶν πάλαι οὕτως ἀσεβεῖς ἦσαν;
2   τῶν κορῶν αἱ μὲν ἐν τῇ ἀγορᾷ εἰσίν, αἱ δὲ ἐν τῇ οἰκίᾳ.
3   ἐπάνειμι πέντε ἡμερῶν.
4   ὁ ἐκεῖσε βαδίζων τὴν συμφορὰν εἶδεν.
5   διὰ τί οὐκ ἐκόλασας τὸν παῖδα, ὦ δέσποτα;
6   τοῦ πίνειν ἕνεκα χρήματα ζητῶ.
7   ἐδίωξα τὸν δοῦλον· ὁ δὲ τέλος ἐξέφυγεν.
8   πότε ἐδέξω τήνδε τὴν ἐπιστολήν;
9   οἱ πλεῖστοι τῶν ἐν τῇ νηὶ ἤδη ἐκάθευδον.
10 τὸ ὄρος τὸ ἐν τῇ νήσῳ κάλλιστόν ἐστιν.

Exercise 6.3

Translate into Greek:

1   The men waiting in the marketplace are prisoners.
2   Did you see the woman who was carrying the food, old man?
3   I enjoy running.
4   Are people now wiser than people long ago?
5   Some of the citizens praised the speaker, others hated him.

Overview of constructions covered in *Greek to GCSE*

Use of participles
- distinction between circumstantial (*while/when*) and bound/attributive (*the one who*, with repeated article)
- tense of participle in relation to that of main verb (before/during/after)
- genitive absolute (noun + participle phrase unconnected grammatically with rest of sentence)
- use of ὡς (*as, since*, or with future participle *in order to*) and καίπερ (*although, despite*) to focus sense of participle

Note here also ἅτε (*inasmuch as, since, seeing that*): more definite than ὡς

Relative clauses
- relative pronoun (ὅς ἥ ὅ) agrees with antecedent in number and gender, but takes case from job done in its own clause

Direct command
- imperative (present or aorist by aspect)
- negative is μή (but negative command [prohibition] for one occasion uses μή with aorist subjunctive)

Indirect command
- infinitive (present or aorist by aspect)

Indirect statement
- three constructions, as in English: ὅτι (*that*) clause, infinitive, participle
- indirect statement *retains tense of the original* (English adjusts if introductory verb is past)
- negative is οὐ
- each construction associated with a particular type of verb:

	verbs of
ὅτι clause	saying, especially λέγω/εἶπον
infinitive construction	thinking, plus φημί (οὐ φημι = *say that ... not*)
participle construction	perception

- with the infinitive and participle versions, a new subject in the indirect statement is accusative; but if the same as that of the introductory verb, nominative (or left out)
- the verb in a ὅτι clause can become optative if the introductory verb is past

Note here also that ὡς can be used for *that*, as an alternative to ὅτι

Indirect question
- follows the same rules as ὅτι clause version of indirect statement
- open question intruduced by εἰ (*whether*), question asking for specific information by one of the interrogative words (mostly beginning π-, e.g. πότε; *when?*), which can (but do not have to) add ὁ- on the front

Purpose clauses
- introduced by ἵνα (less often ὅπως) + subjunctive (primary/vivid) or optative (historic)
- negative is ἵνα μή
- purpose can also be expressed by ὡς + future participle (especially to describe presumed rather than known purpose)

Result clauses

- signpost word in main clause (e.g. οὕτω *so*, τοσοῦτος *so big*)
- result clause introduced by ὥστε
- verb can be either indicative (stressing result that actually happened; negative οὐ) or infinitive (expressing general or likely result, with accusative or nominative subject by same rule as indirect statement; negative μή)

Note here also the following additional idioms involving result clauses:

(1) comparative followed by ἢ ὥστε (lit *more X than so as to do Y*, i.e. *too X to do Y*)
    σοφώτερός ἐστιν ἢ ὥστε τοῦτο ποιεῖν.
    lit   He is wiser than so as to do this (wiser *than would result in* him doing it).
    i.e. He is too wise to do this.

(2) ἐφ᾽ ᾧτε *on the condition that* (ἐπί + dat *on condition of*; neuter relative ᾧ with suffix)
    ἔλυσε τοὺς αἰχμαλώτους ἐφ᾽ ᾧτε μὴ ἐπανελθεῖν.
    He freed the prisoners on the condition that they would not return.
    This idiom can also use the future indicative.

Conditionals

- *Greek to GCSE (2)* introduced two kinds: future open (*if you do X, Y will happen*) and past closed (*if you had done X, Y would have happened*)

Note here also other conditionals - summary table repeated for convenience:

		open (or unknown)	unfulfilled (closed or remote)
future			
	protasis	ἐάν + subjunctive*	εἰ + optative
	apodosis	future indicative	optative + ἄν
present			
	protasis	εἰ + present indicative	εἰ + imperfect indicative
	apodosis	present indicative	imperfect indicative + ἄν
past			
	protasis	εἰ + any past indicative	εἰ + aorist indicative
	apodosis	any past indicative	aorist indicative + ἄν

*or εἰ + future indicative
(particularly for threat or warning)

Exercise 6.4

Translate into English:

1 ἡ γυνὴ οἶδε δεξιὰ οὖσα.
2 μὴ εἰσέλθῃς εἰς τὸν ποταμόν.
3 παραινῶ τοῖς παισὶν ἀεὶ σαφῶς λέξαι.
4 ὁ ξένος, τὸν τοῦ βασιλέως υἱὸν φονεύσας, εὐθὺς ἔφυγεν.
5 ταῦτα μανθάνω ὡς σοφώτερος γενησόμενος.
6 τί ἔδωκας τῷ ξένῳ ὃς χθὲς ἀφίκετο;
7 μείνον ἵνα περὶ σοῦ βουλεύσωμεν.
8 εἰ τὸν χρυσὸν ἔχεις, παραδός μοι.
9 ὁ διδάσκαλος ἠρώτησεν ὅ τι περὶ τούτων ἀκούσαιμι.
10 οὕτως ἀνδρεῖός ἐστιν ὁ παῖς ὥστ᾽ ἔσωσε τοὺς πολίτας.

Exercise 6.5

Translate into English:

1 ἀεὶ τὸ ἀληθὲς ζήτει, ὦ παῖ.
2 πάντες οἱ ἐν τῇ πόλει εἶπον ὡς βούλοιντο μένειν.
3 εἰ παρῆσθα, δεινὰ ἂν ἤκουσας.
4 ὁ κριτὴς σοφώτερός ἐστιν ἢ ὥστε περὶ τούτων λέγειν.
5 ὁ ἄγγελος ἐπέμφθη ἵνα τὰ γενόμενα εἴποι.
6 οὗτος ὁ παῖς ἔφη εὑρεῖν τὰ χρήματα.
7 ἆρ᾽ οὐ θαυμάζεις τὴν τοῦ ποιητοῦ φωνήν;
8 παραινῶ σοι καίπερ νεώτερος ὤν.
9 ὁ δεσμώτης ἐλύθη ἐφ᾽ ᾧτε μηδέποτε δεῦρο ἐπανελθεῖν.
10 αὕτη ἐστὶν ἡ γυνὴ ᾗ ἔδωκα τὴν βίβλον.

Exercise 6.6

Translate into Greek:

1 When the enemy had been defeated, the Athenians rejoiced.
2 I asked the woman if she had read the new book.
3 All the citizens were waiting in order to hear the messenger's words.
4 Is this the slave whom you saw yesterday, friend?
5 The children ate so much food that they suffered badly in the night.

Tense and aspect in the aorist

Remember that *tense* means *time* (in the case of the aorist, *past* rather than present or future) and *aspect* means *type of time* (in the case of the aorist, a *single action* rather than a continuous or repeated one) - but describing a particular usage as *by tense* is shorthand for *by tense as well as aspect* (single action in the past), whilst *by aspect* means by aspect *only* (single action, with no reference to the past).

Indicative	*always by tense (on one occasion in the past)* οἱ ᾿Αθηναῖοι ἐνίκησαν. The Athenians won a victory.
Imperative	*always by aspect (on one occasion - nothing to do with the past)* λαβὲ τοῦτον τὸν ἵππον. Take this horse!
Participle	*nearly always by tense (for one single action that precedes another)* ἀφικόμενοι ἐκάθισαν. Having arrived they sat down.
but:	γελάσας ἔφη He said with a laugh (*momentary, but not necessarily before he started speaking*) *This use purely by aspect applies only to a few idioms, though see note below.* *
Infinitive	*usually by aspect, but by tense in indirect statement (replacing indicative)* οἱ πολῖται ἐπείσθησαν φυγεῖν. The citizens were persuaded to run away.
but:	ὁ ἄγγελος ἐνόμιζε τοὺς πολίτας φυγεῖν. The messenger believed the citizens to have run away.
Subjunctive	*always by aspect* οἱ πολῖται ἐνθάδε μένουσιν ἵνα τὸν βασιλέα ἴδωσιν. The citizens are waiting here in order to see the king.
Optative	*usually by aspect, but by tense in indirect statement/question in historic sequence (replacing indicative) - the tense here being that of the speaker's original words* ἐλύσαμεν τοὺς αἰχμαλώτους ἵνα ὁ πόλεμος παύσαιτο. We released the prisoners so that the war might cease
but:	ὁ ἄγγελος εἶπεν ὅτι ὁ πόλεμος παύσαιτο. The messenger said that the war had ceased.

* Note also:
(a) Use of an aorist participle still logically counts as *by tense* even if one action precedes the other only by a split second - this does not stop it *also* stressing the single and instantaneous character of the action. Compare the use of the aorist participle in a double direct command, e.g. ἐλθὼν λάβε *go and take*, where the participle replaces the (aspectual) imperative ἐλθέ, but one action still precedes the other.
(b) Greek often uses an aorist participle when a present one would be equally acceptable (and the aorist is translated like a present):

νομίσαντες τὸν ποταμὸν χαλεπὸν εἶναι, ἄλλην ὁδὸν εἱλόμεθα.

Believing the river to be dangerous, we chose another road.

Here choice of the aorist stresses the moment of coming to the belief, or the moment when it becomes relevant.
(c) Even where the aorist participle clearly *is* used by tense, English can often *represent* it by a present participle:

ἀκούσας τοὺς τοῦ βασιλέως λόγους, ὁ ἄγγελος ἔφυγεν.

Hearing the king's words, the messenger fled.

Here *hearing* implies *on/after hearing* them (not *while hearing*, which would translate a present participle).

Sequence of tenses and moods

In several constructions, the tense of the main verb determines *what follows on* (the *sequence*) in a subordinate clause. Tenses are divided into the two categories *primary* and *historic*:

> *primary tenses*
> > present
> > future
> > perfect (*describing a continuing present state resulting from a past action*)
>
> *historic tenses*
> > imperfect
> > aorist
> > pluperfect

In its typical form (uses for *purpose clauses*, and after *verbs of fearing*), sequence works as follows:

tense of main verb	mood of verb in subordinate clause	
primary	subjunctive	(present or aorist by aspect)
historic	optative	(present or aorist by aspect)

However the primary construction *can* also be used after a historic main verb, on the grounds of *vividness* (imagining how the situation felt at the time), and so is never wrong.

The difference between primary and historic corresponds to that between *may* and *might* in formal English:

primary	I will read it so that I *may* learn.	I fear that it *may* happen.
historic	I was reading it so that I *might* learn.	I feared that it *might* happen.

Variations of the sequence rule apply to the following constructions:

(1) Indirect statement with ὅτι clause after verbs of *saying*, and indirect question:

primary	indicative	(tense of original direct speech)
historic	optative	(tense of original direct speech)

Here too however the primary construction is often used (i.e. the indicative is retained) even after a historic main verb, again for vividness. Note that when the optative *is* used, it has no sense here of *might* or *would*, but is translated just like the indicative (back a tense from English after a past main verb). See also page 95 on subordinate clauses in indirect speech.

(2) Indefinite construction:

primary	ἄν + subjunctive
historic	optative (without ἄν)

Note that the terms *primary* and *historic* are also used for the basic verb endings which apply (directly or with variations) to most tenses in the category concerned:

		primary active	*primary* middle/passive	*historic* active	*historic* middle/passive
sg	1	-ω	-ομαι	-ον	-ομην
	2	-εις	-ῃ	-ες	-ου
	3	-ει	-εται	-ε(ν)	-ετο
pl	1	-ομεν	-ομεθα	-ομεν	-ομεθα
	2	-ετε	-εσθε	-ετε	-εσθε
	3	-ουσι(ν)	-ονται	-ον	-οντο

Note that all historic tenses have the augment (ἐ-).

Uses of the subjunctive

The subjunctive generally refers to something that *may* happen, as distinct from the indicative (for actual facts) and the optative (for more remote possibilities). In all contexts, the subjunctive operates by *aspect* (present for something that may happen often or generally, aorist for something that may happen once). In constructions involving *sequence*, the subjunctive is *primary* (as it also is in the formation of its endings, easily recognised by their lengthened vowel). The subjunctive is often reflected by English *may* (rather than *might*). The negative for all subjunctive constructions is μή (so remember '*may* and μή').

(1) As the main or only verb of a sentence:

    (i)   exhortation   *let us do X*
           (first person plural command, urging others to join you in doing something)

           ἴωμεν εἰς τὸ τοῦ θεοῦ ἱερόν.
           Let us go into the temple of the god!

    (ii)   prohibition   *do not do X*   μή with second person *aorist* subjunctive
           (negative command *for one occasion*; a more general prohibition is expressed by μή and the present imperative)

           μὴ φάγῃς τοῦτον τὸν σῖτον.
           Do not eat this food!

    (iii) deliberative question   *what am I to do? what should I do?*
           (the speaker is thought of as debating or *deliberating* with himself/herself)

           τί περὶ τοῦ οἴνου εἴπω;
           What am I to say about the wine?

(2) In subordinate clauses:

    (i)   purpose clause (primary sequence or vivid), with ἵνα   *in order that X may happen*

           αἱ γυναῖκες μένουσιν ἵνα τοὺς σοὺς λόγους ἀκούσωσιν.
           The women are waiting in order to (*or* that they may) hear your words.

    (ii)   after verb of fearing (primary sequence or vivid), with μή   *that X may happen*
           (a *negative* fear - *that X may* not *happen* - uses μὴ οὐ)

           οἱ πολῖται φοβοῦνται μή τι κακὸν πάθωσιν.
           The citizens are afraid that they might suffer something bad.

    (iii) indefinite clause (primary sequence), with ἄν   *whenever/until X happens*

           καθίσω ἐνθάδε ἕως ἂν δῷς μοι τὸ ἀργύριον.
           I shall sit here until you give me the money.

    (iv) protasis of future open condition, with ἐάν   *if X happens (Y will happen)*

           ἐὰν εἰς τὴν ὕλην εἰσέλθῃς, ληφθήσῃ.
           If you go into the forest, you will be captured.

Uses of the optative

The optative generally refers to something that *might* happen. It is more remote than the subjunctive in either time or likelihood. It mainly operates by *aspect* (present for something that may happen often or generally, aorist for something that may happen once), but see below for the important exception in indirect speech. In constructions involving *sequence*, the optative is *historic* (as can to some extent be seen also in the formation of its endings, easily recognised by their diphthong οι/αι/ ει). The optative is often reflected by English *might* (rather than *may*), and the negative for most optative constructions is μή, but in both these respects its use in indirect speech is again an exception.

(1) As the main or only verb of a sentence:

   (i)   wish for the future, often with εἴθε (*if only*)   *if only X would happen*

       εἴθε γενοίμην βασιλεύς.
       If only I might become king.

   (ii) potential (putting a hypothesis), with ἄν   *X might happen*
       (this is in effect the same as the apodosis of a future remote condition)

       εἴποι τις ἂν ὅτι τὸ μαντεῖον ἐψεύσατο.
       Someone might say that the oracle lied.

       (This can also be used for a polite request, as in English *you might pass the wine*)

(2) In subordinate clauses:

   (i)   purpose clause (historic sequence), with ἵνα   *in order that X might happen*

       ἐπορεύθην πρὸς τὰς ᾿Αθήνας ἵνα τὰ ἱερὰ ἴδοιμι.
       I travelled to Athens in order to (*or* that I might) see the temples.

   (ii) after verb of fearing (historic sequence), with μή   *that X might happen*
       (a *negative* fear - *that X might* not *happen* - uses μὴ οὐ)

       οἱ πολῖται ἐφοβοῦντο μὴ ἡ πόλις ληφθείη.
       The citizens were afraid that the city might be captured.

   (iii) indefinite clause (historic sequence)

       ὁπότε ἀκούοις, ταχέως ἐμάνθανες.
       Whenever you listened, you used to learn quickly.

   (iv) protasis of future remote condition, with εἰ   *if X were to happen*
       and also
       apodosis of future remote condition, with ἄν   *Y would happen*

       εἰ πλεῖον οἶνον πίοιμι, πέσοιμι ἂν εἰς τὸ ὕδωρ.
       If I were to drink more wine, I would fall into the water.

   (v) in indirect speech (historic seqence)

       Separate rules apply here: the optative is not used by aspect but has the tense of the original direct speech (this explains why there is a future optative); it is translated as if indicative (rather than by *might*); and the negative is οὐ.

(a) indirect statement with ὅτι clause (after verb of saying), or indirect question

ὁ ἡγεμὼν εἶπεν ὅτι ἡ ὁδὸς οὐ χαλεπὴ ἔσοιτο.
The leader said that the journey would not be difficult.

ἡ γυνὴ ἤρετο ὅπου ὁ κίνδυνος εἴη.
The woman asked where the danger was.

(b) subordinate clause within any indirect speech (if part of the original speech)

ἐκέλευσεν αὐτοὺς παραδοῦναι τὸ ἀργύριον ὃ ἔχοιεν.
He ordered them to hand over the money which they had.

These indirect speech rules are for strict sequence, but often in practice the verbs remain indicative (for 'vividness'), and a past indicative in a subordinate clause has to do so.

Uses of ἄν

In general ἄν (which cannot be translated in isolation) has the effect of making a verb or clause *indefinite* or *potential* (often represented in English by words such as *would* or *might*). When used with an optative, this may be felt to reinforce a sense that form of the verb has already, but when used with a past indicative it effects radical transformation, e.g. from *did X* to *would have done X* (but did not).

(i) with the subjunctive as an indefinite in primary sequence

ὃς ἂν δόξαν ἕληται μισθὸν ἕξει.
Whoever chooses glory will have a reward.

This is different from the other uses discussed below (all of which involve the indicative or optative). In this construction the ἄν in origin goes not with the verb at all, but with the pronoun or conjunction introducing the indefinite clause: compare how in words like ὅταν (ὅτε + ἄν) they actually combine. Note also that for an indefinite in historic sequence the optative is used *without* ἄν.

(ii) with the optative expressing potential (putting a hypothesis)

εἴποι τις ἂν ὅτι μῶρός εἰμι.
Someone may say that I am foolish.

(This is also used for a polite request, and it is in effect the same as the apodosis of a future remote condition.)

(iii) with the optative as the apodosis of a future remote condition

εἰ τὸν χρυσὸν εὕροιμι, πλούσιος ἂν γενοίμην.
If I were to find the gold, I would become rich.

(iv) with the imperfect indicative as the apodosis of a present closed condition

εἰ ὁ Σωκράτης παρῆν, ἐθαύμαζεν ἂν τὴν σὴν σοφίαν.
If Socrates were here, he would be amazed at your wisdom.

(v) with the aorist indicative as the apodosis of a past closed condition

εἰ ἠρώτησας, οὐκ ἂν ἀπεκρινάμην.
If you had asked, I would not have answered.

(vi) with an infinitive or participle in indirect statement, representing an optative or indicative with ἄν in the original speech

ὁ Περικλῆς ἐνόμιζε τούς Ἀθηναίους νικηθῆναι ἂν εἰ εξέλθοειν.
Pericles believed the Athenians would be defeated if they went out.

(The infinitive with ἄν representing the apodosis of the original future remote condition. Note here the infinitive as used by aspect, as the optative was, whereas normally in an indirect statement - without ἄν, and representing an original indicative - it would mean *to have been defeated*: in both cases it behaves like what it replaces.)

Uses of οὐ and μή

In general, οὐ is used for *facts* and μή for *possibilities*.
They roughly correspond to *non* and *ne* in Latin.

In more detail, οὐ is found:

• with the indicative, and with the optative or infinitive in indirect statement/question

• with the participle (except as below)

• in the apodosis of any conditional sentence

μή is found:

• with the imperative, the subjunctive, and the optative and infinitive except as above

• with a participle equivalent to a conditional protasis, or a future one expressing purpose

• in the protasis of any conditional sentence

Note the following special idioms:

(1) ἆρ' οὐ (*surely it is the case?* expecting *yes*); ἆρα μή (*surely it is not the case?* expecting *no*)

(2) μή = *that* (no negative force in English) after verbs fearing (μὴ οὐ for *that ... not*)

(3) μή with the future infinitive after the verbs such as *hope, promise, swear*

(4) οὐ φημι with the infinitive in indirect statement = I *say that ... not* (rather than *I do not say*), and οὐ δεῖ + infinitive = *it is necessary not to* (rather than *it is not necessary to*)

All the compound negatives exist in both οὐ and μή forms:

οὐδέ	and not, nor, not even	μηδέ
οὔτε ... οὔτε	neither ... nor	μήτε ... μήτε
οὐδείς οὐδεμία οὐδέν	no-one, nothing, no (not any)	μηδείς μηδεμία μηδέν
οὐδαμοῦ	nowhere	μηδαμοῦ
οὐδαμῶς	in no way	μηδαμῶς
οὐδέποτε οὔποτε	never	μηδέποτε μήποτε
οὐκέτι	no longer	μηκέτι

Notice the peculiarity that οὔκουν is a compound negative predictably meaning *not ... therefore*, but οὐκοῦν (differentiated only by accent) simply means *therefore* (like οὖν): the way to remember them is the accented bit in each case gives the essential meaning.

Greek tends to pile up negatives for emphasis. We cannot reproduce this in correct English (though compare the colloquial *I've not had no tea*, logically implying you have had some, but intended as a strong denial) - we must therefore go down to one in translation:

> οὐκ οὐδὲν ηὑρέθη οὐδαμοῦ.
> *literally* Not nothing was found nowhere.
> *i.e.* Nothing was found anywhere.

153

If however a compound negative *precedes* a simple one, they *do* cancel out to make an affirmative:

> οὐδεὶς οὐ τοῦτο ποιεῖ.
>
> *literally* No-one does not do this
>
> *i.e.* Everyone does this.

Exercise 6.7

Translate into English:

1   τί ἀποκρίνωμαι τῷ ἄρχοντι;
2   ὁ ἄγγελος ἔφη τοὺς πολεμίους φυγεῖν.
3   ὁ στρατηγὸς ἐκέλευσε ἡμᾶς φυγεῖν.
4   ὁπότε ἐκεῖνος ἀφίκοιτο, ἐγὼ ἀπῆλθον.
5   φοβοῦμαι μὴ οὐ τὴν ἐπιστολὴν εἰς καιρὸν δέξωμαι.
6   οὐδεὶς οὐ τὴν τῆς παίδος τέχνην θαυμάζει.
7   εἰ πάντα ἔμαθον, οὐκ ἂν ἥμαρτον.
8   εἴποι τις ἂν ὅτι ταῦτα οὐδαμῶς χρήσιμά ἐστιν.
9   ἐνθάδε μείνον ἕως ἂν ὁ δεσπότης ἐπανέλθῃ.
10 εἴθε εὐτύχης γενοίο.

Exercise 6.8

Translate into English:

1   ἆρα μὴ φιλεῖς ἐκείνην τὴν βίβλον;
2   ὃς ἂν τοιαῦτα λέγῃ μῶρός ἐστιν.
3   εἰ ἄλλος τις τούτους ἔτασσεν, οὐκ ἂν ἐπείθοντο.
4   τῶν συμμάχων μὴ ἀφικομένων, ἐν κινδύνῳ τάχα ἐσόμεθα.
5   εἰ τὴν παῖδα αὖθις ἴδοιμι, ἐπαινέσαιμι ἂν αὐτὴν διὰ τὴν ἀνδρείαν.
6   οἱ ἐν τῇ πόλει ἔφυγον ἵνα μὴ δουλωθεῖεν.
7   εἰ βασιλεὺς ἐν τῇ πόλει πάρεστιν, ἐκεῖσε δράμωμεν.
8   "τὸν σῖτον λαβὼν φαγέ," ἔφη ὁ δεσπότης γελάσας, "εἰ βούλῃ."
9   ὁ διδάσκαλος εἶπεν ὅτι τὸ ἔργον ῥάδιον εἴη.
10 τὴν γυναῖκα ἠρώτησα ὁπόσους τῶν παίδων ἴδοι.

Exercise 6.9

Translate into Greek:

1   I am afraid that we may be forced to retreat.
2   What should we reply to the judge?
3   Whenever I heard about the events in Greece I was amazed.
4   The girls hid in the forest so that they would not be found.
5   Someone might say that we chose a difficult task.

Reference Grammar

The definite article

		masculine	feminine	neuter	
sg	nom	ὁ	ἡ	τό	the
	acc	τόν	τήν	τό	(see also page 142)
	gen	τοῦ	τῆς	τοῦ	
	dat	τῷ	τῇ	τῷ	
pl	nom	οἱ	αἱ	τά	
	acc	τούς	τάς	τά	
	gen	τῶν	τῶν	τῶν	
	dat	τοῖς	ταῖς	τοῖς	

Nouns: First declension

Pattern of endings for singular:

nom	-η/-α	(adds -ς if masculine)
acc	-ην/-αν	
gen	-ης/-ας	(changes to -ου if masculine)
dat	-η/-ᾳ	

All plurals are -αι, -ας, -ων, -αις.

		feminine:			masculine:	
		honour	country	sea	judge	young man
sg	nom	τιμ-ή	χώρ-α	θάλασσ-α	κριτ-ής	νεανί-ας
	acc	τιμ-ήν	χώρ-αν	θάλασσ-αν	κριτ-ήν	νεανί-αν
	gen	τιμ-ῆς	χώρ-ας	θαλάσσ-ης	κριτ-οῦ	νεανί-ου
	dat	τιμ-ῇ	χώρ-ᾳ	θαλάσσ-η	κριτ-ῇ	νεανί-ᾳ
					(voc κριτ-ά)	(voc νεανί-α)
pl	nom	τιμ-αί	χῶρ-αι	θάλασσ-αι	κριτ-αί	νεανί-αι
	acc	τιμ-άς	χώρ-ας	θαλάσσ-ας	κριτ-άς	νεανί-ας
	gen	τιμ-ῶν	χωρ-ῶν	θαλασσ-ῶν	κριτ-ῶν	νεανι-ῶν
	dat	τιμ-αῖς	χώρ-αις	θαλάσσ-αις	κριτ-αῖς	νεανί-αις

Nouns: Second declension

		masculine:* word	neuter: gift
sg	nom	λόγ-ος	δῶρ-ον
	acc	λόγ-ον	δῶρ-ον
	gen	λόγ-ου	δώρ-ου
	dat	λόγ-ῳ	δώρ-ῳ
		(voc λόγ-ε)	
pl	nom	λόγ-οι	δῶρ-α
	acc	λόγ-ους	δῶρ-α
	gen	λόγ-ων	δώρ-ων
	dat	λόγ-οις	δώρ-οις

* feminine nouns such as *νῆσος island* are identical in declension
(the masculine *νοῦς mind* and *πλοῦς voyage* have contracted forms -οῦς, -οῦν for the original -όος, -όον)

Nouns: Third declension

Pattern of endings:

sg	nom	(wide range of possibilities)	
	acc	stem + α	for masc and fem; same as nom if neuter
	gen	stem + ος	
	dat	stem + ι	
pl	nom	stem + ες	for masc and fem; stem + α if neuter
	acc	stem + ας	for masc and fem; stem + α if neuter
	gen	stem + ων	
	dat	stem + σι(ν)*	

* the nu is added if the next word begins with a vowel, or at the end of a sentence

Examples:

		guard (stem φυλακ-)	old man (stem γεροντ-)
sg	nom	φύλαξ	γέρων
	acc	φύλακ-α	γέροντ-α
	gen	φύλακ-ος	γέροντ-ος
	dat	φύλακ-ι	γέροντ-ι
			(voc γέρον)
pl	nom	φύλακ-ες	γέροντ-ες
	acc	φύλακ-ας	γέροντ-ας
	gen	φυλάκ-ων	γερόντ-ων
	dat	φύλαξι(ν)	γέρουσι(ν)
		[*dat pl represents* φυλακ-σι(ν)]	[*dat pl represents* γεροντ-σι(ν)]

(The noun γέρων is the model for the masculine of present, future and second aorist active participles, e.g. παύων: see page 163.)

156

                giant (stem γιγαντ-)

sg   nom   γίγας
     acc   γίγαντ-α
     gen   γίγαντ-ος
     dat   γίγαντ-ι

pl   nom   γίγαντ-ες
     acc   γίγαντ-ας
     gen   γιγάντ-ων
     dat   γίγασι(ν)

     [*dat pl represents* γιγαντ-σι(ν)]

These three examples are all masculine, but feminine nouns e.g. νύξ, νυκτός (stem νυκτ-) *night* decline in the same way.

(The noun γίγας is the model for the masculine of first aorist active participles, e.g. παύσας: see page 163, and also for the adjective πᾶς *all*.)

Neuter example:
                body (stem σωματ-)

sg   nom   σῶμα
     acc   σῶμα
     gen   σώματ-ος
     dat   σώματ-ι

pl   nom   σώματ-α
     acc   σώματ-α
     gen   σωμάτ-ων
     dat   σώμασι(ν)

     [*dat pl represents* σωματ-σι(ν)]

157

Irregular third declension nouns

		fish *(m)*	father *(m)*	man *(m)*	woman *(f)*	Zeus *(m)*
sg	*nom*	ἰχθύς	πατήρ	ἀνήρ	γυνή	Ζεύς
	acc	ἰχθύ-ν	πατέρα	ἄνδρ-α	γυναῖκ-α	Δί-α
	gen	ἰχθύ-ος	πατρός	ἀνδρ-ός	γυναικ-ός	Δι-ός
	dat	ἰχθύ-ι	πατρί	ἀνδρ-ί	γυναικ-ί	Δι-ί
pl	*nom*	ἰχθύ-ες	πατέρες	ἄνδρ-ες	γυναῖκ-ες	
	acc	ἰχθύ-ας	πατέρας	ἄνδρ-ας	γυναῖκ-ας	
	gen	ἰχθύ-ων	πατέρων	ἀνδρ-ῶν	γυναικ-ῶν	
	dat	ἰχθύ-σι(ν)	πατράσι(ν)	ἀνδράσι(ν)	γυναιξί(ν)	

voc sg forms: ἰχθύ, πάτερ, ἄνερ, γύναι, Ζεῦ

		king *(m)*	city *(f)*	ship *(f)*	town *(n)*
sg	*nom*	βασιλεύς	πόλις	ναῦς	ἄστυ
	acc	βασιλέα	πόλιν	ναῦν	ἄστυ
	gen	βασιλέως	πόλεως	νε-ώς	ἄστεως
	dat	βασιλεῖ	πόλει	νη-ί	ἄστει
pl	*nom*	βασιλῆς (/-εῖς)	πόλεις	νῆ-ες	ἄστη
	acc	βασιλέας	πόλεις	ναῦς	ἄστη
	gen	βασιλέων	πόλεων	νε-ῶν	ἄστεων
	dat	βασιλεῦσι(ν)	πόλεσι(ν)	ναυσί(ν)	ἄστεσι(ν)

voc sg forms: βασιλεῦ, πόλι, ναῦ

		trireme *(f)*	race, family *(n)*
sg	*nom*	τριήρ-ης	γέν-ος
	acc	τριήρ-η	γέν-ος
	gen	τριήρ-ους	γέν-ους
	dat	τριήρ-ει	γέν-ει
pl	*nom*	τριήρ-εις	γέν-η
	acc	τριήρ-εις	γέν-η
	gen	τριήρ-ων	γεν-ῶν
	dat	τριήρ-εσι(ν)	γέν-εσι(ν)

Adjectives

2-1-2 declensions*

		masculine	feminine	neuter	
sg	nom	σοφ-ός	σοφ-ή	σοφ-όν	wise
	acc	σοφ-όν	σοφ-ήν	σοφ-όν	
	gen	σοφ-οῦ	σοφ-ῆς	σοφ-οῦ	
	dat	σοφ-ῷ	σοφ-ῇ	σοφ-ῷ	
pl	nom	σοφ-οί	σοφ-αί	σοφ-ά	
	acc	σοφ-ούς	σοφ-άς	σοφ-ά	
	gen	σοφ-ῶν	σοφ-ῶν	σοφ-ῶν	
	dat	σοφ-οῖς	σοφ-αῖς	σοφ-οῖς	

Variant feminine singular if stem ends with a vowel or rho:

sg	nom	φιλί-α	friendly
	acc	φιλί-αν	
	gen	φιλί-ας	
	dat	φιλί-ᾳ	

* i.e. 2(m)-1(f)-2(n): like the three nouns λόγος, τιμή, δῶρον (but in conventional gender order, rather than declension order; the variant feminine φιλία is like the noun χώρα)

Some adjectives (normally *compounds*: stem has a prefix, or more than one element) do not have separate feminine but use masculine form again (i.e. are 2-2 rather than 2-1-2), for example:

ἄδικος -ον	unjust
βάρβαρος -ον	barbarian, foreign

Irregular 2-1-2 (singular starts as if 3-1-3):

		masculine	feminine	neuter	
sg	nom	πολύς	πολλ-ή	πολύ	much, pl many
	acc	πολύν	πολλ-ήν	πολύ	
	gen	πολλ-οῦ	πολλ-ῆς	πολλ-οῦ	
	dat	πολλ-ῷ	πολλ-ῇ	πολλ-ῷ	
pl	nom	πολλ-οί	πολλ-αί	πολλ-ά	
	acc	πολλ-ούς	πολλ-άς	πολλ-ά	
	gen	πολλ-ῶν	πολλ-ῶν	πολλ-ῶν	
	dat	πολλ-οῖς	πολλ-αῖς	πολλ-οῖς	

		masculine	feminine	neuter	
sg	nom	μέγας	μεγάλ-η	μέγα	big, great
	acc	μέγαν	μεγάλ-ην	μέγα	
	gen	μεγάλ-ου	μεγάλ-ης	μεγάλ-ου	
	dat	μεγάλ-ῳ	μεγάλ-η	μεγάλ-ῳ	
pl	nom	μεγάλ-οι	μεγάλ-αι	μεγάλ-α	
	acc	μεγάλ-ους	μεγάλ-ας	μεγάλ-α	
	gen	μεγάλ-ων	μεγάλ-ων	μεγάλ-ων	
	dat	μεγάλ-οις	μεγάλ-αις	μεγάλ-οις	

3-1-3 declensions

		masculine	*feminine*	*neuter*	
sg	nom	βαρ-ύς	βαρ-εῖα	βαρ-ύ	heavy
	acc	βαρ-ύν	βαρ-εῖαν	βαρ-ύ	
	gen	βαρ-έος	βαρ-είας	βαρ-έος	
	dat	βαρ-εῖ	βαρ-είᾳ	βαρ-εῖ	
pl	nom	βαρ-εῖς	βαρ-εῖαι	βαρ-έα	
	acc	βαρ-εῖς	βαρ-είας	βαρ-έα	
	gen	βαρ-έων	βαρ-ειῶν	βαρ-έων	
	dat	βαρε-έσι(ν)	βαρ-είαις	βαρ-έσι(ν)	

The 3-1-3 adjective πᾶς, πᾶσα, πᾶν (παντ-) *all* declines like the first aorist participle: see page 163.

3-3 declensions (no separate feminine): (a) with epsilon contraction

		m/f	*n*	
sg	nom	ἀληθ-ής	ἀληθ-ές	true
	acc	ἀληθ-ῆ	ἀληθ-ές	
	gen	ἀληθ-οῦς	ἀληθ-οῦς	
	dat	ἀληθ-εῖ	ἀληθ-εῖ	
pl	nom	ἀληθ-εῖς	ἀληθ-ῆ	
	acc	ἀληθ-εῖς	ἀληθ-ῆ	
	gen	ἀληθ-ῶν	ἀληθ-ῶν	
	dat	ἀληθ-έσι(ν)	ἀληθ-έσι(ν)	

3-3 declensions (no separate feminine): (b) irregular comparative

		m/f	*n*	
sg	nom	μείζων	μεῖζον	bigger, greater
	acc	μείζον-α	μεῖζον	
	gen	μείζον-ος	μείζον-ος	
	dat	μείζον-ι	μείζον-ι	
pl	nom	μείζον-ες	μείζον-α	
	acc	μείζον-ας	μείζον-α	
	gen	μειζόν-ων	μειζόν-ων	
	dat	μείζοσι(ν)	μείζοσι(ν)	

Alternative forms (losing the nu, and the resultingly adjacent vowels contracting) are:
m/f acc sg and n nom/acc pl μείζω
m/f nom and acc pl μείζους

Comparison of adjectives

'positive' (normal adjective)		comparative	superlative
Regular patterns:			
σοφός -ή -όν	wise	σοφώτερος -α -ον	σοφώτατος -η -ον
φίλιος -α -ον	friendly	φιλιώτερος -α -ον	φιλιώτατος -η -ον
δεινός -ή -όν	strange; terrible	δεινότερος -α -ον	δεινότατος -η -ον
βαρύς -εῖα -ύ	heavy	βαρύτερος -α -ον	βαρύτατος -η -ον
ἀληθής -ές	true	ἀληθέστερος -α -ον	ἀληθέστατος -η -ον
Irregulars:		(* = alternative form)	
ἀγαθός -ή -όν	good	ἀμείνων -ον	ἄριστος -η -ον
		βελτίων -ον*	βέλτιστος -η -ον
αἰσχρός -ά -όν	shameful	αἰσχίων -ον	αἴσχιστος -η -ον
ἐχθρός -ά -όν	hostile	ἐχθίων -ον	ἔχθιστος -η -ον
ἡδύς -εῖα -ύ	sweet	ἡδίων -ον	ἥδιστος -η -ον
ἴσος -η -ον	equal	ἰσαίτερος -α -ον	ἰσαίτατος -η -ον
κακός -ή -όν	bad	κακίων -ον	κάκιστος -η -ον
		χείρων -ον*	χείριστος -η -ον
καλός -ή -όν	fine	καλλίων -ον	κάλλιστος -η -ον
μέγας μεγάλη			
μέγα	big	μείζων -ον	μέγιστος -η -ον
μικρός -ά -όν	small	μικρότερος -α -ον	μικρότατος -η -ον
ὀλίγος -η -ον	small (amount of)	ἐλάσσων -ον	ἐλάχιστος -η -ον
ὀλίγοι -αι -α	few	ἐλάσσονες -α	ἐλαχίστοι -αι -α
πολύς πολλή			
πολύ	much	πλείων -ον/πλέων -ον*	πλεῖστος -η -ον
πολλοί -αί -ά	many	πλείονες -α/πλέονες -α*	πλεῖστοι -αι -α
ῥᾴδιος -α -ον	easy	ῥᾴων -ον	ῥᾷστος -η -ον
ταχύς -εῖα -ύ	swift	θάσσων -ον	τάχιστος -η -ον
φίλος -η -ον	dear	φιλαίτερος -α -ον	φιλαίτατος -η -ον

(1) Comparatives ending -τερος decline like φίλιος; comparatives ending in -ων decline like μείζων; all superlatives decline like σοφός.

(2) Length of last or only syllable of stem determines -οτερος or -ωτερος, by compensation: short adds omega, long adds omicron.

(3) Comparison is expressed either with ἤ (*than*) and same case after as before, or simply by putting the second item in the genitive.

(4) Ordinary adverb is usually formed by changing -ων of genitive plural to -ως; comparative adverb is neuter singular of comparative adjective (e.g. -τερον); superlative adverb is neuter plural of superlative adjective (e.g. -τατα).

Top seven irregular comparatives and superlatives:

ἀγαθός	good	ἀμείνων	better	ἄριστος	best
κακός	bad	κακίων	worse	κάκιστος	worst
μέγας	big	μείζων	bigger	μέγιστος	biggest
ὀλίγοι	few	ἐλάσσονες	fewer	ἐλάχιστοι	fewest
πολλοί	many	πλείονες	more	πλεῖστοι	most
ῥᾴδιος	easy	ῥᾴων	easier	ῥᾷστος	easiest
ταχύς	fast	θάσσων	faster	τάχιστος	fastest

Participles

present *active* παύων -ουσα -ον (3-1-3 decl; m/n gen stem παυοντ-)
stopping
(*indicative:* παύω I stop)

middle/passive παυόμενος -η -ον (2-1-2 decl)
ceasing, stopping oneself (*middle*); being stopped (*passive*)
(*indicative:* παύομαι I cease, I stop myself; I am stopped)

future *active* παύσων -ουσα -ον (3-1-3 decl; m/n gen stem παυσοντ-)
about to stop
(*indicative:* παύσω I shall stop)

middle παυσόμενος -η -ον (2-1-2 decl)
about to cease, about to stop oneself
(*indicative:* παύσομαι I shall cease, I shall stop myself)

passive παυσθησόμενος -η -ον (2-1-2 decl)
about to be stopped
(*indicative:* παυσθήσομαι I shall be stopped)

aorist *first (weak) active* παύσας -ασα -αν (3-1-3 decl; m/n gen stem παυσαντ-)
having stopped
(*indicative:* ἔπαυσα I stopped)

first (weak) middle παυσάμενος -η -ον (2-1-2 decl)
having ceased, having stopped oneself
(*indicative:* ἐπαυσάμην I ceased, I stopped myself)

second (strong) active λαβών -οῦσα, -όν (3-1-3 decl; m/n gen stem λαβοντ-)
having taken
(*indicative:* ἔλαβον I took)

second (strong) middle λαβόμενος -η -ον (2-1-2 decl)
having taken for oneself
(*indicative:* ἐλαβόμην I took for myself)

passive παυσθείς -εῖσα -έν (3-1-3 decl; m/n gen stem παυσθεντ-)
having been stopped
(*indicative:* ἐπαύσθην I was stopped)

perfect *active* πεπαυκώς -υῖα -ός (3-1-3 decl; m/n gen stem πεπαυκοτ-)
having stopped (effect continuing)
(*indicative:* πέπαυκα I have stopped)

middle/passive πεπαυμένος -η -ον (2-1-2 decl)
having ceased, having stopped oneself; having been stopped (*all with effect continuing*)
(*indicative:* πέπαυμαι I have ceased, I have stopped myself; I have been stopped)

Participle declensions: (1) active

present active participle

		masculine	*feminine*	*neuter*	
sg	nom	παύ-ων	παύ-ουσ-α	παῦ-ον	stopping
	acc	παύ-οντα	παύ-ουσ-αν	παῦ-ον	
	gen	παύ-οντος	παυ-ούσ-ης	παύ-οντος	
	dat	παύ-οντι	παυ-ούσ-ῃ	παύ-οντι	
pl	nom	παύ-οντες	παύ-ουσ-αι	παύ-οντα	
	acc	παύ-οντας	παυ-ούσ-ας	παύ-οντα	
	gen	παυ-όντων	παυ-ουσ-ῶν	παυ-όντων	
	dat	παύ-ουσι(ν)	παυ-ούσ-αις	παύ-ουσι(ν)	

similarly:
future participle

	παύσων	παύσουσα	παῦσον	about to stop
	stem (for masc and neut): παυσοντ-			

second (strong) aorist participle

	λαβών	λαβοῦσα	λαβόν	having taken
	stem (for masc and neut): λαβοντ-			

---

first (weak) aorist participle

		masculine	*femimine*	*neuter*	
sg	nom	παύσ-ας	παύσ-ασ-α	παῦσ-αν	having stopped
	acc	παύσ-αντα	παύσ-ασ-αν	παῦσ-αν	
	gen	παύσ-αντος	παυσ-άσ-ης	παύσ-αντος	
	dat	παύσ-αντι	παυσ-άσ-ῃ	παύσ-αντι	
pl	nom	παύσ-αντες	παύσ-ασ-αι	παύσ-αντα	
	acc	παύσ-αντας	παυσ-άσ-ας	παύσ-αντα	
	gen	παυσ-άντων	παυσ-ασ-ῶν	παυσ-άντων	
	dat	παύσ-ασι(ν)	παυσ-άσ-αις	παύσ-ασι(ν)	

---

perfect active participle

		(stem for masculine/neuter πεπαυκοτ-*)*			
		masculine	*feminine*	*neuter*	
sg	nom	πεπαυκώς	πεπαυκυῖ-α	πεπαυκός	having stopped (*effect continuing*)
	acc	πεπαυκότ-α	πεπαυκυῖ-αν	πεπαυκός	
	gen	πεπαυκότ-ος	πεπαυκυί-ας	πεπαυκότ-ος	
	dat	πεπαυκότ-ι	πεπαυκυί-ᾳ	πεπαυκότ-ι	
pl	nom	πεπαυκότ-ες	πεπαυκυῖ-αι	πεπαυκότ-α	
	acc	πεπαυκότ-ας	πεπαυκυί-ας	πεπαυκότ-α	
	gen	πεπαυκότ-ων	πεπαυκυι-ῶν	πεπαυκότ-ων	
	dat	πεπαυκόσι(ν)	πεπαυκυί-αις	πεπαυκόσι(ν)	

Participle declensions: (2) middle and passive

present middle/passive participle

		masculine	feminine	neuter	
sg	nom	παυόμεν-ος	παυομέν-η	παυόμεν-ον	ceasing/being stopped
	acc	παυόμεν-ον	παυομέν-ην	παυόμεν-ον	
	gen	παυομέν-ου	παυομέν-ης	παυομέν-ου	
	dat	παυομέν-ῳ	παυομέν-ῃ	παυομέν-ῳ	
pl	nom	παυόμεν-οι	παυόμεν-αι	παυόμεν-α	
	acc	παυομέν-ους	παυομέν-ας	παυόμεν-α	
	gen	παυομέν-ων	παυομέν-ων	παυομέν-ων	
	dat	παυομέν-οις	παυομέν-αις	παυομέν-οις	

similarly:

future middle participle	παυσόμενος -η -ον
future passive participle	παυσθησόμενος -η -ον
second (strong) aorist middle participle	λαβόμενος -η -ον
perfect middle/passive participle	πεπαυμένος -η -ον
and (substituting alpha for omicron thoughout)	
first (weak) aorist middle participle	παυσάμενος -η -ον

aorist passive participle: *(basic aorist passive stem* παυσθ-; *masculine/neuter genitive stem of participle* παυσθεντ-*)*

		masculine	feminine	neuter	
sg	nom	παυσθείς	παυσθεῖσ-α	παυσθέν	having been stopped
	acc	παυσθέντ-α	παυσθεῖσ-αν	παυσθέν	
	gen	παυσθέντ-ος	παυσθείσ-ης	παυσθέντ-ος	
	dat	παυσθέντ-ι	παυσθείσ-ῃ	παυσθέντ-ι	
pl	nom	παυσθέντ-ες	παυσθεῖσ-αι	παυσθέντ-α	
	acc	παυσθέντ-ας	παυσθείσ-ας	παυσθέντ-α	
	gen	παυσθέντ-ων	παυσθεισ-ῶν	παυσθέντ-ων	
	dat	παυσθεῖσι(ν)	παυσθείσ-αις	παυσθεῖσι(ν)	

Pronouns

First and second person:

	I	you (*sg*)
nom	ἐγώ	σύ
acc	ἐμέ, με	σέ
gen	ἐμοῦ, μου	σοῦ
dat	ἐμοί, μοι	σοί

	we	you (*pl*)
nom	ἡμεῖς	ὑμεῖς
acc	ἡμᾶς	ὑμᾶς
gen	ἡμῶν	ὑμῶν
dat	ἡμῖν	ὑμῖν

αὐτός

Three meanings: (1) self; (2) (*with definite article*) the same; (3) (*not nom*) him, her, it, *pl* them

		masculine	*feminine*	*neuter*
sg	*nom*	αὐτ-ός	αὐτ-ή	αὐτ-ό
	acc	αὐτ-όν	αὐτ-ήν	αὐτ-ό
	gen	αὐτ-οῦ	αὐτ-ῆς	αὐτ-οῦ
	dat	αὐτ-ῷ	αὐτ-ῇ	αὐτ-ῷ
pl	*nom*	αὐτ-οί	αὐτ-αί	αὐτ-ά
	acc	αὐτ-ούς	αὐτ-άς	αὐτ-ά
	gen	αὐτ-ῶν	αὐτ-ῶν	αὐτ-ῶν
	dat	αὐτ-οῖς	αὐτ-αῖς	αὐτ-οῖς

Uses of αὐτός

(1) *self*
- can be used with a noun (with the article but not sandwiched)
  - ὁ δοῦλος αὐτός   *the slave himself* (usually same order as equivalent English)
- or on its own as a pronoun, not necessarily third person
  - αὐτοὶ ἀφικόμεθα   *we ourselves arrived*
- this must be the meaning if part of αὐτός comes first word in a sentence or clause, or is on its own as a pronoun in the nominative

(2) *the same*
- comes immediately after the definite article
- can be used with a noun (sandwiched with the article)
  - ὁ αὐτὸς δοῦλος   *the same slave* (same order as equivalent English)
- or on its own as a pronoun
  - τὰ αὐτὰ αὖθις εἶπον   *they said the same things again*
- the easiest of the three meanings to spot, but the least common

(3) *him/her/it/them*
- on its own as a pronoun, never nominative, always third person
  - εἴδομεν αὐτούς   *we saw them*
- never first word in sentence or clause
- this meaning is the most common of the three

165

Reflexive pronouns (first and second persons):

		myself, *pl* ourselves		yourself, *pl* yourselves	
		masculine	*feminine*	*masculine*	*feminine*
sg	acc	ἐμαυτόν	ἐμαυτήν	σεαυτόν	σεαυτήν
	gen	ἐμαυτοῦ	ἐμουτῆς	σεαυτοῦ	σεαυτῆς
	dat	ἐμαυτῷ	ἐμαυτῇ	σεαυτῷ	σεαυτῇ
pl	acc	ἡμᾶς αὐτούς	ἡμᾶς αὐτάς	ὑμᾶς αὐτούς	ὑμᾶς αὐτάς
	gen	ἡμῶν αὐτῶν	ἡμῶν αὐτῶν	ὑμῶν αὐτῶν	ὑμῶν αὐτῶν
	dat	ἡμῖν αὐτοῖς	ἡμῖν αὐταῖς	ὑμῖν αὐτοῖς	ὑμῖν αὐταῖς

Reflexive pronouns (third person):

		himself, herself, itself, *pl* themselves		
		masculine	*feminine*	*neuter*
sg	acc	ἑαυτόν	ἑαυτήν	ἑαυτό
	gen	ἑαυτοῦ	ἑαυτῆς	ἑαυτοῦ
	dat	ἑαυτῷ	ἑαυτῇ	ἑαυτῷ
pl	acc	ἑαυτούς	ἑαυτάς	ἑαυτά
	gen	ἑαυτῶν	ἑαυτῶν	ἑαυτῶν
	dat	ἑαυτοῖς	ἑαυταῖς	ἑαυτοῖς

There are also alternative plural forms using σφᾶς = *them* (on the pattern of ἡμᾶς αὐτούς etc): hence accusative masculine σφᾶς αὐτούς, feminine σφᾶς αὐτάς; genitive σφῶν αὐτῶν; dative masculine σφίσιν αὐτοῖς, feminine σφίσιν αὐταῖς.

Note the common contracted forms αὐτόν etc (but nom αὐτός is crasis of ὁ αὐτός *the same*)

The reciprocal pronoun ἀλλήλους *each other* (which like the relexives has no nominative) declines as normal 2-1-2 plural.

τίς/τις

Two meanings:

(1) In a question, and with an acute accent on the first syllable: *who? what? which?*

		masculine/feminine	*neuter*	
sg	nom	τίς	τί	
	acc	τίν-α	τί	
	gen	τίν-ος	τίν-ος	
	dat	τίν-ι	τίν-ι	
pl	nom	τίν-ες	τίν-α	
	acc	τίν-ας	τίν-α	
	gen	τίν-ων	τίν-ων	
	dat	τίσι(ν)	τίσι(ν)	*dat pl represents* τιν-σι(ν)

Alternative forms of the genitive and dative singular (τοῦ, τῷ) are distinguishable from the equivalent parts of the article only by context.

(2) As an indefinite adjective/pronoun, with no accent or with an accent on the second syllable, and never as first word in a sentence or clause: *a (certain), some (one/thing)*

		masculine/feminine	neuter	
sg	nom	τις	τι	
	acc	τιν-ά	τι	
	gen	τιν-ός	τιν-ός	
	dat	τιν-ί	τιν-ί	
pl	nom	τιν-ές	τιν-ά	
	acc	τιν-άς	τιν-ά	
	gen	τιν-ῶν	τιν-ῶν	
	dat	τισί(ν)	τισί(ν)	*dat pl represents* τιν-σι(ν)

Alternative forms of the genitive and dative singular (του, τῳ) are distinguishable from equivalent parts of the article by having no accent.

Relative pronoun

who, which

		masculine	feminine	neuter
sg	nom	ὅς	ἥ	ὅ
	acc	ὅν	ἥν	ὅ
	gen	οὗ	ἧς	οὗ
	dat	ᾧ	ᾗ	ᾧ
pl	nom	οἵ	αἵ	ἅ
	acc	οὕς	ἅς	ἅ
	gen	ὧν	ὧν	ὧν
	dat	οἷς	αἷς	οἷς

Parts underlined are distinguishable from equivalent parts of the article only by accent.

Indefinite relative (*whoever, anyone who, whatever, anything which*) and indirect question form of *who, which* (see pages 4-7):

		masculine	feminine	neuter
sg	nom	ὅστις	ἥτις	ὅ τι
	acc	ὅντινα	ἥντινα	ὅ τι
	gen	οὗτινος	ἧστινος	οὗτινος
	dat	ᾧτινι	ᾗτινι	ᾧτινι
pl	nom	οἵτινες	αἵτινες	ἅτινα
	acc	οὕστινας	ἅστινας	ἅτινα
	gen	ὧντινων	ὧντινων	ὧντινων
	dat	οἷστισι(ν)	αἷστισι(ν)	οἷστισι(ν)

This is the relative pronoun and the indefinite τις stuck together, with each bit declined separately. Because some of the resulting forms are cumbersome, alternative versions of the m and n gen and dat sg and pl (ὅτου, ὅτῳ, ὅτων, ὅτοις) are formed as if from a m nom sg ὅτος.

Demonstrative pronouns

Two different words for *this*:

(1)		*masculine*	*feminine*	*neuter*	
sg	*nom*	οὗτος	αὕτη	τοῦτο	this, *pl* these
	acc	τοῦτον	ταύτην	τοῦτο	
	gen	τούτου	ταύτης	τούτου	
	dat	τούτῳ	ταύτῃ	τούτῳ	
pl	*nom*	οὗτοι	αὗται	ταῦτα	
	acc	τούτους	ταύτας	ταῦτα	
	gen	τούτων	τούτων	τούτων	
	dat	τούτοις	ταύταις	τούτοις	

(2)		*masculine*	*feminine*	*neuter*	
sg	*nom*	ὅδε	ἥδε	τόδε	this (often used for *this here*,
	acc	τόνδε	τήνδε	τόδε	or *the following*)

etc: simply the article with -δε attached

That (*compare* ἐκεῖ: literally *the one over there*)

		masculine	*feminine*	*neuter*	
sg	*nom*	ἐκεῖνος	ἐκείνη	ἐκεῖνο	that, *pl* those
	acc	ἐκεῖνον	ἐκείνην	ἐκεῖνο	

etc: declines like αὐτός (or like σοφός with -ο in the neuter nom and acc sg)

Numerals

cardinal		ordinal	
1	εἷς μία ἕν	first	πρῶτος -η -ον
2	δύο	second	δεύτερος -α -ον
3	τρεῖς τρία	third	τρίτος -η -ον
4	τέσσαρες -α	fourth	τέταρτος -η -ον
5	πέντε	fifth	πέμπτος -η -ον
6	ἕξ	sixth	ἕκτος -η -ον
7	ἑπτά	seventh	ἕβδομος -η -ον
8	ὀκτώ	eighth	ὄγδοος -η -ον
9	ἐννέα	ninth	ἔνατος -η -ον
10	δέκα	tenth	δέκατος -η -ον
11	ἕνδεκα		
12	δώδεκα		
13	τρεῖς καὶ δέκα		
14	τέσσαρες καὶ δέκα		
15	πεντεκαίδεκα		
16	ἑκκαίδεκα		
17	ἑπτακαίδεκα		
18	ὀκτωκαίδεκα		
19	ἐννεακαίδεκα		
20	εἴκοσι(ν)		
30	τριάκοντα		
40	τεσσαράκοντα		
50	πεντήκοντα		
60	ἑξήκοντα		
70	ἑβδομήκοντα		
80	ὀγδοήκοντα		
90	ἐνενήκοντα		
100	ἑκατόν		
200	διακόσιοι -αι -α		
300	τριακόσιοι -αι -α		
400	τετρακόσιοι -αι -α		
500	πεντακόσιοι -αι -α		
600	ἑξακόσιοι -αι -α		
700	ἑπτακόσιοι -αι -α		
800	ὀκτακόσιοι -αι -α		
900	ἐνακόσιοι -αι -α		
1000	χίλιοι -αι -α		

Small cardinal numbers (1-4) decline: see below. Hundreds 200-1000 are normal 2-1-2 (like the plural of σοφός). Ordinal numbers are adjectives and decline like σοφός (δεύτερος like φίλιος).

Compounds can be done either way round with καί, or big number first without it, hence 25 can be:

εἴκοσι καὶ πέντε
πέντε καὶ εἴκοσι (compare old-fashioned English *five and twenty*)
εἴκοσι πέντε

Numeral declensions

	masculine	feminine	neuter	
nom	εἷς	μία	ἕν	one (3-1-3 declensions)
acc	ἕνα	μίαν	ἕν	
gen	ἑνός	μιᾶς	ἑνός	
dat	ἑνί	μιᾷ	ἑνί	

	all genders	
nom	δύο	two (dual forms)
acc	δύο	
gen	δυοῖν	
dat	δυοῖν	

	masc/fem	neuter	
nom	τρεῖς	τρία	three (3-3 declensions)
acc	τρεῖς	τρία	
gen	τριῶν	τριῶν	
dat	τρισί(ν)	τρισί(ν)	

	masc/fem	neuter	
nom	τέσσαρες	τέσσαρα	four (3-3 declensions)
acc	τέσσαρας	τέσσαρα	
gen	τεσσάρων	τεσσάρων	
dat	τέσσαρσι(ν)	τέσσαρσι(ν)	

Formed from εἷς, μία, ἕν (preceded by οὐδέ, eliding the epsilon as necessary) is the pronoun/ adjective οὐδείς, οὐδεμία, οὐδέν (*stem* οὐδεν-), literally *not even one*:

	masculine	feminine	neuter	
nom	οὐδείς	οὐδεμία	οὐδέν	no-one/nothing/no (not any)
acc	οὐδένα	οὐδεμίαν	οὐδέν	
gen	οὐδενός	οὐδεμιᾶς	οὐδενός	
dat	οὐδενί	οὐδεμιᾷ	οὐδενί	

Correlatives
(note how accents affect the meaning)

direct	indirect	indefinite	relative	demonstrative

Pronouns/adjectives:

direct	indirect	indefinite	relative	demonstrative
τίς; who?	ὅστις	τις a certain	ὅς (the one) who	οὗτος (or ὅδε), ἐκεῖνος this (this here), that
πότερος; which (of two)?	ὁπότερος			ἕτερος one /the other (of two)
πόσος; how big? *plural* how many?	ὁπόσος		ὅσος the size which all those who	τοσοῦτος* so big so many
ποῖος; what sort of?	ὁποῖος		οἷος the sort which	τοιοῦτος* this sort of

Adverbs:

direct	indirect	indefinite	relative	demonstrative
ποῦ; where?	ὅπου	που somewhere, anywhere	οὗ (the place) where	ἐνθάδε, ἐκεῖ here, there
ποῖ; where to?	ὅποι	ποι to somewhere	οἷ to (the place) where	δεῦρο, ἐκεῖσε to here, to there
πόθεν; where from?	ὁπόθεν	ποθεν from somewhere	ὅθεν from (the place) where	ἐνθένδε, ἐκεῖθεν from here, from there
πότε; when?	ὁπότε	ποτε sometime, ever, once	ὅτε (at the time) when	τότε then, at that time
πῶς; how?	ὅπως	πως somehow	ὡς how, as, in the way in which	οὕτω(ς) or ὧδε so, in this way

* the more predictable forms τόσος and τοῖος also exist, and are common in early Greek, which also has a word τοῦ for *there* (making the ποῦ; set completely regular).

Prepositions

preposition	+ acc	+ gen	+ dat
ἅμα			at the same time as
ἀμφί	around, about		
ἀνά	up		
ἄνευ		without	
ἀντί		opposite, instead of	
ἀπό		from, away from	
διά	on account of, because of	through	
εἰς, ἐς	into, onto, to		
ἐκ, ἐξ		out of	
ἐν			in, on, among
ἕνεκα		on account of (*usu foll noun*)	
ἐπί	against, to, over, for	on; in the time of	on, on condition of
κατά	down, according to, throughout, by	down from	
μετά	after	with	
παρά	along, into the presence of; contrary to	from (a person)	beside
περί	around	about, concerning	
πλήν		except	
πρό		in front of, before	
πρός	towards, to	from, at the hands of; in the name of	in addition to
σύν			with, with the help of
ὑπέρ	beyond, to beyond	above; on behalf of	
ὑπό	under, to under, along under	by (a person)	under
ὡς	to (a person)		

Prepositional phrases:

ἅμ' ἡμέρᾳ	at daybreak, at first light
δι' ὀλίγου	after a short time
διὰ πολλοῦ	after a long time
διὰ πέντε ἐτῶν	every five years
εἰς καιρόν	at the right time
ἐκ τούτου	after this, as a result
ἐξ ἴσου	equally
ἐν τούτῳ	meanwhile (*understand* τῷ χρόνῳ)
ἐπὶ τούτοις	on these terms
καθ' ἡμέραν	daily
κατὰ γῆν	by land
κατὰ θάλασσαν	by sea
κατὰ τοὺς νόμους	according to the laws
μετὰ ταῦτα	after this (*lit* after these things)
οἱ περὶ Ξενοφῶντα	Xenophon and his men (*i.e. including him*)
περὶ πολλοῦ ποιεῖσθαι	to regard as important
ὑπὸ νύκτα	just before nightfall

Verbs (1): ending in -ω

Indicative tenses

		active	middle	passive
				middle/passive
present				
		I stop		I cease/I am stopped
sg	*1*	παύ-ω		παύ-ομαι
	2	παύ-εις		παύ-ῃ *or* -ει
	3	παύ-ει		παύ-εται
pl	*1*	παύ-ομεν		παυ-όμεθα
	2	παύ-ετε		παύ-εσθε
	3	παύ-ουσι(ν)		παύ-ονται

future				
		I shall stop	I shall cease	I shall be stopped
sg	*1*	παύσ-ω	παύσ-ομαι	παυσθήσ-ομαι
	2	παύσ-εις	παύσ-ῃ *or* -ει	παυσθήσ-ῃ *or* -ει
	3	παύσ-ει	παύσ-εται	παυσθήσ-εται
pl	*1*	παύσ-ομεν	παυσ-όμεθα	παυσθησ-όμεθα
	2	παύσ-ετε	παύσ-εσθε	παυσθήσ-εσθε
	3	παύσ-ουσι(ν)	παύσ-ονται	παυσθήσ-ονται

imperfect				
		I was stopping		I was ceasing/I was being stopped
sg	*1*	ἔ-παυ-ον		ἐ-παυ-όμην
	2	ἔ-παυ-ες		ἐ-παύ-ου
	3	ἔ-παυ-ε(ν)		ἐ-παύ-ετο
pl	*1*	ἐ-παύομεν		ἐ-παυ-όμεθα
	2	ἐ-παύετε		ἐ-παύ-εσθε
	3	ἔ-παυον		ἐ-παύ-οντο

first (weak) aorist				
		I stopped	I ceased	I was stopped
sg	*1*	ἔ-παυσ-α	ἐ-παυσ-άμην	ἐ-παύσ-θην
	2	ἔ-παυσ-ας	ἐ-παύσ-ω	ἐ-παύσ-θης
	3	ἔ-παυσ-ε(ν)	ἐ-παύσ-ατο	ἐ-παύσ-θη
pl	*1*	ἐ-παύσ-αμεν	ἐ-παυσ-άμεθα	ἐ-παύσ-θημεν
	2	ἐ-παύσ-ατε	ἐ-παύσ-ασθε	ἐ-παύσ-θητε
	3	ἔ-παυσ-αν	ἐ-παύσ-αντο	ἐ-παύσ-θησαν

second (strong) aorist

		I took	I took for myself	I was taken
sg	*1*	ἔ-λαβ-ον	ἐ-λαβ-όμην	ἐ-λήφ-θην
	2	ἔ-λαβ-ες	ἐ-λάβ-ου	ἐ-λήφ-θης
	3	ἔ-λαβ-ε(ν)	ἐ-λάβ-ετο	ἐ-λήφ-θη
pl	*1*	ἐ-λάβ-ομεν	ἐ-λαβ-όμεθα	ἐ-λήφ-θημεν
	2	ἐ-λάβ-ετε	ἐ-λάβ-εσθε	ἐ-λήφ-θητε
	3	ἔ-λαβ-ον	ἐ-λάβ-οντο	ἐ-λήφ-θησαν

perfect

		I have stopped	I have ceased/I have been stopped
sg	*1*	πέ-παυκ-α	πέ-παυ-μαι
	2	πέ-παυκ-ας	πέ-παυ-σαι
	3	πέ-παυκ-ε(ν)	πέ-παυ-ται
pl	*1*	πε-παύκ-αμεν	πε-παύ-μεθα
	2	πε-παύκ-ατε	πέ-παυ-σθε
	3	πε-παύκ-ασι(ν)	πέ-παυ-νται

pluperfect

		I had stopped	I had ceased/I had been stopped
sg	*1*	ἐ-πε-παύκ-η	ἐ-πε-παύ-μην
	2	ἐ-πε-παύκ-ης	ἐ-πέ-παυ-σο
	3	ἐ-πε-παύκ-ει(ν)	ἐ-πέ-παυ-το
pl	*1*	ἐ-πε-παύκ-εμεν	ἐ-πε-παύ-μεθα
	2	ἐ-πε-παύκ-ετε	ἐ-πέ-παυ-σθε
	3	ἐ-πε-παύκ-εσαν	ἐ-πέ-παυ-ντο

Note:

(1) Verbs with consonant stems make adjustments of spelling in the perfect and pluperfect middle/passive to ease pronunciation (hence e.g. δεδίωγμαι, δεδίωξαι *etc*), with a third person plural made from the perfect participle plus auxiliary verb (e.g. δεδιωγμένοι εἰσί).

(2) The verbs δύναμαι *I am able*, ἐπίσταμαι *I know (how to)*, κεῖμαι *I lie*, μέμνημαι *I remember*, conjugate like a perfect middle/passive.

Root aorists	(so called because they add endings simply to the root or basic stem of the verb)	
		I went (βαίνω)	I got to know (γιγνώσκω)
sg	*1*	ἔβην	ἔγνων
	2	ἔβης	ἔγνως
	3	ἔβη	ἔγνω
pl	*1*	ἔβημεν	ἔγνωμεν
	2	ἔβητε	ἔγνωτε
	3	ἔβησαν	ἔγνωσαν
participle	βάς βᾶσα βάν (βαντ-)	γνούς γνοῦσα γνόν (γνοντ-) (*m like -ων pple after nom*)
infinitive	βῆναι	γνῶναι
subjunctive	βῶ	γνῶ
optative	βαίην	γνοίην

Imperatives

	active	middle
present		
	stop! (*generally*)	cease! (*generally*)
sg	παῦε	παύου
pl	παύετε	παύεσθε

first (weak) aorist

	stop! (*one occasion*)	cease! (*one occasion*)
sg	παῦσον	παῦσαι
pl	παύσατε	παύσασθε

second (strong) aorist

	take! (*one occasion*)	take for yourself! (*one occasion*)
sg	λαβέ	λαβοῦ
pl	λάβετε	λάβεσθε

Participles: summary table

(masculine nominative singular shown here - for grammar details see pages 163-4)

	active	middle	passive
present	παύων	παυόμενος	
future	παύσων	παυσόμενος	παυσθησόμενος
first (weak) aorist	παύσας	παυσάμενος	παυσθείς
second (strong) aorist	λαβών	λαβόμενος	ληφθείς
perfect	πεπαυκώς	πεπαυμένος	

Infinitives

	active	middle	passive
			middle/passive
present	παύειν	παύεσθαι	
	to stop	to cease	to be stopped
future	παύσειν	παύσεσθαι	παυσθήσεσθαι
	to be about to stop	to be about to cease	to be about to be stopped
first (weak) aorist	παῦσαι	παύσασθαι	παυσθῆναι
	to stop (*once*)/ to have stopped	to cease (*once*)/ to have ceased	to be stopped (*once*)/ to have been stopped
second (strong) aorist	λαβεῖν	λαβέσθαι	ληφθῆναι
	to take (once)/ to have taken	to take for onself/to (once)/to have taken for oneself	to be taken (once)/ to have been taken
perfect	πεπαυκέναι	πεπαύσθαι	
	to have stopped (*effect continuing*)	to have ceased (*effect continuing*)	to have been stopped (*effect continuing*)

Correlation of indicative/imperative/infinitive/participle:

		indicative (1 sg)	*imperative* (sg)	*infinitive*	*participle* (m nom sg)
present	active	παύω	παῦε	παύειν	παύων
	middle	παύομαι	παύου	παύεσθαι	παυόμενος
	passive	(all same as middle)			
future	active	παύσω	-	παύσειν	παύσων
	middle	παύσομαι	-	παύσεσθαι	παυσόμενος
	passive	παυσθήσομαι	-	παυσθήσεσθαι	παυσθησόμενος
imperfect	active	ἔπαυον	-	-	-
	middle	ἐπαυόμην	-	-	-
	passive	(same as middle)			
1st (weak) aor	active	ἔπαυσα	παῦσον	παῦσαι	παύσας
	middle	ἐπαυσάμην	παῦσαι	παύσασθαι	παυσάμενος
	passive	ἐπαύσθην	(παύσθητι)	παυσθῆναι	παυσθείς
2nd (strong) aor	active	ἔλαβον	λαβέ	λαβεῖν	λαβών
	middle	ἐλαβόμην	λαβοῦ	λαβέσθαι	λαβόμενος
	passive	ἐλήφθην	(λήφθητι)	ληφθῆναι	ληφθείς
perfect	active	πέπαυκα	-	πεπαυκέναι	πεπαυκώς
	middle	πέπαυμαι	-	πεπαύσθαι	πεπαυμένος
	passive	(same as middle)			

Subjunctive forms

		active	middle	passive
				middle/passive

(column headers: active, middle, passive / middle/passive)

		active	middle/passive	passive
present				
sg	*1*	παύ-ω	παύ-ωμαι	
	2	παύ-ης	παύ-η	
	3	παύ-η	παύ-ηται	
pl	*1*	παύ-ωμεν	παυ-ώμεθα	
	2	παύ-ητε	παύ-ησθε	
	3	παύ-ωσι(ν)	παύ-ωνται	
first (weak) aorist				
sg	*1*	παύσ-ω	παύσ-ωμαι	παυσ-θῶ
	2	παύσ-ης	παύσ-η	παυσ-θῇς
	3	παύσ-η	παύσ-ηται	παυσ-θῇ
pl	*1*	παύσ-ωμεν	παυσ-ώμεθα	παυσ-θῶμεν
	2	παύσ-ητε	παύσ-ησθε	παυσ-θῆτε
	3	παύσ-ωσι(ν)	παύσ-ωνται	παυσ-θῶσι(ν)
second (strong) aorist				
sg	*1*	λάβ-ω	λάβ-ωμαι	ληφ-θῶ
	2	λάβ-ης	λάβ-η	ληφ-θῇς
	3	λάβ-η	λάβ-ηται	ληφ-θῇ
pl	*1*	λάβ-ωμεν	λαβ-ώμεθα	ληφ-θῶμεν
	2	λάβ-ητε	λάβ-ησθε	ληφ-θῆτε
	3	λάβ-ωσι(ν)	λάβ-ωνται	ληφ-θῶσι(ν)

Notes:

(1) Subjunctive endings are simply vowel-lengthened versions of the normal active and middle/passive primary ones (if the vowel is long already, it stays the same, and ambiguous forms have to be determined from context; upsilon disappears). As usual the aorist passive uses active endings.

		active (and aorist passive)		middle/passive (except aorist passive)	
		indicative	*subjunctive*	*indicative*	*subjunctive*
sg	*1*	-ω	-ω	-ομαι	-ωμαι
	2	-εις	-ης	-η*	-η
	3	-ει	-η	-εται	-ηται
pl	*1*	-ομεν	-ωμεν	-ομεθα	-ωμεθα
	2	-ετε	-ητε	-εσθε	-ησθε
	3	-ουσι(ν)	-ωσι(ν)	-ονται	-ωνται

* indicative alternative ending -ει, but subjunctive must be -η

(2) For the subjunctive of contracted verbs see pages 179-81; for the subjunctive of εἰμί and other irregular verbs see pages 182-3; and for the subjunctive of -μι verbs see page 186.

Optative forms

		active	middle/passive	
present				
sg	*1*	παύ-οιμι	παυ-οίμην	
	2	παύ-οις	παύ-οιο	
	3	παύ-οι	παύ-οιτο	
pl	*1*	παύ-οιμεν	παυ-οίμεθα	
	2	παύ-οιτε	παύ-οισθε	
	3	παύ-οιεν	παύ-οιντο	
future				
sg	*1*	παύσ-οιμι	παυσ-οίμην	παυσθησ-οίμην
		etc	etc	etc
first (weak) aorist				
sg	*1*	παύσ-αιμι	παυσ-αίμην	παυσ-θείην
	2	παύσ-ειας/-αις	παύσ-αιο	παυσ-θείης
	3	παύσ-ειε(ν)/-αι	παύσ-αιτο	παυσ-θείη
pl	*1*	παύσ-αιμεν	παυσ-αίμεθα	παυσ-θεῖμεν
	2	παύσ-αιτε	παύσ-αισθε	παυσ-θεῖτε
	3	παύσ-ειαν/-αιεν	παύσ-αιντο	παυσ-θεῖεν
second (strong) aorist				
sg	*1*	λάβ-οιμι	λαβ-οίμην	ληφ-θείην
	2	λάβ-οις	λάβ-οιο	ληφ-θείης
	3	λάβ-οι	λάβ-οιτο	ληφ-θείη
pl	*1*	λάβ-οιμεν	λαβ-οίμεθα	ληφ-θεῖμεν
	2	λάβ-οιτε	λάβ-οισθε	ληφ-θεῖτε
	3	λάβ-οιεν	λάβ-οιντο	ληφ-θεῖεν

Notes:

(1) The optative is easily recognised by the distinctive diphthong in its ending (οι in the present, future and second aorist forms, αι in the first aorist and ει in the aorist passive and in optative forms of some irregular verbs - see next note). The subjunctive endings are lengthened versions of the normal primary ones (used for present and future tenses); it is not so immediately obvious that the optative endings are historic, but compare the middle/passive optative -οιμην -οιο -οιτο etc with the -ομην -ου -ετο of the imperfect middle/passive or second aorist middle indicative. In both cases the form corresponds to the use: subjunctive in primary sequence, optative in historic: see page 148.

(2) For the optative of contracted verbs see pages 179-81; for the optative of εἰμί and other irregular verbs see pages 182-3; and for the subjunctive of -μι verbs see page 186.

Verbs (2): contracted (ending in -αω, -εω, -οω)

(a) With alpha contraction

Rules of contraction:

α followed by an *e* sound (ε or η) becomes long α
α followed by an *o* sound (o or ω) becomes ω
ι becomes subscript, and υ disappears

I honour

present	*active*	*middle/passive*
sg 1	τιμ-ῶ	τιμ-ῶμαι
2	τιμ-ᾷς	τιμ-ᾷ
3	τιμ-ᾷ	τιμ-ᾶται
pl 1	τιμ-ῶμεν	τιμ-ώμεθα
2	τιμ-ᾶτε	τιμ-ᾶσθε
3	τιμ-ῶσι(*ν*)	τιμ-ῶνται

participle	τιμῶν -ῶσα -ῶν	τιμώμενος -η -ον
	(*stem* τιμωντ-)	
infinitive	τιμᾶν	τιμᾶσθαι
imperative	*sg* τίμα *pl* τιμᾶτε	*sg* τιμῶ *pl* τιμᾶσθε

imperfect		
sg 1	ἐ-τίμ-ων	ἐ-τιμ-ώμην
2	ἐ-τίμ-ας	ἐ-τιμ-ῶ
3	ἐ-τίμ-α	ἐ-τιμ-ᾶτο
pl 1	ἐ-τιμ-ῶμεν	ἐ-τιμ-ώμεθα
2	ἐ-τιμ-ᾶτε	ἐ-τιμ-ᾶσθε
3	ἐ-τίμ-ων	ἐ-τιμ-ῶντο

	present subjunctive		present optative	
	active	*middle/passive*	*active*	*middle/passive*
sg 1	τιμ-ῶ	τιμ-ῶμαι	τιμ-ῴην	τιμ-ῴμην
2	τιμ-ᾷς	τιμ-ᾷ	τιμ-ῴης	τιμ-ῷο
3	*etc: as indicative*	*etc: as indicative*	τιμ-ῴη	τιμ-ῷτο
pl 1			τιμ-ῷμεν	τιμ-ῴμεθα
2			τιμ-ῷτε	τιμ-ῷσθε
3			τιμ-ῷεν	τιμ-ῷντο

Other tenses	(not involving contraction, because the sigma/other consonant inserts a barrier)		
	active	*middle*	*passive*
		middle/passive	
future	τιμήσω	τιμήσομαι	τιμηθήσομαι
1st (weak) aor	ἐτίμησα	ἐτιμησάμην	ἐτιμήθην
perfect	τετίμηκα	τετίμημαι	

179

(b) With epsilon contraction

Rules of contraction:
> ε followed by ε becomes ει
> ε followed by o becomes ου
> ε followed by a long vowel or diphthong disappears

I like, I love

present	*active*	*middle/passive*
sg 1	φιλ-ῶ	φιλ-οῦμαι
2	φιλ-εῖς	φιλ-ῇ *or* εῖ
3	φιλ-εῖ	φιλ-εῖται
pl 1	φιλ-οῦμεν	φιλ-ούμεθα
2	φιλ-εῖτε	φιλ-εῖσθε
3	φιλ-οῦσι(ν)	φιλ-οῦνται

participle	φιλῶν -οῦσα -οῦν	φιλούμενος -η -ον
	(*stem* φιλουντ-)	
infinitive	φιλεῖν	φιλεῖσθαι
imperative	*sg* φίλει *pl* φιλεῖτε	*sg* φιλοῦ *pl* φιλεῖσθε

imperfect		
sg 1	ἐ-φίλ-ουν	ἐ-φιλ-ούμην
2	ἐ-φίλ-εις	ἐ-φιλ-οῦ
3	ἐ-φίλ-ει	ἐ-φιλ-εῖτο
pl 1	ἐ-φιλ-οῦμεν	ἐ-φιλ-ούμεθα
2	ἐ-φιλ-εῖτε	ἐ-φιλ-εῖσθε
3	ἐ-φίλ-ουν	ἐ-φιλ-οῦντο

	present subjunctive		present optative	
	active	*middle/passive*	*active*	*middle/passive*
sg 1	φιλ-ῶ	φιλ-ῶμαι	φιλ-οίην	φιλ-οίμην
2	φιλ-ῇς	φιλ-ῇ	φιλ-οίης	φιλ-οῖο
3	φιλ-ῇ	φιλ-ῆται	φιλ-οίη	φιλ-οῖτο
pl 1	φιλ-ῶμεν	φιλ-ώμεθα	φιλ-οῖμεν	φιλ-οίμεθα
2	φιλ-ῆτε	φιλ-ῆσθε	φιλ-οῖτε	φιλ-οῖσθε
3	φιλ-ῶσι(ν)	φιλ-ῶνται	φιλ-οῖεν	φιλ-οῖντο

Other tenses	(not involving contraction, because the sigma/other consonant inserts a barrier)		
	active	*middle*	*passive*
		middle/passive	
future	φιλήσω	φιλήσομαι	φιληθήσομαι
1st (weak) aor	ἐφίλησα	ἐφιλησάμην	ἐφιλήθην
perfect	πεφίληκα	πεφίλημαι	

(c) With omicron contraction

Rules of contraction:
> o followed by a long vowel becomes ω
> o followed by a short vowel becomes ου
> any combination with ι becomes οι

	I show	
	active	*middle/passive*
present		
sg 1	δηλ-ῶ	δηλ-οῦμαι
2	δηλ-οῖς	δηλ-οῖ
3	δηλ-οῖ	δηλ-οῦται
pl 1	δηλ-οῦμεν	δηλ-ούμεθα
2	δηλ-οῦτε	δηλ-οῦσθε
3	δηλ-οῦσι(ν)	δηλ-οῦνται
participle	δηλῶν -οῦσα -οῦν (*stem* δηλουντ-)	δηλούμενος -η -ον
infinitive	δηλοῦν	δηλοῦσθαι
imperative	*sg* δήλου *pl* δηλοῦτε	*sg* δηλοῦ *pl* δηλοῦσθε

imperfect		
sg 1	ἐ-δήλ-ουν	ἐ-δηλ-ούμην
2	ἐ-δήλ-ους	ἐ-δηλ-οῦ
3	ἐ-δήλ-ου	ἐ-δηλ-οῦτο
pl 1	ἐ-δηλ-οῦμεν	ἐ-δηλ-ούμεθα
2	ἐ-δηλ-οῦτε	ἐ-δηλ-οῦσθε
3	ἐ-δήλ-ουν	ἐ-δηλ-οῦντο

	present subjunctive		present optative	
	active	*middle/passive*	*active*	*middle/passive*
sg 1	δηλ-ῶ	δηλ-ῶμαι	δηλ-οίην	δηλ-οίμην
2	δηλ-οῖς	δηλ-οῖ	δηλ-οίης	δηλ-οῖο
3	δηλ-οῖ	δηλ-ῶται	δηλ-οίη	δηλ-οῖτο
pl 1	δηλ-ῶμεν	δηλ-ώμεθα	δηλ-οῖμεν	δηλ-οίμεθα
2	δηλ-ῶτε	δηλ-ῶσθε	δηλ-οῖτε	δηλ-οῖσθε
3	δηλ-ῶσι(ν)	δηλ-ῶνται	δηλ-οῖεν	δηλ-οῖντο

Other tenses	(not involving contraction, because the sigma/other consonant inserts a barrier)		
	active	*middle*	*passive*
		middle/passive	
future	δηλώσω	δηλώσομαι	δηλωθήσομαι
1st (weak) aor	ἐδήλωσα	ἐδηλωσάμην	ἐδηλώθην
perfect	δεδήλωκα	δεδήλωμαι	

Verbs (3): irregular

The verb *to be* - εἰμί I am:

present	indicative	subjunctive	optative
sg 1	εἰμί	ὦ	εἴην
2	εἶ	ᾖς	εἴης
3	ἐστί(ν)	ᾖ	εἴη
pl 1	ἐσμέν	ὦμεν	εἶμεν (*or* εἴημεν)
2	ἐστέ	ἦτε	εἶτε (*or* εἴητε)
3	εἰσί(ν)	ὦσι(ν)	εἶεν (*or* εἴησαν)

participle   ὤν οὖσα ὄν (*stem* ὀντ-)
infinitive   εἶναι
imperative   *sg* ἴσθι *pl* ἔστε

	imperfect	future
sg 1	ἦ (*or* ἦν)	ἔσομαι
2	ἦσθα	ἔσῃ (*or* ἔσει)
3	ἦν	ἔσται
pl 1	ἦμεν	ἐσόμεθα
2	ἦτε	ἔσεσθε
3	ἦσαν	ἔσονται

future participle   ἐσόμενος -η -ον
future infinitive   ἔσεσθαι
future optative   ἐσοίμην *etc*

εἶμι I shall go

	indicative	subjunctive	optative
sg 1	εἶμι	ἴω	ἴοιμι (*or* ἰοίην)
2	εἶ	ἴῃς	ἴοις
3	εἶσι(ν)	ἴῃ	ἴοι
pl 1	ἴμεν	ἴωμεν	ἴοιμεν
2	ἴτε	ἴητε	ἴοιτε
3	ἴασι(ν)	ἴωσι(ν)	ἴοιεν

participle   ἰών ἰοῦσα ἰόν (*stem* ἰοντ-)
infinitive   ἰέναι
imperative   *sg* ἴθι *pl* ἴτε

This is the 'other εἶμι', to be carefully distinguished from the more common εἰμί = *I am* (above). It is used as the future of ἔρχομαι, but note that in parts other than the indicative the meaning is usually present rather than future.

οἶδα I know

present*	indicative	subjunctive	optative
sg 1	οἶδα	εἰδῶ	εἰδείην
2	οἶσθα	εἰδῇς	εἰδείης
3	οἶδε(ν)	εἰδῇ	εἰδείη
pl 1	ἴσμεν	εἰδῶμεν	εἰδεῖμεν (or εἰδείημεν)
2	ἴστε	εἰδῆτε	εἰδεῖτε (or εἰδείητε)
3	ἴσασι(ν)	εἰδῶσι(ν)	εἰδεῖεν (or εἰδείησαν)

participle εἰδώς -υῖα -ός (*stem* εἰδοτ-)
infinitive εἰδέναι
imperative *sg* ἴσθι *pl* ἴστε

past*		
sg 1	ἤδη	
2	ἤδησθα	
3	ἤδει(ν)	
pl 1	ᾖσμεν	
2	ᾖστε	
3	ᾖσαν (*or* ἤδεσαν)	

* the present tense is strictly a perfect (= *I have come to see*, i.e. *I do now know*), the past a pluperfect - from the same root as εἶδον *I saw* (aorist of ὁράω).

φημί I say

present	indicative	subjunctive	optative
sg 1	φημί	φῶ	φαίην
2	φής	φῇς	φαίης
3	φησί(ν)	φῇ	φαίη
pl 1	φαμέν	φῶμεν	φαῖμεν
2	φατέ	φῆτε	φαῖτε (or φαίητε)
3	φασί(ν)	φῶσι(ν)	φαῖεν

participle φάσκων -ουσα -ον (*stem* φασκοντ-; *formed from alternative present* φάσκω)
infinitive φάναι
imperative *sg* φάθι *pl* φάτε

imperfect	
sg 1	ἔφην
2	ἔφησθα
3	ἔφη
pl 1	ἔφαμεν
2	ἔφατε
3	ἔφασαν

Verbs (4): ending in -μι

(a) Active forms

present

		I place	I send	I make to stand	I give	I show
sg	1	τίθημι	ἵημι	ἵστημι	δίδωμι	δείκνυμι
	2	τίθης	ἵης	ἵστης	δίδως	δείκνυς
	3	τίθησι(ν)	ἵησι	ἵστησι(ν)	δίδωσι(ν)	δείκνυσι(ν)
pl	1	τίθεμεν	ἵεμεν	ἵσταμεν	δίδομεν	δείκνυμεν
	2	τίθετε	ἵετε	ἵστατε	δίδοτε	δείκνυτε
	3	τιθέασι(ν)	ἱᾶσι(ν)	ἱστᾶσι(ν)	διδόασι(ν)	δεικνύασι(ν)

imperfect

sg	1	ἐτίθην	ἵην	ἵστην	ἐδίδουν	ἐδείκνυν
	2	ἐτίθεις	ἵεις	ἵστης	ἐδίδους	ἐδείκνυς
	3	ἐτίθει	ἵει	ἵστη	ἐδίδου	ἐδείκνυ
pl	1	ἐτίθεμεν	ἵεμεν	ἵσταμεν	ἐδίδομεν	ἐδείκνυμεν
	2	ἐτίθετε	ἵετε	ἵστατε	ἐδίδοτε	ἐδείκνυτε
	3	ἐτίθεσαν	ἵεσαν	ἵστασαν	ἐδίδοσαν	ἐδείκνυσαν

aorist

sg	1	ἔθηκα	-ἧκα	ἔστησα	ἔδωκα	ἔδειξα
	2	ἔθηκας	-ἧκας	etc (reg aor 1)	ἔδωκας	etc (reg aor 1)
	3	ἔθηκε(ν)	-ἧκε(ν)		ἔδωκε(ν)	
pl	1	ἔθεμεν	εἷμεν		ἔδομεν	
	2	ἔθετε	εἷτε		ἔδοτε	
	3	ἔθεσαν	εἷσαν		ἔδοσαν	

Alternative third-person plurals ἔδωκαν, ἔθηκαν (on the model of the singular) are also found.

Many other parts of these verbs have endings like the equivalent tenses of ordinary verbs:

future	θήσω	-ἥσω	στήσω	δώσω	δείξω
perfect	τέθηκα	-εἷκα	(ἔστηκα see below)	δέδωκα	δέδειχα

imperatives (sg then pl for each)

present	τίθει, τίθετε	ἵει, ἵετε	ἵστη, ἵστατε	δίδου, δίδοτε	δείκνυ, δείκνυτε
aorist	θές, θέτε	ἕς, ἕτε	στῆσον, -ατε	δός, δότε	δεῖξον, -ατε

infinitives

present	τιθέναι	ἱέναι	ἱστάναι	διδόναι	δεικνύναι
aorist	θεῖναι	εἷναι	στῆσαι	δοῦναι	δεῖξαι

present participles

τιθείς -εῖσα -έν (*stem* τιθεντ-)
ἱείς ἱεῖσα ἱέν (*stem* ἱεντ-)
ἱστάς -ᾶσα -άν (*stem* ἱσταντ-)
διδούς -οῦσα -όν (*stem* διδοντ-)
δεικνύς -ῦσα -ύν (*stem* δεικνυντ-)

aorist participles

θείς θεῖσα θέν (*stem* θεντ-)
εἵς εἷσα ἕν (*stem* ἑντ-)
στήσας -ᾶσα -αν (*stem* στησαντ-)
δούς δοῦσα δόν (*stem* δοντ-)
δείξας -ασα -αν (*stem* δειξαντ-)

Intransitive parts of ἵστημι meaning *I stand* (see pages 51-2)

		present (strictly perfect)		aorist	(like root aorist ἔβην)
sg	1	ἕστηκα	I stand	ἔστην	I stood
	2	ἕστηκας		ἔστης	
	3	ἕστηκε(ν)		ἔστη	
pl	1	ἕσταμεν		ἔστημεν	
	2	ἕστατε		ἔστητε	
	3	ἑστᾶσι(ν)		ἔστησαν	

participle	ἑστώς -ῶσα -ός (ἑστωτ-)	στάς στάσα στάν (σταντ-)
infinitive	ἑστάναι	στῆναι
subjunctive	ἑστῶ	στῶ
optative	ἑσταίην	σταίην

(b) Middle and passive forms

present middle/passive

sg	1	τίθεμαι	ἵεμαι	ἵσταμαι	δίδομαι	δείκνυμαι
	2	τίθεσαι	ἵεσαι	ἵστασαι	δίδοσαι	δείκνυσαι
	3	τίθεται	ἵεται	ἵσταται	δίδοται	δείκνυται
pl	1	τιθέμεθα	ἱέμεθα	ἱστάμεθα	διδόμεθα	δεικνύμεθα
	2	τίθεσθε	ἵεσθε	ἵστασθε	δίδοσθε	δείκνυσθε
	3	τίθενται	ἵενται	ἵστανται	δίδονται	δείκνυνται

imperfect middle/passive

sg	1	ἐτιθέμην	ἱέμην	ἱστάμην	ἐδιδόμην	ἐδεικνύμην
	2	ἐτίθεσο	ἵεσο	ἵστασο	ἐδίδοσο	ἐδείκνυσο
	3	ἐτίθετο	ἵετο	ἵστατο	ἐδίδοτο	ἐδείκνυτο
pl	1	ἐτιθέμεθα	ἱέμεθα	ἱστάμεθα	ἐδιδόμεθα	ἐδεικνύμεθα
	2	ἐτίθεσθε	ἵεσθε	ἵστασθε	ἐδίδοσθε	ἐδείκνυσθε
	3	ἐτίθεντο	ἵεντο	ἵσταντο	ἐδίδοντο	ἐδείκνυντο

aorist middle

sg	1	ἐθέμην	εἵμην	ἐστησάμην	ἐδόμην	ἐδειξάμην
	2	ἔθου	εἵσο	(*reg aor 1 mid*)	ἔδου	(*reg aor 1 mid*)
	3	ἔθετο	εἵτο		ἔδοτο	
pl	1	ἐθέμεθα	εἵμεθα		ἐδόμεθα	
	2	ἔθεσθε	εἵσθε		ἔδοσθε	
	3	ἔθεντο	εἵντο		ἔδοντο	

aorist passive (*all regular*)

sg	1	ἐτέθην	-εἵθην	ἐστάθην	ἐδόθην	ἐδείχθην

infinitives:

present middle/passive	τίθεσθαι, ἵεσθαι, ἵστασθαι, δίδοσθαι, δείκνυσθαι
aorist middle	θέσθαι, ἕσθαι, στήσασθαι, δόσθαι, δείξασθαι
aorist passive	τεθῆναι, ἑθῆναι, σταθῆναι, δοθῆναι, δειχθῆναι

participles:

present middle/passive	τιθέμενος (-η -ον), ἱέμενος, ἱστάμενος, διδόμενος, δεικνύμενος
aorist middle	θέμενος (-η -ον), ἕμενος, στησάμενος, δόμενος, δειξάμενος
aorist passive	τεθείς (-εῖσα -έν, *stem* -εντ-), -ἑθείς, σταθείς, δοθείς, δειχθείς

(c) Subjunctive and optative forms

	active	middle	passive
τίθημι (regular subjunctive endings)			
present subjunctive	τιθῶ	τιθῶμαι	(as middle)
aorist subjunctive	θῶ	θῶμαι	τέθω
present optative	τιθείην	τιθείμην	(as middle)
	τιθείης	τιθεῖο	
	τιθείη	τιθεῖτο	
	τιθεῖμεν	τιθείμεθα	
	τιθεῖτε	τιθεῖσθε	
	τιθεῖεν	τιθεῖντο	
aorist optative	θείην	θείμην	τεθείην
	etc	etc	etc

ἵημι (regular subjunctive endings) (hyphen indicates only found in compound forms)

present subjunctive	ἱῶ	ἱῶμαι	(as middle)
aorist subjunctive	-ὧ	-ὧμαι	-ἑθῶ
present optative	ἱείην	ἱείμην	(as middle)
aorist optative	-εἵην	-εἵμην	-

ἵστημι (regular subjunctive endings) (transitive *I make to stand*; for intransitive *I stand* see page 185)

present subjunctive	ἱστῶ	ἱστῶμαι	(as middle)
aorist subjunctive	στήσω	στήσωμαι	σταθῶ
present optative	ἱσταίην	ἱσταίμην	(as middle)
aorist optative	στήσαιμι	στησαίμην	σταθείην

δίδωμι

present subjunctive	sg	1	διδῶ	διδῶμαι	(as middle)
		2	διδῷς	διδῷ	
		3	διδῷ	διδῶται	
	pl	1	διδῶμεν	διδώμεθα	
		2	διδῶτε	διδῶσθε	
		3	διδῶσι(ν)	διδῶνται	
aorist subjunctive	pl	1	δῶ	δῶμαι	δοθῶ
		2	δῷς	δῷ	δοθῇς
			etc (as pres)	etc (as pres)	etc (regular aorist subjunctive)

δίδωμι in the optative uses the -οιην/-οιμην endings like a contracted verb, with the aorist again shortening the stem.

present optative	διδοίην	διδοίμην	(as middle)
aorist optative	δοίην	δοίμην	δοθείην

δείκνυμι (regular subjunctive and optative endings throughout)

present subjunctive	δεικνύω	δεικνύωμαι	(as middle)
aorist subjunctive	δείξω	δείξωμαι	δειχθῶ
present optative	δεικνύοιμι	δεικνυοίμην	(as middle)
aorist optative	δείξαιμι	δειξαίμην	δειχθείην

186

Verbs (5): 30 important irregular aorists

present	meaning	aorist	aorist stem
ἄγω	I lead	ἤγαγον	ἀγαγ-
αἱρέω	I take	εἷλον	ἑλ-
αἰσθάνομαι	I perceive	ἠσθόμην	αἰσθ-
ἀποθνῄσκω	I die	ἀπέθανον	ἀποθαν-
ἀφικνέομαι	I arrive	ἀφικόμην	ἀφικ-
βαίνω	I go	ἔβην	(pple βάς, inf βῆναι)
βάλλω	I throw	ἔβαλον	βαλ-
γίγνομαι	I become, I happen	ἐγενόμην	γεν-
γιγνώσκω	I get to know	ἔγνων	(pple γνούς, inf γνῶναι)
ἐλαύνω	I drive	ἤλασα	ἐλασ-
ἔρχομαι	I come, I go	ἦλθον	ἐλθ-
ἐρωτάω	I ask (a question)	ἠρώτησα or	ἐρωτησ-
		ἠρόμην	ἐρ-
ἐσθίω	I eat	ἔφαγον	φαγ-
εὑρίσκω	I find	ηὗρον	εὑρ-
ἔχω	I have, I hold	ἔσχον	σχ-
λαμβάνω	I take	ἔλαβον	λαβ-
λέγω	I say, I speak	(ἔλεξα or) εἶπον	(λεξ-) εἰπ-
λείπω	I leave	ἔλιπον	λιπ-
μανθάνω	I learn	ἔμαθον	μαθ-
μάχομαι	I fight	ἐμαχεσάμην	μαχεσ-
ὄμνυμι	I swear	ὤμοσα	ὀμοσ-
ὁράω	I see	εἶδον	ἰδ-
πάσχω	I suffer	ἔπαθον	παθ-
πίπτω	I fall	ἔπεσον	πεσ-
πλέω	I sail	ἔπλευσα	πλευσ-
πράσσω	I do, I fare	ἔπραξα	πραξ-
τρέχω	I run	ἔδραμον	δραμ-
ὑπισχνέομαι	I promise	ὑπεσχόμην	ὑποσχ-
φέρω	I carry, I bear	ἤνεγκα or -ον	ἐνεγκ-
φεύγω	I run away, I flee	ἔφυγον	φυγ-

Principal parts of 100 important irregular verbs

present	meaning (* middle)	future	aorist († imperfect)	perfect	aorist passive (** active sense)
ἀγγέλλω	announce	ἀγγελέω	ἤγγειλα	ἤγγελκα	ἠγγέλθην
ἄγω	lead	ἄξω	ἤγαγον	ἦχα	ἤχθην
αἱρέω	take/choose*	αἱρήσω αἱρήσομαι*	εἷλον εἱλόμην*	ᾕρηκα ᾕρημαι*	ᾑρέθην
αἴρω	raise	ἀρέω	ἦρα	ἦρκα	ἤρεθην
αἰσθάνομαι	perceive	αἰσθήσομαι	ᾐσθόμην	ᾔσθημαι	-
αἰσχύνω	disgrace	αἰσχυνέω	ᾔσχυνα	-	ᾐσχύνθην
ἀκούω	hear	ἀκούσομαι	ἤκουσα	ἀκήκοα	ἠκούσθην
ἁμαρτάνω	miss	ἁμαρτήσομαι	ἥμαρτον	ἡμάρτηκα	ἡμαρτήθην
ἀποθνῄσκω	die	ἀποθανέομαι	ἀπέθανον	τέθνηκα	-
ἀποκρίνομαι	answer	ἀποκρινέομαι	ἀπεκρινάμην	-	-
ἀποκτείνω	kill	ἀποκτενέω	ἀπέκτεινα	ἀπέκτονα	-
ἀπόλλυμι	destroy/perish*	ἀπολέω ἀπολέομαι*	ἀπώλεσα ἀπωλόμην*	ἀπολώλεκα ἀπόλωλα*	- -
ἄρχω	rule/begin*	ἄρξω ἄρξομαι*	ἦρξα ἠρξάμην*	ἦρχα	ἤρχθην
ἀφικνέομαι	arrive	ἀφίξομαι	ἀφικόμην	ἀφῖγμαι	-
βαίνω	go	βήσομαι	ἔβην	βέβηκα	-
βάλλω	throw	βαλέω	ἔβαλον	βέβληκα	ἐβλήθην
βλάπτω	harm	βλάψω	ἔβλαψα	βέβλαφα	ἐβλάβην
βούλομαι	wish, want	βουλήσομαι	-	βεβούλημαι	ἐβουλήθην**
γαμέω	marry	γαμέω	ἔγημα	γεγάμηκα	-
γελάω	laugh	γελάσομαι	ἐγέλασα	-	ἐγελάσθην
γίγνομαι	become	γενήσομαι	ἐγενόμην	γέγονα	-
γιγνώσκω	get to know	γνώσομαι	ἔγνων	ἔγνωκα	ἐγνώσθην
γράφω	write	γράψω	ἔγραψα	γέγραφα	ἐγράφην
δεῖ	it is necessary	δεήσει	ἐδέησε(ν) ἔδει†	-	-
δείκνυμι	show	δείξω	ἔδειξα	δέδειχα	ἐδείχθην
δέχομαι	receive	δέξομαι	ἐδεξάμην	δέδεγμαι	ἐδέχθην
διαφθείρω	destroy	διαφθερέω	διέφθειρα	διέφθαρκα	διεφθάρην

present	meaning (* middle)	future	aorist († imperfect)	perfect	aorist passive (** active sense)
διδάσκω	teach	διδάξω	ἐδίδαξα	δεδίδαχα	ἐδιδάχθην
δίδωμι	give	δώσω	ἔδωκα	δέδωκα	ἐδόθην
διώκω	chase	διώξομαι	ἐδίωξα	δεδίωχα	ἐδιώχθην
δοκέω	seem/think	δόξω	ἔδοξα	δέδογμαι	-
δύναμαι	be able	δυνήσομαι	ἐδυνάμην†	δεδύνημαι	ἐδυνήθην**
ἐάω	allow	ἐάσω	εἴασα	εἴακα	εἰάθην
ἐθέλω	be willing	ἐθελήσω	ἠθέλησα	ἠθέληκα	-
εἰμί	be	ἔσομαι	ἦ† or ἦν†	-	-
ἐλαύνω	drive	ἐλάω	ἤλασα	ἐλήλακα	ἠλάθην
ἕλκω	drag	ἕλξω	εἵλκυσα	εἵλκυκα	εἱλκύσθην
ἐλπίζω	hope	ἐλπιέω	ἤλπισα	ἤλπικα	ἠλπίσθην
ἐπαινέω	praise	ἐπαινέσω	ἐπήνεσα	ἐπήνεκα	ἐπηνέθην
ἐπίσταμαι	know how	ἐπιστήσομαι	ἠπιστάμην†	-	ἠπιστήθην**
ἕπομαι	follow	ἕψομαι	ἑσπόμην	-	-
ἔρχομαι	go/come	εἶμι	ἦλθον	ἐλήλυθα	-
ἐρωτάω	ask	ἐρωτήσω ἐρήσομαι	ἠρώτησα ἠρόμην	ἠρώτηκα	ἠρωτήθην
ἐσθίω	eat	ἔδομαι	ἔφαγον	ἐδήδοκα	ἠδέσθην
εὑρίσκω	find	εὑρήσω	ηὗρον	ηὕρηκα	ηὑρέθην
ἔχω	have	ἕξω/σχήσω	ἔσχον εἶχον†	ἔσχηκα	-
ἥδομαι	enjoy	ἡσθήσομαι	-	-	ἥσθην
θάπτω	bury	θάψω	ἔθαψα	τέθαμμαι (pass)	ἐτάφην
θαυμάζω	be amazed	θαυμάσομαι	ἐθαύμασα	τεθαύμακα	ἐθαυμάσθην
ἵημι	send/let go	ἥσω	ἧκα	εἷκα	εἵθην
ἵστημι	(make) stand	στήσω	ἔστησα ἔστην (I stood)	ἕστηκα (I stand intrans)	ἐστάθην
καθεύδω	sleep	καθευδήσω	ἐκάθευδον† καθηῦδον†	-	-
καθίζω	sit	καθίσω	ἐκάθισα	-	-
καίω	burn	καύσω	ἔκαυσα	κέκαυκα	ἐκαύθην
καλέω	call	καλέω	ἐκάλεσα	κέκληκα	ἐκλήθην
κλέπτω	steal	κλέψω	ἔκλεψα	κέκλοφα	ἐκλάπην

present	meaning (* middle)	future	aorist († imperfect)	perfect	aorist passive (** active sense)
κόπτω	hit/cut	κόψω	ἔκοψα	κέκοφα	ἐκόπην
κρίνω	judge	κρινέω	ἔκρινα	κέκρικα	ἐκρίθην
κτάομαι	obtain	κτήσομαι	ἐκτησάμην	κέκτημαι	ἐκτήθην
λαμβάνω	take	λήψομαι	ἔλαβον	εἴληφα	ἐλήφθην
λανθάνω	escape notice	λήσω	ἔλαθον	λέληφα	-
λέγω	say	λέξω ἐρέω	ἔλεξα εἶπον	εἴρηκα	ἐλέχθην ἐρρήθην
λείπω	leave	λείψω	ἔλιπον	λέλοιπα	ἐλείφθην
μανθάνω	learn	μαθήσομαι	ἔμαθον	μεμάθηκα	-
μάχομαι	fight	μαχέομαι	ἐμαχεσάμην	μεμάχημαι	-
μέλλω	be about to	μελλήσω	ἐμέλλησα	-	-
μένω	stay	μενέω	ἔμεινα	μεμένηκα	-
νομίζω	think/consider	νομιέω	ἐνόμισα	νενόμικα	ἐνομίσθην
οἶδα	know	εἴσομαι	ᾔδη†	-	-
ὄμνυμι	swear	ὀμέομαι	ὤμοσα	ὀμώμοκα	ὠμόσθην
ὁράω	see	ὄψομαι	εἶδον ἑώρων (-αο-)†	ἑώρακα	ὤφθην
πάσχω	suffer	πείσομαι	ἔπαθον	πέπονθα	-
πείθω	persuade/obey*	πείσω πείσομαι*	ἔπεισα ἐπιθόμην*	πέπεικα	ἐπείσθην
πειράομαι	try	πειράσομαι	ἐπειρασάμην	πεπείραμαι	ἐπειράθην
πέμπω	send	πέμψω	ἔπεμψα	πέπομφα	ἐπέμφθην
πίνω	drink	πίομαι	ἔπιον	πέπωκα	ἐπόθην
πίπτω	fall	πεσέομαι	ἔπεσον	πέπτωκα	-
πλέω	sail	πλεύσομαι	ἔπλευσα	πέπλευκα	ἐπλεύσθην
πράσσω	do/fare	πράξω	ἔπραξα	πέπραχα πέπραγα (have fared)	ἐπράχθην
πυνθάνομαι	enquire/find out	πεύσομαι	ἐπυθόμην	πέπυσμαι	-
σημαίνω	signal	σημανέω	ἐσήμηνα	-	ἐσημάνθην
σκοπέω	look at	σκέψομαι	ἐσκεψάμην	ἔσκεμμαι	-
στέλλω	send	στελέω	ἔστειλα	ἔσταλκα	ἐστάλην
σῴζω	save	σώσω	ἔσωσα	σέσωκα	ἐσώθην
τάσσω	draw up	τάξω	ἔταξα	τέταχα	ἐτάχθην

present	meaning (* middle)	future	aorist († imperfect)	perfect	aorist passive (** active sense)
τέμνω	cut	τεμέω	ἔτεμον	τέτμηκα	ἐτμήθην
τίθημι	place/put	θήσω	ἔθηκα	τέθηκα	ἐτέθην
τρέπω	turn	τρέψω	ἔτρεψα	τέτροφα	ἐτρέφθην ἐτράπην
τρέχω	run	δραμέομαι	ἔδραμον	δεδράμηκα	-
τυγχάνω	chance	τεύξομαι	ἔτυχον	τετύχηκα	-
τύπτω	hit	τύψω	ἔτυψα	-	ἐτύφθην
ὑπισχνέομαι	promise	ὑποσχήσομαι	ὑπεσχόμην	ὑπέσχημαι	-
φαίνω	show/appear*	φανέω φανέομαι*	ἔφηνα ἐφηνάμην*	πέφηνα	ἐφάνθην
φέρω	carry/win*	οἴσω οἴσομαι*	ἤνεγκα/-ον ἠνεγκάμην/-όμην*	ἐνήνοχα	ἠνέχθην
φεύγω	flee	φεύξομαι	ἔφυγον	πέφευγα	-
φημί	say	φήσω	ἔφησα ἔφην †	-	-
φθάνω	do first	φθήσομαι	ἔφθασα ἔφθην	-	-
φοβέομαι	fear	φοβήσομαι	-	πεφόβημαι	ἐφοβήθην**
φυλάσσω	I guard	φυλάξω	ἐφύλαξα	πεφύλαχα	ἐφυλάχθην
χράομαι	I use	χρήσομαι	ἐχρησάμην	κέχρημαι	ἐχρήσθην
χρή	it is necessary	-	(ἐ)χρῆν†	-	-

Appendix 1: Words easily confused

(including those distinguished only by accent and a few actually identical, which have to be worked out from their context)

ἀγορά	marketplace	γίγνομαι	I become
ἀγρός	field	γιγνώσκω	I get to know
ἄγων	leading (*pres pple of* ἄγω)	δείκνυμι	I show (*aor stem* δειξ-)
ἀγών (-ῶνος)	contest	δέχομαι	I receive (*aor stem* δεξ-)
ἀθυμέω	I am despondent	δηλόω	I show
ἀπορέω	I am at a loss	δουλεύω	I am a slave
		δουλόω	I enslave
αἱρέω	I take		
αἴρω	I raise	εἰ	if
		εἶ	you (*sg*) are (εἰμί)
αἰτέω	I ask for, I beg	εἶ	you (*sg*) will go (εἶμι)
αἴτιος	responsible, to blame for (+ *gen*)		
		εἶδον	I saw (*aor of* ὁράω)
ἀληθής	true	εἶπον	I said (*aor of* λέγω)
ἀσεβής	impious		
ἀσθενής	weak	εἰμί	I am
ἀσφαλής	safe	εἶμι	I shall go (*fut of* ἔρχομαι)
ἀλλά	but	εἰς	into (+ *acc*)
ἄλλα	other things	εἷς	one (*m nom sg*)
ἀνδρεῖος	brave	εἰσί(ν)	they are
ἀνήρ (-δρός)	man	εἶσι(ν)	he/she/it will go
ἀποθνῄσκω	I die, I am killed	ἐκεῖ	there
ἀποκτείνω	I kill	ἐπεί, ἐπειδή	when, since
		ἔπειτα	then, next (*cf* τότε then, at that time)
ἄρα	so then, in that case		
ἆρα;	is it the case that ... ?	Ἑλλάς (-άδος)	Greece
		Ἕλλην (-ηνος)	Greek
αὐτή	she herself *etc* (*f of* αὐτός)		
αὕτη	this (woman) (*f of* οὗτος)	ἐν	in (+ *dat*)
		ἕν	one (*n nom/acc sg*)
αὑτόν	himself (ἑαυτόν *contracted*)		
αὐτός	the same (*crasis of* ὁ αὐτός)	ἐνεγκ-	(*aor stem of* φέρω)
		ἕνεκα	on account of (*foll gen*)
βαθύς	deep		
βαρύς	heavy	ἐξ	out of (+ *gen*) (= ἐκ *before vowel*)
βραδύς	slow	ἕξ	six
βία	force	ἐπαινέω	I praise
βίος	life	παραινέω	I advise
βουλεύω	I discuss, I plan (*oft mid*)	εὐθύς	immediately
βούλομαι	I want, I wish	εὐρύς	broad

192

ἤθελον	I was willing (*impf of* ἐθέλω)	οὐκοῦν	therefore
ἦλθον	I came (*aor of* ἔρχομαι)	οὔκουν	therefore ... not
ἤδη	now, already	πόθεν;	where from?
ἤδη	I knew (*past of* οἶδα)	ποῖ;	where to?
		πότε;	when?
ἡμεῖς	we	ποῦ;	where (at)?
ὑμεῖς	you (*pl*)	πῶς;	how?
ἡμέτερος	our	ποῖος;	what sort of?
ὑμέτερος	your (of you *pl*)	πόσος;	how big? (*pl:* how many?)
ἦν	I/he was	πολέμιοι	enemy
ἤν	if (*contraction of* ἐάν)	πόλεμος	war
ἥν	whom (*f acc sg*)		
		πόλις	city
ἴθι	go! (*sg impv of* εἶμι)	πολίτης	citizen
ἴσθι	be! (*sg impv of* εἰμί)	πολύς	much
ἴσθι	know! (*sg impv of* οἶδα)		
		πότερον	whether
καλέω	I call	πρότερον	previously
κελεύω	I order	προτεραίᾳ, τῇ	on the previous day
κωλύω	I prevent, I hinder		
		πρό	in front of (+ *gen*)
κενός	empty	πρός	towards (+ *acc*)
κοινός	common		
		σαφής	clear
μακρός	long	σοφός	wise
μέγας	big		
μικρός	small	στρατεία	expedition
		στράτευμα	army
ναῦς	ship	στρατιά	army
ναύτης	sailor	στρατός	army
ναυτικόν	fleet	στρατηγός	general
		στρατιώτης	soldier
νῆσος	island	στρατόπεδον	camp
νόμος	law, custom		
νόσος	disease	ταράσσω	I throw into confusion
		τάσσω	I draw up
οἱ	the (*m nom pl of* ὁ)		
οἵ	who (*m nom pl of* ὅς)	ταῦτα	these things
οἷ	to where (*rel of* ποῖ;)	ταὐτά	the same things (*crasis of* τὰ αὐτά)
ὅτε	(at the time) when	ταχύς	swift
ὅτι	that, because	τεῖχος	wall
ὅ τι	what (*ind qu*); whatever		
		τοιοῦτος	of such a sort
οὐ/οὐκ/οὐχ	not	τοσοῦτος	so big (*pl:* so many)
οὖν	therefore		
οὗ	(the place) where	ὥσπερ	just as, as if
		ὥστε	(with the result) that

(see also page 167 for other parts of the definite article and relative pronoun distinguished only by accent, and pages 166-7 for τίς/τις)

Appendix 2: Greek and Latin constructions compared

	GREEK	LATIN
Use of cases:		
- prepositions: motion to	+ accusative	+ accusative
motion from	+ genitive	+ ablative
resting in	+ dative	+ ablative
- time (or distance):		
how long	accusative	accusative
within which	genitive	ablative
at a point	dative	ablative
- person after		
passive verb ('agent')	ὑπό + genitive	*a(b)* + ablative
- thing after		
passive verb ('instrument')	dative (no preposition)	ablative (no preposition)
- participle phrase		
separate from main clause	genitive absolute	ablative absolute
- comparison:		
use word for *than*	ἤ	*quam*
(with same case after as before)		
- or without word for *than*		
comparative adjective +	genitive of comparison	ablative of comparison
Indirect statement:	*(3 methods)*	*(just one method)*
	ὅτι clause (verbs of saying)	
	usu + indicative; can be	
	+ optative if introductory	
	verb is past	
or	participle construction (verbs of	
	perception)	
or	infinitive construction	infinitive construction (*'acc + inf*')
subject of inf (or in Gk participle)		
same as that of main vb:	nom (or nothing) + inf/pple	reflexive acc (e.g. *se*) + inf
	- any of these has tense of	infinitive has tense of
	original direct speech	original direct speech
	- Engl 'moves back a tense'	
	if introductory verb is past	likewise
Direct question:	indicative verb	indicative verb
- asking if a statement true:		
open	ἆρα ... ;	*-ne* ... ? (on end of first word)
expects *yes*	ἆρ' οὐ ... ;	*nonne* ... ?
expects *no*	ἆρα μή ... ;	*num* ... ?
- requesting specific info:	question word usu begins with π	question word usu begins with *q*
Indirect question:	indicative verb; can be optative	subjunctive verb
	if introductory verb is past	
	- has tense of original	
	direct speech (as ind statement)	tense by sense (like English)
- word for *if / whether*	εἰ	*num*
- alternative question	πότερον ... ἤ	*utrum...an*

Direct command:	imperative (aorist imperative if referring to one occasion)	imperative
- negative	μή (with imperative, or with aorist subjunctive if one occasion)	*noli*, plural *nolite* + infinitive
Indirect command:	infinitive (aorist if one occasion)	infinitive only with *iubeo/veto* otherwise *ut* + subjunctive (tense by sequence)
- negative	μή + infinitive (whereas indirect statement has οὐ + infinitive)	*ne* + subjunctive (tense by sequence) (unless using *veto*)
Purpose clause:	ἵνα/ὅπως + subjunctive or (historic sequence) optative - if negative, ἵνα + μή ὡς + future participle (neg. οὐ) (especially for *presumed* purpose)	*ut* + subjunctive (tense by sequence) if negative, *ne* <u>instead of</u> *ut*

Result clause:

- usu a signpost *so...* word or more specific ones	οὕτω(ς) usu begin with τ (e.g.τοσοῦτος)	*tam, adeo* usu begin with *t* (e.g. *tantus*)
- a word for *that*	ὥστε verb is indicative or infinitive (indicative stresses *actual* result) - if negative, ὥστε + οὐ with indicative, ὥστε + μή with infinitive	*ut* verb is subjunctive (tense by sense) negative is *non* (<u>as well as</u> *ut*, i.e. *ut non*)

Conditional clause:

- a word for *if*	εἰ (ἐάν in future open)	*si*
- open/unknown type	indicative verbs (but fut normally has ἐάν + subj in protasis)	indicative verbs
- closed/remote type	always has ἄν in apodosis	
future remote	optative in both halves	present subjunctive in both halves
present closed	imperfect indicative in both	imperfect subjunctive in both
past closed	past (usu aorist) indicative in both	pluperfect subjunctive in both
	- negative for any type is μή in protasis (so e.g. εἰ μή), οὐ in apodosis	- negative for any type is *nisi* in protasis, *non* in apodosis

Vocabulary

English to Greek

Verbs are usually given with present and aorist.
Nouns are given with nominative and genitive, and article to show gender.
Adjectives are given with masculine, feminine, and neuter (if there are only two endings, there is no
separate femimine: the feminine is the same as the masculine).
* = comes second word in sentence or clause.

able	(powerful, capable) δυνατός -ή -όν, (sufficient) ἱκανός -ή -όν
able, I am	οἷός τ᾽ εἰμί, (implying have the power to) δύναμαι impf ἐδυνάμην
about	περί (+ gen)
about to, I am	μέλλω (+ fut inf)
above	ὑπέρ (+ gen)
according to	κατά (+ acc)
account of, on	διά (+ acc), ἕνεκα (foll gen)
accustomed to (doing), I am	φιλέω ἐφίλησα (+ inf)
acquire, I	κτάομαι ἐκτησάμην
act unjustly (to), I	ἀδικέω ἠδίκησα
addition to, in	πρός (+ dat)
admire, I	θαυμάζω ἐθαύμασα
admit, I	ὁμολογέω ὡμολόγησα
advance, I	προχωρέω προὐχώρησα
advise (someone), I	παραινέω (+ dat), συμβουλεύω (+ dat)
afraid (of), I am	φοβέομαι ἐφοβήθην
after (prep)	μετά (+ acc)
after (introducing a clause)	(use aor pple, or ἐπεί clause)
after a short time	δι᾽ ὀλίγου
again	αὖ, αὖθις, πάλιν
against	ἐπί (+ acc)
agora	ἀγορά -ᾶς ἡ
agree (with), I	ὁμολογέω ὡμολόγησα (+ dat)
all	πᾶς πᾶσα πᾶν (παντ-)
all those who	ὅσοι -αι -α
alliance	συμμαχία -ας ἡ
allow, I	ἐάω εἴασα
ally	σύμμαχος -ου ὁ
almost	σχεδόν
alone	μόνος -η -ον
along	παρά (+ acc)
already	ἤδη
also	καί
altar	βωμός -οῦ ὁ
although	καίπερ (+ pple)
always	ἀεί
am, I	εἰμί
amazed (at), I am	θαυμάζω ἐθαύμασα

ambassadors	πρέσβεις -έων οἱ
among	ἐν (+ *dat*)
ancestor	πρόγονος -ου ὁ
ancestral	πατρῷος -α -ον
ancient	ἀρχαῖος -α -ον, παλαιός -ά -όν
and	καί, δέ*
and yet	καίτοι
anger	ὀργή -ῆς ἡ
angry, I get	ὀργίζομαι ὠργίσθην (with, + *dat*)
animal, creature	ζῷον -ου τό
announce, I	ἀγγέλλω ἤγγειλα
another	ἄλλος -η -ο
answer, I	ἀποκρίνομαι ἀπεκρινάμην
anywhere	που
appear (to be), I	φαίνομαι ἐφάνην (+ *inf*)
appoint, I	καθίστημι κατέστησα
approach, I	προσέρχομαι προσῆλθον, προσβαίνω προσέβην
archer	τοξότης -ου ὁ
arm (provide with armour), I	ὁπλίζω ὥπλισα
arms, armour	ὅπλα -ων τά
army	στρατός -οῦ ὁ, στρατιά -ᾶς ἡ, στράτευμα -ατος τό
around	ἀμφί (+ *acc*), περί (+ *acc*)
arrange, I	τάσσω ἔταξα
arrangement	τάξις -εως ἡ
arrive, I	ἀφικνέομαι ἀφικόμην
arrow	τόξευμα -ατος τό
as	ὡς
as far as	μέχρι (+ *gen*)
as great as	ὅσος -η -ον
as if	ὥσπερ
as many as	ὅσοι -αι -α
as quickly as possible	ὡς τάχιστα
as soon as	ὡς/ἐπεὶ τάχιστα (*introducing subordinate clause*)
ashamed, I am	αἰσχύνομαι ᾐσχύνθην
ask (a question), I	ἐρωτάω ἠρώτησα *or* ἠρόμην
ask for, I	αἰτέω ᾔτησα (+ *acc*), δέομαι ἐδεήθην (+ *gen*)
assemble (people/things), I	συλλέγω συνέλεξα
assembly	ἐκκλησία -ας ἡ
at a loss, I am	ἀπορέω ἠπόρησα
at first	πρῶτον
at least, at any rate	γε*
at once	εὐθύς, αὐτίκα
at the hands of	πρός (+ *gen*)
at the same time (as)	ἅμα (+ *dat*)
Athene (goddess)	᾿Αθήνη -ης ἡ
Athenian	᾿Αθηναῖος -α -ον
Athenians, the	᾿Αθηναῖοι -ων οἱ
Athens	᾿Αθῆναι -ῶν αἱ
attack, I	προσβάλλω προσέβαλον (+ *dat*)

avenge (someone), I	τιμωρέω ἐτιμώρησα (+ *dat*)
away, I am	ἄπειμι *impf* ἀπῆν
away from	ἀπό (+ *gen*)
back (again)	πάλιν
bad	κακός -ή -όν
badly, I take (something)	βαρέως φέρω
barbarian	βάρβαρος -ον
battle	μάχη -ης ἡ
be, to	εἶναι
beautiful	καλός -ή -όν
because	διότι, ὅτι (*or use pple*)
because of	διά (+ *acc*)
become, I	γίγνομαι ἐγενόμην
before (*adv* previously)	πρότερον, πρόσθε(ν), ἔμπροσθε(ν)
before (*conj*)	πρίν (*usu* + *inf*)
before (*prep* in front of/prior to)	πρό (+ *gen*), πρόσθε(ν) (+ *gen*), ἔμπροσθε(ν) (+ *gen*)
before (*prep* into presence of)	παρά (+ *acc*)
beg, I	αἰτέω ᾔτησα
begin, I	ἄρχομαι ἠρξάμην (+ *gen*)
beginning	ἀρχή -ῆς ἡ
behalf of, on	ὑπέρ (+ *gen*)
behind	ὄπισθε (+ *gen*)
believe (trust, believe in), I	πιστεύω ἐπίστευσα (+ *dat*)
believe (think to be so), I	νομίζω ἐνόμισα
benefit (someone), I	ὠφελέω ὠφέλησα
beside	παρά (+ *dat*)
besiege, I	πολιορκέω ἐπολιόρκησα
best	ἄριστος -η -ον, (most virtuous) βέλτιστος -η -ον
betray, I	προδίδωμι προὔδωκα
better	ἀμείνων -ον (ἀμεινον-), (more virtuous) βελτίων -ον (βελτιον-)
beyond, to beyond	ὑπέρ (+ *acc*)
big	μέγας μεγάλη μέγα (μεγαλ-)
bigger	μείζων -ον (μειζον-)
biggest	μέγιστος -η -ον
bird	ὄρνις -ιθος ὁ/ἡ
bitter	ὀξύς -εῖα -ύ
blood	αἷμα -ατος τό
boat	πλοῖον -ου τό
body	σῶμα -ατος τό, (dead body, corpse) νεκρός -οῦ ὁ
bold	θρασύς -εῖα -ύ
book	βίβλος -ου ἡ
both	ἀμφότεροι -αι -α
both ... and	τε* ... καί, καί ... καί
bow	τόξον -ου τό
boy	παῖς παιδός ὁ
brave	ἀνδρεῖος -α -ον
breastplate	θώραξ -ακος ὁ
bridge	γέφυρα -ας ἡ

bring, I	κομίζω ἐκόμισα, φέρω ἤνεγκα (or ἤνεγκον)
broad	εὐρύς -εῖα -ύ
bronze	χαλκός -οῦ ὁ, (adj made of bronze) χαλκοῦς -ῆ -οῦν
brother	ἀδελφός -οῦ ὁ
burn (something), I	καίω ἔκαυσα
bury, I	θάπτω ἔθαψα
business	πρᾶγμα -ατος τό
but	ἀλλά, δέ*
by (a person *as agent*)	ὑπό (+ *gen*)
by land	κατὰ γῆν
by sea	κατὰ θάλασσαν
call, I	καλέω ἐκάλεσα
calm, I am	ἡσυχάζω ἡσύχασα
came, I	ἦλθον
camp	στρατόπεδον -ου τό
camp, I (set up)	στρατοπεδεύομαι ἐστρατοπεδευσάμην
campaign	στρατεία -ας ἡ
campaign, I (go on)	στρατεύω ἐστράτευσα
can, I	οἷός τ᾽ εἰμί, (*implying* have the power to) δύναμαι *impf* ἐδυνάμην
captain	λοχαγός -οῦ ὁ
capture, I	αἱρέω εἷλον, λαμβάνω ἔλαβον
care for, I	θεραπεύω ἐθεράπευσα
carry, I	φέρω ἤνεγκα (or ἤνεγκον)
cause, I	παρέχω παρέσχον
cavalry	ἱππεῖς -έων οἱ, (*collective sg*) ἵππος -ου ἡ
cavalryman	ἱππεύς -έως ὁ
cease, I	παύομαι ἐπαυσάμην
certain, a	τις τι (τιν-)
certainly	δή
chain	δεσμός -οῦ ὁ
chance	τύχη -ης ἡ
chariot	ἅρμα -ατος τό
chase, I	διώκω ἐδίωξα
child	παῖς παιδός ὁ/ἡ
choose, I	αἱρέομαι εἱλόμην
circle	κύκλος -ου ὁ
citizen	πολίτης -ου ὁ
city (city-state)	πόλις -εως ἡ
city (as opposed to country)	ἄστυ -εως τό
clear	δῆλος -η -ον, σαφής -ές
clever	σοφός -ή -όν, (skilled) δεξιός -ά -όν
come, I	ἔρχομαι ἦλθον
come, I have	ἥκω (*pres with pf sense*)
come upon, I	ἐντυγχάνω ἐνέτυχον (+ *dat*)
commander	λοχαγός -οῦ ὁ
common	κοινός -ή -όν
community	δῆμος -ου ὁ

199

companion	ἑταῖρος -ου ὁ
compel, I	ἀναγκάζω ἠνάγκασα
complete, I	τελευτάω ἐτελεύτησα
concerning	περί (+ *gen*)
confident, I am	θαρρέω/θαρσέω ἐθάρρησα/ἐθάρσησα
confusion, I throw into	ταράσσω ἐτάραξα
conquer, I	νικάω ἐνίκησα
consider, I	(think to be so) νομίζω ἐνόμισα, ἡγέομαι ἡγησάμην, (deliberate) βουλεύομαι ἐβουλευσάμην, (examine) σκοπέω ἐσκεψάμην, (contemplate) ἐννοέω ἐνενόησα
contest	ἀγών -ῶνος ὁ
contrary to	παρά (+ *acc*)
control, I	κρατέω ἐκτράτησα (+ *gen*)
converse (with), I	διαλέγομαι διελεξάμην (+ *dat*)
corpse	νεκρός -οῦ ὁ
correct	ὀρθός -ή -όν
corrupt, I	διαφθείρω διέφθειρα
council	βουλή -ῆς ἡ
country, land	χώρα -ας ἡ
countryside	ἀγροί -ῶν οἱ
courage	ἀνδρεία -ας ἡ, ἀρετή -ῆς ἡ
craft	τέχνη -ης ἡ
creature	ζῷον -ου τό
criminal (*adj*)	ἄδικος -ον
crowd	πλῆθος -ους τό
cry, I	δακρύω ἐδάκρυσα
custom	νόμος -ου ὁ
cut, I	κόπτω ἔκοψα, τέμνω ἔτεμον
daily	καθ' ἡμέραν
damage, I	βλάπτω ἔβλαψα
danger	κίνδυνος -ου ὁ
danger, I am in	κινδυνεύω ἐκινδύνευσα
dangerous	χαλεπός -ή -όν
dare, I	τολμάω ἐτόλμησα
daring	τόλμα -ης ἡ
darkness	σκότος -ου ὁ
daughter	θυγάτηρ -τρος ἡ
day	ἡμέρα -ας ἡ
daybreak, at	ἅμ' ἡμέρα
day by day	καθ' ἡμέραν
dead body	νεκρός -οῦ ὁ
dear	φίλος -η -ον
death	θάνατος -ου ὁ
deceive, I	ἐξαπατάω ἐξηπάτησα, ψεύδω ἔψευσα
decide, I	(*lit* it seems good to me) δοκεῖ ἔδοξε (+ *dat, e.g.* μοι)
deed	ἔργον -ου τό
deep	βαθύς -εῖα -ύ

defend, I	ἀμύνω ἤμυνα (+ *dat*), (defend myself) ἀμύνομαι ἠμυνάμην
deliberate, I	βουλεύομαι ἐβουλευσάμην
deprive, I	ἀποστερέω ἀπεστέρησα (someone *acc* of something *gen*)
deserted	ἐρῆμος -η -ον
deserving (of)	ἄξιος -α -ον (+ *gen*)
despise, I	καταγρονέω κατεφρόνησα (+ *gen*)
despite (being)	καίπερ (+ *pple*)
despondent, I am	ἀθυμέω ἠθύμησα
destroy, I	διαφθείρω διέφθειρα, ἀπόλλυμι ἀπώλεσα
device	μηχανή -ῆς ἡ
devise, I	μηχανάομαι ἐμηχανησάμην
die, I	ἀποθνήσκω ἀπέθανον, τελευτάω ἐτελεύτησα
difficult	χαλεπός -ή -όν
difficulty, with	μόλις
dinner	δεῖπνον -ου τό
disaster	συμφορά -ᾶς ἡ
discuss, I	βουλεύομαι ἐβουλευσάμην
disease	νόσος -ου ἡ
disgraceful	αἰσχρός -ά -όν
disheartened, I am	ἀθυμέω ἠθύμησα
distant (from), I am	ἀπέχω ἀπέσχον (+ *gen*)
do, I	δράω ἔδρασα, πράσσω ἔπραξα, ποιέω ἐποίησα
do something first, I	φθάνω ἔφθασα
do wrong (to), I	ἀδικέω ἠδίκησα
doctor	ἰατρός -οῦ ὁ
door	θύρα -ας ἡ
doubt, I am in	ἀπορέω ἠπόρησα
down	κατά (+ *acc*)
down from	κατά (+ *gen*)
drag	ἕλκω εἵλκυσα
draw up, I	τάσσω ἔταξα
drink, I	πίνω ἔπιον
drive, I	ἐλαύνω ἤλασα
each	ἕκαστος -η -ον, (of two) ἑκάτερος -α -ον
each other	ἀλλήλους -ας -α
eager	πρόθυμος -ον
early	πρῴ
earth	γῆ γῆς ἡ
easier	ῥᾴων -ον (ῥᾷον-)
easiest	ῥᾷστος -η -ον
easy	ῥᾴδιος -α -ον
eat, I	ἐσθίω ἔφαγον
educate, I	παιδεύω ἐπαίδευσα
eight	ὀκτώ
eight hundred	ὀκτακόσιοι -αι -α
eighth	ὄγδοος -η -ον
eighty	ὀγδοήκοντα
either ... or	ἤ ... ἤ

eleven	ἕνδεκα
empire	ἀρχή -ῆς ἡ
empty	κενός -ή -όν
encamp, I	στρατοπεδεύομαι ἐστρατοπεδευσάμην
end	τέλος -ους τό, τελευτή -ῆς ἡ
enemy	(personal) ἐχθρός -οῦ ὁ, (in war) πολέμιοι -ων οἱ
enjoy, I	ἥδομαι ἥσθην (+ dat)
enough	(adj) ἱκανός -ή -όν, (adv) ἅλις
enquire, I	πυνθάνομαι ἐπυθόμην
enslave, I	δουλόω ἐδούλωσα
entrust, I	ἐπιτρέπω ἐπέτρεψα (something acc to someone dat)
envy	φθόνος -ου ὁ
equal	ἴσος -η -ον
equipment	σκεύη -ῆς ἡ
escape	ἐκφεύγω ἐξέφυγον
escape (the) notice (of), I	λανθάνω ἔλαθον
especially	μάλιστα
even	καί
evening	ἑσπέρα -ας ἡ
event	συμφορά -ᾶς ἡ
ever	ποτε
every	πᾶς πᾶσα πᾶν (παντ-), (each) ἕκαστος -η -ον
everywhere	πανταχοῦ
examine, I	σκοπέω ἐσκεψάμην
excellence	ἀρετή -ῆς ἡ
except	πλήν (+ gen)
excessively, too much	ἄγαν
exile	(person in exile) φυγάς -άδος ὁ, (state of exile) φυγή -ῆς ἡ
expect (to), I	ἐλπίζω ἤλπισα (usu + fut inf)
expedition (military)	στόλος -ου ὁ, στρατεία -ας ἡ
experience, I	πάσχω ἔπαθον
explain, I	διηγέομαι διηγησάμην
eye	ὀφθαλμός -οῦ ὁ
fair (with justice)	δίκαιος -α -ον
faithful	πιστός -ή -όν
fall, I	πίπτω ἔπεσον
family	γένος -ους τό
far as, as	μέχρι (+ gen)
fare, I	πράσσω ἔπραξα (foll adv)
farthest	ἔσχατος -η -ον
father	πατήρ -τρός ὁ
fatherland	πατρίς -ίδος ἡ
fear	φόβος -ου ὁ
fear, I	φοβέομαι ἐφοβήθην
festival	ἑορτή -ῆς ἡ
few	ὀλίγοι -αι -α
fewer	ἐλάσσονες -α
fewest	ἐλάχιστοι -αι -α

field	ἀγρός -οῦ ὁ, (plain) πεδίον -ου τό
fifth	πέμπτος -η -ον
fifty	πεντήκοντα
fight, I	μάχομαι ἐμαχεσάμην
fight a sea-battle, I	ναυμαχέω ἐναυμάχησα
fill, I	πληρόω ἐπλήρωσα
finally	τέλος
find, I	εὑρίσκω ηὗρον
find out, I	γιγνώσκω ἔγνων, (*implying* by enquiry) πυνθάνομαι ἐπυθόμην
fine	καλός -ή -όν
fire	πῦρ πυρός τό
fire at, I	βάλλω ἔβαλον, (with arrows) τοξεύω ἐτόξευσα
firm	βέβαιος -α -ον
first (*adj*)	πρῶτος -η -ον
first (*adv*), at first	πρῶτον
first light, at	ἅμ᾽ ἡμέρᾳ
fish	ἰχθύς -ύος ὁ
five	πέντε
five hundred	πεντακόσιοι -αι -α
flee, I	φεύγω ἔφυγον
fleet	ναυτικόν -οῦ τό
follow, I	ἕπομαι ἑσπόμην (+ *dat*)
following way, in the	ὧδε
food	σῖτος -ου ὁ
foolish	μῶρος -α -ον
foot	πούς ποδός ὁ
foot, on	πεζῇ
footsoldiers	πεζοί -ῶν οἱ
for	γάρ*
force	βία -ας ἡ
force, I	ἀναγκάζω ἠνάγκασα
foreign	βάρβαρος -ον
foreigner	ξένος -ου ὁ
forest	ὕλη -ης ἡ
forget (about), I	ἐπιλανθάνομαι ἐπελαθόμην (*usu* + *gen*)
fort, fortification	τείχισμα -ατος τό
fortify, I	τειχίζω ἐτείχισα
fortunate	εὐτυχής -ές
forty	τεσσαράκοντα
forward, I go	προχωρέω προὐχώρησα
forwards	πόρρω/πρόσω
four	τέσσαρες τέσσαρα
four hundred	τετρακόσιοι -αι -α
fourth	τέταρτος -η -ον
free	ἐλεύθερος -α -ον
freedom	ἐλευθερία -ας ἡ
friend	(male) φίλος -ου ὁ, (female) φίλη -ης ἡ
friendly	φίλιος -α -ον

friendship	φιλία -ας ἡ
from	ἀπό (+ gen), (from a person) παρά (+ gen)
from here	ἐνθένδε
from then	ἐντεῦθεν
from there	ἐκεῖθεν
from (the place) where	ὅθεν
from where?	πόθεν; (indirect qu) ὁπόθεν
front of, in	πρό (+ gen)
furthest (part of adj)	ἄκρος -α -ον
future, in the	ὄπισθε(ν)
gate	πύλη -ης ἡ
gather (something together), I	ἀθροίζω ἤθροισα, σύλλεγω συνέλεξα
general	στρατηγός -οῦ ὁ
general, I am a	στρατηγέω ἐστρατήγησα
get, I	κτάομαι ἐκτησάμην
get angry, I	ὀργίζομαι ὠργίσθην (with, + dat)
get to know, I	γιγνώσκω ἔγνων
giant	γίγας -αντος ὁ
gift	δῶρον -ου τό
girl	κόρη -ης ἡ, παῖς παιδός ἡ
give, I	δίδωμι ἔδωκα
glad	ἄσμενος -η -ον
gladly	ἡδέως
glory	δόξα -ης ἡ
go, I	ἔρχομαι ἦλθον, βαίνω ἔβην (usu in compounds), χωρέω ἐχώρησα
go, I shall	εἶμι
go away, I	ἀποβαίνω ἀπέβην
go forward, I	προχωρέω προὐχώρησα
go out, I	ἐκβαίνω ἐξέβην
go to(wards), I	προσβαίνω προσέβην
god	θεός -οῦ ὁ
goddess	θεά -ᾶς ἡ
going to, I am	μέλλω (+ fut inf)
gold	χρυσός -οῦ ὁ, (adj golden, made of gold) χρυσοῦς -ῆ -οῦν
good	ἀγαθός -ή -όν
grasp, I	λαμβάνομαι ἐλαβόμην (+ gen)
grateful, I am	χάριν ἔχω (to someone dat for something gen)
great	μέγας μεγάλη μέγα (μεγαλ-)
greater	μείζων -ον (μειζον-)
greatest, very great	μέγιστος -η -ον
Greece	Ἑλλάς -άδος ἡ
Greek, Greek man	Ἕλλην -ηνος ὁ
grudge	φθόνος -ου ὁ
grudge, I	φθονέω ἐφθόνησα
guard	φύλαξ -ακος ὁ
guard, I	φυλάσσω ἐφύλαξα
guest	ξένος -ου ὁ

guide	ἡγεμών -όνος ὁ
hand	χείρ χειρός ἡ
hand over, I	παραδίδωμι παρέδωκα
hands of, at the	πρός (+ gen)
happen, I	(occur) γίγνομαι ἐγενόμην, (chance to) τυγχάνω ἔτυχον (+ pple)
happy	εὐδαίμων -ον (εὐδαιμον-)
harbour	λιμήν -ένος ὁ
harm, I	βλάπτω ἔβλαψα
hate, I	μισέω ἐμίσησα
hatred	μῖσος -ους τό
have, I	ἔχω ἔσχον
have come, I	ἥκω
have power over, I	κρατέω ἐκράτησα (+ gen)
head	κεφαλή -ῆς ἡ
hear, I	ἀκούω ἤκουσα (+ acc of thing, gen of person)
heaven	οὐρανός -οῦ ὁ
heavy	βαρύς -εῖα -ύ
help	βοήθεια -ας ἡ
help, I	(often implying run to help) βοηθέω ἐβοήθησα (+ dat), (implying benefit) ὠφελέω ὠφέλησα
her (acc pronoun)	αὐτήν
herald	κῆρυξ -υκος ὁ
here	ἐνθάδε
here, I am	πάρειμι impf παρῆν
here, to	δεῦρο
herself (reflexive)	ἑαυτήν
hesitate (to), I	μέλλω (+ fut inf)
hesitation	ἀπορία -ας ἡ
hide (something), I	κρύπτω ἔκρυψα, (hide myself) κρύπτομαι ἐκρυψάμην
high	ὑψηλός -ή -όν
hill	ὄρος -ους τό
him	αὐτόν
himself (reflexive)	ἑαυτόν
hinder, I	κωλύω ἐκώλυσα
hit, I	(strike) τύπτω ἔτυψα, (pelt) βάλλω ἔβαλον
hit upon, I	τυγχάνω ἔτυχον (+ gen)
holy	ἱερός -ά -όν
home, at	οἴκοι
home, from	οἴκοθεν
homewards, to home	οἴκαδε
honour	τιμή -ῆς ἡ
honour, I	τιμάω ἐτίμησα
hope (to), I	ἐλπίζω ἤλπισα (usu + fut inf)
hoplite (heavy-armed soldier)	ὁπλίτης -ου ὁ
horn	κέρας -ατος τό
horse	ἵππος -ου ὁ
horseman	ἱππεύς -έως ὁ

host	ξένος -ου ὁ
hostile	(as personal enemy) ἐχθρός -ά -όν, (in war) πολέμιος -α -ον
hour	ὥρα -ας ἡ
house	οἰκία -ας ἡ, οἶκος -ου ὁ
how?	πῶς;
how big?	πόσος; -η; -ον; (indirect qu) ὁπόσος -η -ον
how many?	πόσοι; -αι; -α; (indirect qu) ὁπόσοι -αι -α
however	μέντοι*
human being	ἄνθρωπος -ου ὁ/ἡ
hundred, a	ἑκατόν
hunt, I	θηρεύω ἐθήρευσα
husband	ἀνήρ -δρός ὁ
I	ἐγώ
if	εἰ (+ indic or opt), ἐάν (+ subj)
if only ... !	εἴθε (+ opt)
illness	νόσος -ου ἡ
immediately	εὐθύς
impious	ἀσεβής -ές
in	ἐν (+ dat)
in addition to	πρός (+ dat)
in front of	πρό (+ gen)
in no way	οὐδαμῶς
in order to	ἵνα (+ subj/opt), ὅπως (+ subj/opt), ὡς (+ fut pple)
in some way	πως
in the following way	ὧδε
in the time of	ἐπί (+ gen)
in this way	οὕτω(ς)
in vain	μάτην
inasmuch as	ἅτε (+ pple)
increase (something), I	αὐξάνω ηὔξησα
indeed	δή
infantry	πεζοί -ῶν οἱ
inhabit, I	οἰκέω ᾤκησα
inhabitant	ἔνοικος -ου ὁ
instead of	ἀντί (+ gen)
insult, I	ὑβρίζω ὕβρισα
intend to, I	μέλλω (+ fut inf)
into	εἰς (+ acc)
invade, I	εἰσβάλλω εἰσέβαλον (+ εἰς + acc)
invasion	εἰσβολή -ῆς ἡ
invite, I	καλέω ἐκάλεσα
island	νῆσος -ου ἡ
it (acc pronoun)	αὐτό
it is necessary (for X to ...)	δεῖ impf ἔδει (+ acc + inf), (implying moral obligation) χρή impf (ἐ)χρῆν (+ acc + inf)
it is possible (for X to ...)	ἔξεστι(ν) impf ἐξῆν (+ dat + inf)
journey	ὁδός -οῦ ἡ

judge	κριτής -οῦ ὁ
judge, I	κρίνω ἔκρινα
judgement	γνώμη -ης ἡ
just (with justice)	δίκαιος -α -ον
just as, just like	ὥσπερ
justice	δικαιοσύνη -ης ἡ, δίκη -ης ἡ
kill, I	ἀποκτείνω ἀπέκτεινα
killed, I am	ἀποθνῄσκω ἀπέθανον
king	βασιλεύς -έως ὁ
know, I	οἶδα *impf* ᾔδη, (*implying* know how to) ἐπίσταμαι *impf* ἠπιστάμην (+ *inf*)
know, I do not	ἀγνοέω ἠγνόησα
know, I get to	γιγνώσκω ἔγνων
know how (to), I	ἐπίσταμαι ἠπιστάμην (+ *inf*)
labour, I	κάμνω ἔκαμον, πονέω ἐπόνησα
land	(country) χώρα -ας ἡ, (earth) γῆ γῆς ἡ
land, by	κατὰ γῆν
language	γλῶσσα -ης ἡ
last (farthest)	ἔσχατος -η -ον
later	(*adv*) ὕστερον, (*adj*) ὕστερος -α -ον
laugh, I	γελάω ἐγέλασα
law	νόμος -ου ὁ
lawsuit	δίκη -ης ἡ
lead, I	ἄγω ἤγαγον, ἡγέομαι ἡγησάμην
leader	ἡγεμών -όνος ὁ
leap, I	πηδάω ἐπήδησα
learn, I	μανθάνω ἔμαθον
learn by enquiry, I	πυνθάνομαι ἐπυθόμην
least	(*adj*) ἐλάχιστος -η -ον, (*adv*) ἥκιστα
least, at	γε*
leave, I	λείπω ἔλιπον
left (on the left hand side *adj*)	ἀριστερός -ά -όν
left (over)	λοιπός -ή -όν
less	ἐλάσσων -ον (ἐλασσον-)
letter	ἐπιστολή -ῆς ἡ
lie (be laid down), I	κεῖμαι *impf* (ἐ)κείμην
lie (tell a lie), I	ψεύδομαι ἐψευσάμην
life	βίος -ου ὁ
light, at first	ἅμ᾽ ἡμέρᾳ
light-armed soldier	πελταστής -οῦ ὁ
like, just as	ὥσπερ
like, I	φιλέω ἐφίλησα
likely, what/that which is	εἰκός -ότος τό
likely to, I am	κινδυνεύω ἐκινδύνευσα (+ *inf*)
lion	λέων -οντος ὁ
listen (to), I	ἀκούω ἤκουσα (+ *acc of thing, gen of person*)
little of, a	ὀλίγος -η -ον

live, I	(be alive) ζάω ἔζησα, (live in, inhabit) οἰκέω ᾤκησα
long	μακρός -ά -όν
long ago	πάλαι
look, I	βλέπω ἔβλεψα
look at, I	σκοπέω ἐσκεψάμην, θεάομαι ἐθεασάμην
lose, I	ἀπόλλυμι ἀπώλεσα
loss, I am at a	ἀπορέω ἠπόρησα
love, I	φιλέω ἐφίλησα
lucky	εὐτυχής -ές
madness	μανία -ας ἡ
magistrate	ἄρχων -οντος ὁ
mainland	ἤπειρος -ου ἡ
make, I	ποιέω ἐποίησα
man, human being	ἄνθρωπος -ου ὁ
man, male	ἀνήρ -δρός ὁ
many	πολλοί -αί -ά
march, I	πορεύομαι ἐπορεύθην, (go on military campaign or expedition) στρατεύω ἐστράτευσα
marketplace	ἀγορά -ᾶς ἡ
marry (someone), I	(m subject) γαμέω ἔγημα (+ acc), (f subject) γαμέομαι ἐγημάμην (+ dat)
marsh	λίμνη -ης ἡ
master	δεσπότης -ου ὁ
matter (affair, business)	πρᾶγμα -ατος τό
meanwhile	ἐν τούτῳ
meet (someone), I	ἐντυγχάνω ἐνέτυχον (+ dat)
messenger	ἄγγελος -ου ὁ
middle, middle bit of (adj)	μέσος -η -ον
might (power, authority)	κράτος -ους τό
mind	νοῦς νοῦ ὁ
miss (target etc), I	ἁμαρτάνω ἥμαρτον
mistake, I make a	ἁμαρτάνω ἥμαρτον
mistress	δέσποινα -ης ἡ
money	χρήματα -ων τά, (cash, coinage) ἀργύριον -ου τό
more	(sg) πλείων -ον (πλειον-), (pl) πλείονες -α, (adv) μᾶλλον
most	(sg) πλεῖστος -η -ον, (pl) πλεῖστοι -αι -α
mother	μήτηρ -τρος ἡ
mountain	ὄρος -ους τό
mouth	στόμα -ατος τό
much	πολύς πολλή πολύ (πολλ-)
murder, I	φονεύω ἐφόνευσα
Muse (goddess of inspiration)	Μοῦσα -ης ἡ
my	ἐμός -ή -όν
myself (reflexive)	ἐμαυτόν -ήν
naked	γυμνός -ή -όν
name	ὄνομα -ατος τό
name of, in the	πρός (+ gen)

narrate, I	διηγέομαι διηγησάμην
narrow	στενός -ή -όν
nation	ἔθνος -ους τό
near	ἐγγύς (+ gen)
nearly	σχεδόν
necessary (for X to ...), it is	δεῖ impf ἔδει (+ acc), (implying moral obligation) χρή impf (ἐ)χρῆν (+ acc)
necessity	ἀνάγκη -ης ἡ
need, I	δέομαι ἐδεήθην (+ gen)
neither ... nor	οὔτε ... οὔτε, μήτε ... μήτε
never	οὔποτε/οὐδέποτε, μήποτε/μηδέποτε
nevertheless	ὅμως
new	νέος -α -ον
next	ἔπειτα, εἶτα
next day, on the	τῇ ὑστεραίᾳ
night	νύξ νυκτός ἡ
nine	ἐννέα
nine hundred	ἐνακόσιοι -αι -α
ninety	ἐνενήκοντα
ninth	ἔνατος -η -ον
no ... , not any	οὐδείς οὐδεμία οὐδέν (οὐδεν-), μηδείς μηδεμία μηδέν (μηδεν-)
no longer	οὐκέτι, μηκέτι
no way, in	οὐδαμῶς, μηδαμῶς
no-one	οὐδείς (οὐδεν-) οὐδεμία, μηδείς (μηδεν-) μηδεμία
noble	εὐγενής -ές
non-Greek	βάρβαρος -ον
not	οὐ (οὐκ before smooth breathing, οὐχ before rough breathing), (in contexts other than statements of fact) μή
not at all	ἥκιστα, (in no way) οὐδαμῶς
not even	οὐδέ, μηδέ
not only ... but also	οὐ μόνον ... ἀλλὰ καί
nothing	οὐδέν, μηδέν
notice, I	αἰσθάνομαι ᾐσθόμην
now	(at this time) νῦν, (already, by now) ἤδη, (just recently) ἄρτι
number	ἀριθμός -οῦ ὁ, (large number, crowd) πλῆθος -ους τό
oath	ὅρκος -ου ὁ
obey, I	πείθομαι ἐπιθόμην (+ dat)
obtain, I	κτάομαι ἐκτησάμην
obvious	δῆλος -η -ον
often	πολλάκις
old	ἀρχαῖος -α -ον, παλαιός -ά -όν
old man	γέρων -οντος ὁ, πρέσβυς -εως ὁ
on	ἐπί (+ dat)
on account of	διά (+ acc)
on behalf of	ὑπέρ (+ gen)
on condition that	ἐφ' ᾧτε (usu + inf)
on the one hand ... on the other	μέν* ... δέ*

209

once (at some time)	ποτε
one	εἷς μία ἕν (ἑν-)
one/the other (of two)	ἕτερος -α -ον
only	(adj) μόνος -η -ον, (adv) μόνον
opinion	γνώμη -ης ἡ, δόξα -ης ἡ
opportunity	καιρός -οῦ ὁ
opposite	(adj) ἐναντίος -α -ον, (prep) ἀντί (+ gen)
or	ἤ
oracle (place or response)	μαντεῖον -ου τό, χρηστήριον -ου τό
order, I	κελεύω ἐκέλευσα
other	ἄλλος -η -ο
our	ἡμέτερος -α -ον
ourselves (reflexive)	ἡμᾶς αὐτούς -άς
out of	ἐκ (ἐξ before vowel) (+ gen)
outside	ἔξω

part	μέρος -ους τό
pass (over/through mountains)	εἰσβολή -ῆς ἡ
pay	μισθός -οῦ ὁ
peace	εἰρήνη -ης ἡ
pelt, I	βάλλω ἔβαλον
penalty	δίκη -ης ἡ
people (community)	δῆμος -ου ὁ
perceive, I	αἰσθάνομαι ἠσθόμην
perhaps	ἴσως, τάχα, τάχ' ἄν
perish, I	ἀπόλλυμαι ἀπωλόμην
perplexity	ἀπορία -ας ἡ
person	ἄνθρωπος -ου ὁ/ἡ
persuade, I	πείθω ἔπεισα
pious	εὐσεβής -ές
pity, I	οἰκτείρω ᾤκτειρα
place	τόπος -ου ὁ, χωρίον -ου τό
place, I	τίθημι ἔθηκα
plain	πεδίον -ου τό
plan	βουλή -ῆς ἡ
plan, I	βουλεύομαι ἐβουλευσάμην
pleasant	ἡδύς -εῖα -ύ
pleased	ἄσμενος -η -ον
pleased (with), I am	ἥδομαι (+ dat)
poet	ποιητής -οῦ ὁ
point out, I	δείκνυμι ἔδειξα
politician	ῥήτωρ -ορος ὁ
possession	κτῆμα -ατος τό
possibility	εἰκός -ότος τό
possible	δυνατός -ή -όν
possible, as quickly as	ὡς τάχιστα
possible (for X to ...), it is	ἔξεστι(ν) impf ἐξῆν (+ dat + inf), πάρεστι impf παρῆν (+ dat + inf)
power	δύναμις -εως ἡ

power over, I have	κρατέω ἐκράτησα (+ *gen*)
praise, I	ἐπαινέω ἐπήνησα
pray, I	εὔχομαι ηὐξάμην
prepare, I	παρασκευάζω παρεσκεύασα
presence of, into the	παρά (+ *acc*)
present, I am	πάρειμι *imperf* παρῆν
press, I	πιέζω ἐπίεσα
prevent, I	κωλύω ἐκώλυσα (from, + *gen or inf*)
previous day, on the	τῇ προτεραίᾳ
previously	πρότερον
priest	ἱερεύς -έως ὁ
prison	δεσμωτήριον -ου τό
prisoner	δεσμώτης -ου ὁ, (of war) αἰχμάλωτος -ου ὁ
prize	ἆθλον -ου τό
probably	ἴσως
proclaim, I	κηρύσσω ἐκήρυξα
produce, I	παρέχω παρέσχον
promise (to), I	ὑπισχνέομαι ὑπεσχόμην (+ *fut inf*)
provide, I	παρέχω παρέσχον
prophet	μάντις -εως ὁ
prudent	σώφρων -ον (σωφρον-)
public speaker	ῥήτωρ -ορος ὁ
public square	ἀγορά -ᾶς ἡ
punish, I	κολάζω ἐκόλασα, (take vengeance on) τιμωρέω ἐτιμώρησα
purpose	γνώμη -ης ἡ
pursue, I	διώκω ἐδίωξα
put, I	τίθημι ἔθηκα
put out to sea, I	ἀνάγομαι ἀνηγαγόμην
queen	βασίλεια -ας ἡ
quick	ταχύς -εῖα -ύ
quicker	θάσσων -ον (θασσον-)
quickest	τάχιστος -η -ον
quickly	ταχέως
quickly as possible, as	ὡς τάχιστα
race (nation *etc*)	γένος -ους τό, ἔθνος -ους τό
raise, I	αἴρω ἦρα
rank	τάξις -εως ἡ
ransom, I	λύομαι ἐλυσάμην
rather	μᾶλλον
read, I	ἀναγιγνώσκω ἀνέγνων
ready	ἕτοιμος -η -ον
reason	λόγος -ου ὁ
receive, I	δέχομαι ἐδεξάμην
recent	νέος -α -ον
recently	ἄρτι
regard as important, I	περὶ πολλοῦ ποιέομαι
rejoice, I	χαίρω ἐχαίρησα

211

related (as family)	συγγενής -ές
release, I	λύω ἔλυσα
reliable	πίστος -η -ον
remain, I	μένω ἔμεινα
remaining, left	λοιπός -ή -όν
remember, I	μέμνημαι ἐμεμνήμην (+ gen)
reply, I	ἀποκρίνομαι ἀπεκρινάμην
report, I	ἀγγέλλω ἤγγειλα
resent, I	φθονέω ἐφθόνησα
resist, I	ἀμύνομαι ἠμυνάμην (+ dat)
respect, I	αἰδέομαι ᾐδεσάμην
responsible (for)	αἴτιος -α -ον (+ gen)
result	τέλος -ους τό
result, as a	ὥστε
retreat, I	ἀναχωρέω ἀνεχώρησα
return, I	ἐπανέρχομαι ἐπανῆλθον
reveal, I	φαίνω ἔφηνα
revolt, I	ἀφίσταμαι ἀπέστην
revolt, I make/cause to	ἀφίστημι ἀπέστησα
reward	μισθός -οῦ ὁ
rich	πλούσιος -α -ον
ride, I	ἱππεύω ἵππευσα
right hand	δεξιά -ᾶς ἡ
right (hand side) (adj)	δεξιός -ά -όν
right (just)	δίκαιος -α -ον
right time	καιρός -οῦ ὁ
risk, I run a	κινδυνεύω ἐκινδύνευσα
river	ποταμός -οῦ ὁ
road	ὁδός -οῦ ἡ
rob, I	ἀποστερέω ἀπεστέρησα (someone acc of something gen)
rout, I	τρέπω ἔτρεψα
rule	ἀρχή -ῆς ἡ
rule, I	ἄρχω ἦρξα (+ gen), κρατέω ἐκράτησα (+ gen)
ruler	(chief, magistrate) ἄρχων -οντος ὁ, (king) βασιλεύς -έως ὁ
run (act of running)	δρόμος -ου ὁ
run, I	τρέχω ἔδραμον
run away, I	φεύγω ἔφυγον
run to help, I	βοηθέω ἐβοήθησα (+ dat)
sacrifice, I	θύω ἔθυσα
safe	ἀσφαλής -ές
safety	ἀσφάλεια -ας ἡ, σωτηρία -ας ἡ
said, he/she (usu interrupting direct quotation)	ἔφη
sail, I	πλέω ἔπλευσα
sailor	ναύτης -ου ὁ
same, the	ὁ αὐτός, ἡ αὐτή, τὸ αὐτό
same time, at the ... (as)	ἅμα (+ dat, or as adv)
save, I	σῴζω ἔσωσα

saw, I	εἶδον
say, I	λέγω εἶπον or *(less commonly)* ἔλεξα, φημί *impf* ἔφην
scarcely	μόλις
sea	θάλασσα -ης ἡ
sea-battle	ναυμαχία -ας ἡ
sea-battle, I fight a	ναυμαχέω ἐναυμάχησα
second	δεύτερος -α -ον
secretly	λάθρα
see, I	ὁράω εἶδον
seeing that (since, inasmuch as)	ἅτε (+ *pple*)
seek, I	ζητέω ἐζήτησα
seem, I	δοκέω ἔδοξα, (it seems good to X, *i.e.* X decides to ...) δοκεῖ ἔδοξε (+ *dat* + *inf*)
seize, I	ἁρπάζω ἥρπασα
self	αὐτός -ή -ό
self-controlled	σώφρων -ον (σωφρον-)
send, I	πέμπω ἔπεμψα, (let go, hurl) ἵημι ἧκα, (despatch expedition *etc*) στέλλω ἔστειλα
send for, I	μεταπέμπομαι μετεπεμψάμην
servant	(male) θεράπων -οντος ὁ, (female) θεράπαινα -ης ἡ
serve, I	θεραπεύω ἐθεράπευσα
set free, I	ἐλευθερόω ἠλευθέρωσα
set out, I	ὁρμάομαι ὡρμησάμην
seven	ἑπτά
seven hundred	ἑπτακόσιοι -αι -α
seventh	ἕβδομος -η -ον
seventy	ἑβδομήκοντα
shame (someone), I	αἰσχύνω ᾔσχυνα
shameful	αἰσχρός -ά -όν
share, I have a	μετέχω μετέσχον (of + *gen*)
sharp	ὀξύς -εῖα -ύ
shield	ἀσπίς -ίδος ἡ
ship	ναῦς νεώς ἡ
shoot (fire an arrow), I	τοξεύω ἐτόξευσα
shore	ἀκτή -ῆς ἡ
short time, after a	δι᾽ ὀλίγου
shout, shouting	βοή -ῆς ἡ
shout, I	βοάω ἐβόησα
show, I	(make clear) δηλόω ἐδήλωσα, (point out) δείκνυμι ἔδειξα, (reveal) φαίνω ἔφηνα
sign, signal	σῆμα -ατος τό
signal, I	σημαίνω ἐσήμηνα
silence	σιγή -ῆς ἡ, (*adv* in silence) σιγῇ
silent, I am	σιγάω ἐσίγησα
similar	ὅμοιος -α -ον
silver	ἄργυρος -ου ὁ, (*adj* made of silver) ἀργυροῦς -ᾶ -οῦν
since (as, because)	ἐπεί, ἐπειδή (*introducing subordinate clause*), ἅτε (*with pple, or pple alone*)
since (from the time when)	ἐξ οὗ

213

sit, I	καθίζω ἐκάθισα
six	ἕξ
six hundred	ἑξακόσιοι -αι -α
sixth	ἕκτος -η -ον
sixty	ἑξήκοντα
skilful	δεξιός -ά -όν
skill	τέχνη -ης ἡ
sky	οὐρανός -οῦ ὁ
slave	(male) δοῦλος -ου ὁ, (female) δούλη -ης ἡ
slave, I am a	δουλεύω ἐδούλευσα
sleep	ὕπνος -ου ὁ
sleep, I	καθεύδω *impf* ἐκάθευδον *or* καθηῦδον
slow	βραδύς -εῖα -ύ
small	μικρός -ά -όν
small amount of	ὀλίγος -η -ον
snatch, I	ἁρπάζω ἥρπασα
so	οὕτω(ς)
so big, so great	τοσοῦτος -αύτη -οῦτο
so many	τοσοῦτοι -αῦται -αῦτα
soldier	στρατιώτης -ου ὁ
somehow, in some way	πως
someone	τις τινός
something	τι τινός
sometime	ποτε
sometimes	ἐνίοτε
somewhere	που
somewhere, from	ποθέν
somewhere, to	ποι
son	υἱός -οῦ ὁ
soon	(quickly) τάχα, (after a short time) δι' ὀλίγου
sort, of such a	τοιοῦτος -αύτη -οῦτο
sort of, what?	ποῖος; -α; -ον; *(indirect qu)* ὁποῖος -α -ον
sort which, of the	οἷος -α -ον
Spartans, the	Λακεδαιμόνιοι -ων οἱ
speak, I	λέγω εἶπον *or (less commonly)* ἔλεξα
speaker	ῥήτωρ -ορος ὁ
spear	λόγχη -ης ἡ
spy	κατάσκοπος -ου ὁ
stade *(about 180 metres)*	στάδιον -ου τό, *m pl* στάδιοι -ων οἱ
stand, I	ἕστηκα *(pf with pres sense)* ἔστην, (stand something *acc* up) ἵστημι ἔστησα
state, I am in a certain	καθίσταμαι κατέστην
state, I put in a certain	καθίστημι κατέστησα
stay, I	μένω ἔμεινα
steady	βέβαιος -α -ον
steal, I	κλέπτω ἔκλεψα
still, even now	ἔτι
stone	λίθος -ου ὁ
stop, I	(stop something) παύω ἔπαυσα, (stop myself) παύομαι

	ἐπαυσάμην
storm	χειμών -ῶνος ὁ
story	(myth, fable) μῦθος -ου ὁ, (factual account) λόγος -ου ὁ
straight	ὀρθός -ή -όν
straightaway	αὐτίκα
strange	δεινός -ή -όν
stranger	ξένος -ου ὁ
strength	βία -ας ἡ
strike, I	τύπτω ἔτυψα
strong	ἰσχυρός -ά -όν
stupid	μῶρος -α -ον
such, of such a kind	τοιοῦτος -αύτη -οῦτο
suddenly	ἐξαίφνης
suffer, I	(experience) πάσχω ἔπαθον, (toil) πονέω ἐπόνησα
suffering	πόνος -ου ὁ
sufficient	ἱκανός -ή -όν
summer	θέρος -ους τό
sun	ἥλιος -ου ὁ
supplies	ἐπιτήδεια -ων τά
surely	δή, δήπου
surely ...?	ἆρ' (= ἆρα) οὐ;
surely ... not?	ἆρα μή;
swear, I	ὄμνυμι ὤμοσα (usu + fut inf)
sweet	γλυκύς -εῖα -ύ, ἡδύς -εῖα -ύ
swift	ταχύς -εῖα -ύ
swifter	θάσσων -ον (θασσον-)
swiftest	τάχιστος -η -ον
sword	ξίφος -ους τό
take, I	λαμβάνω ἔλαβον, (often implying capture) αἱρέω εἷλον
take hold of, I	λαμβάνομαι ἐλαβόμην (+ gen)
take (something) badly, I	βαρέως φέρω
task	ἔργον -ου τό
teach, I	διδάσκω ἐδίδαξα
teacher	διδάσκαλος -ου ὁ
tell, I	(say, speak) λέγω εἶπον or (less commonly) ἔλεξα, (report) ἀγγέλλω ἤγγειλα, (order) κελεύω ἐκέλευσα
temple	ἱερόν -οῦ τό
ten	δέκα
tent	σκηνή -ῆς ἡ
tenth	δέκατος -η -ον
terrible	δεινός -ή -όν
than	ἤ
thank, I	χάριν ἔχω (someone dat for something gen)
that (pronoun that one there)	ἐκεῖνος -η -ο
that (conjunction)	(the fact that) ὅτι or ὡς, (with the result that) ὥστε
the	ὁ ἡ τό
their (own)	σφέτερος -α -ον
them (acc pronoun)	αὐτούς -άς, σφᾶς

215

themselves (*reflexive*)	ἑαυτούς -άς, σφᾶς αὐτούς -άς
then	(next) ἔπειτα, εἶτα, (at that time) τότε, ἔνθα, (drawing an inference) ἄρα
there	ἐκεῖ, ἔνθα, (to there) ἐκεῖσε, (from there) ἐκεῖθεν
therefore	οὖν*, οὐκοῦν
therefore ... not	οὔκουν
these	οὗτοι αὗται ταῦτα, (*implying* here present *or* the following) οἵδε αἵδε τάδε
thing	χρῆμα -ατος τό, (matter, business) πρᾶγμα -ατος τό
think, I	(think to be so) νομίζω ἐνόμισα, ἡγέομαι ἡγησάμην, (think about) ἐννοέω ἐνενόησα
third	τρίτος -η -ον
thirty	τριάκοντα
this	οὗτος αὕτη τοῦτο, (*implying* here present *or* the following) ὅδε ἥδε τόδε
this way, in	οὕτω(ς)
those	ἐκεῖνοι -αι -α
thousand, a	χίλιοι -αι -α
threaten	ἀπειλέω ἠπείλησα
three	τρεῖς τρία
three hundred	τριακόσιοι -αι -α
through	δία (+ *gen*), (on account of) δία (+ *acc*)
throughout	κατά (+ *acc*)
throw, I	βάλλω ἔβαλον, ῥίπτω ἔρριψα
time	χρόνος -ου ὁ
time, at the same ... (as)	ἅμα (+ *dat, or as adv*)
time of, in the	ἐπί (+ *gen*)
time, right *or* appropriate	καιρός -οῦ ὁ
to	(towards) πρός (+ *acc*), (into) εἰς (+ *acc*), (to a person) ὡς (+ *acc*)
to here	δεῦρο
to (the place) where	οἷ
today	σήμερον
toil	πόνος -ου ὁ
toil, I	κάμνω ἔκαμον, πονέω ἐπόνησα
tomb	τάφος -ου ὁ
tomorrow	αὔριον
tongue	γλῶσσα -ης ἡ
too much	ἄγαν
top, top bit of (*adj*)	ἄκρος -α -ον
touch, I	ἅπτομαι ἡψάμην (+ *gen*)
towards	πρός (+ *acc*)
town	ἄστυ -εως τό
train, I	παιδεύω ἐπαίδευσα
travel, I	πορεύομαι ἐπορεύθην
treat (someone *e.g.* well), I	ποιέω ἐποίησα (*foll adv,* + *acc*), χράομαι ἐχρησάμην (*foll adv,* + *dat*)
treaty	σπονδαί -ῶν αἱ
tree	δένδρον -ου τό

216

trial (in court)	ἀγών -ῶνος ὁ
tribe	ἔθνος -ους τό
trick, trickery	δόλος -ου ὁ
trireme (warship)	τριήρης -ους ἡ
trophy	τρόπαιον -ου τό
true	ἀληθής -ές
trust, I	πιστεύω ἐπίστευσα (+ *dat*)
trustworthy	πιστός -ή -όν
try, I	πειράομαι ἐπειρασάμην
turn, I	τρέπω ἔτρεψα
turn, in	αὖ
twelve	δώδεκα
twenty	εἴκοσι
two	δύο
two hundred	διακόσιοι -αι -α
type	γένος -ους τό
ugly	αἰσχρός -ά -όν
under	(going/to under) ὑπό (+ *acc*), (resting under/subject to) ὑπό (+ *dat*)
unexpected	ἀπροσδόκητος -ον
unfortunate	δυστυχής -ές
unjust	ἄδικος -ον
unjustly (to), I act	ἀδικέω ἠδίκησα (+ *acc*)
unlucky	δυστυχής -ές
until	(*prep*) μέχρι (+ *gen*), (*conj*) ἕως *or* πρίν
unwilling, unwillingly	ἄκων -ουσα -ον (ἀκοντ-)
up	ἀνά (+ *acc*)
urge, I	ἀξιόω ἠξίωσα
use, I	χράομαι ἐχρησάμην (+ *dat*)
useful	χρήσιμος -η -ον
vain, in	μάτην
value (at), I	ποιέομαι ποιησάμην (+ περί + *gen*)
very	μάλα
very much (*adv*)	(especially) μάλιστα, (strongly) σφόδρα
victory	νίκη -ης ἡ
village	κώμη -ης ἡ
virtue	ἀρετή -ῆς ἡ
voice	φωνή -ῆς ἡ
voyage	πλοῦς πλοῦ ὁ
wait (for), I	μένω ἔμεινα
walk, I	βαδίζω ἐβάδισα
wall	τεῖχος -ους τό
want, I	βούλομαι *impf* ἐβουλόμην (*less common aor* ἐβουλήθην)
war	πόλεμος -ου ὁ
war, I make/fight a	πολεμέω ἐπολέμησα
ward off, I	ἀμύνω ἤμυνα

watch, I	θεάομαι ἐθεασάμην
water	ὕδωρ -ατος τό
way	(route) ὁδός -οῦ ὁ, (manner) τρόπος -ου ὁ
way, in no	οὐδαμῶς
way, in this	οὕτω(ς), (implying as follows) ὧδε
we	ἡμεῖς
weak	ἀσθενής -ές
wealthy	πλούσιος -α -ον
weapons	ὅπλα -ων τά
weather, bad	χειμών -ῶνος ὁ
weep, I	δακρύω ἐδάκρυσα
well	εὖ
went, I	ἦλθον
what?	τί; τίνος;
what sort of?	ποῖος; -α; -ον; (indirect qu) ὁποῖος -α -ον
when?	πότε;
when	(since) ἐπεί, ἐπειδή (or use pple), (at the time when) ὅτε, ἔνθα (or use pple)
whenever	ὁπότε, ἐπειδάν (+ subj), ὅταν (+ subj)
where (at)?	ποῦ; (indirect qu) ὅπου
where (in the place in which)	οὗ
where from?	πόθεν; (indirect qu) ὁπόθεν
where to?	ποῖ; (indirect qu) ὅποι
whether ... or	εἴτε ... εἴτε, πότερον ... ἤ
which?	τίς; τί; (τίν-;)
which (of two)?	πότερος; -α; -ον; (indirect qu) ὁπότερος -α -ον
which (relative the one which)	ὅς ἥ ὅ
while	ἕως (or use pres pple)
who?	τίς; (τιν-;)
who, which (relative)	ὅς ἥ ὅ (or use pple)
whoever, whichever	ὅστις ἥτις ὅ τι
whole (of adj)	ἅπας -ασα -αν (ἁπαντ-)
why?	διὰ τί;
wide	εὐρύς -εῖα -ύ
wife	γυνή γυναικός ἡ
willing, willingly	ἑκών -οῦσα -όν (ἑκοντ-)
willing, I am	ἐθέλω ἠθέλησα
win, I	(conquer, am victorious) νικάω ἐνίκησα, (win prizes) φέρομαι ἠνεγκάμην/-όμην
wind	ἄνεμος -ου ὁ
wine	οἶνος -ου ὁ
wing (of army)	κέρας -ατος τό
winter	χειμών -ῶνος ὁ
wisdom	σοφία -ας ἡ
wise	σοφός -ή -όν
wish, I	βούλομαι impf ἐβουλόμην (less common aor ἐβουλήθην), ἐθέλω ἠθέλησα
with	μετά (+ gen), (often implying with the help of) σύν (+ dat), (at the same time as) ἅμα (+ dat)

with difficulty	μόλις
with the result that	ὥστε
withdraw, I	ἀναχωρέω ἀνεχώρησα
without	ἄνευ (+ *gen*)
woman	γυνή γυναικός ἡ
wood (forest)	ὕλη -ης ἡ
wooden, made of wood	ξύλινος -η -ον
word	λόγος -ου ὁ
work	ἔργον -ου τό
worse	κακίων -ον (κακιον-), (*implying* inferior) χείρων -ον (χειρον-)
worst	κάκιστος -η -ον, (*implying* most inferior) χείριστος -η -ον
worthy (of)	ἄξιος -α -ον (+ *gen*)
worthy, I think (something)	ἀξιόω ἠξίωσα
wound	τραῦμα -ατος τό
wound, I	τραυματίζω ἐτραυμάτισα
wretched	δυστυχής -ές
write, I	γράφω ἔγραψα
wrong, wrongdoing	ἀδικία -ας ἡ
wrong, I do	ἀδικέω ἠδίκησα
year	ἔτος -ους τό, ἐνιαυτός -οῦ ὁ
yes	ναί
yesterday	χθές
yet	ἔτι
you (*sg*)	σύ
you (*pl*)	ὑμεῖς
young	νέος -α -ον
young man	νεανίας -ου ὁ
your (of you *sg*)	σός σή σόν
your (of you *pl*)	ὑμέτερος -α -ον
yourself (*reflexive*)	σεαυτόν -ήν
yourselves (*reflexive*)	ὑμᾶς αὐτούς -άς
Zeus	Ζεύς Διός ὁ

;iven with present and aorist (see pages 188-91 for principal parts of irregular verbs).
Nou.... given with nominative and genitive.
Adjectives are given with masculine, feminine (if different), and neuter (some also with stem in brackets)

ἀ-	(as 'privative' prefix makes word negative)
ἀγαγ-	(aor stem of ἄγω)
ἀγαθός -ή -όν	good
ἄγαν	too much, excessively
ἀγγέλλω ἤγγειλα	I announce
ἄγγελος -ου ὁ	messenger
ἀγνοέω ἠγνόησα	I do not know
ἀγορά -ᾶς ἡ	marketplace, public square, agora
ἀγρός -οῦ ὁ	field, (pl) countryside
ἄγω ἤγαγον	I lead
ἀγών -ῶνος ὁ	contest, trial
ἀδελφή -ῆς ἡ	sister
ἀδελφός -οῦ ὁ	brother
ἀδικέω ἠδίκησα	I wrong (someone), I act unjustly
ἀδικία -ας ἡ	wrong, wrongdoing, injustice
ἄδικος -ον	criminal, unjust
ἀδύνατος -ον	impossible; incapable, unable
ἀεί	always
᾿Αθῆναι -ῶν αἱ	Athens
᾿Αθηναῖος -α -ον	Athenian, pl ᾿Αθηναῖοι -ων οἱ the Athenians
᾿Αθήνη -ης ἡ	Athene (goddess)
ἆθλον -ου τό	prize
ἀθροίζω ἤθροισα	I gather together
ἀθυμέω ἠθύμησα	I am despondent, I am disheartened
αἰδέομαι ᾐδεσάμην	I respect, I revere, I feel shame in front of
αἷμα -ατος τό	blood
αἱρέω εἷλον	I take
mid αἱρέομαι εἱλόμην	I choose
αἴρω ἦρα	I raise
αἰσθ-	(aor stem of αἰσθάνομαι)
αἰσθάνομαι ᾐσθόμην	I perceive, I notice
αἰσχρός -ά -όν	disgraceful, shameful; ugly
αἰσχύνω ᾔσχυνα	I disgrace, I shame
mid αἰσχύνομαι ᾐσχύνθην	I am ashamed
αἰτέω ᾔτησα	I ask for, I beg
αἴτιος -α -ον	responsible for, guilty of (+ gen)
αἰχμάλωτος -ου ὁ	prisoner, prisoner of war
ἀκούω ἤκουσα	I hear, I listen to (+ gen of person)
ἄκρος -α -ον	top (bit of), furthest
ἀκτή -ῆς ἡ	shore
ἄκων -ουσα -ον (ἀκοντ-)	unwilling
ἀληθής -ές	true
ἅλις	enough

ἀλλά	but
ἀλλήλους -ας -α	each other
ἄλλος -η -ο	other, another
ἅμα	at the same time (as), with (+ *dat*)
ἁμαρτάνω ἥμαρτον	I make a mistake, I miss (target *etc*)
ἀμείνων -ον (ἀμεινον-)	better (*comp of* ἀγαθός)
ἀμύνω ἥμυνα	I ward off, I defend (+ *dat*)
mid ἀμύνομαι ἡμυνάμην	I defend myself; I resist (+ *gen*)
ἀμφί	(+ *acc*) around, about
ἀμφοτέροι -αι -α	both
ἄν	(*particle making clause indefinite/potential e.g.* would, could ...)
ἀνά	(+ *acc*) up
ἀναγιγνώσκω ἀνέγνων	I read
ἀναγκάζω ἡνάγκασα	I compel
ἀνάγκη -ης ἡ	necessity
ἀνάγομαι ἀνηγαγόμην	I put out to sea
ἀναχωρέω ἀνεχώρησα	I retreat, I withdraw
ἀνδρεία -ας ἡ	courage
ἀνδρεῖος -α -ον	brave
ἄνεμος -ου ὁ	wind
ἄνευ	without (+ *gen*)
ἀνήρ ἀνδρός ὁ	man, male, husband
ἄνθρωπος -ου ὁ(/ἡ)	man, person, human being
ἀντί	opposite, instead of, for, counterbalancing (+ *gen*)
ἄξιος -α -ον	worthy (of), deserving (+ *gen*)
ἀξιόω ἡξίωσα	I think worthy; I urge, I demand
ἅπας -ασα -αν (ἁπαντ-)	all, the whole of
ἀπειλέω ἡπείλησα	I threaten
ἄπειμι	(1) I am away (εἰμί); (2) I go away (εἶμι)
ἀπέχω ἀπέσχον	I am distant (from + *gen*)
ἀπό	from (+ *gen*), (*in compounds*) away
ἀποθαν-	(*aor stem of* ἀποθνῃσκω)
ἀποθνῄσκω ἀπέθανον	I die, I am killed
ἀποκρίνομαι ἀπεκρινάμην	I answer, I reply
ἀποκτείνω ἀπέκτεινα	I kill
ἀπόλλυμι ἀπώλεσα	I lose; I destroy
mid ἀπόλλυμαι ἀπωλόμην	I perish
ἀπορέω ἡπόρησα	I am at a loss, I am in doubt
ἀπορία -ας ἡ	perplexity, hesitation
ἀποστερέω ἀπεστέρησα	I deprive, I rob X (*acc*) of Y (*gen*)
ἀπροσδόκητος -ον	unexpected
ἅπτομαι ἡψάμην	I lay hold of, I touch (+ *gen*)
ἄρα	then (*inferential*), so then, in that case; moreover
ἄρα;	*e.g.* is it? (*open direct qu*)
ἀρ᾽ οὐ;	surely ... ? (*expects* Yes)
ἄρα μή;	surely ... not ? (*expects* No)
ἀργύριον -ου τό	money
ἄργυρος -ου ὁ	silver

ἀργυροῦς -ᾶ -οῦν	made of silver
ἀρετή -ῆς ἡ	excellence, courage, virtue
ἀριθμός -οῦ ὁ	number
ἀριστερός -ά -όν	left (hand side)
ἄριστος -η -ον	best, very good (*sup of* ἀγαθός)
ἅρμα -ατος τό	chariot
ἁρπάζω ἥρπασα	I seize, I snatch
ἄρτι	recently, just now
ἀρχαῖος -α -ον	old, ancient
ἀρχή -ῆς ἡ	rule, empire; beginning
ἄρχω ἦρξα	I rule
mid ἄρχομαι ἠρξάμην	I begin
ἄρχων -οντος ὁ	ruler, chief, magistrate
ἀσεβής -ές	impious
ἀσθενής -ές	weak
ἄσμενος -η -ον	glad, pleased
ἀσπίς -ίδος ἡ	shield
ἄστυ -εως τό	city, town
ἀσφάλεια -ας ἡ	safety
ἀσφαλής -ές	safe
ἅτε	inasmuch as, since, seeing that
αὖ *or* αὖθις	in turn, again
αὐξάνω ηὔξησα	I increase
αὔριον	tomorrow
αὐτίκα	at once, straightaway
αὐτός -ή -ό	self; (+ *article*) same; (*pronoun, not nom*) him *etc*
ἀφικ-	(*aor stem of* ἀφικνέομαι)
ἀφικνέομαι ἀφικόμην	I arrive
ἀφίστημι ἀπέστησα	I make to revolt
mid ἀφίσταμαι ἀπέστην	I revolt
βαδίζω ἐβάδισα	I walk
βαθύς -εῖα -ύ	deep
βαίνω ἔβην	I go
βαλ-	(*aor stem of* βάλλω)
βάλλω ἔβαλον	I throw; I pelt
βάρβαρος -ον	non-Greek, foreign, barbarian
βαρύς -εῖα -ύ	heavy
βαρέως φέρω	I take (something) badly
βασίλεια -ας ἡ	queen
βασιλεύς -έως ὁ	king
βέβαιος -α -ον	firm, steady
βία -ας ἡ	force, strength
βίβλος -ου ἡ	book
βίος -ου ὁ	life
βλάπτω ἔβλαψα	I harm, I damage
βλέπω ἔβλεψα	I look
βοάω ἐβόησα	I shout
βοή -ῆς ἡ	shout, shouting

βοήθεια -ας ἡ	help, assistance
βοηθέω ἐβοήθησα	I help, I run to help (+ *dat*)
βουλεύω ἐβούλευσα	I discuss, I plan, I consider (*often mid*)
βουλή -ῆς ἡ	council; counsel, plan
βούλομαι *impf* ἐβουλόμην	I wish, I want
βραδύς -εῖα -ύ	slow
βωμός -οῦ ὁ	altar
γαμέω ἔγημα	I marry (*m subject*, + *acc*)
mid γαμέομαι ἐγημάμην	I marry (*f subject*, + *dat*)
γάρ	for
γέ	at least, at any rate
γελάω ἐγέλασα	I laugh
γεν-	(*aor stem of* γίγνομαι)
γένος -ους τό	type, family, race
γέρων -οντος ὁ	old man
γέφυρα -ας ἡ	bridge
γῆ γῆς ἡ	earth, land
γίγας -αντος ὁ	giant
γίγνομαι ἐγενόμην	I become, I happen
γιγνώσκω ἔγνων	I get to know
γλυκύς -εῖα -ύ	sweet, delightful
γλῶσσα -ης ἡ	tongue, language
γνώμη -ης ἡ	mind, opinion, judgement, purpose
γοῦν	at least, at any rate
γράφω ἔγραψα	I write, I draw
γυμνός -ή -όν	naked; unarmed
γυνή -αικός ἡ	woman, wife
δακρύω ἐδάκρυσα	I weep, I cry
δέ	and; but
δεῖ *impf* ἔδει	it is necessary (+ *acc* + *inf*)
δείκνυμι ἔδειξα	I show
δεινός -ή -όν	strange; terrible; clever
δεῖπνον -ου τό	meal, dinner
δέκα	ten
δέκατος -η -ον	tenth
δένδρον -ου τό	tree
δεξ-	(*aor stem of* δέχομαι)
δεξιά -ᾶς ἡ	right hand
δεξιός -ά -όν	right, on the right side; skilled
δέομαι ἐδεήθην	I ask (for), I need (+ *gen*)
δεσμός -οῦ ὁ	chain, bond, fastening
δεσμωτήριον -ου τό	prison
δεσμώτης -ου ὁ	prisoner
δέσποινα -ης ἡ	mistress
δεσπότης -ου ὁ	master
δεῦρο	hither, to here
δεύτερος -α -ον	second

δέχομαι ἐδεξάμην	I receive, I accept, I welcome
δή *or* δῆτα	*e.g.* indeed, certainly (*emboldens preceding word*)
δῆλος -η -ον	clear, obvious
δηλόω ἐδήλωσα	I show
δῆμος -ου ὁ	people, community
δήπου	of course, surely
διά	(+ *acc*) on account of
	(+ *gen*) through
διὰ τί;	why?
δι' ὀλίγου	soon, after a short time
διακόσιοι -αι -α	200
διαλέγομαι διελεξάμην	I converse (with + *dat*)
διαφθείρω διέφθειρα	I destroy, I corrupt
διδάσκαλος -ου ὁ	teacher
διδάσκω ἐδίδαξα	I teach
δίδωμι ἔδωκα	I give
διηγέομαι διηγησάμην	I narrate, I explain
δίκαιος -α -ον	just, moral, fair
δικαιοσύνη -ης ἡ	justice
δίκη -ης ἡ	justice; lawsuit; penalty
Δίος	(*irreg gen of* Ζεύς)
διότι	because
διώκω ἐδίωξα	I chase, I pursue; I prosecute (in court)
δοκέω ἔδοξα	I seem, I consider (myself to be)
impsnl δοκεῖ ἔδοξε(ν)	(+ *dat*) it seems good to X, X decides
δόλος -ου ὁ	trick, trickery
δόξα -ης ἡ	opinion; glory
δουλεύω ἐδούλευσα	I am a slave
δούλη -ης ἡ	female slave
δοῦλος -ου ὁ	slave
δουλόω ἐδούλωσα	I enslave
δραμ-	(*aor stem of* τρέχω)
δράω ἔδρασα	I do
δρόμος -ου ὁ	run, act of running
δύναμαι *impf* ἐδυνάμην	I can, I am able
δύναμις -εως ἡ	power, capacity
δυνατός -ή -όν	capable, able; possible
δύο δυοῖν	two
δυστυχής -ές	unfortunate
δώδεκα	twelve
δῶρον -ου τό	gift
ἐάν *or* ἤν	if (+ *subj, in fut open conditions*)
ἑαυτόν -ήν -ό *or* αὑτόν -ήν -ό	himself, herself, itself (*refl*)
ἐάω εἴασα	I allow
ἑβδομήκοντα	70
ἕβδομος -η -ον	seventh
ἐγγύς	(+ *gen*) near
ἐγώ	I

ἔγωγε	I, I at least, I for my part (*emph*)
ἐθέλω ἠθέλησα	I wish, I am willing
ἔθνος -ους τό	tribe, race, nation
εἰ	if
εἰδώς (εἰδοτ-)	(*pple of* οἶδα)
εἴθε	if only ... ! (+ *opt, introducing wish*)
εἰκός -ότος τό	possibility, what is likely
εἴκοσι(ν)	20
εἰμί *impf* ἦ *or* ἦν	I am
εἶμι *impf* ᾖα *or* ᾖειν	I shall go
εἰπ-	(*aor stem of* λέγω)
εἰρήνη -ης ἡ	peace
εἰς	into (+ *acc*)
εἷς μία ἕν (ἑν-)	one
εἰσβάλλω εἰσέβαλον	I invade
εἰσβολή -ῆς ἡ	invasion; pass (*through mountains*)
εἶτα	then, next
εἴτε ... εἴτε	whether ... or
ἐκ, ἐξ	out of (+ *gen*)
ἐξ οὗ	since, from the time when
ἕκαστος -η -ον	each
ἑκάτερος -α -ον	each (of two)
ἑκατόν	100
ἐκεῖ	there
ἐκεῖθεν	from there
ἐκεῖσε	to there
ἐκεῖνος -η -ο	that, *pl* those
ἐκκλησία -ας ἡ	assembly
ἕκτος -η -ον	sixth
ἐκφεύγω ἐξέφυγον	I escape
ἑκών -οῦσα -όν (ἑκοντ-)	willing
ἑλ-	(*aor stem of* αἱρέω)
ἐλασ-	(*aor stem of* ἐλαύνω)
ἐλάσσων -ον (ἐλασσον-)	smaller (amount), *pl* fewer (*comp of* ὀλίγος)
ἐλαύνω ἤλασα	I drive
ἐλάχιστος -η -ον	smallest (amount), *pl* fewest (*sup of* ὀλίγος)
ἐλευθερία -ας ἡ	freedom
ἐλεύθερος -α -ον	free
ἐλευθερόω ἠλευθέρωσα	I free, I set free
ἐλθ-	(*aor stem of* ἔρχομαι)
ἕλκω εἵλκυσα	I drag
Ἑλλάς -άδος ἡ	Greece
Ἕλλην -ηνος ὁ	Greek, Greek man
ἐλπίζω ἤλπισα	I hope, I expect
ἐλπίς -ίδος ἡ	hope, expectation
ἐμαυτόν -ήν	myself (*refl*)
ἐμός -ή -όν	my
ἔμπροσθεν	previously, before (+ *gen*)
ἐν	in, on, among (+ *dat*)

ἐνακόσιοι -αι -α	900
ἐναντίος -α -ον	opposite
ἔνατος -η -ον	ninth
ἕνδεκα	eleven
ἐνεγκ-	(*aor stem of* φέρω)
ἕνεκα	on account of (+ *gen; usu comes after noun*)
ἐνενήκοντα	90
ἔνθα	there, then, when
ἐνθάδε	here
ἐνθένδε	from here, from then
ἐνιαυτός -οῦ ὁ	year
ἐνίοτε	sometimes
ἐννέα	nine
ἐννοέω ἐνενόησα	I consider, I think of
ἔνοικος -ου ὁ	inhabitant
ἐνταῦθα	here, there, then
ἐντεῦθεν	from then, thereupon, from here, from there
ἐντυγχάνω ἐνέτυχον	I meet, I come upon (+ *dat*)
ἕξ	six
ἐξαίφνης	suddenly
ἑξακόσιοι -αι -α	600
ἐξαπατάω ἐξηπάτησα	I deceive
ἔξεστι *impf* ἐξῆν	it is possible, it is allowed (+ *dat* + *inf*)
ἑξήκοντα	60
ἔξω	outside
ἑορτή -ῆς ἡ	festival
ἐπαινέω ἐπήνεσα	I praise
ἐπανέρχομαι ἐπανῆλθον	I return
ἐπεί	when, since
ἐπεὶ τάχιστα	as soon as
ἐπειδάν	when, whenever (*indef,* + *subj*)
ἐπειδή	when, since
ἔπειτα	then, next
ἐπί	(+ *acc*) to, against, over, for
	(+ *gen*) on; in the time of
	(+ *dat*) on, on condition of
ἐφ᾽ ᾧτε	on condition that (+ *acc* + *inf*)
ἐπιλανθάνομαι ἐπελαθόμην	I forget
ἐπίσταμαι ἠπιστάμην	I understand, I know (how to)
ἐπιστολή -ῆς ἡ	letter
ἐπιτήδεια -ων τά	supplies, provisions
ἐπιτρέπω ἐπέτρεψα	I entrust X (*acc*) to Y (*dat*)
ἕπομαι ἑσπόμην	I follow (+ *dat*)
ἕπτα	seven
ἑπτακόσιοι -αι -α	700
ἔργον -ου τό	work, task, deed
ἐρῆμος -η -ον	deserted
ἔρχομαι ἦλθον	I go, I come
ἐρωτάω ἠρώτησα *or* ἠρόμην	I ask (a question)

ἐσθίω ἔφαγον	I eat
ἑσπέρα -ας ἡ	evening
ἕστηκα	I stand (*pf of* ἵστημι *with present meaning*)
ἔσχατος -η -ον	last, farthest
ἑταῖρος -ου ὁ	companion
ἕτερος -α -ον	one/the other (of two); different
ἔτι	yet, still
ἑτοῖμος -η -ον	ready
ἔτος -ους τό	year
εὖ	well
εὐγενής -ές	noble
εὐδαίμων -ον (εὐδαιμον-)	happy, blessed, prosperous
εὐθύς	at once, immediately
εὑρ-	(*aor stem of* εὑρίσκω)
εὑρίσκω ηὗρον	I find
εὐρύς -εῖα -ύ	broad
εὐσεβής -ές	pious
εὐτυχής -ές	fortunate, lucky
εὔχομαι ηὐξάμην	I pray
ἐχθρός -ά -όν	hostile, *noun* ἐχθρός -οῦ ὁ personal enemy
ἔχω ἔσχον	I have, I hold; (+ *adv*) I am
χάριν ἔχω	I am grateful, I thank
ἑώρων	(*impf of* ὁράω)
ἕως	while, until
ζάω ἔζησα	I live
Ζεύς Διός ὁ	Zeus
ζητέω ἐζήτησα	I seek, I enquire about
ζῷον -ου τό	animal, creature
ἤ	or; than
ἤ ... ἤ	either ... or
ἡγεμών -όνος ὁ	leader, guide
ἡγέομαι ἡγησάμην	I lead (+ *dat*); I think, I consider
ἤδη	now, already
ἥδομαι ἥσθην	I enjoy, I am pleased with (+ *dat*)
ἡδύς -εῖα -ύ	sweet, pleasant
ἥκιστα	least (*adv*); not at all
ἥκω *impf as plpf* ἧκον	I have come
ἥλιος -ου ὁ	sun
ἡμεῖς	we
ἡμᾶς αὐτούς -άς	ourselves (*refl*)
ἡμέρα -ας ἡ	day
ἡμέτερος -α -ον	our
ἤπειρος -ου ἡ	mainland
ἡσυχάζω ἡσύχασα	I am calm
θάλασσα -ης ἡ	sea
θάνατος -ου ὁ	death

θάπτω ἔθαψα	I bury
θαρρέω ἐθάρρησα *or* θαρσέω ἐθάρσησα	I am confident
θάσσων -ον (θασσον-)	quicker, swifter (*comp of* ταχύς)
θαυμάζω ἐθαύμασα	I am amazed, I wonder (at), I admire
θεά -ᾶς ἡ	goddess
θεάομαι ἐθεασάμην	I look at, I watch
θεός -οῦ ὁ	god (*or can be used as f* goddess, *like* θεά)
θεράπαινα -ης ἡ	(female) servant
θεραπεύω ἐθεράπευσα	I care for, I serve
θεράπων -οντος ὁ	(male) servant
θέρος -ους τό	summer
θηρεύω θήρευσα	I hunt
θρασύς -εῖα -ύ	bold, reckless
θυγάτηρ -τρος ἡ	daughter
θύρα -ας ἡ	door
θύω ἔθυσα	I sacrifice
θώραξ -ακος ὁ	breastplate
ἰατρός -οῦ ὁ	doctor
ἰδ-	(*aor stem of* ὁράω)
ἱερεύς -έως ὁ	priest
ἱερόν -οῦ τό	temple
ἱερός -ά -όν	holy
ἵημι ἧκα	I send, I let go, I hurl
ἱκανός -ή -όν	sufficient, capable, able (to + *inf*)
ἵνα	(+ *subj/opt*) in order to, so that; (+ *indic*) where
ἱππεύς -έως ὁ	cavalryman
ἱππεύω	I ride
ἵππος -ου ὁ/ἡ	horse, (*f collective sg*) cavalry
ἴσος -η -ον	equal
ἵστημι ἔστησα	I make to stand, I set up
intrans ἔστηκα (*pf as pres*) ἔστην	I stand
ἰσχυρός -ά -όν	strong
ἴσως	perhaps, probably
ἰχθύς -ύος ὁ	fish
καθεύδω *impf* καθηῦδον *or* ἐκάθευδον	I sleep
καθίζω ἐκάθισα	I sit
καθίστημι κατέστησα	I place, I make, I appoint, I put into a state of ...
mid καθίσταμαι κατέστην	I am placed, I am appointed, I am in a state of ...
καί	and, even, also, actually
καίπερ	although, despite
καιρός -οῦ ὁ	right time, opportunity
καίτοι	and yet
καίω ἔκαυσα	I burn, I set on fire
κακίων -ον (κακιον-)	worse (*comp of* κακός)
κάκιστος -η -ον	worst, very bad (*sup of* κακός)
κακός -ή -όν	bad; cowardly
καλέω ἐκάλεσα	I call, I invite

228

καλός -ή -όν	fine, beautiful
κάμνω ἔκαμον	I toil
κατά	(+ acc) down; according to; throughout; by (e.g. κατὰ γῆν by land)
	(+ gen) down from
κατάσκοπος -ου ὁ	spy, scout
καταφρονέω κατεφρόνησα	I despise, I look down on (+ gen)
κατηγορέω κατηγόρησα	I accuse, I prosecute (X gen on a charge of Y acc)
κεῖμαι impf (ἐ)κείμην	I lie, I am situated, I am established
κελεύω ἐκέλευσα	I order
κενός -ή -όν	empty
κέρας -ατος τό	horn; wing (of army)
κεφαλή -ῆς ἡ	head
κῆρυξ -υκος ὁ	herald
κηρύσσω ἐκήρυξα	I proclaim
κινδυνεύω ἐκινδύνευσα	I am in danger, I run a risk; I am likely (to + inf)
κίνδυνος -ου ὁ	danger
κλέπτω ἔκλεψα	I steal
κοινός -ή -όν	common, shared
κολάζω ἐκόλασα	I punish
κομίζω ἐκόμισα	I bring, I convey; mid I regain
κόπτω ἔκοψα	I cut; I hit, I knock
κόρη -ης ἡ	girl
κρατέω ἐκράτησα	I control, I have power over (+ gen)
κράτος -ους τό	might, authority
κρίνω ἔκρινα	I judge
κριτής -οῦ ὁ	judge
κρύπτω ἔκρυψα	I hide (something)
κτάομαι ἐκτησάμην	I obtain, I acquire
κτῆμα -ατος τό	possession
κυβερνήτης -ου ὁ	helmsman
κύκλος -ου ὁ	circle
κωλύω ἐκώλυσα	I prevent (from + inf), I hinder
κώμη -ης ἡ	village
λαβ-	(aor stem of λαμβάνω)
λάθρα	secretly
Λακεδαιμόνιοι -ων οἱ	the Spartans
λαμβάνω ἔλαβον	I take, I capture
λανθάνω ἔλαθον	I escape (the) notice (of)
λέγω (ἔλεξα or) εἶπον	I say, I speak, I tell
λείπω ἔλιπον	I leave (behind)
λέων -οντος ὁ	lion
λίθος -ου ὁ	stone
λιμήν -ένος ὁ	harbour
λίμνη -ης ἡ	marsh
λιπ-	(aor stem of λείπω)
λόγος -ου ὁ	word, account, reason, story
λόγχη -ης ἡ	spear

λοιπός -ή -όν	left, remaining
λοχαγός -οῦ ὁ	commander
λύω ἔλυσα	I loose, I release
mid λύομαι ἐλυσάμην	I ransom
μαθ-	(*aor stem of* μανθάνω)
μακρός -ά -όν	long
μάλα	very
μάλιστα	especially, very much; (*with numbers*) about
μᾶλλον	more (*adv*), rather
μανθάνω ἔμαθον	I learn
μανία -ας ἡ	madness
μαντεῖον -ου τό	oracle
μάντις -εως ὁ	prophet
μάτην	in vain
μαχεσ-	(*aor stem of* μάχομαι)
μάχη -ης ἡ	battle, fight
μάχομαι ἐμαχεσάμην	I fight
μέγας μεγάλη μέγα (μεγαλ-)	great, big
μέγιστος -η -ον	greatest, biggest, very big (*sup of* μέγας)
μείζων -ον (μειζον-)	greater, bigger (*comp of* μέγας)
μέλλω ἐμέλλησα	I intend, I am going to; I hesitate
μέμνημαι (*pf as pres*) ἐμεμνήμην	I remember (+ *gen*)
μέν ... δέ	on the one hand ... on the other
μέντοι	however; certainly
μένω ἔμεινα	I remain; I await
μέρος -ους τό	part, share, turn
μέσος -η -ον	middle, middle bit of
μετά	(+ *acc*) after
	(+ *gen*) with
μεταπέμπομαι μετεπεμψάμην	I send for
μετέχω μετέσχον	I have a share (of + *gen*)
μέχρι	until, as far as (+ *gen*)
μή	not (*for ideas/possibilities;* οὐ *for facts*)
μηδαμοῦ	nowhere
μηδαμῶς	in no way
μηδέ	and not, nor, not even
μηδείς μηδεμία μηδέν (μηδεν-)	no-one, nothing, no
μηδέποτε	never
μηκέτι	no longer
μήποτε	never
μήτε ... μήτε	neither ... nor
μήτηρ -τρος ἡ	mother
μηχανάομαι ἐμηχανησάμην	I devise, I contrive
μηχανή -ῆς ἡ	device
μικρός -ά -όν	small
μισέω ἐμίσησα	I hate
μισθός -οῦ ὁ	reward, fee, pay
μῖσος -ους τό	hatred

μόλις	scarcely, with difficulty
μόνον	only (*adv*)
μόνος -η -ον	alone, only (*adj*)
Μοῦσα -ης ἡ	Muse
μῦθος -ου ὁ	word, story
μῶρος -α -ον	foolish, stupid
ναί	yes
ναυμαχέω ἐναυμάχησα	I fight a sea-battle
ναυμαχία -ας ἡ	sea-battle
ναῦς νεώς ἡ	ship
ναύτης -ου ὁ	sailor
ναυτικόν -οῦ τό	fleet
νεανίας -ου ὁ	young man
νεκρός -οῦ ὁ	corpse, dead body
νέος -α -ον	new; young; recent
νῆσος -ου ἡ	island
νικάω ἐνίκησα	I conquer, I win
νίκη -ης ἡ	victory
νομίζω ἐνόμισα	I think, I believe
νόμος -ου ὁ	law, custom
νοσέω ἐνόσησα	I am ill
νόσος -ου ἡ	illness, disease
νοῦς νοῦ ὁ	mind
νῦν	now
νύξ νυκτός ἡ	night
ξένος -ου ὁ	stranger, foreigner, host, guest, friend
ξίφος -ους τό	sword
ξύλινος -η -ον	wooden, made of wood
ὁ ἡ τό	the
ὀγδοήκοντα	80
ὄγδοος -η -ον	eighth
ὅδε ἥδε τόδε	this, this here, the following
ὁδός -οῦ ἡ	road, way
ὅθεν	from where (*rel*)
οἷ	to where (*rel*)
οἶδα (*pf as pres*) ᾔδη (*plpf as past*)	I know (how to + *inf*)
οἴκαδε	homewards
οἰκέω ᾤκησα	I dwell, I inhabit
οἰκία -ας ἡ	house
οἴκοθεν	from home
οἴκοι	at home
οἶκος -ου ὁ	house, home
οἰκτείρω ᾤκτειρα	I pity
οἶνος -ου ὁ	wine
οἷος -α -ον	such, of the kind which
οἷός τ' εἰμί	I can, I am able (to)

ὀκτακόσιοι -αι -α	800
ὀκτώ	eight
ὀλίγος -η -ον	small (amount of), *pl* few
ὄμνυμι ὤμοσα	I swear
ὅμοιος -α -ον	similar, of the same sort
ὁμολογέω ὡμολόγησα	I agree, I admit
ὀμοσ-	(*aor stem of* ὄμνυμι)
ὅμως	nevertheless
ὄνομα -ατος τό	name
ὀξύς -εῖα -ύ	sharp, bitter
ὄπισθε(ν)	behind (+ *gen, or as adv*); in the future
ὅπλα -ων τά	arms, armour, weapons
ὁπλίζω ὥπλισα	I arm
ὁπλίτης -ου ὁ	hoplite, heavy-armed soldier
ὁπόθεν	from where (*ind qu, rel or indef*)
ὅποι	to where (*ind qu, rel or indef*)
ὁποῖος -α -ον	what sort of (*ind qu*), of the sort which (*rel*)
ὁπόσος -η -ον	how big, *pl* how many (*ind qu*), of the size which, as many as (*rel*)
ὁπότε	when (*ind qu or rel*), whenever (*indef*)
ὁπότερος -α -ον	which of two (*ind qu*)
ὅπου	where (*ind qu, rel or indef*)
ὅπως	(as to) how (*ind qu*); so that, in order to (+ *subj or opt*)
ὁράω εἶδον	I see
ὀργή -ῆς ἡ	anger
ὀργίζομαι ὠργίσθην	I become angry
ὀρθός -ή -όν	straight, correct
ὅρκος -ου ὁ	oath
ὁρμάομαι ὡρμησάμην	I set out
ὄρνις -ιθος ὁ/ἡ	bird
ὄρος -ους τό	hill, mountain
ὅς ἥ ὅ	who, which, what (*rel*)
ὅσος ὅση ὅσον	the size which, how/as big/much as, *pl* as many as, all those who (*rel*)
ὅστις ἥτις ὅ τι	who, which, what (*ind qu*), whoever, whichever, whatever (*indef*)
ὅταν	whenever (*indef*)
ὅτε	when (*rel*)
ὅτι	that; because
οὐ (οὐκ, οὐχ, οὐχι)	not (*for facts;* μή *for ideas/possibilities*)
οὗ	where (*rel*)
οὐδαμοῦ	nowhere
οὐδαμῶς	in no way
οὐδέ	and not, nor, not even
οὐδείς οὐδεμία οὐδέν (οὐδεν-)	no-one, nothing, no
οὐδέποτε	never
οὐκέτι	no longer
οὐκοῦν	therefore

οὔκουν	not ... therefore
οὖν	therefore, and so
οὔποτε	never
οὐρανός -οῦ ὁ	sky, heaven
οὔτε ... οὔτε	neither ... nor
οὗτος αὕτη τοῦτο	this
οὕτω(ς)	thus, so
ὀφθαλμός -οῦ ὁ	eye
παθ-	(aor stem of πάσχω)
παιδεύω ἐπαίδευσα	I educate, I train
παῖς παιδός ὁ/ἡ	boy, girl, child
πάλαι	long ago, formerly
παλαιός -ά -όν	ancient, (of) old, former
πάλιν	again, back
πανταχοῦ	everywhere
παρά	(+ acc) along; into the presence of; contrary to
	(+ gen) from (a person)
	(+ dat) beside
παραδίδωμι παρέδωκα	I hand over
παραινέω (+ dat)	I advise
παρασκευάζω παρεσκεύασα	I prepare
πάρειμι impf παρῆν	I am present
impsnl πάρεστι impf παρῆν	it is possible (+ dat + inf)
παρέχω παρέσχον	I provide, I produce, I cause
παρθένος -ου ἡ	maiden, virgin; (adj) unmarried
πᾶς πᾶσα πᾶν (παντ-)	all, every
πάσχω ἔπαθον	I suffer, I experience
πατήρ -τρος ὁ	father
πατρίς -ίδος ἡ	fatherland, homeland
πατρῷος -α -ον	of a father, ancestral
παύω ἔπαυσα	I stop (something)
mid παύομαι ἐπαυσάμην	I stop (myself), I cease (from + gen)
πεδίον -ου τό	plain, field
πεζῇ	on foot
πεζοί -ῶν οἱ	infantry
πείθω ἔπεισα	I persuade
mid πείθομαι ἐπιθόμην	I obey (+ dat)
πειράομαι ἐπειρασάμην	I try
πελταστής -οῦ ὁ	light-armed soldier
πέμπτος -η -ον	fifth
πέμπω ἔπεμψα	I send, I fire (arrow etc)
πεντακόσιοι -αι -α	500
πεντήκοντα	50
πέντε	five
περί	(+ acc) around
	(+ gen) about, concerning
πεσ-	(aor stem of πίπτω)
πηδάω ἐπήδησα	I leap

233

πιέζω ἐπίεσα	I press, I oppress
πίνω ἔπιον	I drink
πίπτω ἔπεσον	I fall
πιστεύω ἐπίστευσα	I trust, I believe (+ *dat*)
πιστός -ή -όν	faithful, reliable
πλείονες -α *or* πλέονες -α	more (*pl comp of* πολύς)
πλεῖστοι -αι -α	most (*pl sup of* πολύς)
πλευσ-	(*aor stem of* πλέω)
πλέω ἔπλευσα	I sail
πλῆθος -ους τό	crowd, large number
πλήν	except (+ *gen*)
πληρόω ἐπλήρωσα	I fill
πλοῖον -ου τό	boat
πλοῦς -οῦ ὁ	voyage
πλούσιος -α -ον	rich
πόθεν;	from where?
ποῖ;	to where?
ποιέω ἐποίησα	I make, I do; (+ *adv*) I treat
mid ποιέομαι ἐποιησάμην	I value, I reckon (+ περί + *gen*)
ποιητής -οῦ ὁ	poet
ποῖος -α -ον	what sort of?
ὁποῖος -α -ον	of what sort, of the sort which (*ind qu or rel*)
πολεμέω ἐπολέμησα	I make war, I fight a war
πολέμιοι -ων οἱ	enemy
πολέμιος -α -ον	hostile, (of the) enemy
πόλεμος -ου ὁ	war
πολιορκέω ἐπολιόρκησα	I besiege
πόλις -εως ἡ	city, city-state
πολίτης -ου ὁ	citizen
πολλάκις	often
πολλοί -αί -ά	many
οἱ πολλοί	the majority
πολύς πολλή πολύ (πολλ-)	much
πονέω ἐπόνησα	I toil, I labour; I suffer
πόνος -ου ὁ	toil, business; suffering, distress
πορεύομαι ἐπορεύθην	I march, I travel
πόρρω *or* πρόσω	forwards
πόσος -η -ον	how great? (*pl*) how many?
ποταμός -οῦ ὁ	river
πότε;	when?
ποτε	once, at some time, ever
πότερον ... ἤ	whether (*but omit in direct qu*) ... or
πότερος -α -ον	which of two?
ποῦ;	where?
που	somewhere, anywhere; I suppose
πούς ποδός ὁ	foot
πρᾶγμα -ατος τό	thing, matter, business
πραξ-	(*aor stem of* πράσσω)
πράσσω ἔπραξα	I do, (+ *adv*) I fare

πρέσβυς -εως ὁ	old man; *pl* πρέσβεις -έων οἱ ambassadors
πρίν	before, until
πρό	in front of (+ *gen*)
πρόγονος -ου ὁ	ancestor
προδίδωμι προὔδωκα	I betray
πρόθυμος -ον	eager
πρός	(+ *acc*) to, towards
	(+ *gen*) from, at the hands of; in the name of
	(+ *dat*) at; in addition to
προσβάλλω προσέβαλον	I attack (+ *dat*)
πρόσθε(ν) ἔμπροσθεν	previously, before (+ *gen*)
προτεραίᾳ τῇ	on previous day
πρότερον	formerly, previously
προχωρέω προὐχώρησα	I advance, I go forward
πρῴ	early
πρῶτον	first (*adv*), at first
πρῶτος -η -ον	first
πυθ-	(*aor stem of* πυνθάνομαι)
πύλη -ης ἡ	gate
πυνθάνομαι ἐπυθόμην	I enquire, I ascertain, I learn
πῦρ πυρός τό	fire
πῶς;	how?
πως	in some way
ῥᾴδιος -α -ον	easy
ῥᾷστος -η -ον	easiest, very easy (*sup of* ῥᾴδιος)
ῥᾴων -ον (ῥᾳον-)	easier (*comp of* ῥᾴδιος)
ῥήτωρ -ορος ὁ	speaker, politician
ῥίπτω ἔρριψα	I throw, I hurl
σαφής -ές	clear
σεαυτόν -ήν	yourself (*refl*)
σῆμα -ατος τό	sign, signal
σημαίνω ἐσήμηνα	I signal, I show, I tell
σήμερον	today
σιγάω ἐσίγησα	I am silent
σιγή -ῆς ἡ	silence
σῖτος -ου ὁ	food, bread, corn
σκευή -ῆς ἡ	equipment
σκηνή -ῆς ἡ	tent
σκοπέω ἐσκεψάμην	I look at, I examine
σκότος -ου ὁ	darkness
σός σή σόν	your (of you *sg*)
σοφία -ας ἡ	wisdom, cleverness
σοφός -ή -όν	wise, clever
σπονδαί -ῶν αἱ	treaty
στα-	(*basic stem of* ἵστημι)
στάδιον -ου τό (*pl* στάδιοι -ων οἱ)	stade (*approx 180 metres*)
στέλλω ἔστειλα	I send

στενός -ή -όν	narrow
στόλος -ου ὁ	expedition
στόμα -ατος τό	mouth
στρατεία -ας ἡ	campaign, expedition
στράτευμα -ατος τό	army
στρατεύω ἐστράτευσα	I march
στρατηγέω ἐστρατήγησα	I am (a) general
στρατηγός -οῦ ὁ	general
στρατιά -ᾶς ἡ	army
στρατιώτης -ου ὁ	soldier
στρατοπεδεύομαι ἐστρατοπεδευσάμην	I encamp
στρατόπεδον -ου τό	camp, army
στρατός -οῦ ὁ	army
σύ	you (*sg*)
συγγενής -ές	related, kin
συλλέγω συνέλεξα	I gather, I assemble
συμβουλεύω συνεβούλευσα	I advise (+ *dat*)
συμμαχία -ας ἡ	alliance
σύμμαχος -ου ὁ	ally
συμφορά -ᾶς ἡ	event; disaster
σύν	with, with the help of (+ *dat*)
σφᾶς	them
σφᾶς αὐτούς -άς	themselves (*refl*)
σφέτερος -α -ον	their, their own
σφόδρα	very much
σχ-	(*aor stem of* ἔχω)
σχεδόν	nearly, almost
σῴζω ἔσωσα	I save
σῶμα -ατος τό	body
σωσ-	(*aor stem of* σῴζω)
σωτηρία -ας ἡ	safety
σώφρων -ον (σωφρον-)	prudent, self-controlled
τάξις -εως ἡ	arrangement, rank
ταράσσω ἐτάραξα	I throw into confusion
τάσσω ἔταξα	I draw up, I arrange
τάφος -ου ὁ	tomb
τάχα	quickly, soon; perhaps
τάχ' ἄν	perhaps
τάχιστος -η -ον	quickest, swiftest, very quick (*sup of* ταχύς)
ταχύς -εῖα -ύ	quick, swift
τε	and
τε ... καί ...	both ... and
τε ... τε ...	both ... and
τειχίζω ἐτείχισα	I fortify
τείχισμα -ατος τό	fort, fortification
τεῖχος -ους τό	wall
τελευτάω ἐτελεύτησα	I end, I complete; I die
τελευτή -ῆς ἡ	end

236